Too Good to Be Altogether Lost

Too Good to Be Altogether Lost

Rediscovering Laura Ingalls Wilder's Little House Books

PAMELA SMITH HILL

University of Nebraska Press | Lincoln

Manufactured in the United States of America

The University of Nebraska Press is part of a land-grant institution with campuses and programs on the past, present, and future homelands of the Pawnee, Ponca, Otoe-Missouria, Omaha, Dakota, Lakota, Kaw, Cheyenne, and Arapaho Peoples, as well as those of the relocated Ho-Chunk, Sac and Fox, and Iowa Peoples.

Publication of this volume was assisted by the Virginia Faulkner Fund, established in memory of Virginia Faulkner, editor in chief of the University of Nebraska Press.

For customers in the EU with safety/GPSR concerns, contact:
gpsr@mare-nostrum.co.uk
Mare Nostrum Group BV
Mauritskade 21D
1091 GC Amsterdam
The Netherlands

Library of Congress Control Number: 2024043472

Jacket: *Cottage in the Woods*, by Laura Ingalls Wilder. Courtesy of Laura Ingalls Wilder Home Association, Mansfield, Missouri. *Cottage in the Woods* was painted on cardboard when Wilder was a teenager in Dakota Territory and given its name decades after her death. According to Ingalls family lore it was Wilder's attempt to illustrate a wooded landscape for her baby sister Grace Ingalls, a child of the prairie who had never seen a forest.

Designed and set in Questa by K. Andresen.

In memory of Jean Coday

Contents

Illustrations

Preface

IN 1937, WHEN LAURA INGALLS WILDER WAS NOT YET A LITerary legend, she told her audience at the Detroit Book Fair that she'd launched her Little House series because the stories from her childhood were "too good to be altogether lost."[1]

Those stories seemed far from being lost during the remainder of her lifetime and well into the twenty-first century. They were translated into dozens of languages. First Ladies from Eleanor Roosevelt to Laura Bush embraced the Little House books; generations of children read them at school; dedicated readers made pilgrimages to Little House locations. With the release of NBC's *Little House on the Prairie* in 1974, Wilder was well on her way to becoming an international literary icon.

Then almost simultaneously, the novels themselves began to slip from view, replaced by assumptions and questions about Wilder's values and politics, and even about the authenticity of the books themselves. From the 1980s onward, a slow but steady critical crescendo began to assail Wilder's literary reputation. During the summer of 2018, the American Library Association (ALA) stripped Wilder's name from the literary legacy medal created in her honor in 1954.

The ALA's Association for Library Service to Children issued this statement: "The decision was made in consideration of the fact that Wilder's legacy, as represented by her body of work, includes expressions of stereotypical attitudes inconsistent with ALSC's core values of inclusiveness, integrity and respect, and responsiveness."[2]

On the surface—if you look only at words on the page and not their meaning or context—it appears the ALA's assessment is accurate. As the *Washington Post* reported, the book at the heart of the controversy, *Little House on the Prairie*, "includes multiple statements from characters saying, 'The only good Indian is a dead Indian.'"[3]

Did Laura Ingalls Wilder intend for readers to embrace this idea? Is this how she viewed Native Americans? And if so, how could a mainstream publisher—Harper and Brothers—publish such a writer, such a book, even in 1935?

The glib answer, the one often found on social media, is that Wilder lived in a different time, that her world and its values fail to measure up to our own. Her books are consequently obsolete.

Wilder certainly lived in a different time, and her experiences were indeed very different than ours. She was born in 1867, not quite two years after the American Civil War ended. She was a young mother when federal troops fired on unarmed Lakota civilians at Wounded Knee in 1890. She was fifty-three in 1920, when the Nineteenth Amendment was ratified, giving women the right to vote. Her books were published during the Great Depression and World War II.

But living in a different time is precisely the point of Wilder's work. She wrote the Little House books to enlighten readers about the past, to illustrate how life *had* changed—what people once valued and what they once questioned in an era fading from memory. As she explained to her audience at the Detroit Book Fair, "I realized that I had seen and lived it all—all the successive phases of the frontier, first the frontiersman then the pioneer, then the farmers and towns."[4]

Yet Laura Ingalls Wilder chose *not* to write historical nonfiction; instead, she wrote historical *fiction*, which focuses not only on differences between past and present but similarities between them. Literary historical fiction, at its best, serves as a bridge between past and present, linking us all in an ongoing narrative—sometimes inspiring, sometimes uncomfortable—but always with the view to enrich readers, to make them think, to make them ask questions.

By choosing to write historical fiction, Wilder was able to immerse readers into her past, allowing them to experience it directly through her characters. Readers in essence *become* the fictional Laura Ingalls; with her, they toss a ball made from a pig's bladder, feel hundreds of grasshoppers crawling over their skin, or struggle to find their way home in a blinding blizzard. Historical fiction also gave Wilder the freedom to shape and transform the facts of her life, giving them more drama, immediacy, and depth. "All I have told is true," she confessed, "but it is not the whole truth."[5]

The ALA's Wilder decision relates directly to historical fiction—and the role it plays in readers' literary and everyday lives: Should it attempt to present the culture and social conventions of the period it depicts or should it instead re-create the past in the image of present-day society and its current social conventions? One of the underlying principles in this debate is the concept of presentism: interpreting and assessing the past through the lens of contemporary values. Since the late twentieth century, this concept has evolved in literary circles and gained traction beyond academia, in part supported by the argument that contemporary writers of historical fiction can't authentically re-create an objective portrait of a historical world they haven't directly experienced. Presentism has now become a kind of literary yardstick. Authors of historical fiction are measured and valued by how closely their work conforms to twenty-first century attitudes. Artistry and context become less important than inclusiveness and responsiveness.

The concept of presentism casts a slightly different, more moralistic shadow when applied specifically to fiction directed at young readers and raises a different set of literary questions. Should historical fiction for young readers teach twenty-first century moral lessons? If so, should authors spell out the appropriate answers for them? Can young readers be trusted to make their own decisions about uncomfortable, unsettling historical issues?

Wilder's Little House books predate the concept of literary presentism as we understand it today, and they defy quick and easy interpretation.[6] The characters and themes in her novels are complex and nuanced, often gritty, and rough around the edges. Wilder introduced a new kind of historical realism in fiction for young readers in the 1930s and 1940s, a realism that was intrinsically complex, despite the apparent simplicity of her prose. Her books pose difficult questions for young readers, yet she resisted the urge to provide answers. Instead she trusted her audience to draw their own conclusions about the dynamic, harsh, and sometimes bewildering American frontier.

The emotional and historical realism in Wilder's novels—for example, how pioneers interacted with Native Americans, the prevalence of blackface and the minstrel tradition in the nineteenth century—is now perceived as a fatal flaw in her work. Yet these aspects of the Little House books reflect prevailing social and cultural attitudes of the period and can lead to essential discussions, not only about the past but about the present—and the underlying and overt racism young readers encounter today.

COMPOUNDING THE CURRENT PREOCCUPATION WITH PRESENTISM and its impact on literary historical fiction for young readers is the steady decline in the genre itself. From the late twentieth century onward, the demand for new and even classic titles has dwindled. Since J. K. Rowling's *Harry Potter and the Sorcerer's Stone* was published in 1998, younger readers have been drawn to fantasy, dystopian, horror, contemporary, and science fiction titles. During one of my literature courses on Laura Ingalls Wilder at Missouri State University, a twenty-something student admitted she signed up for the course only because it fulfilled a requirement. She'd never read the Little House books, and frankly wasn't interested in them. Covered wagons and sun bonnets, she said, weren't as exciting as dragons, sorcerers, and zombies. A young participant in the Wilder pageant at De Smet, South Dakota, echoed a similar sentiment to the producers of iHeartMedia's *Wilder* podcast in 2023. Historical fiction, she said, was "not my genre." She preferred to read "fantasy" and "gay romance."[7]

Although a historical novel—*Freewater* by Amina Luqman-Dawon—won the Newbery Medal in 2023, during the previous five years, only six historically themed titles out of twenty-two were named either Newbery Medal or Honor books. The remaining titles were contemporary, fantasy, or science fiction books. Furthermore, according to a definitive article by Nathan Heller titled "The End of the English Major," today's younger readers now have "an orientation to the present" and seem to "lose their bearings in the past."[8]

Underlying this contemporary disinterest in historical fiction is often an assumption that "the unenlightened past" is irrelevant or offensive.[9] Again, as the Heller article points out, younger readers are more likely to seek out and identify "problematic" ideas in classic texts than delve into the historical or cultural contexts that produced them.[10] In an episode of the *Wilder* podcast, for example, a very young reader criticized Wilder because she didn't use the term "Native American" in the Little House books. The young reader's mother praised her son's critical observation, but like him, she apparently didn't realize the term wasn't used during the nineteenth century and wasn't coined until the 1960s, over twenty years after the last Little House book was published.[11]

BY CONTRAST, WHEN I WAS A YOUNG READER, LITERARY HIStorical fiction was an essential and popular pillar in children's literature. So was biography. By the time I discovered my first Laura Ingalls Wilder book—*Little Town on the Prairie*—in the juvenile section at the back of the bookmobile, I had already devoured the Betsy-Tacy books by Maud Hart Lovelace and perhaps a dozen biographies in the Childhood of Famous Americans series. I was nine.

Readers from my generation were grounded in historical fiction, from *Little Women* to the Little House books, from *Johnny Tremain* to *Island of the Blue Dolphins*. Even the Nancy Drew mysteries gave us a sense of history, with quaint references to frocks and roadsters. Well into the 1970s, 1980s, and 1990s, Newbery Award medalists wrote historical fiction. During the 1990s, before J. K. Rowling's first novel in the Harry Potter series was published, fifteen titles in historical fiction and nonfiction were named as Newbery medal winners or honor books. My first two young adult novels, published in the late 1990s, were historical, one set during the American Civil War, the other at the turn of the twentieth century.

Perhaps this is why today's most passionate Wilder fans are adults, who grew up reading historical fiction. As I toured the country after the publication of *Pioneer Girl: The Annotated Autobiography*, I met hundreds of her fans—men as well as women—who remained devoted to Wilder's books. Perhaps it was the adventure they found in those pages that has stayed with them—images of living in a dugout on the banks of Plum Creek, riding wild black ponies across the prairie, or surviving the Long Winter. Or maybe it was the devoted and loving family Wilder depicted in her books. Or was it the hardships the family endured with courage, hard work, and optimism? Or Wilder's vivid descriptions of the natural world? Whatever the touchstone, readers felt they had a personal connection with Laura Ingalls Wilder, that her work not only spoke directly and personally to them but had somehow transformed their lives and continued to influence them.

But even among Wilder's most passionate fans, the context, meaning, and themes of her novels are fading. Adult readers now seem to be drawn to her work because they believe she wrote about a "simpler time," or they're intrigued with Wilder's family history, not the fiction she created.

Yet Wilder's work is never simple, nor was the historical period at the heart of the Little House books. Writing from the perspective of a child and eventually a young woman on the American frontier, Wilder wasn't afraid to confront the ambiguities of western American history and the difficult issues we still confront today. When Ma reveals not just her fear but her dislike of Native Americans in *Little House on the Prairie*, five-year-old Laura asks, "What did we come to their country for, if you don't like them?"[12] Pa and Ma can't answer Laura's question, but it remains the fundamental issue about the settling of the American West: the clash between Native peoples and the settlers who ultimately prevailed. And it is fearlessly center stage in the novel.

Contrary to popular perceptions, the Little House books aren't sunny, moralistic, or blindly optimistic. Nor was Wilder herself. She was a conscientious and ambitious writer, who transformed American literature for young readers in the 1930s and 1940s; in fact, her groundbreaking work in young adult literature helped formalize the category itself. The themes Wilder pioneered in her fiction—sacrifice and survival, growth and maturity, illness and disability, feminism, coming-of-age, sexuality and marriage—remain central themes in twenty-first-century middle grade and Young Adult fiction. The artistry of Wilder's work has largely been overlooked—or forgotten.

DESPITE HER GROUNDBREAKING CONTRIBUTIONS TO HISTORical fiction for young readers, Wilder wasn't the first or only author in the 1930s and 1940s to write semi-autobiographical fiction about pioneers in the American West. In fact, she was part of a larger trend in popular American fiction during this period. In 1929 Bess Streeter Aldrich published *A Lantern in Her Hand*, a pioneer novel for adult readers, which is loosely based on her grandmother's pioneer experiences.[13] In 1931, a year before the publication of Wilder's first novel, *Little House in the Big Woods*, Florence Crannell Means published *A Candle in the Mist: A Story for Girls* and dedicated it to the women in her family who contributed to the writing of the book.[14] Janey Grant, its main character, along with her family battles a deadly blizzard, grasshoppers, and a prairie fire on the Minnesota frontier in the 1870s. *Caddie Woodlawn* was published the same year as *Little House on the Prairie*. Its author, Carol Ryrie Brink, based her main character on her grandmother, Caddie Woodhouse.[15] Set in Wisconsin during "those pioneer days," Caddie, like Janey Grant and Laura Ingalls, is free spirited, unconventional, and tomboyish. The novel won the Newbery Medal in 1936, while *Little House on the Prairie* was passed over by the Newbery committee that year.

Then there are the pioneer novels by Wilder's daughter, Rose Wilder Lane. Because Lane was an established and best-selling author by the time she published these two books, *Let the Hurricane Roar* in 1932 and *Free Land* in 1938, a chorus of Wilder scholars and critics now maintain that Lane was the creative genius behind the Little House books, further undermining Wilder's literary reputation. Yet Lane's pioneer novels, published for adults, lack the immediacy, authenticity, emotional realism, and artistry of Wilder's Little House series. As we'll see, Lane borrowed heavily from Wilder, lifting characters, dialogue, and descriptions from her mother's unpublished autobiography.

Wilder's books, however, transcended this Depression-era trend. They endured as her contemporaries' work did not. It's unlikely, for example, that Lane's pioneer novels would be in print today if Laura Ingalls Wilder hadn't been her mother. In fact, the Little House books spilled off the page and into popular culture, well into the twenty-first century. Random references to Wilder and her work appear not just in such mainstream print and broadcast media as the BBC, NPR, the *Wall Street Journal*, the *Smithsonian*, and the *New York Times*. They also appear in such irreverent television series as *The Simpsons*, *The Big Bang Theory*, and *Derry Girls*.[16]

Like Jane Austen, L. Frank Baum, and J. K. Rowling, Wilder remains a cultural icon. This status, however, has come with a price. Like J. K. Rowling, in particular, Wilder is now a cultural flash point, a polarizing literary figure. People from one hemisphere to another adore or revile her. And in part, thanks to the rise of social media, it's easier than ever to revile her. Misinformation about Wilder is now so prevalent that the most offensive line in *Little House on the Prairie* is commonly attributed to Ma or Pa—not as it should be to Mrs. Scott, a somewhat unappealing secondary character in the novel.

IN THE SWIRL OF RACIAL CONTROVERSY ABOUT THE LITTLE House books, the enduring appeal of Wilder's work has largely been forgotten. Why did generations of readers wholeheartedly admire the Little House novels? Why did her work endure and become embedded in American culture? Is it because the books seem to embrace what we now call traditional family values? Is it because they explore an inherently dramatic period of American history? Is it because the American West is itself so mythic? Is it because the novels feel real and true? Or does it have something to do with the intriguing intersection Wilder created between her fiction and her own life?

Yes—to all those questions.

These questions also underscore the complexity of the Little House series. Wilder's novels aren't predictable, one-dimensional books for very young and very inexperienced readers, although her first four Little House titles can certainly appeal to this group. Wilder's books—a total of eight in the Little House series—explore meaty, serious issues and illustrate a masterful understanding of plot, structure, theme, character, description, and dialogue.

Children's and Young Adult (YA) authors are rarely proclaimed artists, no matter their artistic contributions to the field; instead, if their literary legacy passes muster in this current cultural moment, they are usually deemed "beloved," which implies a sweetness and wholesomeness to their body of work. Yet the new realism Wilder brought to children's and YA literature made her novels "edgy" for the period in which she wrote them, and they remain thematically edgy and often dark even now. The fictional Ingalls family, for example, faces one existential crisis after another throughout the series, and Wilder doesn't cheerfully gloss over these threats, as her contemporary children's book authors usually did. In *Little House on the Prairie*, for example, six-year-old Laura realizes that if the family's wagon had been swept away in rushing flood water on their trek into Kansas, the "river would have rolled them over and over and carried them away and drowned them, and nobody would ever have known what became of them."[17]

Wilder's novels bring emotional depth to the page and so does the artistry of her voice. It contains unexpected complexity, speaking to young readers on one level, to adults on another. The Little House voice is sometimes subversive, an essential quality in fiction for young readers. In *On the Banks of Plum Creek*, Laura tells Mary she could be even meaner than Nellie Oleson "if Ma and Pa would let me."[18]

Over the course of the Little House books Wilder's voice evolves with her main character, subtly and gradually maturing as Laura herself matures (and by extension, as do Wilder's readers). Wilder didn't write the Little House books exclusively for six- or seven-year-olds. Her goal was that her readers would mature and grow over time, and like Laura, would be ready for what Wilder called the "adult stuff" in the final Little House books.[19]

WHEN READERS OF THE LITTLE HOUSE SERIES FIRST MEET Laura Ingalls, she is an intrepid preschooler. Seven books later, she is a somewhat reluctant eighteen-year-old bride. For any author, such a transition would pose an almost insurmountable creative challenge. Yet Wilder ages Laura Ingalls credibly. Her voice remains consistent as it seamlessly evolves from one book to the next, subtly and gradually maturing as Laura herself matures. Perhaps this is why the most fundamental and compelling reason readers across generations and across the world have embraced Wilder's work hinges on the fictional character of Laura Ingalls herself. She is an unconventional girl with warmth, passion, and grit. Her character is timeless and so compelling that many readers have come to feel not only a personal connection with the girl at the heart of the Little House series but with the author who created her. Wilder's books break down the barrier between author and reader, between the reality of the printed page and the imagined world that exists beyond it. This is a rare artistic achievement.

In many ways, Wilder was a literary rebel, perhaps because she had been something of a rebel herself as a girl. She broke literary rules in her books, and delved deeply into emotional truths, sometimes over the objections of her editors. Her voice was original; her achievements—both personal and literary—resonate through the decades. Yet over time her original voice and her innovative achievements became so much a part of the literary mainstream that they've now been largely forgotten.

For these reasons and more, the Little House books are too good, too important, to be altogether lost. And the best way to appreciate these stories is to read them again, and see what they're really about.

Acknowledgments

THIS BOOK HAD ITS BEGINNING OVER TEN YEARS AGO IN A conference room on the Missouri State University campus in Springfield, Missouri. At the time, I was researching and writing my second book on Laura Ingalls Wilder, a project titled *Laura Ingalls Wilder's Pioneer Girl: The Annotated Autobiography*, and had been invited to campus as a guest member of a committee to brainstorm interdisciplinary ideas for the university's Ozarks Studies program. Someone mentioned Laura Ingalls Wilder, and by the end of the meeting, faculty members decided to pursue two new classes, both on Wilder. One would be an online literature class for the university's traditional undergraduate students; the other would be a massive open online class for anyone interested in Wilder and her work. Both classes sprang to life in 2014, and the massive open online class was more successful than anyone could have imagined. During its two-year run, the class reached over ten thousand students worldwide. My lectures for those classes form the foundation of this book.

I'm grateful to Dr. Kathy Pulley, Dr. Kris Sutliff, Dr. Joye Norris, and Dr. W. D. Blackmon of Missouri State University for inviting me to be part of that Ozarks Studies committee all those years ago and then entrusting their new Wilder classes to me. I am also indebted to the MSU team assigned to support the massive open online classes: Lacey Geiger, Jessica Farrow, Hannah Julien, and Dan Rowland. Their tireless work, even as enrollments mushroomed unexpectedly, allowed me to focus on class content and, ultimately, the content of this book.

The late Jean Coday, the longtime director of the Laura Ingalls Wilder Historic Home and Museum in Mansfield, Missouri, was an essential part of the MSU team, allowing us to film class segments on location in Wilder's historic homes, where the Little House books were written. But Mrs. Coday's support for my Wilder research actually began in 2006, as I researched *Laura Ingalls Wilder: A*

Writer's Life, and continued throughout the four-year publication process for *Pioneer Girl*. During our last meeting shortly before her death in 2018, we discussed my vision for this book and Wilder's lasting influence on American middle grade and Young Adult fiction. Jean's diligent stewardship of the Wilder archives, homes, and museum ensured that researchers, as well as devoted readers of the Little House books, would have access to materials that not only preserved Wilder's literary legacy but inspired ongoing reading and research. Her insights into Wilder's life and work were indispensable.

Much of this book was written during the pandemic, when many Wilder institutions were closed to visitors and researchers. But librarians and archivists remained at work and responded promptly to my questions about primary materials in their collections. Supervisory archivist Craig Wright and archives technician Spencer Howard at the Herbert Hoover Presidential Library-Museum sent me numerous scans, including scans of Wilder's original manuscript for *The First Four Years*. I'm enormously grateful for their ongoing support over the years for my Wilder projects.

Nicholas Inman, the current director of the Laura Ingalls Wilder Historic Home and Museum, curator and special projects director Tana Melton, and staff assistant Kim Miller tirelessly fielded my ongoing requests about archival materials in their collection. They tracked down answers to even my most obscure questions and helped locate photographs that captured important moments in Wilder's writing life.

Haley Frizzle-Green, archivist with the State Historical Society of Missouri, located the microfilm copy of Wilder's 1894 travel diary and made special arrangements for my niece Holly Atkinson, acting as my research assistant, to scan it at the Springfield Research Center on the Missouri State University campus. My heartfelt thanks to both of them.

Anne Marie Baker, assistant professor at the MSU Meyer Library, and Brian Grubbs, local history and genealogy manager at the Springfield-Greene County Library, contributed useful advice on Wilder photographs in the Betty Love collection. Amos Bridges, editor of the *Springfield News-Leader*, and Jessica La Bozetta, reference archivist at the American Heritage Center at the University of Wyoming, helped locate elusive but essential images for this book.

Throughout the pandemic, my critique group in Portland, Oregon—authors Ellen Howard, Carmen T. Bernier Grand, Carolyn Conahan, Eric Kimmel, Susan Fletcher, Becky Hickox, Winnie Morris, and Nicole Rubel—provided constructive criticism and enthusiastic support for this book. Monthly Chez Zoom conversations with playwright Cynthia Whitcomb and authors Laura Whitcomb and Wendela Whitcomb Marsh were inspirational and made the writing life feel less lonely during the darkest days of the pandemic.

I'm deeply grateful to my friend and colleague William Anderson for his insights into not only Wilder's life and work but for the many lively and meaningful discussions we've shared over the years about All Things Wilder. Bill generously read my manuscript; his observations and suggestions have made this a better book. His knowledge, his books and articles, his presentations and interviews on Wilder have consistently strengthened my own work in this field. My sincere thanks to author Nancy McCabe, who also read my manuscript. Her encouragement and support mean more than I can say.

Wilder scholarship evolves, but all three of my books on Wilder are indebted to the work of biographers who published definitive books over twenty years ago—William Holtz and then John Miller, whose death in 2020 cast a shadow over this project. I'm also grateful to Noel Silverman at the Little House Heritage Trust for his ongoing support of Wilder scholarship and the legal team at Authors Guild for their excellent counsel.

The pandemic wasn't the only obstacle fate placed in my path during the writing of this book. My father's health declined dramatically from the moment I began work on chapter 1. As he faced one health crisis after another, my parents were forced to leave their home of fifty-nine years and move into an assisted living apartment, then into a nursing home. In 2023 my mother died unexpectedly. My father died a few months later. Throughout my family's ordeal, editor Bridget Barry remained patient, supportive, and committed to this project.

The editorial staff at the University of Nebraska Press provided outstanding professional support as the book approached publication. I'm especially grateful to project editor Sara Springsteen and copy editor Amy Pattullo.

Finally, I thank my immediate family—Chris Jacobson, my daughter Emily, her husband Jamie, and my sister Angela—for never losing faith in me or my work. And Opal and Callie, my flat-coated retrievers, who shared their office with me and made every writing day less solitary.

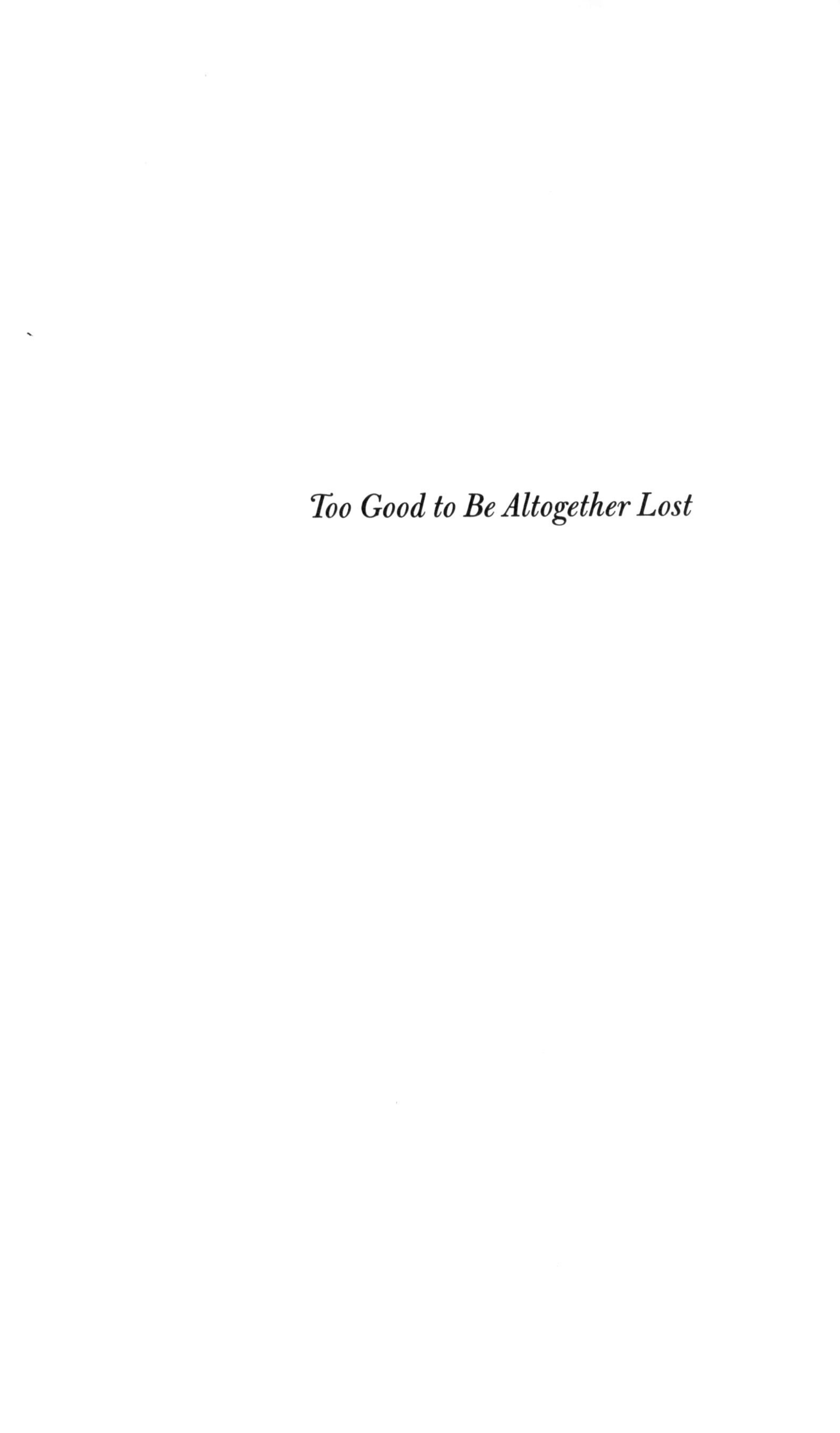

Too Good to Be Altogether Lost

1

Ambition

Sustaining a Dream

LAURA ELIZABETH INGALLS WAS BORN ON FEBRUARY 7, 1867, in Pepin County, Wisconsin, to a family that valued education, books, and music. She described her father, Charles Ingalls, as "a hunter and trapper, a musician and poet."[1] Her mother, Caroline Ingalls, had been a schoolteacher before she married, and instilled in her four daughters—Mary Amelia, Laura, Caroline Celestia, and Grace Pearl—a passion for learning. They were a literary family, despite their poverty.

As a preschooler, Laura taught herself to read, thanks to her older sister Mary, who "would show me the letters and the words she had learned that day [at school], until, to Ma's surprise, I could read as well as Mary."[2] Laura vividly remembered the gift she received for her fifth birthday, "a pretty little book of verses called 'The Floweret.'"[3] The family often read aloud together, and their modest library followed them across the frontier—from Wisconsin, possibly to Missouri, then to Kansas, back to Wisconsin, on to Minnesota, east to Iowa, back to Minnesota, and finally to Dakota Territory, where Charles and Caroline permanently settled in 1879. Laura was twelve. The town of De Smet sprang up around them. Its thriving township school—and one teacher in particular—would inspire Laura Ingalls, top student in the class, to become Laura Ingalls Wilder, the influential, groundbreaking American author. Thc transformation took almost fifty years. Wilder's ambition to write, born as a teenager, spanned decades and never quite failed her.

IN THE FALL OF 1883, SIXTEEN-YEAR-OLD LAURA INGALLS faced a dilemma common to most high school students: completing an assignment she didn't understand. She'd missed school the day before, when her teacher, V. S. L. (Ven) Owen, had assigned her class to write their "first compositions" on the subject of "Ambition." Unlike her classmates, who "had prepared their papers at home the night before," she had to write hers quickly in class—before Mr. Owen called on her to read her composition aloud.[4] Adding to the pressure: she feared she'd lose her standing in class if her composition failed. Mr. Owen felt she "had a wonderful mind and memory."[5] She didn't want to disappoint him or herself.

A Flawed Original

Writing an original composition was an unusual assignment in 1883, even for advanced students. Usually they were expected to memorize and then recite multiplication tables, important dates and events in American history, or long passages from such books as *The Independent Fifth Reader*. But Ven Owen was an unusual educator. Hired as teacher and principal of the De Smet's township school no. 2 in September 1883, he was neat and dapper with a quick, sharp intellect. He ran an efficient school but challenged scholars with innovative techniques and assignments—like writing an original composition.

"I couldn't make a start," Wilder remembered years later, "and in despair went to the dictionary to see what it had to say about ambition, hoping to get an idea."[6] She went back to her desk and wrote quickly.

Her original draft began, "Ambition denotes a desire of preferment, or of honor. It is also used to denote an inordinate desire of power or eminence."[7] From there, Wilder turned to the word's origins but soon realized something wasn't right. She drew lines across her first draft, turned the page over, and started again. Instinctively, she had recognized an essential principle of professional writing: ruthless revision.

For her second and final draft, Wilder interpreted the dictionary's definition more personally: "Ambition is, like other good things, a good only when used in moderation." She embellished this idea and for her new conclusion, turned to Shakespeare: "Ambition is a good servant but a hard master; and if you think it is likely to become your master: I would say to you in the world of the immortal Shakespeare: Cromwell, I charge thee fling away ambition, by the sin fell the angels." Wilder had apparently written her revision so quickly that she unintentionally wrote "world" instead of "words."[8] She finished just in time to read her composition aloud:

> Mr. Owen looked sharply at me when I had finished reading it, and said, "You have written compositions before."
>
> "Oh no Sir!" said I, "This is my first."
>
> "Well you should write more of them," he said. "I wouldn't have believed any one could have done so well the first time."[9]

A Privately Nurtured Ambition

Wilder kept this composition for the rest of her life. "First composition I ever wrote," she noted in pencil in the margins of the original, adding the date and place, "De Smet, Dak Ter, 1883."[10] Why did she keep it decade after decade? It was nothing more than a school assignment, not a published piece of writing. What meaning could it have held for her?

Like Wilder, I aspired to become a writer when I was young. Although I didn't keep any high school assignments or compositions, I still have bound issues of the high school and college newspapers I edited. They symbolized a promise I made to myself as a teenager: that someday I would become a real writer, earning my living by my pen. Perhaps "Ambition" symbolized something similar for Wilder, a dream formed when she was young and inexperienced, an ambition privately nurtured over decades. Ven Owen's assignment, after all, had given Wilder her first audience, and her first public praise from an informed and perceptive reader, a reader who encouraged her to write more. "Ambition" held the promise of what she might someday become: a writer with something important to say.

An Ideal Literary Opportunity

"Ambition's" story, however, didn't end in Ven Owen's classroom back in 1883, or in Wilder's personal collection of papers, newspaper clippings, and letters. Sixty years later, when Wilder was a successful children's book author, she rewrote "Ambition" one more time, placing it in a pivotal scene in *These Happy Golden Years*, her last Little House book. By then, her personal literary ambitions had been fulfilled. She had already published seven Little House books, a series of historically realistic novels built around a fictional version of her own family. A fiercer, braver, more accomplished fictional Laura Ingalls emerged as the main character. Within the context of these novels, however, Wilder hadn't yet dropped her readers a hint that the Laura Ingalls of the books might grow up to become an author. "Ambition" gave her the ideal literary opportunity.

When the fictional Laura Ingalls writes her version of "Ambition," it is more polished, more skillfully written than Wilder's original from 1883. Laura doesn't need a rough draft. She writes perfectly under pressure: "Ambition is necessary to accomplishment. Without an ambition to gain an end, nothing could be done. Without an ambition to excel others and to surpass one's self there would be no superior merit. To win anything we must have the ambition to do so."[11] Perhaps the fictional "Ambition" of *These Happy Golden Years* reflects Wilder's more mature insight into her own ambition to write, a dream she sustained over a lifetime and finally accomplished.

Kind Reader, Be Judge

Wilder's initial adolescent ambition, however, went beyond writing compositions for Ven Owen. She also wrote verse, influenced perhaps not only by the poems the family read together but by Caroline Ingalls herself, who made a "book" from "writing paper" in which she wrote "some of her own poetry" and also "copied some that she liked."[12] As a teenager Wilder made a similar book, and one of her earliest verses reveals a budding writer's preoccupation with voice and vocabulary, concepts essential to all writers. In the poem, the writer compares her preference for simple, direct vocabulary to her friend's more pretentious choices:

> . . . I go to the school
> Which she attends
> In which I have "chums"
> And she has "friends."

She works "difficult problems"
While I do "hard sums"
She says it "continues"
While I say it "runs."[13]

Wilder also appears to have written poems throughout her courtship and engagement to Almanzo Wilder. One seems to refer to their separation in 1884, when she was seventeen. Almanzo and his brother had left Dakota Territory for a lengthy trek through Nebraska and Iowa "with a covered hack and a stock of notions to sell on the road."[14] The poem reads:

You're far away and yet so near,
In word, and deed, and thought.
Your pleasant voice, I seem to hear
And feel the joy it brought.

I seem to hear your manly tread;
Your happy smile to see;
And distance loses half its dread;
You seem so near to me.[15]

The line "I seem to hear your manly tread" is both clever and sentimental: throughout their courtship and sixty-four years of marriage, Wilder called her husband "Manly," not Almanzo. The line is especially moving, given that just four years later, Manly "suffered a slight stroke of paralysis" after a life-threatening battle with diphtheria.[16] As their daughter later observed, "He limped through the rest of his ninety years."[17] His "manly tread" was forever altered.

A Series of Tragedies

As she had done with "Ambition," Wilder saved her adolescent verse. But she appeared to set aside her literary ambitions when she and Manly married on August 25, 1885. She was eighteen; he was twenty-eight.

Over the next four years, the couple endured a series of merciless personal tragedies: a hailstorm ruined their wheat crop in 1886; a fire burned their barn to the ground in 1887; diphtheria and Manly's stroke left them both weakened and frail in 1888; an infant son died in 1889; and another fire that same year destroyed their house. If Wilder continued to write privately during these years, this work is lost to the historical record. But it's hard to imagine she had the time or inclination to write, given the crushing circumstances she endured during this period.

The one bright spot in Wilder's first four years of marriage was the birth of her daughter Rose, born December 5, 1886. She was named for the wild prairie roses that flower across eastern South Dakota in June. Forty-four years later, Wilder described them as "the sweetest roses that ever bloomed," and told her daughter, "You are their namesake, my dear."[18]

By her own account, Rose was headstrong and willful, right from the beginning. She recalled an argument with a photographer when she was five years old: "The photographer . . . kept putting my right hand on top of the left, and I kept changing them back because I wanted my carnelian ring to show. And in the end, I won out."[19]

The family gave up on farming in South Dakota in 1890 and moved to Spring Valley, Minnesota, where Manly's parents lived. From there they moved to Florida in October 1891, then back to South Dakota in August 1892. There Wilder and Manly saved enough money for one final move—to the Missouri Ozarks in 1894, to give farming one last try.

To Tell in Plain Prose

The move to Missouri apparently rekindled Wilder's writing ambitions, and she determined to keep a diary along the way. Among the possessions she packed in their two-seated hack, which would take them to Missouri: her pearl-handled pen and a portable writing desk Manly had made for her. They set out from De Smet, South Dakota, on July 17, 1894. Her first entry was brief and factual, without a hint of regret at leaving family and friends behind: "Started at 8^{40}. Three miles out Russian thistles. Harvesting wheat. Crossed the line into Miner County at 2 o'clock. . . . Camped by a spring that cannot be pumped but plenty of feed [for the horses]. Grain about 8 inches high, will go about 1½ bu[shels] for acre. Hot wind."[20] Wilder recorded her observations of the seven-hundred-mile journey in a four-inch by six-and-a-half-inch notebook from the Mutual Life Insurance Company of New York. She wrote almost every day, from July 17 until August 30.

An edited version of this diary was published posthumously in 1962 as *On the Way Home*. It features an introduction by Rose Wilder Lane, who appears to have copyedited her mother's diary, replacing sentence fragments with complete sentences, standardizing punctuation and grammar, and reorganizing passages for better clarity. She also appears to have invented entries, including one of my favorites: "The sky seems lower here, and it is the softest blue," a description of an Ozark sky.[21] The result is a polished, sophisticated diary, one that gives Wilder a calm, self-assured, and experienced voice. But it robs the original of its immediacy and spontaneity. Gone is the sense that Wilder was writing in the moment, uncertain of her family's future, yet curious, interested, and engaged with what she observed along the road.

Despite its raw, unfinished style, the original diary foreshadows the kind of writer Wilder would eventually become, a writer with an eye for detail, dialogue, character, and description. In the following passage, for example, Wilder clearly was writing in haste, yet she combines precise details with description and even dialogue: "Crossed the line into Hutchinson Co at 10. They are mowing buffalo grass for hay. Passed a great pile of stone that had been cleared of[f] the land. Some good wheat. 12 o'clock Russian settlement. Adobe houses & barns & chicken houses and piles of peat to burn. . . . Houses are mostly back from the road and a good many of them are built long[,] the house on one end & the barn in the other. . . . This is a nice country but 'nix good this year, nix good last year' as one Russian said."[22] Throughout this diary, Wilder describes the crops, livestock, farming practices, soil, and weather conditions she saw along the way. Her insights and observations on the business of farming would prove useful to her writing career later on.

On rare occasions, Wilder's diary entries include her own emotional responses to the scenes she observed on this journey. One passage in particular leaps out. It hints at her ambition to become a writer and foreshadows a subject that now colors perceptions of Wilder's literary legacy: "We crossed the James River & reached the top of the bluffs on the other side in 20 minutes. We all stopped & looked back at the scene & I wished for an artist hand or a poet brain or even to be able to tell in good plain prose how beautiful it was. If I had been the Indians I would have scalped more white folks before I would have left it."[23] The passage is revealing. It illustrates not only how the beauty of the West inspired Wilder but suggests that at least on some level, she recognized what Native Americans had lost.

At this point in the diary, Wilder appears to have attempted an experiment in "plain prose," struggling to find the right words and phrases to capture the natural beauty of the moment: "We could see the water gleaming between the trees which ~~seemed to wind back and around and across the valley like [illegible]~~ grew on the banks as[?] the river [moved?] along down the valley. The bluffs rose high & bare, on the other side brown & burned & the ~~little~~ lovely green trees & grass and shining water at their feet & on this side the bluffs again like ~~brown~~ gigantic brown waves tumbled & tossed about." The crossed-out words and phrases are Wilder's. But before she could revise and refine her description, the family was on the move again, passing cornfields and "cottonwood hedges."[24]

Wilder didn't intend to publish this travel diary, but from its pages she produced her first published piece—a letter to the editor of De Smet's *News and Leader*. Posted from Lamar, Missouri, on August 28, 1894, and signed simply "Laura Wilder," the one-column newspaper clipping includes just nine short paragraphs. It's well written but otherwise unremarkable—except that in the clipping's left-hand margin, written in pencil in Wilder's hand are the words, "First I ever had published."[25] Those nine published paragraphs were clearly important to her.

Simply Glorious

The family arrived in Mansfield, Missouri, on August 30, 1894. Wilder was twenty-seven. Both she and her husband fell almost immediately under the spell of the Missouri Ozarks. As she recorded in her diary, "Driving along a lovely road through the woods shaded by oak trees. The farther we go east the better we like it. Parts of Nebraska & Kansas were nice but Mo. is simply glorious." Manly interrupted her as she was writing to say, "It is a beautiful country."[26] Until her death, sixty-three years later, the Ozarks would be Wilder's home.

On the outskirts of Mansfield, she and Manly bought a forty-acre farm, which included a log cabin, two hundred young apple trees that had been "set out" on land "so poor it would not raise a stalk of corn over 4 feet high," and an additional eight hundred young apple trees that, once planted, would cover "an additional twenty acres."[27] They named their newly acquired property Rocky Ridge Farm. Over time, they increased their holdings to two hundred acres, and transformed the cabin into a remarkable farmhouse, unlike any in the county. But their success in Mansfield didn't come quickly or easily. They rented and eventually bought a small house in town, where Wilder occasionally prepared homecooked meals for local businessmen. Manly ran a draying business. In between, they worked the farm.

Rose, who was seven when her parents moved to Missouri, wasn't happy in the Ozarks. "I lived through a childhood that was a nightmare," she claimed. "No sensitive child who has gone to school from a poverty-besieged home, in patched clothes, with second-hand books, fails to learn that human beings are barbarous."[28]

As an adult, Rose was given to hyperbole and invention, but her displeasure with Ozark life appears to have been real. Wilder apparently recognized her daughter's unhappiness, and allowed her to finish high school in Crowley, Louisiana. Manly's widowed sister Eliza lived there with her son. Rose returned to Mansfield briefly after graduation in 1904 but quickly moved north—to Kansas City, where she became what she called a "bachelor girl" and went to work as a telegraph operator. The move propelled her into a more cosmopolitan environment, and would profoundly transform her professional life—and her mother's.

A Tale of Mystery

Between 1894 and 1910, Wilder's own ambition to write appears to have stalled, although one especially intriguing writing fragment, what Wilder described as "a tale of mystery," could date from this period. It may have been her first attempt to use her own experiences from childhood—"when the two Dakotas were still one territory"—in a work of fiction. The fragment appears on the backs of stock requisition order forms for the Waters Pierce Oil Company, one dated February 20, 1903, the other February 22, 1903.[29] Almanzo Wilder made deliveries for the company and Wilder herself kept its books.

At first glance, the fragment seems unlike anything readers have come to associate with Laura Ingalls Wilder and her work:

> In the days of old when black magic was practiced, by aid of Devil, magacins [*sic*] were credited with being able to transport themselves long distances almost instantly.
>
> Let me tell you a weird tale of later days when it was thought the Black Art had long since been abandoned.
>
> I make no attempt at explanation, leaving you free to form your own conclusion from the facts, which are vouched for by persons yet in the prime of life. If names were given they could also be verified by court proceedings. No this is a tale of mystery and it remains a mystery to the end.[30]

A tale of the supernatural from Laura Ingalls Wilder? Where is her pioneer realism and its authenticity? How could a story touching on "black magic" have autobiographical underpinnings? Even the voice of Wilder's narrator in this fragment feels slightly jarring, perhaps even derivative as it attempts to persuade readers that this "weird" tale can be "verified." It echoes Washington Irving's narrator in "The Legend of Sleepy Hollow" or Charles Dickens's voice in *A Christmas Carol*.

Yet Wilder's narrator quickly transitions to a setting and a voice that predicts the writer she would become: "It was December . . . and the wind was howling outside and the snow was drifting as only the wind can howl and the snow drift across an unbroken prairie. We were just a little lonely that eve for it was nearing Christmas time and we were 40 miles from our nearest neighbor at the little RR station to the East." From there, the scene moves into even more familiar territory: "We sat close to the fire for warmth for the house was only a pioneer cabin with thin walls unfinished. Mother was reading to us by the light of the kerosene lamp on the small table beside her and we were listening interestedly when we were startled by a rap on the door."[31]

This scene is based on Wilder's memory of the Christmas her family spent in the surveyors' house on Silver Lake in 1879. As Wilder later wrote in *Pioneer Girl*, the Ingalls family's nearest neighbors "were forty miles away to the east," and on Christmas Eve they were alone, "sitting around the fire and the lamp on the table reading and talking" until they "heard a shout outside." As devoted Wilder readers know, the shout is from the family's friend Robert Boast, who along with his wife Ella, has braved the "deep drifts" of snow all the way from Iowa to spend Christmas and the rest of the winter with the Ingalls family.[32]

In Wilder's mystery story, however, the door swings "slowly open" to reveal "in the dim light from the small lamp, with midnight blackness behind," the shape of a very tall man with "flashing black eyes & a droopy black mustache covered with frost and snow." He has arrived at the family's door, through the bitter cold and drifting snow "without overcoat or overshoes."[33] And here the fragment ends.

Despite its brevity, the fragment is revealing, and suggests that perhaps Wilder retained an ambition to write even as her duties as a farm wife and part-time bookkeeper demanded most of her energy. And despite the fragment's supernatural plot, Wilder was clearly inspired by her own frontier memories. This fragment also reveals that she was conscious of getting every word right. Wilder didn't just dash out this story idea. She revised as she wrote, crossing out phrases and rearranging key details to improve the rhythm and flow of her paragraphs. Here, for example, is her complete description of the stranger at the door: "He was extremely tall and thin with flashing black eyes & a droopy black mustache covered with frost and snow ~~and~~ [this next phrase is circled and a line indicates it should follow 'flashing black eyes'] rather long black hair ~~also full of snow~~ His face was dead white and very thin with a prominent beak like nose."[34] Wilder was thinking like a professional, revising and editing even her roughest drafts.

What motivated Wilder to pursue a supernatural story in the first place? It seems like an unusual genre for her. Yet several of her abbreviated story lines that also appear on the backs of Waters Pierce order forms have a supernatural emphasis. In one, for example, a "lone man" sits "waiting for a train." He feels a "presence" touch his face and then runs "frantically" searching for its source but finds "nothing." There's another about a haunted house, and a third about an "old professor"—a "spiritualist"—running over the prairie.[35]

Of course, Wilder could have been motivated to write about the supernatural for purely commercial reasons. Maybe she felt this kind of story might sell, although there's no evidence that she developed any of them further or attempted to market them. There's also one other tantalizing possibility: Charles Ingalls's death in June 1902 may have influenced Wilder's impulse to merge a supernatural plot with her own girlhood memories of Dakota Territory. Her father was a gifted storyteller; Wilder may have been attempting to carry on that tradition.

Ideas for Work

Still, as tempting as it may be to interpret Wilder's motivation for her "tale of mystery" in this light, it's impossible to know with any certainty why or even *when* Wilder wrote this piece. It appears as part of a random collection of what Wilder labeled "Ideas for work" and stored in a letter-sized envelope from the editor's office of *Farm World*, a publication headquartered in Chicago. The envelope's postmark reads 1912. The ideas in the envelope appear to span several decades, including a humorous piece about the "first car that came to the Ozarks," written on the back of a young reader's fan letter from May 1940.[36]

This envelope also contains six pages of typewritten letter fragments from Lane, written a few years after her marriage to Claire Gillette Lane in 1909, and several years before she launched her own successful writing career with the *San Francisco Bulletin* in 1915. With characteristic self-confidence, Lane advises her mother on how to monetize her writing talents by writing promotional and advertising copy for local newspapers "similar to Claire's [scheme] in Oklahoma," but doesn't refer to Wilder's interest in writing fiction or to her supernatural story ideas.[37]

Given the range of material in the "Ideas for work" file, dating Wilder's "tale of mystery" to 1903 is admittedly guesswork. It's equally plausible that Wilder may have tucked her Waters Pierce bookkeeping records away, then years later when those forms had outlived their usefulness, decided to put them to a new, more creative use. A letter from Wilder to Lane in 1937 even suggests this scenario.

In the letter Wilder offers Lane "some notes I made years ago, thinking I would use them sometime. I never will, I am sure, but perhaps you can use them . . . , so I have copied them and here they are." Wilder goes on to explain that these "anecdotes" date from "when Wilson was president"—between 1913 and 1921. Unfortunately, the notes Wilder copied for Lane haven't survived. All that remains now is Wilder's obscure and brief description of them within the text of the letter itself, summarized in just three sentences: "I saw the Mt. Zion and Mt. Pleasant meetings myself. Mrs. Frink told of the woman who wouldn't look in the glass. She knew of her and said it actually happened that way."[38]

This description doesn't correspond to Wilder's "tale of mystery" or the other supernatural story ideas she wrote on the backs of those Waters Pierce forms from 1903. The woman "who wouldn't look in the [looking?] glass" appears nowhere in any of Wilder's existing papers except here, in this one intriguing phrase. Still, there's a catch. Written on the front of those forms from 1903 are a pair of fragments that may be about meetings—revival meetings.

A fragment that appears on the front of the form dated February 20, 1903, opens this way: "Oh Sister Boggs have you heard the news? The Baptists have sued us for $2 apiece for the converts they say we [Methodists] coaxed away from them."[39] This fragment, however, doesn't refer to either a Mt. Zion or a Mt. Pleasant congregation. While a pair of churches with those names had a long history in Wright County, Missouri, a short drive from Rocky Ridge Farm, both were *Baptist* congregations.[40] It's possible, of course, that in this fragment, Wilder chose to pit the Baptists against the Methodists to disguise a Baptist versus Baptist rivalry, but this too is pure conjecture.

The second fragment, written on the front of the Waters Pierce form dated February 22, 1903, doesn't have a specific setting, but like Wilder's Dakota "tale of mystery," it reveals a writer at work, searching for the right word or phrase: "Those who have never heard the old fashioned revival hymn sung ~~enthusiastically~~ by a half frenzied crowd with their ~~for that time being fanatical~~ minds all ~~bent on~~ concentrated on the one ~~idea~~ object can have no idea of the lilt and swing and compelling force of it. No battle music ever created a greater enthusiasm for the charge than this."[41] Undoubtedly, this fragment is about a revival meeting, but since it has no specific setting—no church or denomination is mentioned—it's impossible to know if it was one of the anecdotes Wilder copied out for Lane in 1937.

Whatever their history, Wilder's early creative experiments exploring Ozark religious fervor, the supernatural, or even her adolescent memories of Dakota Territory played no meaningful role in launching her professional writing career. Instead, her writing career was built on her experiences at Rocky Ridge Farm with Manly.

Wake Up to Your Opportunities

In 1910 Wilder published a column in the *St. Louis Star Farmer* about raising Leghorn hens. The following year, her first article appeared in the *Missouri Ruralist*, a weekly agricultural newspaper published in Kansas City, Missouri. Writing from a farm woman's perspective as Mrs. A. J. Wilder, she concluded, "If there are any country women who are wasting their time envying their sisters in the city—don't do it. Such an attitude is out of date. Wake up to your opportunities."[42]

A short verse by Mrs. A. J. Wilder appeared in an April issue, and then on July 22, 1911, the *Missouri Ruralist* featured an article headlined "The Story of Rocky Ridge Farm" by A. J. Wilder. Its opening line was intriguing and accomplished. "To appreciate fully the reason why we named our place Rocky Ridge Farm, it should have been seen at the time of the christening." The writer noted that the land "was and is, uncompromisingly ridge land, on the very tip top of the ridge at that, within a very few miles of the highest point in the Ozarks."[43]

In fact, the writer wasn't A. J. Wilder—Manly, or "the Man of the Place," as readers of the *Missouri Ruralist* later came to know him. It was Wilder herself. She apparently submitted the article in response to the *Ruralist*'s "farm home story contest." But as the newspaper's editor explained to his readers, the writer had submitted the story not "for any prize," but only for publication—if it was found "worthy." The editor added, "We certainly believe it worthy . . . and believe all contributors to this feature will approve of our giving it good position on this page since we cannot give it a prize."[44] The story appeared on page three. Wilder was forty-four.

She was not an introspective writer. No letters or diaries exist that convey her feelings about fulfilling what appears to have been an ambition she had sustained for decades. But she must have found the editor's admiration for "The Story of Rocky Ridge Farm" gratifying. It was the first public praise her writing had earned since Ven Owen had told her, twenty-eight years earlier, "You should write more."

Still, this major breakthrough wasn't one she could publicly own. Wilder initially published her *Ruralist* work under a genderless pseudonym. Although farm women were an important part of its audience (the newspaper had endorsed women's suffrage by the time Wilder became a contributor), she must have surmised that male readers in the early twentieth century would be more inclined to read a serious article about farming experiences and practices if it appeared under a presumably male byline. Using her husband's initials initially gave Wilder's published work more credibility. In June 1912 another feature article by A. J. Wilder appeared in the *Missouri Ruralist*, along with a front-cover photograph of Manly, posing in their apple orchard.

She Writes Well

In 1913 the *Missouri Ruralist* hired a new editor—John F. Case. He set out to create "a more friendly, interesting, and personable style" at the newspaper.[45] He also wanted to engage more women readers. Wilder's talent and voice matched Case's mission, and in 1913, she began publishing regularly under her own byline, "Mrs. A. J. Wilder."

Most of her published work for the *Ruralist* was directed toward the newspaper's female audience. In "A Plain Beauty Talk," for example, she admonished farm women to look their best: "It is not vanity to wish to appear pleasing to the eyes of our home folks and friends. . . . To be well groomed and good to look at will give us an added self respect and a greater influence over others."[46] Wilder's article "All in the Day's Work" opens with praise for the impressive contributions Missouri farm women made to the state's economy: "How many persons when reading the astonishing amount received in a year for Missouri poultry and eggs think of the fact that it is practically all produced by the women, and as a sideline at that!"[47] In "What the War Means to Women," published in May 1918, Wilder wrote passionately about World War I and its implications for women: "All over the world women are bravely taking their part in the conflict and doing what they can to defend those things they hold most sacred."[48]

Under Case's editorial direction, Wilder became a columnist and page editor for the *Missouri Ruralist*. Eventually her columns were published under the title "The Farm Home" and later "As a Farm Woman Thinks." In 1918 Case profiled Wilder for the *Ruralist*. Published alongside a handsome studio photograph of Wilder, his article was titled "Let's Visit Mrs. Wilder." Noting that she had been part of the *Missouri Ruralist* longer than anyone else on its editorial staff, Case wrote that Wilder "knows farm folks and their problems as few women who write know them. And having sympathy with the folks whom she serves she writes well."[49]

Essential Writing Concepts

By then, Wilder had grasped the essentials of farm journalism. She wrote about topics that interested her audience in an engaging and personable style. She had also perfected essential journalistic techniques. Her columns usually began with what's known in journalism as a compelling "lead." For a feature story or column, a good lead involves creating a hook, a memorable line or opening that will draw readers into a story and keep them reading. She also had learned how to capture essential qualities about the personalities she sometimes profiled in her columns, including Manly. A column from July 1917 illustrates Wilder's grasp of both these principles: "The Man of the Place brought me a bouquet of wild flowers this morning. It has been a habit of his for years."[50]

Another essential concept Wilder mastered during her *Ruralist* years was an effective use of dialogue and quotations. By capturing someone's speech, she provided readers with a glimpse into his or her character. Dialogue also brought more color and humor into her writing. In 1916, for example, she began her column "So

We Moved the Spring" with a series of anecdotes, which included comic dialogue: "'Why don't you dig a well,' asked a stranger, 'and not haul water so far?' 'Well,' said the farmer, 'it's about as fur to water one way as 'tis t'other.'"[51] Wilder sprinkled quotations throughout more serious columns as well. In a profile about a successful Wright County cattle and hog farm, she used quotations from the farm's manager—a Mrs. Wilson—to convey her subject's agricultural knowledge and perspective: "The Shorthorns [cattle] have all other breeds beaten when it comes to making money for their owners," Mrs. Wilson observed. "Besides they are aristocrats and we think them the most beautiful of any."[52]

The Right to Self-Expression

Wilder wrote several columns based on personal experiences, but few of them provide direct insight into her writing life, or what drew her to write for the *Ruralist* in the first place. But in her column, "If We Only Understood," Wilder references the first professional writer she knew, Mrs. Laura Brown, wife of the minister who had officiated at Wilder and Manly's marriage in Dakota Territory. The column begins with a compelling lead: "Mrs. Brown was queer. The neighbors all thought so and, what was worse, they all said so." As the column unfolds, readers learn that Mrs. Brown is "queer" because she's forsaken the conventional role of keeping house, and instead is writing professionally. The column then pleads for tolerance and understanding. "We should be willing to allow others the freedom we demand for ourselves. Everyone has the right to self expression."[53]

Wilder later wrote about Mrs. Brown in her memoir, "Pioneer Girl," and her portrait there is sharper, less tolerant: "Mrs. Brown was literary and wrote for several church papers, neglecting her personal appearance and her house which was always in a dirty disorder."[54] Taken together, these two references to Mrs. Brown could provide a clue into the long delay between Wilder's adolescent writing ambitions and their fulfillment decades later. Perhaps Wilder needed to find the right balance between the responsibilities she felt compelled to perform for her family and the more personal desire for self-expression as a published writer.

Wilder continued to write for the *Missouri Ruralist* through 1924, when she was fifty-seven. She didn't publish a farewell column to readers, nor did she leave behind a written explanation for her decision to stop contributing to the newspaper. But it's possible that by the end of 1924, a bigger, more ambitious writing project was beginning to take shape in Wilder's imagination. Her final regular column for the *Missouri Ruralist* appears to provide an essential clue to this project's subject.

The column, published on December 15, 1924, is autobiographical and focuses on a harrowing sleigh ride Wilder made with Manly when she was just sixteen, two years before they were married. In the column, Wilder records that they covered twelve miles over isolated prairie:

> When we reached the journey's end, it was 40 degrees below zero, the snow was blowing so thickly that we could not see across the street and I was so chilled that I had to be half carried into the house. But I was home for Christmas and cold and danger were forgotten.
>
> Such magic there is in Christmas to draw the absent ones home and if unable to go in the body the thoughts will hover there! Our hearts grow tender with childhood memories and love of kindred.[55]

Wilder's ambitions appear to have turned to drawing "the absent ones home" through "childhood memories and love of kindred," a project outside the scope of the *Missouri Ruralist*.

Caroline Quiner Ingalls, Wilder's mother, had died unexpectedly in 1924 on Easter Sunday. To mark her mother's passing, Wilder wrote one of her shortest columns for the *Missouri Ruralist*. Published in June 1924, the column includes a line that suggests Wilder was beginning to revisit her past even then: "The world seems a lonesome place when mother has passed away and only memories of her are left us."[56] By the following year, those memories had taken on a new urgency. In June 1925 Wilder wrote her mother's sister, asking for "any special stories" about "what you and mother and Aunt Eliza and Uncle Tom and Uncle Henry did as children and young folks." Wilder had hoped to collect these stories from her mother, but as she wrote her aunt, "Now it is too late to ever get them from her."[57]

Wilder's request for stories about her mother's past carried a professional component as well as a personal one. Not only did Wilder instruct her aunt to relate those stories "in your own words as you would . . . if only you could talk to me," she offered to pay a stenographer to more easily and accurately record her aunt's memories.[58] Her aunt responded—no stenographer was needed—but Wilder filed the letter away and her writing career idled, waiting to be ignited by yet another loss.

Getting People Down on Paper

The same year Wilder published her story about keeping chickens in the *St. Louis Star Farmer*, her daughter landed a reporting job with the *Kansas City Star*. Mother and daughter seemed to be on parallel career paths. But the daughter—Rose Wilder Lane—had professional connections unavailable to her mother.

The year before—in 1909—Lane had moved to San Francisco. She met and married a reporter for the *San Francisco Call*, Claire Gillette Lane (known as Gillette). Perhaps his experience as a journalist influenced Lane's decision to become a reporter after the couple moved to Kansas City. But the coincidence between the timing of Wilder's debut as a farm journalist and her daughter's start as a cub reporter is striking.

Like her mother, Lane had grown up in a household that valued books and storytelling. As she later recalled, "My mother loves courage and beauty and books."[59] The Rocky Ridge farmhouse even had its own its library, a paneled nook off the living room with built-in bookshelves. Lane wrote that she "was brought up on [my mother's] pioneer stories," but they didn't inspire her: "never a spark from me," she observed.[60] Yet Lane couldn't quite escape those stories; nor, apparently, could she escape an ambition to become a storyteller, like her mother.

When she and Gillette returned to San Francisco in 1911, Lane used his contacts at the *San Francisco Bulletin* to eventually establish herself as a freelance writer. Just four years later, she began writing a regular column on the new women's page for the *Bulletin*, using it as a springboard for freelance assignments with *Sunset*, a notable regional magazine even then. Lane published her first book, *Henry Ford's Own Story*, in 1917, and produced one book after another through the 1920s. She transitioned from writing nonfiction to fiction, publishing her first novel in 1919. Just a year after the publication of her first book, *Sunset* asked Lane to produce an autobiographical profile for its readers. While her profile doesn't explain why she had become a writer, it does address what interested and challenged her creatively. "I like people—clerks and farmers and highwaymen and tramps and elevator girls and poets and lawyers—all sorts of people. I would like better to write about them if only I could get them down on paper exactly as they really are."[61]

Yet Lane struggled to get people down on paper exactly as they really were. Among her earliest published feature articles for the *Bulletin* were fictionalized accounts of invented characters and their situations, presented to readers as true stories. Lane seemed drawn toward the sensational, imagining dialogue, scenes, and motivations, even for the public figures she later profiled—from Henry Ford to Jack London. London's widow, for example, charged Lane with publishing a "misleading" biographical series on her husband, filled with misrepresentations and "false impressions" about his life and work.[62] Lane herself admitted that, "Of course the whole thing is fictionalized," and added that she was simply trying to get "at the truth rather than at the facts."[63] Lane's biographer has characterized this aspect of her writing life as an "easy ethical slide" from truth to fiction, even when writing nonfiction.[64] This ethical slide characterized much of Lane's work, and would later influence the way she represented her mother's Little House books.

But Wilder herself was proud of her daughter's accomplishments. In one of her last *Ruralist* columns, titled, "What Makes My Country Great," Wilder included Lane in a list of "distinguished" people from Mansfield and Wright County, Missouri. Without directly identifying Lane as her daughter, Wilder described "Rose Wilder Lane" as a "writer and world traveler, whose books and short stories are published in the United States and England and have been translated into foreign languages."[65]

Yet earlier in her career, when mother and daughter were both still relatively new to their writing lives, Wilder wasn't sure she was ready to pursue publication as aggressively as Lane. "I intend to try to do some writing that will count," she wrote Manly from San Francisco, where she was visiting their daughter in 1915, "but would not be driven by the work as she is for anything and I do not see how she can stand it." In a line that perhaps sums up the balance Wilder sought to make between her personal and professional ambitions, she noted, "The more I see of how Rose works the better satisfied I am to raise chickens."[66]

2

Pioneer Girl

Literary Mother Lode

ON MAY 7, 1930, LAURA INGALLS WILDER FINISHED THE FIRST draft of her first book-length manuscript, an autobiography titled, "Pioneer Girl."[1] Written on tablet paper in pencil, the manuscript describes Wilder's childhood and adolescence in the American West. She told her daughter that she hoped this book would earn her "prestige rather than money."[2] Wilder had been haunted by the idea of autobiographical writing for decades, and as early as 1919 she was apparently working on a semi-autobiographical story for *McCall's* magazine, tracing "the contrast between girls today and girls in . . . [her] youth." The draft of this article no longer survives, but a lengthy letter from Lane, filled with editorial suggestions to improve it, hints at its contents: "Your log cabin in the Great Woods . . . , your trip through Kansas . . .—the building of the railroad through the Dakotas . . .—Make it all real, because you saw it with your own eyes."[3]

Wilder, however, abandoned the project, and instead published several columns, centering on memories from her childhood and adolescence, for the *Missouri Ruralist*. Her older sister Mary died in October 1928, and perhaps motivated by a sense of her own mortality, Wilder finished "Pioneer Girl" just over eighteen months later at the age of sixty-three, the same age as Mary at the time of her death. Lane edited the manuscript, producing several different versions, and submitted them to two literary agents. "Pioneer Girl" was politely rejected by one magazine after another, from the *Ladies Home Journal* to the *Saturday Evening Post*. The manuscript was finally published fifty-seven years after Wilder's death as *Pioneer Girl: The Annotated Autobiography* in 2014. But even as an unpublished manuscript, "Pioneer Girl" earned Wilder and Lane prestige as well as money during their lifetimes. It served as the foundation for all Wilder's Little House books and for Lane's two pioneer novels, *Let the Hurricane Roar* and *Free Land*. Lane also used material from "Pioneer Girl" for several short stories published in national magazines throughout the 1930s.

THE ORIGINAL VERSION OF WHAT WOULD BE PUBLISHED AS *Pioneer Girl* begins with the traditional storytelling phrase, "Once upon a time." The setting is Indian Territory—southeastern Kansas—in 1869. Pa and Ma find the place they've "been looking for" and decide to camp. In the fifth paragraph, readers glimpse the author and her unique voice for the first time: "I lay and looked through the opening in the wagon cover at the campfire and Pa and Ma sitting there. It was lonesome and so still with the stars shining down on the great, flat land where no one lived."[4]

This beginning was so promising that just two days after receiving her mother's handwritten, rough draft, Lane sent sample pages off to her literary agent, Carl Brandt. His first impression was positive; the work was "very fine."[5] In the days that followed, Lane lightly edited and typed the entire first draft, correcting spelling errors, grammatical glitches, and rearranging scenes, based on her mother's notes in the manuscript's margins.[6] On May 17 Lane sent Brandt the entire manuscript.

He wasn't impressed. "No good news in mail," Lane recorded in her diary roughly a month later, "nothing sold, Carl returns my mother's story."[7] But Lane persevered that summer, editing and revising "Pioneer Girl," including the final revision, known now as the George T. Bye version. In the fall of 1930, Lane probably showed this final version to Carl Brandt. He remained unimpressed. "Carl advises not to try to sell mother's story," Lane confided in her diary.[8]

But Lane tried to market "Pioneer Girl" herself, and eventually fired Brandt that fall. She then hired literary agent George Bye, who reluctantly took on the task of marketing Wilder's memoir. "'Pioneer Girl' didn't warm me enough at the first reading," he wrote Lane. "It didn't seem to have enough high points or crescendo. A fine old lady was sitting in a rocking chair and telling a story chronologically but with no benefit of perspective or theatre."[9]

A Fatal Flaw

As a marketable manuscript, the fatal flaw in "Pioneer Girl"—from Wilder's original rough draft to the final Bye version—is its lack of narrative focus, that absence of perspective or theater. "Pioneer Girl" moves from one scene to another with no apparent theme, little introspection, and dozens of digressions. It introduces readers not just to Wilder and her family but to one set of characters after another. They sometimes appear to influence the course of Wilder's life, but just as often they don't. The main characters age as "Pioneer Girl" progresses but without a sense of forward momentum, a central conflict, or a dramatic resolution. Scenes are often linked by bland narrative threads—or nothing at all.

A number of contemporary critics of *Pioneer Girl* share Carl Brandt's and George Bye's opinions of the book. As Judith Thurman wrote in the *New Yorker*, "the tedium of Wilder's style" in *Pioneer Girl* is "a leaden pot cover that smothers her stew's flavor."[10] For some, it also confirms the idea that Wilder had absolutely no talent, and supports the contention that Lane was the creative genius behind the Little House books. William Holtz, whose biography of Lane essentially launched the question of Little House authorship in 1993, describes Wilder as having "a commonplace mind and a commonplace style."[11]

Yet a closer examination of "Pioneer Girl" reveals that its literary shortcomings mask creative triumphs, and that Lane relied as much on her mother's creative vision as Wilder relied on her daughter's editorial skill. For both women, "Pioneer Girl" became a literary mother lode.

Divine Dictation

The published version of *Pioneer Girl* is based on Wilder's original, handwritten draft with its misspellings, false starts, and grammatical glitches. Although readers expect a more polished work from an iconic writer like Wilder, an unedited, rough draft can reveal how writers have developed over time and can display their inherent strengths and weaknesses. But a rough manuscript, especially for audiences unfamiliar with the writing process, may be hard to assess, difficult to appreciate or understand.

When I was a very young reader, for example, I assumed authors simply wrote down their stories perfectly—the first time. Because I was a preacher's daughter who grew up on Bible stories, I envisioned the writing process a little like Moses on Mount Sinai, a kind of divine dictation from an inspired source. By the time I landed my first newspaper job in college, I knew better.

Writing is hard work, a craft, a discipline that demands dedication and mastery—even when writing on deadline. The secret to accomplished writing, however, as most writers will tell you, is to give yourself permission to write a seemingly hopeless first draft and then, with grit, ruthlessness, and determination, revise and improve it. As Wilder herself eventually described this process, "The only way I can write is to wander along with the story, then rewrite and re-arrange and change it everywhere."[12] *Pioneer Girl*, viewed in this context, illustrates Wilder's grit and determination as a writer. Her rough draft is certainly rough and sometimes unformed, but she hadn't yet flexed her deeper creative muscles.

Scraps of Memory

Wilder appears to have written the original draft of "Pioneer Girl" very quickly, perhaps motivated by the creative release she discovered in finally—after letting the idea simmer for decades—committing her life story to paper. As often happens when writing a first draft, Wilder sometimes lost track of her story. She amended her narrative on the fly with cross-outs, inserts, and even instructions to Lane (as a first reader) to jump ahead a page or two, or to backtrack for a scene Wilder initially forgot to include. Such meanderings in a first draft aren't unusual. What is somewhat more unusual, however, is that the original draft of "Pioneer Girl" has no section or chapter breaks, nothing to separate episodes or emphasize one more than another. Even the final Bye version of "Pioneer Girl" contains only random, untitled section breaks.[13]

But "Pioneer Girl" was Wilder's first attempt at a book-length manuscript, which perhaps further explains its ragged, loose, and unformed structure. Most of it unfolds in short, often episodic scenes that read like bursts of memory from early childhood. This structure could reflect Wilder's creative process as she wrote "Pioneer Girl," summoning up distant scraps of memory and quickly committing them to paper. After all, Wilder had been just two years old when the family moved to Indian Territory. What kind of coherent story could she weave from such memories?

The *Missouri Ruralist* Connection

The episodic structure of "Pioneer Girl" also corresponds to Wilder's experience as a columnist and editor for the *Missouri Ruralist*. Her columns were short, episodic, and thematically diverse. And perhaps because she was writing as a farm journalist, she minimized emotion and introspection. In those rare instances when her stories for the newspaper were more subjective, they usually expressed ideas that would clearly resonate with her audience, primarily (but not exclusively) the newspaper's women readers. As the *Ruralist*'s editor noted, "Mrs. Wilder writes well for farm folks because she knows them."[14] "Pioneer Girl" adopts a similar approach.

Wilder's last regular *Ruralist* column, published in December 1924, illustrates her transition from newspaper columnist to memoirist. It centers on her memory as a sixteen-year-old schoolteacher, stranded on Christmas Eve with her students in Dakota Territory. "The snow was scudding low over the drifts of the white world outside the little claim shanty," the column opens. "It was blowing through the cracks in its walls and forming little piles and miniature drifts on the floor and even on the desks."[15] The writing is vivid, but the piece is short—just over five hundred words. The only emotional insight comes at the conclusion of the column, a kind of Christmas card message to her readers: "Our hearts grow tender with childhood memories and love of kindred and we are better throughout the year for having in spirit become a child again at Christmas-time."[16]

Wilder initially applied this creative model to "Pioneer Girl," building scenes around brief, episodic memories with journalistic detachment. She targeted the manuscript toward a national, adult audience. Like her most successful columns, "Pioneer Girl" would include passages of description interspersed with dialogue and interesting characters. These stylistic embellishments, however, would be based on the facts as Wilder remembered them; scenes from her childhood would appear in the manuscript more or less as they had actually happened—chronologically. But Wilder's creative model for "Pioneer Girl" deviated from her *Ruralist* work in one vital and ultimately enduring way: her daughter would be the manuscript's first reader and, ultimately, its editor.

The Big Market Experience

Wilder and Lane had formed this creative partnership years before, not for Wilder's work at the *Ruralist* but for what Lane called the "big market." She praised her mother's journalistic work: "It is extraordinarily good [your] Ruralist stuff; always did stand out in the paper like a skyscraper on a plain," she wrote Wilder. But Lane also felt her mother's work wasn't good enough for national audiences, and from 1915 onward, she began an aggressive and sometimes patronizing attempt to teach Wilder how to write for national magazines, which in the early twentieth century published short as well as long-form manuscripts (like "Pioneer Girl"). "I'm trying to train you as a writer for the big market," she wrote in 1919.[17]

Wilder eventually published three "big market" articles. In June 1919 Wilder's article "Whom Will You Marry?" was published in *McCall's*. The article was an extension of her work for the *Missouri Ruralist*, centering on a fictional scenario that allowed Wilder to champion her view of farm women as equal partners with their husbands in the business of farming. In 1925 Wilder published two articles in *Country Gentleman*, "My Ozark Kitchen" and "The Farm Dining Room." Both articles focused on Wilder's farmhouse at Rocky Ridge Farm, its design innovations, unique décor, and integration with the surrounding Ozark landscape.

What's most significant about Wilder's work for the big magazine markets, however, isn't the published work itself; it's the editorial process that was forged at this turning point in her career. Lane, at least when reviewing other people's work, had become supremely self-confident in her own editorial abilities. Her experience on the *San Francisco Bulletin* had made her a ruthless editor, who performed one "ordinary re-write job" after another on her colleagues' work—and eventually on her mother's work as well, sometimes to Wilder's dismay.[18] Yet Lane became her mother's trusted first reader and editor on projects unrelated to the *Missouri Ruralist*, reviewing Wilder's manuscripts before anyone on the editorial staff at *McCall's* or *Country Gentleman* saw them. This editorial partnership continued with "Pioneer Girl."

Wilder initially took her daughter's editorial advice religiously, painful as it often was. Marginal notes and parenthetical statements directed to Lane within the rough draft of "Pioneer Girl" indicate that Wilder expected her daughter's editorial guidance on the project. But also, given later editorial correspondence between the two women, it's unlikely that she would have expected Lane to simply rewrite the manuscript. "Pioneer Girl" may have been Wilder's first attempt at writing a book, but she had been writing professionally for as long as Lane. Wilder brought a unique set of skills to "Pioneer Girl," skills she had honed on her own at the *Missouri Ruralist*.

Perfect in Describing Landscapes and Things

Even Lane herself acknowledged Wilder's inherent creative strengths. "I don't see how anybody could improve on your use of words," she once wrote her mother. "You are perfect in describing landscapes and things."[19] Wilder brought these essential, writerly "things" to the original draft of "Pioneer Girl": a skillful use of dialogue, vivid descriptions, meaningful details, and memorable characters. These aspects of "Pioneer Girl" illustrate that Wilder's talents were far from commonplace. They also illustrate that her ability to deploy these writing essentials often outstripped her daughter's.

Wilder's skillful use of dialogue is apparent right from the beginning of "Pioneer Girl." Pa's voice sounds believable, effortless, and natural: "'Well, Caroline,' he said, 'here's the place we've been looking for. Might as well camp.'"[20] Wilder uses a sentence fragment here, a subtle but important clue that reveals she understood that dialogue should sound the way real people talk. The lines also exhibit a conversational rhythm. This approach is consistent in Pa's dialogue throughout "Pioneer Girl," even when Wilder quotes him indirectly: "Jerry, Pa said was a half breed, Indian and French, a gambler, some said a horse thief, but a darned good fellow."[21] As for Ma, her dialogue, often presented indirectly in "Pioneer Girl," is more emotionally restrained, yet firm and decisive. When Pa wants to move to Oregon, "Ma said she was tired of wandering around 'from pillar to post' and would not go."[22]

In addition to providing immediacy and color to a narrative, dialogue can also reveal essential qualities about character, a concept Wilder appears to have understood more clearly than her daughter. As Wilder explained to Lane, "But of course a lady like Ma would never use such expressions [as 'I'll be darned' or 'great Gehosaphat']," for she "was a school teacher and well educated for her time and place, rather above Pa socially."[23] Good dialogue shouldn't draw attention to itself; most readers skim right over it, taking in its meaning, color, and context almost unconsciously. But they'll notice a piece of dialogue that sounds forced or unnatural.

Most of the dialogue in Lane's frontier novels is solid, but unlike her mother, Lane sometimes overreached, trying too hard to give her characters colorful and memorable lines. In an early scene in *Let the Hurricane Roar*, Charles, a character Lane based on Charles Ingalls, tells his wife: "Come here, squaw! Give me a kiss. Oh, little squaw, little squaw, your baby's going to be a papoose!"[24] The line is memorable, though most contemporary readers will also find it objectionable. From the standpoint of craft, the lines seem forced and unnatural, Lane's misguided attempt to capture frontier idiom.

The opening passage from "Pioneer Girl" also illustrates another skill Wilder had carried over from her *Ruralist* experience: mastery of a good lead, opening lines that capture a reader's attention and spark curiosity. Although Wilder may have struggled with overall structure in "Pioneer Girl," she knew where to start her memoir: in the middle of unfolding action. The opening scene doesn't stop to explain who Pa and Ma are or what they are looking for; instead, it allows readers to figure this out on their own, pulling them into the story immediately. It's an accomplished beginning.

By contrast, Lane's *Hurricane*, which relies heavily on material from "Pioneer Girl," opens with an explanation and a description of the main characters: "While they were children playing together, they said they would be married as soon as they were old enough, and when they were old enough they married. Charles liked to remind her [Caroline] that he had never asked her to marry him;

he liked to see her smile sedately, as she always smiled at his teasing."[25] The novel's action doesn't really begin for another two pages, when Lane tells readers the main characters "went west."[26] Even then, the action is buried in what's known as exposition—background details an author feels readers need to know to make sense of a story. This is not an accomplished beginning.

Wilder's gift for description appears throughout her *Missouri Ruralist* columns and clearly shines through in "Pioneer Girl." One of her most lyrical, unedited descriptions in the manuscript appears at a pivotal moment as the Ingalls family witnesses a Dakota prairie sunset for the first time. Flocks of ducks and geese fly low overhead, and then, Wilder writes, "the sun sank lower and lower until, looking like a ball of pulsing, liquid light it sank gloriously in clouds of crimson and silver. Cold purple shadows rose in the east; crept slowly around the horizon, then gathered above in depth on depth of darkness from which the stars swung low and bright."[27] In later edited drafts of "Pioneer Girl," Wilder and Lane made minor changes to the description, and a slightly edited version of the original "Pioneer Girl" passage appears in *By the Shores of Silver Lake*, Wilder's fifth Little House novel.[28] But her rough draft description is stronger, more immediate, and more eloquent than the revisions.

Lane apparently found something to admire in this original passage too. She wrote variations on her mother's prairie sunset in "Pioneer Girl" and placed them in her own pioneer novels. In *Let the Hurricane Roar*, published in 1932, Caroline (patterned on Caroline Ingalls in "Pioneer Girl") observes a glorious prairie sunset at a pivotal moment in her life: "The sunset had never been so gorgeous. Great banners of crimson, rose and orange unfurled to the zenith. Their reflections colored the air and land, and the putrid water in the creek glowed like jewels."[29] This description's structure, context, and vocabulary echo Wilder's original.

Lane returned to her mother's description of that Dakota sunset when writing *Free Land* in 1938. Its context is virtually identical to the original scene in "Pioneer Girl." Lane's David Beaton (patterned on Almanzo Wilder) rides west into Dakota Territory for the first time and, like the Ingalls family, observes "geese and ducks flying south." In the following paragraph, "Sunset spread in rainbow colors around the level rim of the earth and purple shadows rose. The low stars were huge and quivering."[30]

Lane's sunset descriptions in both *Let the Hurricane Roar* and *Free Land* lack the lyricism, style, and grace of Wilder's original in "Pioneer Girl." Lane couldn't quite match her mother's instinctive perfection in describing landscapes and things.

Another instinctive storytelling talent Wilder exhibits in "Pioneer Girl" is her grasp of essential detail, although she doesn't use it to full effect, perhaps because she hadn't yet broken free of the newspaper columnist's mandate to write crisp, concise prose. In "Pioneer Girl," for example, she uses only a short paragraph to describe the "house of logs" Pa built in Indian Territory "from the trees in the nearby creek bottom."[31] In *Little House on the Prairie*, her third novel in the Little House series, Wilder devotes five chapters to this cabin. But by then, she had begun to embrace the freedom of writing fiction.

That's not to say that "Pioneer Girl" isn't rich in detail. It is. After a description of the hotel the family had come to manage in Iowa, Wilder includes one brief but sobering detail: "It was all a very pretty place, but in the door between the dining room and kitchen were several bullet holes made by the son of the man who had sold us the hotel, when he shot at his wife as she ran from him through the door."[32]

Sustained, Powerful Scenes

As Wilder moved deeper into "Pioneer Girl," she integrated description, dialogue, and detail more effectively, creating sustained and powerful scenes that foreshadow some of her most vivid writing in the Little House books. Here, for example, is an excerpt from one of the strongest scenes in "Pioneer Girl":

> Just then we heard some one call and Mrs. Nelson was in the doorway. She was all out of breath with running, wringing her hands and almost crying, "The grasshoppers are coming! The grasshoppers are coming!" she shrieked. "Come and look!"
>
> We all ran to the door and looked around. Now and then a grasshopper dropped on the ground, but we couldn't see anything to be so excited about.

> "Look at the sun! Yoost look at the sun!" cried Mrs. Nelson, pointing to the sky.
>
> We raised our faces and looked straight into the sun. It had been shining brightly but now there was a light colored, fleecy cloud over its face so it did not hurt our eyes.
>
> And then we saw that the cloud was grasshoppers, their wings a shiny white making a screen between us and the sun. They were dropping to the ground like hail in a hailstorm faster and faster.[33]

Lane essentially lifted this scene from "Pioneer Girl" and placed it in *Let the Hurricane Roar*. By contrast, however, Lane's version is almost all description. It lacks the pacing and action of Wilder's original; it also lacks the power of her mother's deceptively simple prose. Wilder's light-colored, fleecy cloud becomes Lane's "ineffably beautiful" cloud.[34]

In Lane's scene the Mrs. Nelson character—Mrs. Svenson—has no dialogue. Readers never hear her voice directly. Instead, she falls "on her knees, sobbing, her apron over her head." As Caroline realizes the cloud is full of grasshoppers, "dropping by dozens," Charles cries, "Good—God—Almighty!"[35] His lines are credible but not exactly original. The scene seems melodramatic and contrived when compared to Wilder's unedited original.

Inclined to Be Fatalistic

Admittedly, "Pioneer Girl" doesn't sparkle with one gem of a scene after another. Memorable episodes are sometimes under-written or buried between passages of forgettable narrative. One of the most under-written scenes in the original "Pioneer Girl" manuscript is also chilling and deeply disturbing. It unfolds in Walnut Grove, Minnesota, in the late 1870s. Wilder, who was then between ten and twelve, had hired out to Will and Nannie Masters, a troubled young married couple from a prosperous family (Will was the husband responsible for those bullet holes in the hotel dining room door). Wilder writes that working in their home "was not pleasant." Nannie, who had fainting spells, "would fall without a word or a sign and lie as dead." Will had started drinking again, and his behavior was menacing:

I hadn't stayed with Nannie very long when one night I waked from a sound sleep to find Will leaning over me. I could smell the whiskey on his breath. I sat up quickly.

"Is Nannie sick," I asked.

"No," he answered, ["]lie down and be still!"

"Go away quick," I said, "or I will scream for Nannie."

He went and the next day Ma said I could come home.[36]

The implication is clear: Wilder was threatened with sexual assault. But she doesn't provide additional context to the scene or reflect on how the experience affected her. The scene is startling, stark, and emotionally unresolved. Still, it illustrates the gritty reality of life in a raw and new frontier town; it also reveals a childhood trauma Wilder endured and apparently overcame. Subsequent edited versions of "Pioneer Girl," however, don't include this episode. Wilder and Lane must have decided it was too disturbing, too sexually suggestive for adult readers in the 1930s. The scene has no parallel in the Little House novels.

The emotional detachment of "Pioneer Girl" may relate to what Wilder later described as an inherent family reticence: "We were not excitable, usually. . . . It seems to me we were rather inclined to be fatalistic—to just take things as they came. I know we all hated a fuss, as I still do."[37] Lane felt that even her mother's Little House books lacked emotional impact between characters and, by extension, on readers. But Lane couldn't convince her mother to move away from the pioneer stoicism Wilder felt was both realistic and essential to her novels. And while Wilder's fictional characters certainly have more emotional depth and focus than do their counterparts in "Pioneer Girl," Wilder erred on the side of restraint. For her, it was an essential aspect of the pioneer spirit.

In her own pioneer novels, however, Lane chose a different path, allowing her characters to freely act out their emotions. Here, for example, is a passage from Lane's *Let the Hurricane Roar*: "In a rage of pity, an outbursting cry against the universal cruelty, she plunged through the snow to the nearest patiently dying creature; she wrenched the ice from its eyes."[38] Lane's pioneer characters also express their emotions directly. Charles in *Let the Hurricane Roar* tells Caroline, "I'm not a baby! Losing a little sleep won't hurt me!"[39]

A Family Standing Together

Despite Lane's role as editor of "Pioneer Girl"—and her experience as an author of both fiction and nonfiction—she failed to suggest a meaningful solution to the central creative weakness in all versions of the manuscript: the absence of a sustained story arc. So other than a loose chronology, does anything hold its seemingly random episodes together? What is "Pioneer Girl" about?

A close reading of "Pioneer Girl" reveals that its heart—its central focus—is the survival of a nurturing, loving family despite seemingly insurmountable hardships. Pa emerges as a heroic figure, capable, courageous, and resourceful. Like his fictional counterpart in the Little House books, he hunts, traps, plays the fiddle, and tells funny, wise, and sometimes scary stories. But the Pa of "Pioneer Girl" is also leaner, hungrier, more desperate to provide for his family. He fails at managing a hotel, briefly opens a butcher shop, and skips town with the family at night to avoid paying a "skinflint" landlord.[40]

Ma is resourceful, more refined than her husband, long suffering but resilient, and determined to carve out a better life for her daughters. A former schoolteacher herself, she believes in the transformative power of education. Her girls—Mary and Laura—become exemplary students, despite the family's poverty. In a poignant, two-paragraph episode, Wilder captures both the desperation of the family—living in "rooms over a grocery store"—and her parents' determination to support their daughters' education:

> Mary and I . . . liked our reading lessons very much and used to practice reading them aloud at home nights.
>
> Pa knew, but did not tell us until later, that a crowd used to gather in the store beneath to hear us read.

Wilder then recalls looking out from those rooms over the grocery store "into the beautiful, terraced, lawn of a big, white house across the street" without envy or malice.[41]

Despite the gap between her neighbors' wealth and her family's poverty, the Laura of "Pioneer Girl" has everything she needs. She is perfectly contented with the "very pleasant and sunny and clean" rooms she shares with her family.[42]

Wilder's neighbors in town, however, appear to have viewed the Ingallses' plight very differently. In one of "Pioneer Girl"'s most revealing scenes, Wilder illustrates this point dramatically, and simultaneously underscores the family's devotion and commitment to each other: "Coming home . . . , I found our Dr's wife Mrs. Starr visiting with Ma. As I came in the door she put her arm around me. . . . She said she wanted me to go and live with her; that her own girls, Ida and Fanny, were grown . . . and she wanted a little girl to help her around the house and keep her from being lonesome. She said if I would come she would adopt me and treat me just like her own. But Ma smiled at me and said she couldn't possibly spare me."[43] In the Bye version of "Pioneer Girl," the scene ends with this additional and rare introspective observation: "But afterward, whenever I thought of her [Mrs. Starr], the queer feeling came back. It seemed to be possible that I could go on being me—Laura Ingalls—even without Pa and Ma and Mary and Carrie and Grace. Mrs. Starr might have taken me away from them. It seemed strange and I always tried to forget about it as quickly as I could."[44]

Throughout "Pioneer Girl," Wilder's family stands together while other families disintegrate—through drink, adultery, greed, abuse, or isolation. The contrast is striking. Despite their poverty, the Ingalls family remains committed to each other and to the principles of fairness, hard work, self-improvement, and even generosity. During the long, hard winter of 1880–81, for example, Pa and Ma take in George and Maggie Masters, part of that large, often dysfunctional Masters clan. In a letter to Lane, Wilder later explained that the couple's first child was due "too soon" after their marriage and the newlyweds had headed west to Dakota Territory to avoid disgrace. "Then winter set in and caught them. There was no where else they could stay. Every house was full and Pa couldn't put them out in the street."[45] Charles and Caroline shared their dwindling supply of food and fuel with George, Maggie, and their baby that entire winter. Wilder's parents emerge in "Pioneer Girl" as compassionate and forgiving, qualities their wealthier neighbors rarely demonstrate.

Literary Triumph or Flop?

When Wilder began writing fiction, she learned to sharpen her thematic focus, and eventually used the idea of a devoted family finding their way west as a foundation for her Little House books. "Pioneer Girl" served as a rough outline for all of them, even providing a memorable episode for *Farmer Boy*, Wilder's novel about her husband's childhood on a farm near Malone, New York. From this perspective, "Pioneer Girl" could be deemed a triumphant literary experiment. As for her growth as a writer, literary agent George Bye's change of heart about Wilder and her work perhaps illustrates how far from commonplace she was. From initially describing her as a fine old lady telling drab stories about her childhood, Bye came to consider Wilder an iconic American author. "If you write for children," he confessed after reading Wilder's seventh novel, *Little Town on the Prairie*, "then I am in my second childhood."[46] When she sent him her last Little House manuscript in 1942, Bye wrote back predicting that the series "will become an American fixture, something like Little Women and Little Men."[47] The praise he heaped on Wilder is unmatched in his existing correspondence with Lane about her pioneer novels.

But would we read "Pioneer Girl" today if the Little House books didn't exist? Probably, not. On its own, the manuscript is too rough and unformed. Viewed independently from Wilder's Little House books, "Pioneer Girl" doesn't stand on its own merits for contemporary readers. And it apparently didn't stand on its own merits ninety years ago when editor after editor rejected the manuscript. "Pioneer Girl" was a literary flop.

Yet in 1932, two years after the *Saturday Evening Post* had initially rejected "Pioneer Girl," the magazine apparently reconsidered. Its publisher, Graeme Lorimer, contacted George Bye, who then represented Wilder as well as Lane. Something about "Pioneer Girl" had stuck with Lorimer, and he was now interested in an article with "first person experience" about "pioneer conditions in the middle west."[48] Since Lane usually represented her mother's interests to Bye at this time, he forwarded Lorimer's letter to her and observed, "I think Graeme Lorimer confused your mother's ['Pioneer Girl'] manuscript with your authorship."[49]

Lane apparently didn't tell her mother about the magazine's renewed interest in her manuscript, perhaps because Lane herself was secretly working on a pioneer-themed project of her own, a novel for adult readers drawn directly from "Pioneer Girl." Despite Lane's professional success, she hadn't yet been published in the prestigious *Saturday Evening Post*. Perhaps she thought she could use Lorimer's confusion over authorship to her advantage and persuade him that the market was right, not for a memoir about pioneer experiences but for a serialized novel based on such memories—and written not by an unknown author like her mother but by an accomplished novelist, Lane herself. Whatever her motivation, it appears that in 1932, she sacrificed the possible sale of "Pioneer Girl" to serve her own professional interests.

But by then, Laura Ingalls Wilder had published her first novel and found her voice—one that would speak to young readers for generations to come, a voice that would have remained silent if not for "Pioneer Girl."

3

"When Grandma Was a Little Girl"

A Little House Prelude

LAURA INGALLS WILDER RECEIVED A PAIR OF LIFE-CHANGING letters in mid-February 1931, shortly after her sixty-fourth birthday. The first, dated February 12, was written by editor Marion Fiery of Alfred A. Knopf Borzoi Books. It praised a manuscript Wilder had never seen before but was credited with writing. "I like the material you have used," Fiery wrote. "It covers a period in American history about which very little has been written, and almost nothing for boys and girls."[1]

The second letter was from Lane, explaining the existence of the manuscript Fiery had praised. "It is your father's stories, taken out of the long PIONEER GIRL manuscript, and strung together as you will see," she wrote. Seemingly to provide reassurance, Lane noted, "It is really your own work, practically word for word."[2]

Nothing exists in the historical record to document Wilder's response to these extraordinary letters, but after a string of rejections for what Lane called the long "Pioneer Girl" manuscript, Wilder must have felt both encouraged and confused—encouraged by the admiration from an editor at a major publishing house and by the prospect, at long last, of publishing a book for children; confused by the messages both letters carried. And while Fiery admired this juvenile manuscript, she hadn't exactly offered to publish it. Instead, Fiery asked, "Would you be willing to make some editorial changes to the manuscript?"[3]

THE MANUSCRIPT IN QUESTION—TYPEWRITTEN AND TWENTY pages long—was titled "When Grandma Was a Little Girl." Its opening line reads, "When Grandma was a little girl, she lived in a little gray house made of logs."[4] Lane had pieced the manuscript together from episodes she'd cut from the final edited version of "Pioneer Girl," stories she apparently considered too juvenile to appeal to editors at such big-market magazines as the *Saturday Evening Post* or the *Ladies Home Journal.*

At the time Lane lived in the farmhouse with her companion Helen Boylston on Rocky Ridge Farm; Wilder and Almanzo lived in the Rock House, about half a mile away. A path across the top of the ridge and through the woods connected the two houses. According to her diary entries, Lane and her parents crossed this path almost daily for visits, lunches, teas, suppers—and presumably consultations about "Pioneer Girl."

My Mother's Juvenile

Lane had launched into the final edit for the adult "Pioneer Girl" manuscript on July 31, 1930, although her literary agent—Carl Brandt—wasn't enthusiastic about the earlier version he'd seen. He was, at best, lukewarm about the project. Still, Lane's journal entries from this period suggest that she made her initial cuts very quickly, eliminating many of the stories about her mother's early childhood memories in Wisconsin. Nothing remains to indicate whether Wilder approved of her daughter's editorial decisions, but reading between the lines in Lane's diary, it appears Lane's cuts may have gone too deep. Six days later, she set "Pioneer Girl" aside.[5]

A few days after Lane abandoned work on "Pioneer Girl," her parents made one of their customary visits. It was August 14, 1930, and the Wilders' forty-sixth wedding anniversary was approaching. According to Lane's diary, Lane and her mother argued about how to celebrate the anniversary. Lane wanted to give her parents an anniversary trip to South Dakota; her parents, however, had had second thoughts about the trip and instead wanted to spend the travel money Lane had offered on improvements at the farm. But could mother and daughter also have argued about the juvenile scenes Lane had cut from the final revision of "Pioneer Girl"?

Lane's diary entries are short, no more than four or five lines per day; she didn't record events in detail. But something appears to have shifted after that argument on the fourteenth, because just two days later, on August 16, Lane wrote that she had once again "worked on her mother's copy." On the next day, she'd finished her "mother's juvenile," and on the next, it was in the mail to someone Lane's diary doesn't identify.[6] These entries are significant, and reveal something new and different in the way Lane approached "Pioneer Girl": she had inexplicably decided to create a juvenile adaptation of her mother's memoir.

Expanding Opportunities in Children's Stories

Wilder had long been interested in writing for children. In 1915, while visiting Lane in San Francisco for the Panama-Pacific International Exposition, Wilder published a series of children's poems in the *San Francisco Bulletin*, and for the first time in print identified herself as Laura Ingalls Wilder.[7] Her interest in writing for young readers persisted and she sent Lane some children's stories to review in 1919. Those stories are now lost, but Lane's response to them remains. They were "good," she wrote, but "there is no opportunity to make a name with children's stories."[8]

By August 1930, however, Lane had obviously changed her mind. What had shifted? Other than her mother's persistent interest in writing for young readers, why did Lane create a juvenile version of "Pioneer Girl"?

Lane's diaries and letters from this period provide no direct answer to this question, but she undoubtedly understood that children's publishing had evolved over the previous decade and that by 1930, there were expanding opportunities for writers to make a name for themselves with children's stories. Such publishing houses as Macmillan, Harper & Brothers, and Alfred Knopf had established children's departments. In 1922 the American Library Association had created the John Newbery Award to recognize outstanding works of American literature for young readers. Furthermore, Lane herself had a personal connection to the children's publishing world. Her friends Berta and Elmer Hader from San Francisco had moved to Nyack, New York, where they were building a reputation as a successful children's book writing and illustrating team.

Lane probably sent "When Grandma Was a Little Girl" to Berta Hader in August 1930, because at some point in late 1930 or early 1931, Hader had, in turn, submitted the manuscript to Knopf. In February 1931 she invited Lane to her home in Nyack for a meeting with Fiery to discuss "When Grandma Was a Little Girl." The meeting went well. On February 15, 1931, Lane wrote in her diary that Marion Fiery "takes Pioneer Girl juvenile."[9]

A Definite Interest

"When Grandma Was a Little Girl" relates an episodic story of a pioneer family living on the Wisconsin frontier in the Big Woods. "Grandma's name was Laura. She called her father, Pa, and her mother, Ma."[10] Laura's older sister is Mary; her baby sister is Carrie. Their story takes place during one winter in the family's life, and features renditions of episodes today's Little House readers will recognize: Grandpa and the panther, Pa and the owl in the woods, Christmas with the cousins, Grandpa's irresistible new sled, Ma's and Pa's unique encounters with real and imaginary bears.

As charming as Fiery found these stories, she actually didn't "take" the manuscript at all. Instead, her letter to Wilder that February asked for a longer, fuller manuscript and significant editorial changes and additions to "Grandma." In a follow-up letter to Wilder, Fiery more clearly explained her position: "Our interest in having this book is very definite. . . . Of course, you understand a definite contract cannot be made until we receive the complete [and revised] manuscript."[11] What went unsaid in this letter: if Fiery didn't like Wilder's revisions, she could reject the manuscript without any obligation, a tactic that editors still employ today.

Accepting Fiery's terms would be risky: Wilder might spend months rewriting and expanding the manuscript only to have it rejected. On the other hand, if Wilder declined, she might permanently lose an opportunity to publish a story for children. How likely was it that other publishers might be interested in her pioneer memories? After all, several magazine editors had already rejected the adult version of "Pioneer Girl."[12] Lane felt that her mother should take the risk: "You will have those stories preserved in book form, and beautifully, which after all is the main thing."[13]

But Lane remained skeptical about "Grandma's" financial prospects. While Lane's ideas about children's book publishing had modified somewhat over the years, her view of its financial rewards hadn't. She told Wilder, "I do not think you will make a great deal of money out of this book."[14]

It's also clear that Lane wasn't sure her mother was up to the challenge of revising and expanding "When Grandma Was a Little Girl." As she had done over ten years earlier, Lane inserted herself into Wilder's writing and revising process. "I wish you would just get another tablet, and put down in it somehow the other 15,000 words that Marian [*sic*] wants," Lane wrote. "When I come home I will go through the whole thing and we will send it off to her."[15]

Despite Lane's editorial assurance, she had virtually no experience writing for young readers. She had published just four profiles for this audience in the *Junior Red Cross News* shortly after the close of World War I, and her inexperience in the field was responsible for "Grandma's" central creative flaw, one Fiery identified in the manuscript and hoped Wilder would address.

The True Character of the Book

Although Fiery wanted a longer, meatier book, one with more details "about the everyday life of the pioneers," she also wanted a more subtle but creatively challenging change, a change in what writers and editors now call the "voice" of a novel. In her letter to Wilder, Fiery hinted at this issue with a reference to the manuscript's working title, "When Grandma Was a Little Girl." She told Wilder that it "does not convey the true character of the book."[16] And it was the true character of a children's book that Lane herself had failed to capture when she pasted together those juvenile stories from the adult "Pioneer Girl." The stories *were* ideal for children, but the voice—even the main character—wasn't.

On the opening page of "When Grandma Was a Little Girl," a wolf howls in the night and "Grandma knew that wolves ate little girls. But Grandma was safe inside the log house.'"[17] Grandma is the main character in this manuscript and her memories spark its action. The entire premise of the story and its narrative perspective focuses on a grandma looking back through time at her childhood memories. A children's book, however, usually needs a young protagonist—and certainly a young voice—from the very beginning, a voice that can express the true character of a book.

Writing a children's story from an adult perspective is a common pitfall for aspiring children's book writers, so it isn't surprising that Lane would make this mistake herself. Perhaps Lane had settled on this approach for "Grandma" because it maintained a semblance of consistency with the original adult "Pioneer Girl" manuscript—an older woman looking back on her childhood.[18] When Lane decided to create a juvenile version, however, she had not only changed audiences but genres. She jumped from an adult memoir to juvenile autobiographical fiction, "a true story—in fictional form."[19]

The literary conventions that apply to writing fiction for children are very different from those that govern writing memoir for adults. Lane apparently hadn't fully grasped these differences, at least initially. Her meeting with Fiery—and perhaps conversations with Berta and Elmer Hader—provided Lane with a clearer understanding of the literary conventions necessary to write memorable and marketable fiction for young readers. The original "Grandma" manuscript—with its adult voice and main character—placed too much narrative distance between young readers, the protagonist, and her story. "Grandma" lacked immediacy and a child's sense of wonder.

A Little Change Which Will Only Take a Minute

Without claiming any responsibility for "Grandma"'s shaky opening, and striking her usual authoritative editorial tone, Lane took up this issue directly with Wilder. "I am not satisfied with the lead," Lane wrote, "and that will be changed. We will start right off with Laura, and not say anything about Grandma." As almost an afterthought, Lane added, "That is a very little change which will only take a minute though."[20]

From there, Lane launched into a more technical discussion about point-of-view, switching from "Pioneer Girl"'s original first-person perspective to third person. Probably paraphrasing something Fiery had said during their meeting at the Haders',

Lane told Wilder that "for juveniles you can not use the first person, because the 'I' books do not sell well." Lane implied, however, that her mother might not have the creative muscle to tackle this editorial change, and observed, "If you find it easier to write in the first person, write that way. I will change it into the third person [for you]."[21]

This passage reveals that perhaps Lane herself didn't understand, at least initially, the depth of the revision Fiery wanted. Changing pronouns from "I" in first-person nonfiction narratives to "she" in third-person juvenile fiction can't on its own transform the voice of a novel or deepen the depiction of its main characters. After all, Lane's original "Grandma" manuscript was already written in third person—and it hadn't completely satisfied Fiery. She wanted more depth, more immediacy, and an authentic young voice.

We Are Wrong

Finding the right voice for "When Grandma Was a Little Girl" would be Wilder's biggest creative challenge, and its biggest barrier to publication. The future of the project hinged on Wilder's ability to grasp Fiery's editorial insights and apply them to an expanded and revised manuscript which, technically speaking, Wilder hadn't created in the first place.

But as she read and reviewed those letters in February 1931, it may be that Wilder wasn't completely in the dark, at least conceptually, about the idea of a juvenile "Pioneer Girl." A clue about "Grandma"'s origin seems to appear on the second page of Lane's letter. After telling her mother where to find a carbon copy of the manuscript (in Lane's filing cabinet on the sleeping porch in the farmhouse), Lane wrote, "We are wrong in thinking they are stories for <u>little</u> children; it is not picture book material, but must be for children from 8 to 10, who are beginning to read."[22] The implication here is clear: at some point, Lane and Wilder must have previously discussed a "Pioneer Girl" adaptation for children, but their initial ideas for it as a picture book had been "wrong."

If Wilder wrote back to Lane, addressing the issue of voice, point-of-view, or the other issues raised in those letters from February 1930, that correspondence no longer survives. But she did dive into revisions herself. Wilder also ignored Lane's offer to make changes in point-of-view. Wilder tackled this challenge on her own, partially restoring her original opening of "Pioneer Girl," and on her first attempt getting closer to just the right voice for a children's book: "Once upon a time, long ago, a little girl lived in the Big Woods of Wisconsin, in a little gray house made of logs."[23]

4

Little House in the Big Woods

Once Upon a Time

IN LATE MAY 1931, LANE WROTE MARION FIERY THAT "MY mother is just sending you the revised manuscript of those tales in the Big Woods. I do so much hope you will like it." With Lane as her editor and typist, Wilder had spent almost three months revising and expanding the manuscript. As Lane told Fiery, the "manuscript runs a bit longer than 25,000 words, but I advised her not to cut it until you'd seen it as it stands."[1]

Fiery liked the revised manuscript, although wasn't satisfied with the titles Wilder and Lane had proposed: "Trundle-bed Tales," "Little Pioneer Girl," "Long Ago Yesterday," "Little Girl in the Big Woods."[2] Instead, she proposed "Little House in the Woods" and offered Wilder a three-book contract in September. The book was scheduled for publication the following year—1932.

The offer was remarkable: in the depths of the Great Depression, a three-book deal with an unknown children's book writer. As children's book editor Virginia Kirkus later recalled, "The 'depression' was making its impress on our sales; people were thinking that new books for children were unnecessary, while old ones could serve."[3] Perhaps Fiery already envisioned a series of books based on the characters in Wilder's first novel, but her offer certainly reflected the confidence she had in Wilder's ability to produce exceptional literary work, even when times were tough in American publishing.

Again, the historical record doesn't reveal Wilder's response to Fiery's offer. But she must have felt thrilled; it's hard to imagine any first-time novelist, then or now, feeling anything but excitement when offered a three-book deal. But the excitement quickly wore off. On November 3, 1931, before Wilder had signed the Knopf contract, Fiery sent Lane a handwritten three-page letter that began, "This is just a little note to tell you that Mr. Knopf has decided to give up the children's department the first of this year, so I shall not be here after that time." If this news wasn't bad enough, Fiery added, "Under the circumstances I do not believe it would be wise for you to sign a three book contract here for your mother as heaven knows what will happen in the next three years."[4]

In a surviving draft of a letter Lane wrote to Fiery, she told her to expect a telegram from Wilder with instructions "to hold up on the contract." Still, Lane said, "My mother does not know what to do. . . . She is afraid that if Knopf does not publish it, she may not find another publisher." And with uncharacteristic self-doubt about her own professional insights, Lane wrote, "I dare not advise her, because I know nothing whatever about the juvenile field."[5]

Amid this confusion, however, Fiery made a strategic decision: she called Virginia Kirkus, who directed the Department of Books for Boys and Girls at Harper & Brothers, and pitched "Little House in the Woods." On December 8, 1931, Wilder received yet another life-changing letter. Kirkus wrote that Harper & Brothers had accepted her manuscript: "It is always a pleasant surprise to find something that gives so graphically as does your manuscript a picture of the early days on our own frontier." But perhaps not surprisingly, she also wrote, "May I take for granted your permission to make certain editorial changes?"[6]

The contract was for only one book, which was released in April 1932, with a revised title, *Little House in the Big Woods*. Kirkus later called it "the book no depression could stop."[7] One of the slight editorial changes Kirkus apparently suggested to *Little House in the Big Woods* appears in its opening line: "Once upon a time, sixty years ago, a little girl lived in the Big Woods of Wisconsin, in a little gray house made of logs."[8] The revision is slight—"Once upon a time, sixty years ago" instead of Wilder's original "Once upon a time, long ago." In hindsight, Wilder's original line is more timeless and would have been a more effective opening for the generations of readers to come *after* 1932.

The change was probably an attempt to frame the story historically, to place *Little House in the Big Woods* within a specific period of American history for Depression-era readers. But it also reflects the expectations for the novel: that like most children's books, it would—at best—sell steadily for a few years and then be forgotten.

Little House in the Big Woods wasn't the Newbery medal winner the year it was eligible (1933), nor was it an honor book. The winning title that year, *Young Fu of the Upper Yangtze*, by Elizabeth Foreman Lewis, remains in print, but none of the books or authors chosen by the Newbery committee in 1933 have had the lasting impact of *Little House in the Big Woods*. Although it was an exceptionally polished and accomplished children's book, no one in American publishing at the time guessed how deeply the fictional Ingalls family would influence generations of readers to come.

Why is the book important and what did Wilder do in this novel that her contemporaries—even those Newbery authors—did not? Why do we still read *Little House in the Big Woods* today? After all, countless children's books have been published about American frontier families, and none of them have achieved the iconic status of the Little House books in general, or *Little House in the Big Woods* in particular.

Carol Ryrie Brink's *Caddie Woodlawn* received the Newbery Medal in 1936, and like *Little House in the Big Woods*, is based on a real frontier family's experiences living in Wisconsin. On its surface, Brink's approach is virtually identical to Wilder's. "The facts of the book," Brink explained, "are mainly true but have sometimes been slightly changed to make them fit better into the story."[9] Yet *Caddie Woodlawn*, beloved by generations of readers, doesn't have the powerful resonance or enduring influence of *Little House in the Big Woods*. Wilder's first novel stands apart from other children's books about the pioneer experience because it at once idealizes the American frontier and embraces its reality. From the ordinary but forgotten tasks of frontier life, Wilder builds an extraordinary story with archetypal underpinnings. The novel's structure, setting, themes, and even its characters take on a mythic quality that taps into the memories, dreams, and aspirations—conscious and unconscious—of its readers. Wilder brings such dreams and situations to life in *Little House in the Big Woods*, beginning with the fictional family itself.

An Archetypal Pioneer Family

The characters Wilder creates in *Little House in the Big Woods* are uniquely themselves, often captured in a simple phrase, a single action, or a vivid scene. The game of mad dog in the book's second chapter, for example, establishes the main characters' unique personalities in just a few brief paragraphs. Pa runs his fingers "through his thick, brown hair, standing up on end" and then drops down on all fours, growling like a mad dog. He corners Laura and Mary against the woodbox.[10] The episode's action defines Pa. He's imaginative, playful, unpredictable, and a devoted father. Ma, on the other hand, is capable, reserved, and gentle. She sits "in her rocking chair, sewing," an observer to her family's wild, imaginative play.[11]

The mad dog game also establishes Laura's and Mary's personalities: "Mary was so frightened that she could not move. But as Pa came nearer Laura screamed, and with a wild leap and a scramble she went over the woodbox, dragging Mary with her."[12] Mary is timid, passive, a more conventional nineteenth-century girl. Laura, on the other hand, is as impulsive as Pa. She's courageous and even protective, dragging her older sister to safety from Pa's make-believe mad dog.

Throughout the novel, the Ingalls family functions as a tightly knit ensemble. And as an ensemble, they represent something bigger, something almost mythic that extends well beyond their individual personalities. Wilder's initial description of the family reinforces this image: "So far as the little girl could see, there was only the one little house where she lived with her Father and Mother, her sister Mary and baby sister Carrie. A wagon track ran before the house, turning and twisting out of sight in the woods, where the wild animals lived, but the little girl did not know where it went, nor what might be the end of it."[13] The family is isolated, the walls of their little house providing their only shelter against the wilds of the Big Woods. Civilization is unimaginably far away. This is an archetypal family, at once taming the wild and living as part of it. They also represent essential American values. The Ingalls family is resourceful, independent, devoted to each other, and fearless in the face of danger and hardships.

Although the opening line establishes that the story will be told from the perspective of that little girl in the Big Woods, the focus of the novel isn't exclusively on Laura's actions, feelings, and conflicts. In fact, Wilder rarely lingers on Laura's internal thoughts and emotions, as she does in later Little House books. Instead, the novel examines how the entire family lives its life together in those Big Woods of Wisconsin. Pa, Ma, Mary, Laura, and (to a lesser extent) Baby Carrie share Wilder's spotlight. Even the secondary characters are part of this archetypal family—Grandpa and Grandma, the aunts and uncles, all the cousins. They are essential to the novel's unfolding action and its storybook atmosphere.

Throughout *Little House in the Big Woods*, extended family gatherings take on a larger-than-life resonance. As the "Christmas" chapter unfolds, for example, Wilder's spotlight moves from Laura, Mary, and their cousins making "pictures in the snow" to Aunt Eliza and Uncle Peter telling a spine-tingling story about a panther and the giant tracks it left just beyond their door. Then Pa takes out his fiddle. As Laura, Mary, and the cousins drift off to sleep, the "flickering firelight" creates its own magic, casting "big and quivering shadows" of Ma, Aunt Eliza, and Uncle Peter against the darkened walls.[14] This is an ensemble scene with an ensemble cast, and it captures those dreamy childhood moments that somehow transcend everyday experience.

Young readers, of course, aren't aware that episodes like this one convey such deep and profound meaning, but generations of them carried memories of iconic moments from *Little House in the Big Woods* with them into adulthood—from Laura and Mary playing catch with that pig's bladder to the image of Grandma out-jigging Uncle George at the dance at Grandpa's. The images are at once distinctly American and yet universal.

While Wilder creates these indelible moments with an ensemble cast, she places one character at the center of almost every scene—and it isn't Laura. It's Charles Ingalls. If there *is* a central character in *Little House in the Big Woods*, it's Pa, the character around whom most of the action swirls.

Those Stories of My Father's

As we've already seen, Wilder herself was motivated to write "Pioneer Girl" and ultimately *Little House in the Big Woods* because she wanted to preserve her father's stories. "I would be especially glad to have Knopf publish those stories of my father's," Wilder wrote Marion Fiery in 1931. "They impressed me very much as a child and I still have great affection for them."[15] Wilder thought of her father—the real Charles Ingalls—in almost mythic terms. As she wrote Lane, Pa "was a hunter and trapper, a musician and poet."[16] In *Little House in the Big Woods*, the fictional Pa is all of this and more. He becomes the quintessential American pioneer, providing for and protecting his family, able to take on any challenge and succeed. Pa is heroic. He is "big and swift and strong," with his gun on his shoulder, his hatchet and powderhorn at this side. His "tall boots" make "great tracks" in the snow.[17]

From the very beginning of the novel, the action revolves around Pa. When Laura is frightened by wolves howling in the distance, she knows she is safe because "Her father's gun hung over the door," and one night, when wolves gather outside the family's cabin, Pa scoops Laura up in his arms and takes her to the window to see them.[18] In Pa's strong arms, Laura knows she has nothing to fear.

Throughout *Little House in the Big Woods*, Pa remains center stage, even when the narrative sweeps other members of the family into the action. When Laura misbehaves one Sunday afternoon, the action pivots from her to Pa: he tells her "The Story of Grandpa's Sled and the Pig." In the chapter "Sugar Snow," Pa again controls the action, relating in detail how Grandpa harvests sap from trees in the forest and makes maple syrup. At the dance that follows, Grandma and Grandpa, Uncle George, Aunt Docia, and Aunt Ruby share the spotlight, but Pa binds all these characters together. He plays his fiddle and calls out "the figures" for the square dancers.[19] He literally directs the action of the scene. Even on the last pages of *Little House in the Big Woods*, Pa and his fiddle orchestrate its memorable finale: "Laura lay awake a little while, listening to Pa's fiddle softly playing and to the lonely sound of the wind in the Big Woods."[20]

Danger and Survival

Pa's dominant role in the book reinforces one of its major themes, which also underscores its archetypal atmosphere. *Little House in the Big Woods* is a novel about danger and survival, how a family carves out a meaningful, secure life and livelihood in a wild, primeval place. Wilder establishes this idea right from the beginning: "As far as a man could go to the north in a day, or a week, or a whole month, there was nothing but woods. There were no houses. There were no roads. There were no people. . . . Wolves lived in the Big Woods, and bears, and huge wild cats."[21] Pa stands between the family and the wild beasts just outside their door. Laura and Mary know when Pa ventures out alone into the Big Woods that "he could always kill bears and panthers with the first shot."[22] As for those wild beasts themselves—the bears and panthers and wolves—they were as exotic to young readers of the Depression (and to future generations) as giants, dragons, and fairytale wolves.

Pa engages the entire family in this struggle against the wilderness. He makes his own bullets, but Laura and Mary are his assistants. Laura hands him "the smooth, polished cowhorn full of gunpowder," while Mary gives him "the little tin box full of little pieces of greased cloth" when Pa loads his long rifle.[23] Ma is Pa's capable and fearless partner in this art of survival. She has mastered the domestic arts and works her own kind of magic, making sausages and cheese, churning butter, supplying the family with "good things to eat."[24] Laura and Mary help Ma with her chores. They wipe the morning dishes, make their own bed, and Mary is even big enough to help Ma churn butter. Survival on the frontier demands that children work alongside their parents.

To underscore the importance of the survival theme, Wilder strategically places action scenes, packed with tension and danger, throughout the novel. In the third chapter, for example, Pa matter-of-factly shoots a bear, but a few chapters later, Wilder reveals the risks he takes every time he goes out alone into the woods: "When he shot at a bear or a panther, he must kill it with the first shot. A wounded bear or panther could kill a man before he had time to load his gun again."[25] And midway through the book, Pa finds himself alone in the woods without his rifle. As dark falls, he glimpses a bear "standing up on his hind legs." Pa sees the bear's shining eyes, his "pig-snout," even "one of his claws in the starlight.'"[26] Pa arms himself with a solid, broken-off tree branch and heroically rushes the bear—only to discover it isn't a bear at all. It's a "big, black, burned stump!"[27] Pa laughs at himself and so do Laura and Mary when he later relates the story. But the danger had been real. As Pa tells the girls, he had seen bear tracks nearby earlier that same day.[28]

To reinforce the danger and its randomness in the Big Woods, Pa's encounter with that nonbear appears in the same chapter as Ma and Laura's experience with a very real one, "standing at the barnyard gate." In the dark, Ma mistakes a bear for their cow. She actually reaches across the gate and slaps the bear's shoulder before light from Laura's lantern reveals "long, shaggy, black fur, and two little glittering eyes." Just as Pa knows how to arm himself against what ultimately is an imaginary bear, Ma knows what to do when faced with a real one. She remains calm. Not until they're well away from the bear does Ma snatch Laura up, "lantern and all," and run to the house, slamming the door behind them.[29] Later, when Pa hears the story, he doesn't say anything. Instead, he hugs Laura tight, then "tighter."[30] The Big Woods are full of danger, and the entire family—Pa, Ma, Mary, Laura, and even Baby Carrie—must live every day in the shadow of its many perils. They all must be heroic, as the best storybook characters always are.

A Mythic Structure

The structure of *Little House in the Big Woods* is episodic, moving from one scene to another seemingly at random. It captures the timelessness of childhood, a child's sense of life's ongoing wonder. The novel also mirrors the way many of us recall our earliest childhood memories—as sharp, fragmentary flashes or impressions that aren't necessarily connected to anything else. Through Laura, Wilder conveys a seemingly fragmented narrative of vivid, almost dreamlike images: wolves outside the cabin window, a ragdoll at Christmas time, making cheese with Ma. This approach at once creates and reinforces the underlying mythic qualities at play in the novel. Laura doesn't grow and change as the novel progresses; instead, she moves through a series of timeless experiences with her family. Their life together is cyclical. Pa sets his traps in the winter. The extended family gathers at Christmas. Laura and Mary play house under those two big oak trees in the summer. And Pa and Uncle Henry harvest their crops together in the autumn. Life in the Big Woods has a natural yet somehow magical rhythm.

This is, in part, because the rhythm of the Big Woods is essentially seasonal. Wilder builds the novel around a year in the natural world—from fall to winter, winter to spring, spring to summer, summer to yet another fall. The novel brings the family full circle, and essentially spans that magical period, often found in fairy and folk tales, of a year and a day.

Lane suggested this structure to her mother after meeting with editor Marion Fiery to discuss "When Grandma Was a Little Girl" during February 1931. "As it stands," Lane wrote Wilder, "the action [in 'Grandma'] covers only one winter. My own idea for expansion would be to make it cover a year. . . . Just carry on through the summer, with any stories you can think of, and then through the beginning of school and your going to school for the first time."[31]

Wilder took Lane's advice but structured her novel not ending with the adventure of going to school. Instead, she anchors all the stories she could think of to the natural world, making the family's rhythm of life seasonal in the most elemental sense. This narrative structure reinforces the image of the Ingalls family as archetypal pioneers, struggling to create a safe and secure life for themselves on the wild and dangerous frontier.

Wilder brings the family full circle, from one autumn to the next. And the book's ending echoes its beginning: "She was glad that the cozy house, and Pa and Ma and the firelight and the music, were now. They could not be forgotten, she thought, because now is now. It can never be a long time ago."[32] *Little House in the Big Woods* is thus a moment in time that somehow transcends time, a child's eternal Now.

A Voice Full of Wonder

The novel's mythic quality comes filtered through a narrative voice that is childlike, full of wonder, yet never sentimental. When Laura has been punished for slapping Mary, for example, Laura sits in the corner sobbing: "At last, when it was getting dark, Pa said again, 'Come here Laura.' His voice was kind, and when Laura came he took her on his knee and hugged her close. She sat in the crook of his arm, her head against his shoulder and his long brown whiskers partly covering her eyes, and everything was all right again."[33] The moment is tender and real, not sentimental or cloying. Pa and Laura may be quintessential pioneers on the frontier, but their relationship seems contemporary, even to twenty-first-century readers. Wilder's voice narrows the distance between past and present, her fictional world and our own.

Her style is at once childlike and profound. She uses spare, concrete vocabulary that gives her work unexpected depth. Perhaps most importantly, Wilder doesn't talk down to young readers. She never tells them what to think or how to feel; she trusts that they will draw their own conclusions, thus strengthening her readers' identification with her characters and their extraordinary world. When Cousin Charley, for example, screams as if he's been bitten by a snake, repeatedly pulling Pa and Uncle Henry away from the harvest, Wilder doesn't tell readers that Charley is a "bad boy," as she does in *Pioneer Girl*.[34] Instead, she lets the scene unfold. As the grownups in the scene fall for his stunt time and time again, Charley laughs—until in another pivotal moment, poetic justice is served. Hundreds of yellow jackets sting Charley when he tramples over their nest.

Still, Wilder resists the urge to preach. She doesn't stoop to moralize. Pa, who relates Charley's story, tells Mary and Laura, "It served the little liar right." But as the chapter ends, Laura mulls over all she's heard about Charley and reaches her own unique conclusions: "She thought about what the yellow jackets had done to Charley. She thought it served Charley right too. It served him right because he had been so monstrously naughty. And the bees had a right to sting him, when he jumped on their home."[35]

Readers know exactly what Laura thinks about Charley, and by extension, they probably feel the same way. But notice that Wilder doesn't interrupt the narrative to preach a sermon about Charley, or instruct readers on the virtues of hard work, obedience, and being truthful. If there is a message, it comes indirectly, through Laura, and in this passage Laura takes sides not exactly with Pa but, unexpectedly, with the yellow jackets. In fact, Laura's confused by Pa's condemnation of Charley. She doesn't understand "why Pa had called him a little liar. She didn't understand how Charley could be a liar, when he had not said a word."[36]

The story becomes less an instructive tale about Bad Boy Charley and more a rare revelation of Laura's character and her way of viewing the world. As we'll see later on, Wilder uses this approach throughout the rest of the Little House books, trusting her readers to draw their own conclusions about her characters and their stories.

Setting as Character

Most young readers prefer to read about characters who are older than they are. But in *Little House in the Big Woods*, Laura turns five roughly midway through the book. She's significantly younger than most of Wilder's readers—third and fourth graders who can handle the sometimes challenging vocabulary ("monstrous," "suspicious," and "catechism"). Why does this work? How is it that young readers identify with characters who are clearly younger than they are? The key is Wilder's setting. The frontier becomes a kind of character in itself, a wild, exotic, and dangerous character who introduces Laura, Mary, and, by extension, readers themselves to unforgettable experiences and adventures. Together they explore a world filled with the unexpected, where a bear can be mistaken for a cow, a panther can ride on the back of a horse, or a doe and her fawn can suddenly step "daintily out of the shadows."[37]

This is an approach Wilder perfects and deepens in the later Little House books. The frontier and ultimately the West—from its dark, deep forests to its endless prairies and big sky; its relentless blizzards and violent summer storms—will be as essential to the Little House books as the Ingalls family itself. The West is capricious and powerful—sometimes lively and playful, sometimes breathtaking and majestic, sometimes dark and terrible. Ultimately, Wilder's West is an unforgiving place, beyond the control of even her most heroic human characters who endeavor to tame it.

Beyond the Big Woods

Modern readers are used to reading *Little House in the Big Woods* as the first book in the Little House series, yet it was initially written as a self-contained, stand-alone book. Its style, tone, and structure are unique to the series. Still, Wilder lays the foundation here for characterizations, concepts, and ideas she develops more fully in her later books. A perfect example is Wilder's preoccupation with nineteenth-century fashion.

In the chapter "Dance at Grandpa's," Wilder painstakingly describes how Aunt Docia and Aunt Ruby style their hair, tighten their corsets, and don their best calico dresses. Wilder lingers on nineteenth-century fashion details—the color and pattern of the calico, the design of a bodice, the flounces on a skirt. Ma is the belle of the ball, even more beautiful than Laura's unmarried aunts, "in her dark green delaine, with the little leaves that looked like strawberries scattered over it." Ma looks "so rich and fine" that Laura is "afraid to touch her."[38] As Ma, Aunt Docia, and Aunt Ruby sail over the dance floor in their flowing skirts, they are transformed into frontier goddesses, with rosy cheeks and bright eyes, "under the wings of shining sleek hair."[39]

Their transformation, however, serves a larger purpose. True, the scene feels magical, but by lingering on a few key fashion details, Wilder not only contrasts past with present, she uses these details as a symbol of women's unfailing attempts to bring beauty into their lives on the frontier, to soften the hardships of everyday life. Later in the Little House series, as we shall see, Wilder also uses fashion as a measure of financial stability.

Fashion, of course, is linked to the idea of feminine beauty, another theme that makes its first appearance in *Little House in the Big Woods*. When Aunt Lotty arrives, wearing a "beautiful pink" dress and matching sunbonnet, Mary immediately demands that Aunt Lotty decide which of her nieces has the prettiest curls—Mary's golden or Laura's brown ones.[40] Lotty answers wisely: "I like both best."[41] But the issue doesn't go away, and becomes the foundation for an argument that turns unexpectedly physical between the two girls. Laura slaps Mary when she declares, "Golden hair is lots prettier than brown."[42] Although Laura agrees with Mary, Laura longs to be considered pretty too.

This theme surfaces again when Laura ventures into the world beyond the Big Woods for the first time. Here it takes on a timeless, more haunting resonance: "The storekeeper said to Pa and Ma, 'That's a pretty little girl you've got there,' and he admired Mary's golden curls. But he did not say anything about Laura, or about her curls. They were brown and ugly."[43]

Wilder doesn't linger on Laura's feelings, nor does she stop the action to relay a lesson about the fundamental injustice of judging people—girls in particular—by their appearance. But readers then and now recognize the injury Laura suffers in this scene. She is invisible to the shopkeeper, judged not by who she is but how she looks.

The theme of feminine beauty returns throughout the Little House novels, sometimes masking an ugly spirit (in Nellie Oleson) and sometimes revealing a generous one (in Mrs. Boast and Ida Brown)—but always encouraging readers to think about how beauty defines and shapes a character's expectations of herself, of others, and ultimately her place in the world.

In *Little House in the Big Woods*, Laura repents of her jealousy of Mary but Wilder builds on this initial rivalry between the two girls throughout the rest of the series. Mary's beauty, relative goodness, and ladylike behavior define her. Laura, on the other hand, is defined by her strength. Pa tells her, "You're only a little half-pint of cider half drunk up, but by Jinks! you're as strong as a little French horse!"[44] These characterizations—"Half-pint" and "Little French Horse"—follow Laura as endearments throughout the rest of the series.

Wilder builds on the contrast between the two girls in the Little House books, deepening their characters, refining them, and ultimately bringing the sisters together to transcend their differences. Literature has given readers many memorable sisters in conflict—Jane Austen's Elinor and Marianne in *Sense and Sensibility*, the March girls in Louisa May Alcott's *Little Women*, even Cinderella and her wicked stepsisters. Laura and Mary Ingalls are just as memorable, and their literary journey through the Little House books—from rivals to soul mates—is iconic, one of the essential elements of Wilder's work.

Another essential element also makes its first appearance in *Little House in the Big Woods*: the music of the frontier. Wilder uses music not just as a characteristic that defines Pa but as a way to underscore setting, mood, action, and theme. Often Wilder includes lyrics in addition to song titles, especially when the lyrics are entertaining, revealing, or atmospheric.[45] Music wraps itself into the fabric of *Little House in the Big Woods*. It becomes an indispensable part of the family's pioneer experience.

"Yankee Doodle Dandy" is the first song that appears in the

novel. Pa chooses to play it on his fiddle after that rousing game of mad dog. The choice seems at once authentic and strategic. What other song would the definitive American pioneer father choose to play on a cold winter's night for his girls? It's also a song that young readers would know and recognize, bringing Wilder's fictional world closer to their own. At the end of the book, Wilder makes another musical choice that feels both authentic and strategic when Pa plays "Auld Lang Syne." Laura asks, "What are days of auld lang syne, Pa?" He answers, "They are the days of a long time ago, Laura."[46]

His answer defines *Little House in the Big Woods*.

Moving West: An Unexpected Absence

One major theme we've come to associate with the Little House books doesn't make an appearance in *Little House in the Big Woods*: the idea of a pioneer family always moving west. Pa's restless pioneer spirit, that irresistible yearning to move west that dominates later books in the series, is completely absent here. Instead, he is the hero who defends and nurtures what the family already has. He doesn't long to follow that wagon trace out of the Big Woods and beyond. When he leaves that little house in the Big Woods, he always returns home, without complaint. Pa is the family's anchor.

In 1931, when Wilder revised and submitted her first novel to Harper & Brothers, she hadn't envisioned a series of books about the American West. True, she was working on another book, but it would be a different kind of novel—still historical but not strictly autobiographical. She wanted to write a boy's book about life in the nineteenth century, one that would complement *Little House in the Big Woods* and yet illustrate how a settled, more prosperous family back east went about the business of living. *Little House in the Big Woods* had brought Wilder's memories of early childhood to life for young readers; now she wanted to do the same thing for her husband in a book she would title *Farmer Boy*.

5

Farmer Boy

Mirror Image

A MONTH BEFORE *LITTLE HOUSE IN THE BIG WOODS* WAS PUBlished, Wilder finished the first draft of her second novel, *Farmer Boy*. The story would be essentially free of autobiographical underpinnings, a fictional slice of Almanzo's childhood, set on the family's farm near Malone, New York. Wilder had never seen this part of the country and the story's action would take place before Wilder had been born; Almanzo was, after all, ten years her senior and his fictional counterpart would be "not quite nine years old" at the beginning of the book.[1] Lane edited the manuscript in May and June, typed it in August, then sent it off to Harper & Brothers later that month.

Lane was also working on a novel of her own that summer, one for adults based entirely on episodes from "Pioneer Girl." She told her mother nothing about it.

Lane had begun writing this novel in October 1931, shortly after Marion Fiery at Alfred Knopf had accepted Wilder's manuscript for *Little House in the Big Woods*. Although Lane had previously been uninterested in her mother's pioneer stories, she apparently began to recognize their potential to jump-start her own career. On the day before Lane's first reference to her new novel, she wrote that she had "walked over to my mother's in the afternoon and contemplated what I'm coming to in twice ten years."[2]

Whatever future Lane contemplated for herself in the distant future, her immediate future seemed suddenly clear. This new novel, Lane's first since the publication of *Cindy: A Romance of the Ozarks* in 1928, would provisionally be titled "Courage."[3] Its main characters would be a newly married pioneer couple named Charles and Caroline. He "was laughing and bold, a daring hunter, fiddler, and fighter." She was "a quiet person" who never lost the wonder that she had won "such a man as Charles."[4]

IN THE SPRING OF 1932, BEFORE LANE HAD FINISHED "COURAGE," she received a letter from her literary agent with news that Graeme Lorimer of the *Saturday Evening Post* had changed his mind about "Pioneer Girl." He now wanted to publish a "first person experience" about "pioneer conditions in the middle West."[5] As mentioned earlier, Lane's agent noted, "I think that Graeme Lorimer confused your mother's manuscript with your authorship."[6]

Let the Hurricane Roar

Although Wilder still hoped to publish the adult version of "Pioneer Girl," Lane didn't share this news with her mother. Instead, Lane finished writing "Courage," fictionalizing such "Pioneer Girl" episodes as the grasshopper plague at Plum Creek, the building of the railroad across Dakota Territory, and a blizzard from the Hard Winter. Lane finished her novel and gave it a new title, *Let the Hurricane Roar*, a line from a hymn Wilder and her sister Carrie remembered from their childhoods. Through her literary agent, Lane submitted it to the *Saturday Evening Post*. Lorimer bought the manuscript and the news reached Lane on September 6. She was "too excited to sleep" that night.[7]

About two weeks later, Wilder learned that her new editor at Harper & Brothers, Ida Louise Raymond, had rejected "Farmer Boy." The refusal must have stung, but again, there's no record of Wilder's reaction. Even Lane's diary is silent on the subject. In fact, Lane's diary from September 24 through October 31 (and for much of the remaining year) is blank, perhaps in part because she left Rocky Ridge Farm for an extended road trip that would ultimately take her to New York. But the gap could also reflect the rift that had developed between Wilder and Lane even before she packed her bags.

Let the Hurricane Roar was no longer a secret.

Even before Lane left Rocky Ridge Farm that fall, she received a check of $2,700 (the equivalent of over $48,000 today) for the sale of the manuscript, and Wilder herself deposited it.[8] The *Saturday Evening Post* published *Let the Hurricane Roar* almost immediately in its October and November issues. This was quickly followed by an offer from Longmans, Green to publish Lane's novel in book form.[9]

It became clear to Wilder that Lane, whose book sprang from the pages of "Pioneer Girl," had achieved exactly what Wilder herself had originally envisioned when she wrote "Pioneer Girl"—publication in a prestigious national magazine followed by a subsequent book deal. Furthermore, Lane's success had effectively killed "Pioneer Girl"'s future. Why would anyone agree to publish a memoir from a relatively unknown writer that essentially dealt with the same material as a novel from a bestselling author?[10] Even Wilder's future as a children's book author seemed murky. After all, "Farmer Boy" had failed to land a contract.

The historical record provides us with just one glimpse into the tension that developed between Wilder and Lane during late 1932 and early 1933. In an extended journal entry, Lane wrote that out of a sense of self-preservation, she'd hidden an advertisement for *Let the Hurricane Roar*, dreading her mother's "resentment" of the book's success. Inevitably, Wilder saw the ad and "read it with an air of distaste," Lane recorded. Her mother objected to the names Caroline and Charles. "They don't belong in that place at that time," Wilder apparently told Lane. "I don't know—it's all wrong. They've got it wrong somehow." In that moment, Lane felt her mother had robbed her of "the simple perfection of my pleasure."[11] Was Wilder's reaction selfish and unreasonable? Or was Lane insensitive to her mother's perspective?

Certainly an argument can be made that Lane had simply been inspired by her mother's work. But an equally compelling argument can be made that she plagiarized it. If Wilder and Lane hadn't been mother and daughter, Lane's appropriation of "Pioneer Girl" material—major characters, scenes, and sometimes specific passages of dialogue and description—would have been seen as a clear case of plagiarism. After all, without Wilder's knowledge or permission, Lane had lifted creative material from her unpublished manuscript, a manuscript Wilder herself still hoped to publish.

Yet Lane and Wilder remained remarkably professional during

this crisis. While Lane was back east, Wilder apparently began revising "Farmer Boy." And Lane, knowing that her mother was at work on this revision, visited Malone, New York, on her mother's behalf. She sent her descriptions of the Wilder family's farm and the surrounding countryside. In one postcard she wrote, "There are old lilac bushes in the yard, and I send you with this a twig from the balsam tree."[12] Lane's observations about Malone made it more real, more tangible, a place Wilder could envision in more concrete detail. As for Wilder, she helped Lane track down the lyrics to the hymn, "Let the Hurricane Roar," which her daughter needed for the Longmans, Green version of the book.[13]

Lane returned to Rocky Ridge Farm in December, and took to her bed for much of the month ("sick with an agonizing headache, vomiting, and fever").[14] Her symptoms slowly subsided and she celebrated the holidays with her parents, friends, and neighbors. Wilder finished the revised draft of *Farmer Boy* on January 19, 1933, and despite the continuing tension between them, asked Lane to edit and type this new draft. Lane agreed. The final draft was finished and submitted to Harper & Brothers in late February. On March 19, 1933, Lane's diary reads, "Farmer Boy sold."[15]

Relief and Disappointment

Farmer Boy's sale came with relief—and disappointment: Harper & Brothers offered Wilder only a 5 percent royalty for the manuscript, half of what Wilder had received with *Little House in the Big Woods*. Louise Raymond at Harper & Brothers explained that the publishing house had "much less money to manufacture the [second] book" and assured Wilder and Lane that other authors had accepted similar terms.[16] The 50 percent cut in royalties, Raymond maintained, was a reflection of the realities of the Great Depression, not the quality of *Farmer Boy* itself.

It's likely that Wilder felt, however, that the contract *did* reflect some inherent deficiency in *Farmer Boy*. Raymond had also told Wilder and Lane that *Little House in the Big Woods* had "set a very, very high standard, quite enough to have reached once in a lifetime."[17] This comment, added to the fact that Harper & Brothers had initially rejected *Farmer Boy*, seemed to indicate some fundamental flaw in the book. And yet, what Wilder and Lane may not have understood (since both had minimal experience in children's publishing at this point) is that it wasn't unusual for children's book editors to initially reject a manuscript from an established writer, then ask for revisions and a subsequent resubmission. This remains a standard practice in children's publishing ninety years later.

Having a new editor on board at Harper & Brothers could also have complicated *Farmer Boy*'s acceptance process. Here again, the situation wasn't unusual. Editors come and go at publishing houses, and when an editor inherits a writer, even one with publishing history, the editor may wait to make an offer until *after* she's seen how willing and how thoroughly a writer can revise. What's important is an editor's final decision, and Raymond, after asking Wilder to resubmit her revised manuscript in January 1933, ultimately concluded that "FARMER BOY is excellent—different, sincere, authentic."[18]

Echoes in Time and Place

Raymond made one other memorable observation about *Farmer Boy*. It was "not quite another LITTLE HOUSE."[19] True, *Farmer Boy* is very different from its predecessor. It deals with different characters in a different setting. And most readers today also feel that *Farmer Boy* strikes a different tone, with a different set of themes than the rest of Wilder's Little House books. But if you read the Little House series sequentially, it becomes clear that *Little House in the Big Woods* and *Farmer Boy* are companion books. *Little House in the Big Woods* is about a frontier family living in the West. *Farmer Boy* is about a farm family living in the East. Despite the contrast in setting, the books showcase how both families live their everyday lives during the late 1860s and early 1870s.

The parallels between the two books begin in their opening lines. *Farmer Boy*'s first sentence reads, "It was January in northern New York State, sixty-seven years ago."[20] The book has shed the fairytale opening of "once upon a time" that establishes the mythic atmosphere of *Little House in the Big Woods*, but otherwise *Farmer Boy* echoes its predecessor, which begins, "Sixty years ago, a little girl lived in the Big Woods of Wisconsin, in a little gray house made of logs."[21] These paired opening lines simultaneously mirror and contrast with each other. One book is about a girl's family from long ago, and the other is about a boy's from even longer ago.

As the two novels unfold, it's also clear that both focus on accomplished and self-reliant families. Both books explore what life was like for these families and feature detailed descriptions of their everyday chores and pleasures. For the Wilders of New York this includes shearing sheep and planting potatoes, popping corn and going fishing.

Similar Themes and Approaches

The tightly knit family in *Farmer Boy* mirrors the fictional Ingalls family. While the Wilder household is slightly larger—two boys and two girls—and the children are older, both fictional families value honest work, craftsmanship, and proficiency.[22] In *Farmer Boy*, for example, Mother has a "large and bright" workroom, complete with a spinning wheel and loom.[23] She is an accomplished weaver and homemaker. Father is a prosperous farmer and a skilled woodworker. In his attic workroom, he crafts projects that not only keep the farm running efficiently but delight his children. In *Farmer Boy*, he makes Almanzo a practical, farm-boy gift—a "little calf-yoke" of red cedar for his calves Star and Bright.[24] But Father also builds Almanzo a "beautiful sled . . . made of hickory."[25] Like Charles Ingalls (who balances his chores with the pleasures of music and storytelling), Father in *Farmer Boy* encourages his children to work hard yet enjoy life.

Again like the fictional Ingalls family, all of the Wilders pitch in to help with everyday chores. Almanzo and his sister Alice plant carrots in the springtime. Royal helps Father plant seed corn, their "hand and their hoes" making "exactly the same movements every time."[26] Eliza Jane and Alice know how to make butter, cook, and sew. They routinely help Mother with household chores. Father and Mother in Malone—like Pa and Ma in the Big Woods—expect their children to learn the value of work and self-sufficiency.

Farmer Boy—like *Little House in the Big Woods*—also explores a variety of experiences unique to nineteenth-century life. Entire chapters are devoted to the tin-peddler's and cobbler's visits, the ice-house, a county fair. And like *Little House in the Big Woods*,

Farmer Boy includes an episode about harvesting maple sap as "the snow softened . . . and the icicles dripped."[27]

Farmer Boy also touches on the idea of feminine beauty and what it means to be a girl, a theme Wilder introduced in *Little House in the Big Woods*. When Almanzo asks Alice if "she didn't want to be a boy," Alice at first says yes, then no:

> "Boys aren't pretty like girls, and they can't wear ribbons."
>
> "I don't care how pretty I be," Almanzo said. "And I wouldn't wear ribbons anyhow."
>
> "Well, I like to make butter and I like to patch quilts. And cook, and sew, and spin. Boys can't do that. But even if I be a girl, I can drop potatoes and sow carrots and drive horses as well as you can."[28]

Farmer Boy and *Little House in the Big Woods* clearly share similar themes and approaches; both also draw inspiration from "Pioneer Girl."

The Smartest Man in the World

The opening scene in *Farmer Boy* illustrates how dramatically Wilder could not only transform material from her "Pioneer Girl" manuscript into fiction, but how she could transplant it into an entirely different fictional world, one that didn't spring directly from her own memories. The transformation is seamless.

The novel opens on the Wilder children's first day of school on a cold January day. Their new teacher is Mr. Corse, "a slim, pale young man."[29] How would he confront the Bill Richie gang? Everyone knew that "Bill could thrash school-teachers and break up the school."[30]

When the confrontation comes, Bill Richie and the entire community of Malone get a big surprise. As Bill rushes down the aisle, Mr. Corse "stepped away from his desk. His hand came from behind the desk lid, and a long-thin, black streak hissed through the air. . . . It was a blacksnake ox-whip fifteen feet long. . . . The thin, long lash coiled around Bill's legs, and Mr. Corse jerked. Bill lurched and almost fell. Quick as black lightning the lash circled and struck and coiled again."[31] Bill bawls "like a calf," blubbering and begging for the whipping to end, but the "lash kept on hissing, circling, jerking," until Bill finds himself at the school door, and Mr. Corse throws him out, locking the door behind him. The rest of the gang is quickly subdued and the school runs efficiently for the rest of the term.[32]

This episode, however, has its origins in Burr Oak, Iowa, not Malone, New York. According to *Pioneer Girl*, a young Laura and Mary Ingalls watched as a "slim young man"—Mr. William Reed—faced down a gang of "big men 24 and 25 years old," who "always before the winter was over . . . started a fight with the teacher and drove him away." Although Mr. Reed's weapon of choice—a handmade ruler—isn't as dramatic as Mr. Corse's blacksnake ox-whip, the outcome is the same. The gang is thoroughly defeated and never returns to the school again.[33]

The account in *Farmer Boy* is far more dramatic and violent than the original scene in *Pioneer Girl*, but it also serves an important thematic purpose in the novel. As it turns out, the real hero of this episode isn't Mr. Corse; it's Father. The blacksnake ox-whip belongs to him. He orchestrated Mr. Corse's actions. Almanzo decides "that Father was the smartest man in the world, as well as the biggest and strongest."[34]

And toward the end of the book, Father delivers a life-changing speech to Almanzo: "A farmer depends on himself, and the land and the weather. . . . You work hard, but you work as you please, and no man can tell you to go or come. You'll be free and independent, son, on a farm."[35] At the end of the speech, Almanzo squirms but admits that he "wanted to be just like Father. But didn't say so."[36]

Just as Pa is idolized in *Little House in the Big Woods*, Father emerges as a heroic character in *Farmer Boy*. He is "a big man."[37] But unlike Pa, Father isn't at the center of the action in *Farmer Boy*. He isn't the book's main character, and this fundamental distinction is one of many between Wilder's first two novels. They are mirror images, yet they aren't . . . quite.

Distinctly Different

Wilder considered *Farmer Boy* a boys' book, and its focus is always on one particular boy, one particular character—Almanzo Wilder, the youngest in his family. From the beginning, readers sense the book will center not so much on the Wilder family as an ensemble cast but almost exclusively on just one member of the family: Almanzo—and his experiences, his feelings, his hopes and dreams. On the novel's opening pages, for example, Almanzo walks "fast to keep up" with his older brother and sisters as he hurries to school for the first time.[38] What follows is a lengthy description—not of Almanzo's brothers and sisters—but of the clothes Almanzo wears to keep warm on that walk to school. The action and descriptions revolve around Almanzo and no one else.

The Wilders don't face mythic struggles as do the Ingalls in *Little House in the Big Woods*. They don't inhabit a wild, fairytale place where almost anything might happen—and sometimes does. Instead, the Wilders of *Farmer Boy* are solid, prosperous characters, respectable and hardworking, but not mythic. Almanzo's father is "an important man." He has "a good farm" and drives "the best horses in the county." He puts "money in the bank," and townsfolk speak to him "respectfully."[39]

Almanzo's mother is equally respectable and important. When the family goes to church on Sunday, Almanzo takes pride in his mother's finery: "Poor people had to wear homespun on Sundays. . . . But Father and Mother and the girls were very fine, in clothes that Mother had made of store-boughten cloth, woven by machines."[40] The family's clothes, expertly handmade by Mother, are a measure of the family's success and prosperity.

The world of *Farmer Boy* is a civilized and secure place, a world with a school and a bank and a church. The Wilders live a settled life without the dangers the fictional Ingalls family encounters in the Big Woods. There aren't any panthers and wolves in Malone; there isn't mortal danger when the family steps outside their farmhouse door. Perhaps this is one reason why the Wilders don't possess the storybook qualities of the Ingalls family in *Little House in the Big Woods*.

Granted, the Wilders are industrious and frugal, even Almanzo's stylish sisters, who refashion their "old dresses and bonnets, sponging and pressing them and sewing them together again the other side out, to look new."[41] But the Wilders of Malone are not as fiercely independent or quite as self-reliant as are the Ingalls in *Little House in the Big Woods*. They don't have to be because the world of *Farmer Boy* is established and settled, a world that seems more familiar to young readers, despite the nineteenth-century setting. Chapter titles have a familiar ring: "School Days," "Birthday," "Independence Day."

New Creative Challenge

Despite its more conventional historical setting, *Farmer Boy* provided a new creative challenge for Wilder and marks an important transition in her career as a novelist. In Almanzo of *Farmer Boy*, Wilder had to create a main character—and an entire fictional world—that existed outside her own experiences. She had to fully and completely imagine nearly every character, scene, and setting in the novel. With the exception of the episode with Mr. Corse and Bill, Wilder couldn't draw from her own memories or flesh out scenes that already existed in "Pioneer Girl." Of course, she knew the man on whom *Farmer Boy* was based very well. In 1931, when she began work on the novel, she and Almanzo Wilder had been married for forty-six years.

But creating characters from the outside in—rather than from the inside out, as she does in *Little House in the Big Woods*—is a very different process. Wilder had to imagine Almanzo as a boy, decades before she knew him, and create a convincing personality for him—his feelings, his observations, his dreams, his desires. As Eloise Jarvis McGraw, author of several Newbery Award Honor Books, observed, "Writers can't write books if they don't know why their characters do what they do, feel as they feel, fear what they fear. And they don't have readers if the reasons aren't clear and believable on the page."[42]

Almanzo's character springs to life in a vivid scene in *Farmer Boy*'s second chapter. The episode reveals not only who he is but what he wants:

> He loved horses. There they stood in their roomy box-stalls, clean and sleek and gleaming brown, with long black manes and tails. . . . The three-year-olds . . . all knew Almanzo. Their ears pricked up and their eyes shone softly when they saw him. . . .

> Their necks arched proudly, firm and round, and the black manes fell over them like a heavy fringe. You could run your hand along those firm, curved necks, in the warmth under the mane.
>
> But Almanzo hardly dared to do it. He was not allowed to touch the beautiful three-year-olds. . . . He was only eight years old, and Father would not let him handle the young horses or the colts. . . .
>
> A boy who didn't know any better might scare a young horse, or tease it, or even strike it, and that would ruin it. . . . Almanzo did know better; he wouldn't ever scare or hurt one of those beautiful colts. He would always be quiet, and gentle, and patient; he wouldn't startle a colt or shout at it, not even if it stepped on his foot. But Father wouldn't believe this.
>
> So Almanzo could only look longingly at the eager three-year-olds. He just touched their velvety noses, and then he went quickly away from them.[43]

The scene is filled with longing and revelation—a boy who loves and understands horses, respects them, respects his father, and despite all he desires will wait quietly, patiently, until he earns his father's confidence and trust. The details in the scene not only provide readers with a clear image of the Wilders' horse barn in Malone and those achingly beautiful horses, they also reveal Almanzo's vision of his world. They reinforce Almanzo's character, who he is, how he views his place in this world, and what he most desires. This approach—a tight focus on a single main character—is a fundamental shift away from *Little House in the Big Woods* and its ensemble cast of characters.

Growth and Change

From the opening lines to the end of the book, the narrative arc of *Farmer Boy* follows Almanzo. Readers never lose sight of him. And this is perhaps the most striking artistic difference between *Farmer Boy* and *Little House in the Big Woods*. It isn't that *Farmer Boy* is a "boys' book" or that it centers on the Wilders instead of the Ingalls family. It's that Wilder's focus in *Farmer Boy* is on a single character, and how over time, he achieves what he desires.

Laura and Mary in *Little House in the Big Woods* are unchanged by the end of the novel. They are perpetual little girls living a kind of enchanted frontier existence. *Farmer Boy*'s Almanzo, on the other hand, changes and grows over the course of the novel. He is not the same boy who, in the beginning of *Farmer Boy*, had to carry the dinner-pail to school for his siblings. Instead, he finds the courage to speak to Father directly, wins his confidence, and fulfills a long-awaited dream:

> "If it's a colt you want, I'll give you Starlight."
>
> "Father!" Almanzo gasped. "For my very own?"
>
> "Yes, son. You can break him, and drive him, and when he's a four-year-old you can sell him or keep him, just as you want to. We'll take him out on a rope, first thing tomorrow morning, and you can begin to gentle him."

In that moment, "the whole world was a great, shining, expanding glow of warm light" for Almanzo.[44] He is poised to become the master horseman he has always dreamed of growing up to be.

A Linear Structure

Farmer Boy is a middle-grade coming-of-age novel, and as these books usually are, its structure is linear, not cyclical. The book does follow the course of one year—from January to January—but unlike *Little House in the Big Woods*, *Farmer Boy* never falters in its clear, forward motion, building momentum as it nears the end.

The central storyline running through *Farmer Boy* (with a few deviations) follows the fulfillment of Almanzo's dream: to one day be responsible and old enough to "gentle" his own colt. While this is a more traditional approach to middle-grade fiction, it also marks a significant deviation from *Little House in the Big Woods*, which doesn't have a traditional plot at all. Instead, its action flows from one season to the next, creating a kind of natural rhythm, a seasonal ebb and flow. The book's lyrical ending presents an image of the Ingalls family captured in an eternal Now and a past that can never be "a long time ago."[45] In contrast, the last line in *Farmer Boy* refers to the future: "We'll take him [Starlight] out on a rope, first thing tomorrow morning, and you can begin to gentle him."[46] Almanzo's story continues to move forward, even on the final page of the book.

This difference is important because it signals a shift in Wilder's creative vision. Although *Farmer Boy* began as a kind of mirror image to *Little House in the Big Woods*—a way Wilder could explore the parallel nineteenth-century childhoods of a girl living on the frontier in the West and a boy growing up on a farm in the East—it ultimately inspired her to see beyond a cyclical, ensemble cast for the fictional Ingalls family. While writing *Farmer Boy*, Wilder began to envision a way to write an ongoing story about growth, maturity, and change that would center on the fictional Ingalls family. But this time, Wilder would place Laura at the center of the action. She would be a strong, three-dimensional character with her own clear story arc. And simultaneously Wilder would weave the changes in Laura's character over time into her family's larger-than-life desire to move west. This thematic and structural shift would allow Wilder to tell a more sweeping story, a story she later described as representing "a whole period of American history."[47]

'Way out beyond Kansas

In the middle of *Farmer Boy*, Wilder plants an intriguing reference to the West. After the family has celebrated Independence Day in Malone, Almanzo and Father milk the cows together, and as they carry the milk into the house, they talk about the role farmers have played in American history. As they reach the house, Father finishes Almanzo's history lesson this way: "This country goes three thousand miles west now. It goes 'way out beyond Kansas, and beyond the Great American Desert, over mountains bigger than these mountains, and down to the Pacific Ocean. It's the biggest country in the world, and it was farmers who took all that country and made it America."[48] This is Wilder's first oblique reference in her novels to Manifest Destiny, the idea that the United States was divinely destined to expand across the continent from coast to coast. This belief permeated American society from the mid-nineteenth century well into the early twentieth. Perhaps this reference to the West, which occurs in *Farmer Boy*—but nowhere in *Little House in the Big Woods*—reflects another significant creative shift that sprang from Wilder's work on her second novel.

By the time *Farmer Boy* was published in late 1933, Wilder was already working on another manuscript, a manuscript that even

Lane was excited about, one that would establish the themes that now characterize Wilder's literary legacy: growth, change, and a restless pioneering spirit played out in the American West. As Lane wrote their literary agent in March 1933, "My mother is now doing another book about her childhood experiences among the Indians. . . . [It] promises to beat Little House all hollow."[49]

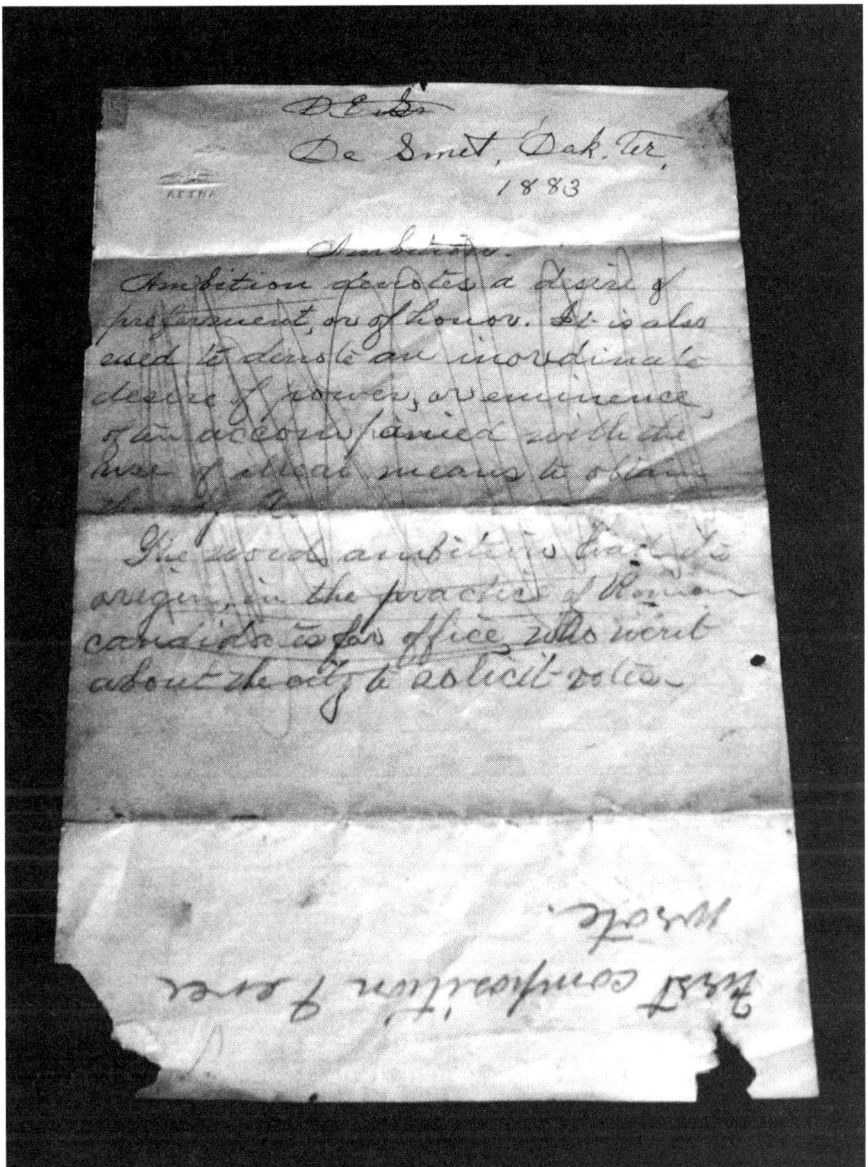
De Smet, Dak. Ter.
1883

Ambition.

Ambition denotes a desire of preferment, or of honor. It is also used to denote an inordinate desire of power, or eminence, often accompanied with the use of illegal means to obtain them.

The word ambition has its origin in the practice of Roman candidates for office who went about the city to solicit votes.

First composition I ever wrote.

1. Wilder's original "Ambition" essay, dated 1883. Courtesy of Laura Ingalls Wilder Home Association, Mansfield, Missouri.

MISSOURI RURALIST

WITH WHICH IS COMBINED THE BREEDERS SPECIAL

A WEEKLY JOURNAL FOR MISSOURI FARMERS AND BREEDERS

Vol. IX. Whole No. 503 | Saturday, June 1, 1912 | Price $1.00 Per Year

FROM this 12 year old apple tree in the Ozark country of Missouri were gathered at one time five barrels of No. 1, and three barrels of No. 2 apples. They were highly colored and of most excellent flavor. This tree is a sample of the trees on the hundred-acre orchard farm of A. J. Wilder, who is shown standing at the side of the tree. After a fruitless struggle on the plains of Dakota, Mr. Wilder came to Missouri, settling at Mansfield. He purchased 40 acres of undeveloped land by going in debt for it and went to work. Mother Nature rewarded his well meant if not well directed efforts—he knew nothing of orcharding at the time. Mr. Wilder has since added another 60 acres. He is out of debt, his land has more than doubled in value and his orchard is regarded by nurserymen and apple buyers as one of the best in the Ozark country.

2. Wilder's cover story for the *Missouri Ruralist*, featuring a photograph of Almanzo Wilder, June 1912. Microfilm. University of Missouri, Columbia.

3. What appears to be a rare mother-daughter photograph of Wilder and Lane at Rocky Ridge Farm, circa 1912. Courtesy of Laura Ingalls Wilder Home Association, Mansfield, Missouri.

4. Laura Ingalls Wilder during her tenure with the *Missouri Ruralist*, circa 1918. Herbert Hoover Presidential Library.

5. Rose Wilder Lane's studio portrait published with her profile in *Sunset* magazine, 1918. Herbert Hoover Presidential Library.

6. The Rock House, where Wilder wrote *Pioneer Girl* and the first three Little House books. Photo by Chris Jacobson.

7. Rose Wilder Lane, circa 1928–30, when *Pioneer Girl* was written. Herbert Hoover Presidential Library.

8. Wilder and Almanzo Wilder, circa 1933, when her career as a novelist was just beginning. Courtesy of Laura Ingalls Wilder Home Association, Mansfield, Missouri.

9. Helen Sewell's frontispiece for *Little House in the Big Woods*, 1932. Used by permission of HarperCollins Publishers.

10. Lane's *Let the Hurricane Roar*, published in book form in 1933. Author's collection.

11. Virginia Kirkus, Wilder's first editor at Harper & Brothers, at her desk. Virginia Kirkus Papers, collection 10953, box 1. American Heritage Center, University of Wyoming, Laramie.

12. The book that launched the Little House novels as a series, 1935. Used by permission of HarperCollins Publishers.

13. "The little Indians did not have to wear clothes," the only Native American illustration in the original edition of *Little House on the Prairie*, 1935. Used by permission of HarperCollins Publishers.

6

Little House on the Prairie, Part One

A Series Is Born

THROUGHOUT HER LIFETIME, LAURA INGALLS WILDER WAS thrifty. When money was tight at Rocky Ridge Farm in the early 1930s, for example, she suggested—to her daughter's irritation—that they could economize by shutting off the electricity.[1] Kerosene and candles were cheaper. So perhaps it isn't surprising that throughout her writing career, Wilder wrote her rough drafts on inexpensive Big Chief and Fifty-Fifty school tablets. Unlike Virginia Woolf, who preferred to use a "dipping pen and ink" (often paired with an elegant, textured paper stock), Wilder's instrument of choice was a pencil.[2]

Even after the publication of her first two novels, Wilder used resources carefully. A case in point: in 1933 Wilder received a letter from an admiring young fan. "My teacher has read us the book of *The Little House in the Big Woods*, and I would like to know if you have anymore books like it for I enjoyed the book very much."[3] The young writer of this letter would have been surprised to learn that on the back of her letter, Wilder wrote a draft of the opening lines for her next book. In fact, Wilder scribbled slightly different variations for the opening of the book she called "Indian Country" on the backs of letters from that enthusiastic young reader, her editor, her former editor at the *Missouri Ruralist*, and even from her daughter. Success hadn't fundamentally changed Laura Ingalls Wilder. She was still a frugal woman who remained true to those early pioneer lessons of conserving and making do.

Those scraps of rough drafts also illustrate that Wilder took her responsibilities to her readers seriously. She worked hard at her craft, revising and rewriting her work. She didn't take success for granted. As she wrote Lane several years later, when she was well into the Little House series, "The only way I can write is to wander along with the story, then rewrite and re-arrange and change it everywhere."[4]

As she wandered along with the story for her third novel, she faced a monumental creative challenge: how to begin this new book, a book that would take the fictional Ingalls family west into "Indian Country." And while the opening lines of any novel are critically important, this new beginning was especially daunting. *Little House in the Big Woods* had ended perfectly, even magically, with a timeless portrait of a pioneer family content with itself and its place in the world. Why would the Ingalls family ever want to leave?

EDITORS WILL TELL YOU THAT THE OPENING LINES OF A MANuscript often determine not only whether they'll read it but ultimately whether they'll publish it. If editors don't find a manuscript's opening pages compelling, how can they expect readers—young or old—to stick with the story once it's in print?

This principle is especially important in children's literature, and was as true when Wilder was writing in the 1930s as it is today. A vivid, memorable beginning will draw young readers into a story and then ideally keep them turning page after page until they reach its very last line. But in 1932, as Wilder sketched out ideas for her third novel, her challenge was somewhat unique. Her opening lines not only had to entice young readers (and her editor, Ida Louise Raymond at Harper & Brothers), they had to transition from her first novel to this new one. And this transition also had to be so smooth, so seamless that readers wouldn't suspect there had been a novel—*Farmer Boy*—in between.

Adding to the challenge was Raymond's guarded response to *Farmer Boy* itself, and her conclusion that *Little House in the Big Woods* had set a once-in-a-lifetime standard. Wilder's creative challenge was indeed ambitious: How to begin a sequel to a novel her editor considered incomparable?

The Quest for a Good Lead

When Wilder sketched out those opening lines on the back of that fan letter, she experimented with slightly different variations. "It was late afternoon as the white-topped covered wagon moved slowly across the prairie," she wrote. "The two black ponies seemed tired of pulling it and Mary and Laura were tired of riding in it." Wilder crossed out these lines and began again: "A white-topped covered wagon moved slowly across the prairie drawn by two black ponies. A man and a woman sat on the wagon seat in front. The man was driving, his bright blue eyes looking along the wagon trail ahead."[5]

But Wilder still wasn't happy with that beginning. She scratched out phrases she didn't like, circled words she wanted to change, and inserted whole sentences. Her more polished first draft begins this way:

> A white-topped, covered wagon, drawn by two black ponies moved slowly across the prairie in Southern Kansas. A brindle bulldog trotted in the shade underneath.
>
> A man and a woman sat on the spring-seat at the very front of the wagon. The man was driving, his bright blue eyes looking ahead along the wagon trail, his brown beard blowing in the wind.[6]

There's nothing wrong with this opening scene. It is well written and vivid, from the brindle bulldog to the spring-seat. But its voice lacks a sense of childlike wonder, and it doesn't bridge the gap between that cozy log cabin in the Big Woods and the white-topped covered wagon moving slowly across the prairie.

Actually, Wilder's rough draft beginning for "Indian Country" reads more like the opening lines for an adult novel about the West. It strikes a similar style and tone to Willa Cather's beginning for *O Pioneers!*, published in 1913: "One January day, thirty years ago, the little town of Hanover, anchored on a windy Nebraska tableland, was trying not to be blown away. A mist of fine snowflakes was curling and eddying about the cluster of low drab buildings huddled on the gray prairie, under a gray sky."[7] In fact, "Indian Country"'s rough draft beginning is actually stronger and more vivid than Lane's opening lines in *Let the Hurricane Roar*: "While they were children playing together, they said they would be married as soon as they were old enough, and when they were old enough they married."[8]

Despite the lackluster opening lines in her own novel, Lane understood the importance of what she called a good lead in children's books; it was one of the concepts Marion Fiery had emphasized back in 1931, when she and Lane had met to discuss "When Grandma Was a Little Girl." Lane recognized the inherent flaws in her mother's rough-draft opening scene in "Indian Country"—its adult voice and its failure to connect a Kansas prairie to the Big Woods of Wisconsin. As Wilder's first reader and editor, Lane convinced her mother to use a totally different approach. When the manuscript was published in 1935 under its new title, *Little House on the Prairie*, its opening lines were unforgettable:

> A long time ago, when all the grandfathers and grandmothers of today were little boys and little girls or very small babies, or perhaps not even born, Pa and Ma and Mary and Laura and Baby Carrie left their little house in the Big Woods of Wisconsin. They drove away and left it lonely and empty in the clearing among the big trees, and they never saw that little house again.
>
> They were going to the Indian country.[9]

The narrative voice in this passage is intimate, inviting, and almost playful. It establishes a connection to the family's little house in the Big Woods, but it carries the action forward, toward a new adventure. It also identifies the novel's main characters right away, creating a bridge between that first Little House book and this one. But unlike *Little House in the Big Woods* and *Farmer Boy* (with their specific references to sixty and sixty-seven years ago), the first paragraph in *Little House on the Prairie* gives readers a sense of historic timelessness, a past that is long ago but bound to no specific point in time. It's almost as if Wilder and Lane recognized that *Little House on the Prairie* would cast a spell over generations of young readers.

A Breakthrough Novel

Little House on the Prairie is Wilder's breakthrough novel. It's where the Little House series actually begins, and where Wilder introduces creative and thematic elements that have since come to define her literary legacy. Laura Ingalls emerges as a clearly defined main character, and the world she inhabits is an ever-changing, sweeping, sometimes terrible but always magnificent American West. The supporting cast—Pa, Ma, Mary, and even Baby Carrie—provide depth, balance, and perspective to Laura's perceptions and experiences. Together they face the challenges in the West with courage, hard work, grit, and optimism. Wilder also brings a stronger dose of realism to *Little House on the Prairie* but with a twist: the realism somehow heightens the mythic qualities of the novel. The past she creates is at once historic and timeless, real and mythic.

Historic Timelessness

The timelessness of Wilder's opening lines in *Little House on the Prairie* extends well beyond the opening page and reflects both a creative and practical solution to the fundamental problem she faced with the novel: how to manipulate her own life story to fit the fictional framework and sequencing she had essentially inherited from Lane in "When Grandma Was a Little Girl."

Wilder's earliest childhood memories probably sprang from "Indian country"—the Osage Diminished Reserve in Kansas—not the Big Woods of Wisconsin. "Pioneer Girl," after all, begins in "Indian country," and on the second page of her handwritten original draft, Wilder describes what may have been her earliest memory: Pa carrying her to the window to see the wolves "sitting in a ring around the house, with their noses pointed up at the big, bright moon, howling as loud and long as they could."[10] But when Lane pieced together "When Grandma Was a Little Girl" from scenes she and her mother had cut from the adult version of "Pioneer Girl," Lane moved the action to the Big Woods, mixing scenes that had originated in Kansas with others from Wisconsin. Wilder maintained this chronological memory meld when she transformed "Grandma" into *Little House in the Big Woods*. She apparently had no qualms then about transporting "Pioneer Girl"'s wolves from Kansas to Wisconsin, where, in *Little House in the Big Woods*, they also "pointed their noses at the big, bright moon, and howled."[11]

But back in 1931, when Wilder inherited Lane's fictional chronology for "Grandma," she hadn't yet envisioned a series of books based on her past. Now, two years later, as Wilder began work on *Little House on the Prairie*, she had to create yet another and more challenging memory meld, one that would sustain a plausible fictional chronology with enough momentum to carry the Ingalls family forward—into "Indian country" and beyond. Eliminating specific historical markers gave Wilder more freedom to reshape the past, to fuse fact with fiction, and ultimately to more seamlessly edit her own personal history to conform to the fictional future she envisioned for her characters. This new chronology would propel the family through book after book, all the way to Dakota Territory.

It also gave Wilder the creative freedom to amplify the image she had created for her characters in *Little House in the Big Woods*. In that novel, Pa, Ma, Mary, Laura, and Baby Carrie represent the archetypal pioneer family building a secure life for themselves on the frontier. In *Little House on the Prairie*, they step into an even bigger role as the rootless American pioneer family, always moving west, striving through one hardship after another to attain a better life for themselves. They envision a West of boundless opportunities, a place that remains wild and free, where there is room to dream. In the opening chapter of *Little House on the Prairie*, Pa talks to Ma during long winter evenings about the "Western country," describing its sweeping grandeur and freedom: "In the West the land was level, and there were no trees. The grass grew thick and high. There the wild animals wandered and fed as though they were in a pasture that stretched much farther than a man could see."[12] Ma doesn't "object" to Pa's dream, so he sells their farm in the Big Woods, for "enough to give us a new start in a new country."[13] The fictional family moves west with virtually no markers to pinpoint their place in time.

Going West

Unlike their fictional counterparts, the real Ingalls family moved away from their little house in the Big Woods twice—first in 1869, when Wilder was two, and then again in 1874, when Wilder was seven. In between, from 1869 until 1871, the real Ingalls family lived on the Osage Diminished Reserve in present-day Kansas.[14]

But on the first page of *Little House on the Prairie*, Wilder signals her creative decision to abandon the facts of her life for a larger thematic vision. When the fictional family leaves their little house in the Big Woods of Wisconsin, they drive away, leaving it "lonely and empty in the clearing among the big trees, and they never saw that little house again."[15] They move west to "Indian country," permanently turning their backs on the East, where "too many people" were pushing wildlife away. Pa, Wilder writes, "liked a country where the wild animals lived without being afraid."[16]

"Going West," the first chapter in *Little House on the Prairie*, literally establishes the direction, not just for the novel but for the remaining books Wilder intended to write over the coming decade. The chapter title also predicts the setting, theme, and central conflicts ahead in *Little House on the Prairie* and beyond. Wilder sprinkles iconic images of the American West throughout this first chapter too, beginning with the covered wagon itself, alone in a vast landscape: "Kansas was an endless flat land covered with tall grass blowing in the wind. Day after day they traveled in Kansas, and saw nothing but the rippling grass and the enormous sky. In a perfect circle the sky curved down to the level land, and the wagon was in the circle's exact middle."[17] Flooded creeks, brilliant sunsets, jackrabbits, and even the defining boundaries of the Mississippi and Missouri Rivers make an appearance in this first chapter, along with several references to Native people.

Throughout the rest of the novel, the West defines every aspect of the fictional family's life, from their little house built from a "load of logs from the creek bottoms" to the prairie fire with its "twists of flame" traveling on the wind; from the longhorn cattle and the cowboys who "burst out of the prairie" in a cloud of dust to the Indians who "often came to the house."[18] The West even transforms Christmas. When Santa Claus appears on the street in Independence, Kansas, he has left his reindeer and sleigh behind. In the "southwest," Wilder writes, he travels with a pack-mule and rides a "fine bay horse."[19]

A Transformative Landscape

Throughout the novel, Wilder writes eloquently about the western landscape and its transformative influence on the fictional family.

Unlike the closed-in spaces of the Big Woods, the prairie—the West—works a different kind of magic. It is a storybook landscape in its own right, vast, dangerous, beautiful, and unpredictable, a landscape of overwhelming dimensions. As the family goes "farther and farther into the vast prairie," Laura feels "smaller and smaller." She observes that "even Pa did not seem as big as he really was."[20]

The power of the West even promises to transform Pa, to calm the restlessness that drove him west in the first place. He says:

> "This is a great country. This is a country I'll be contented to stay in the rest of my life."
>
> "Even when it's settled up?" Ma asked.
>
> "Even when it's settled up. No matter how thick and close the neighbors get, this country'll never feel crowded. Look at that sky!"[21]

Although Ma clings to the trappings of civilization, carefully placing her beloved china shepherdess on the mantle-shelf in their new house, and insisting that Laura and Mary wear their sunbonnets, she can't control how the West changes and inspires her children, especially Laura. Laura lets her sunbonnet "dangle down her back" and fully embraces the freedom and beauty of the her new surroundings.[22] Like Pa, Laura likes "the enormous sky and the winds, and the land that you couldn't see to the end of."[23]

This focus on Laura and her feelings marks another major departure from *Little House in the Big Woods*. For Wilder, *Little House on the Prairie* would be the beginning of not just the fictional Ingalls family's adventures in the West; it would launch the story of one member of the Ingalls family in particular. Although Charles Ingalls—Pa—would maintain the heroic and influential role Wilder gave him in *Little House in the Big Woods*, her spotlight in *Little House on the Prairie* would shift from Pa and an ensemble cast to her own fictional counterpart—Laura, a six-year-old who likes "going out west."[24]

A Distinct Voice

Although *Little House on the Prairie* opens with a direct reference to the ensemble cast from Wilder's first novel, it quickly establishes Laura as the main character with a distinct voice and story of her own: "Pa promised that when they came to the West, Laura should see a papoose. 'What is a papoose?' she asked him, and he said, 'A papoose is a little, brown Indian baby.'"[25] This simple exchange signals a shift in Wilder's creative vision for her fiction and corresponds to the direction she took in *Farmer Boy*. Just as Almanzo's desire to gentle a colt in *Farmer Boy* propels the forward action in that novel, Laura's desire to see a papoose drives and unites the action in *Little House on the Prairie*. Her curiosity about the Indigenous people who live around her in Indian country becomes part of the greater mystery of the West, a place that stirs something deep and elemental in six-year-old Laura. She "had never seen a place she liked so much as this place."[26]

The next chapter will explore the racial complexities and contemporary interpretations of Wilder's depiction of Native Americans in more detail, but in general, Wilder uses Laura's perspective as a bright, precocious preschooler to bring a sense of wonder, confusion, and detachment to the complexities of life in the West. As Laura asks Ma, "This is Indian country, isn't it? . . . What did we come to their country for, if you don't like them?"[27]

In *Little House on the Prairie*, readers experience the action directly through Laura. The novel, and indeed the rest of the Little House books (with a few strategic exceptions), are written in third-person limited point-of-view. In other words, the story is told from the perspective of just one character—in this case, Laura. Readers see, feel, hear, think, and dream from Laura's point-of-view. They experience the West exclusively through Laura's eyes. As the family leaves the Big Woods, for example, and passes through the town of Pepin one last time, readers share Laura's vision: "The town grew smaller and smaller behind, till even the tall store was only a dot. All around the wagon there was nothing but empty and silent space. Laura didn't like it. But Pa was on the wagon seat and Jack was under the wagon; she knew that nothing could hurt her while Pa and Jack were there."[28] This small, personal moment feels real and true, a believable response for a six-year-old, leaving the security of home behind and venturing into the unknown.

Epic scenes in the novel come filtered through Laura's perceptions as well. In the chapter "Crossing the Creek," Pa decides to cross a flooded creek at what he assumes is a ford. But the West is far from predictable, and Pa misjudges the danger. As the rushing water lifts the wagon and it begins to sway, Ma orders Laura and Mary to lie down.

> Mary did not move; she was trembling and still. But Laura could not help wriggling a little bit. She did so want to see what was happening. She could feel the wagon swaying and turning. . . . Then Pa's voice frightened Laura. It said, "Take them, Caroline!"
>
> The wagon lurched; there was a sudden heavy splash beside it. Laura sat straight up and clawed the blanket from her head.
>
> Pa was gone.[29]

Laura, who can now observe everything Mary can't, faintly hears Pa's voice "through the rushing water" and sees Ma's face, "white and scared," gripping the reins.[30] Simultaneously, readers are in the wagon with Laura, experiencing the danger, fear, and uncertainty with her. The suspense grows as Ma again orders Laura to lie down. "She felt cold and sick. Her eyes were shut tight, but she could still see the terrible water and Pa's brown beard drowning in it."[31]

The scene appears to end well. The family, the team of horses, the wagon, and all it carries ultimately make it safely to the other side of the creek, but that feeling of relief is brief. Laura suddenly realizes that Jack didn't make the crossing with them: "Laura swallowed hard, to keep from crying. She knew it was shameful to cry, but there was crying inside her."[32]

Wilder's depiction of Laura's feelings is understated, unsentimental, and yet all the more powerful for that. She gives readers emotional space on the page to grieve for Jack themselves—along with Laura. It is a masterful emotional moment, the first of many such moments in the Little House series. Laura's voice—its authenticity, curiosity, and restraint—draws readers into the narrative. It also brings a sense of realism and immediacy to the novel. This is how a plucky six-year-old on the frontier *would* respond to such a heart-wrenching discovery. After Pa goes "far up and down the creek bank, looking for Jack," it's clear that Jack is gone. "At last," Wilder writes, "there was nothing to do but to go on."[33]

A New Realism

The scene in "Crossing the Creek" illustrates one more creative leap Wilder makes in *Little House on the Prairie*. It illustrates the new realism she brings to this novel, a marked contrast to the storybook quality of *Little House in the Big Woods*. Although the Big Woods of Wisconsin is a dangerous place, filled with panthers and bears and wolves, it remains a kind of fantasy world, where an idyllic pioneer family lives an idyllic pioneer life. The crafts Wilder describes with such detail in *Little House in the Big Woods* give the novel a gloss of reality, but its cyclical structure, its mythic hero (in Pa), and its cozy, storytelling voice create a charming, fairytale atmosphere. Despite the encounters with wolves, bears, and panthers, readers never quite believe the family's very existence is at stake.

By contrast, the dangers in *Little House on the Prairie* are existential. True, there are wolves and panthers in "Indian country," and they certainly threaten the family. But the dangers in "Indian country" are often unexpected, random, and even mundane—crossing a creek, raising a cabin, digging a well. The dangers here are part of a pioneer's everyday existence. They are real and potentially deadly: "If Pa had not known what to do, or if Ma had been too frightened to drive, or if Laura and Mary had been naughty and bothered her, then they would all have been lost. The river would have rolled them over and over and carried them away and drowned them, and nobody would ever have known what became of them. For weeks, perhaps, no other person would come along that road."[34] The Ingalls family escapes not only death but oblivion. This is very chilling stuff for a children's book—then or today. Indeed, in 1935, when *Little House on the Prairie* was published, Wilder's realistic approach to the American West was a major departure from children's books of the period. *Little House on the Prairie* and Carol Ryrie Brink's *Caddie Woodlawn* were published during the same year. But their representations of the pioneer experience are totally different.

Both books include scenes depicting visits from Native Americans, dangerous and unpredictable weather, lost dogs, prairie fires, and perceived attacks from neighboring Indigenous people. Both feature memorable young heroines from pioneering families. Both are written from their main character's point-of-view. And yet the two books strike radically different tones. Brink's characters take a more lighthearted, adventurous approach to the dangers that befall them. When Caddie and her siblings narrowly miss being struck by lightning, they stand "dazed and crying," looking back at a giant oak, split down the middle by lightning. "Another moment under its shelter," Brink writes, "and all of them might have been killed." But the implications of their brush with death pass as quickly as that bolt of lightning itself:

> How they ran that last half mile! No one had ever run so quickly before. Even Hetty could not outstrip the others to be the first to tell. Breathless and wild-eyed, with wet and muddy clothes, they rushed into the kitchen.
>
> "*Mother!*" they shouted all together. "Mother, listen to what happened to us."[35]

This isn't an existential experience. It lacks the gritty realism of Laura's realization after her family has safely crossed the flooded creek.

Wilder gives six-year-old Laura more emotional self-awareness than Brink gives eleven-year-old Caddie. In another revealing scene in *Little House on the Prairie*, Laura risks her life to save Mary and Carrie from a fire in the chimney. Ma comforts Laura when the danger has passed, but Wilder doesn't brush over the implications of what might have happened. Laura, as a six-year-old, understands it all quite well. Her throat is choked up and one tear "ran out of each eye," as she admits to Ma that she was afraid: "I was afraid Mary and Carrie would burn up. I was afraid the house would burn up and we wouldn't have any house."[36]

Throughout *Little House on the Prairie* and the subsequent Little House books, Wilder gives Laura these flashes of insight, realizations that life in the West is not only dangerous and adventurous but potentially life-changing and deadly. These moments are usually understated but packed with memorable details. Long after a log falls on Ma's foot as she helps Pa build their cabin, Laura sees that "Ma's ankle was not well yet. When she unwrapped it in the evenings, to soak it in hot water, it was all purple and black and green and yellow." Laura understands then that Ma's injury had been very serious. "It was Providential that the foot was not crushed."[37] When Pa tries to rescue their neighbor Mr. Scott, who has collapsed at the bottom of the well they're digging, Laura goes cold with fear. When both men are safely out of the well, Ma "covered her face with her apron and burst out crying," one of the few times Ma cries in the Little House books. The detail is telling. Laura realizes, "That was a terrible day."[38]

Certainly, Wilder balances these moments of existential darkness with scenes of optimism and hope. Their neighbor Mr. Edwards, for example, helps Pa finish framing the cabin not long after Ma's accident, and at the end of that chapter, they celebrate. Pa plays his fiddle and Mr. Edwards dances "like a jumping-jack in the moonlight."[39] But even in scenes like these, the West asserts itself. It is bigger, vaster than the family's achievements: "When Pa's fiddle stopped, they could not hear Mr. Edwards any more. Only the wind rustled in the prairie grasses. The big, yellow moon was sailing high overhead. The sky was so full of light that not one star twinkled in it, and all the prairie was a shadowy mellowness."[40]

In 1935 Brink's creative approach to the American frontier was much more mainstream, and she received the Newbery Medal for *Caddie Woodlawn* the following year. The Newbery committee skipped over *Little House on the Prairie*.[41] But the emotional realism Wilder pioneered in *Little House on the Prairie* ultimately had a lasting impact, not just on the remaining Little House novels but on American children's literature as well.

A Character with an Unfinished Story

Laura's character in *Little House on the Prairie* is consistent with her depiction in *Little House in the Big Woods*. She is daring, loyal, and quick; inquisitive and impulsive; less conventional than Mary. Laura remains the "little half-pint of sweet cider half drunk up," as Pa calls her.[42] But in *Little House on the Prairie*, Laura emerges as a character who not only grows and evolves within its pages but can sustain an entire series. A single book doesn't resolve Laura's story.

Like Almanzo in *Farmer Boy*, Laura in *Little House on the Prai-*

rie has one overriding desire that unifies the book's action. Her longing to see a papoose parallels his dream of gentling a colt. By the end of the book, Laura's wish is fulfilled, but unlike Almanzo's, hers takes an unexpected turn. Once she sees the baby, she imagines a deep connection between them: "Its head turned and its eyes kept looking into Laura's eyes."[43] She even asks Pa to take the infant from its mother. Of course, he refuses, and as the baby rides away, Laura begins to cry.

Laura cries as she didn't cry for Jack at the beginning of the novel, or even for her family after the fire in the chimney. She cries so hard she "could hardly see at first. Her eyes were full of tears and sobs kept jerking out of her throat."[44] Ma reprimands Laura, not for crying but for wanting the unattainable (as children sometimes do). Yet Laura remains unrepentant—until Pa helps her see the larger world around her, to experience the moment more completely and set her fixation aside. It is a subtle moment of growth and recognition: Laura must put away childish things. When the last Indian pony passes by, Laura remains in the doorway of the family's little house, "looking till that long line of Indians slowly pulled itself over the western edge of the world. And nothing was left but silence and emptiness. All the world seemed very quiet and lonely."[45] The Osages have been forced out of "Indian country," and the West is forever changed, just as (by implication) Laura will be forever changed by her continuing experiences there. Laura's story is unfinished. Her character has more room—much more room—to grow.

The real agent of change in Laura's life isn't the fulfillment of her dream to see a papoose; it's the West itself. At the beginning of *Little House on the Prairie*, Laura shares Mary's opinion of the West. It is a dull, changeless place, where "the land was the same, the sky was the same. . . . There was nothing new to do and nothing new to look at."[46] Over time, however, the West works its magic on Laura. She begins to see the West differently: "Thickly, in front of the open wagon-top hung the large, glittering stars. Pa could reach them, Laura thought. She wished he would pick the largest one from the thread on which it hung from the sky and give it to her."[47]

Laura's thoughts, feelings, and reactions are the soul of the novel. She emerges as an introspective character, far more introspective than Almanzo in *Farmer Boy*. And Wilder gives Laura's feelings a kind of realistic lyricism. Her thoughts remain grounded in what a six-year-old could conceivably think and feel. So does her vocabulary. But Laura's observations are often original, beautiful, and profound. Wilder, for example, returns one more time in *Little House on the Prairie* to that childhood memory of wolves howling outside the family's little house. But this time, she expands the scene and lets readers experience her memory more directly through Laura's eyes. The biggest wolf, Wilder writes, is taller than Laura: "Everything about him was big—his pointed ears, and his pointed mouth with the tongue hanging out, and his strong shoulders and legs, and his two paws side by side, and his tail curled around the squatting haunch. His coat was shaggy gray and his eyes were glittering green. . . . The moonlight made little glitters in the edges of the shaggy fur, all around the big wolf. . . . Laura could hear their breathing."[48]

The scene is intimate and immediate. The danger is immediate too. Although Laura, Pa, and the rest of the family are inside the cabin, it has no door, only a quilt to keep out the elements. And yet, by the end of the chapter, Laura isn't afraid of the wolves. And ultimately, this memorable chapter isn't about fear. It's about wonder and power and beauty—the wonder and power and beauty of the West, the wonder and power and beauty of family:

> She heard the scratch of their claws on the ground, and the snuffling of a nose at a crack [in the cabin's walls]. She heard the big gray leader howl again, and all the others answering him.
>
> But Pa was walking quietly from one window hole to the other, and Jack did not stop pacing up and down before the quilt that hung in the doorway. The wolves might howl, but they could not get in while Pa and Jack were there. So at last Laura fell asleep.

Laura experiences the power of a wild, untamed West simultaneously with the power of a safe and secure family. And the storybook magic of wolves and their howls that "shuddered through the house and filled the moonlight and quavered away across the vast silence of the prairie" once again brings a mythic atmosphere to Wilder's work.[49]

But this magic—Wilder's wild and untamed West—is rarely romanticized. There's an undercurrent of darkness, ambivalence, and danger. Wilder's natural world is always real, and Laura's responses to it may be lyrical but never fanciful. She is not like L. M. Montgomery's Anne Shirley, who revels in nature, imagining fairies, ghosts, and dryads in the forests, fields, and orchards of Green Gables. Wilder doesn't abandon realism to create her magic, and Laura is always at the center of it. She is a daring character, a little girl with grit, who embraces the West's danger and beauty. Throughout the rest of the Little House books, this dichotomy will shape and define Laura's character.

Another Transitional Novel

Little House on the Prairie, like *Farmer Boy*, is a transitional novel in the Little House series. While it is where the Little House series truly begins, the novel maintains structural and thematic connections to *Little House in the Big Woods*. Like Wilder's first novel, *Little House on the Prairie* continues to explore lost or forgotten pioneer skills and crafts. She devotes entire chapters to how Pa and Ma, sometimes with the help of neighbors, build a log cabin, craft a pair of doors, dig a well, and construct a chimney.

But in *Little House on the Prairie*, the how-to's of pioneer life are woven more seamlessly into the plot. For example, in the chapter "The House on the Prairie," the construction of the cabin serves as a backdrop to the chapter's main action: the accident that badly injures Ma's foot and the introduction of their neighbor, Mr. Edwards, who plays an important role, not just in this chapter but throughout the rest of the novel and in a later Little House book. Pa builds those "Two Stout Doors" in the eighth chapter in response to the wolf pack's appearance in the previous chapter. In "Fresh Water to Drink," building the well leads directly to the introduction of another neighbor—Mr. Scott. His carelessness endangers both himself and Pa, who ultimately rescues Mr. Scott from the bottom of the well. In later chapters, Mr. Scott's poor judgment and lack of understanding about the West and the people who live there contribute to the settlers' misinterpretation of the prairie fire and add to the mounting tensions in the chapter "Indian War-Cry."

Furthermore, the skills Wilder showcases in *Little House on the Prairie* relate to a central image of the book—the little house itself. Raising a cabin, building its doors and windows, digging a well, and crafting a fireplace are physical manifestations of the family's dream to establish a secure and stable life for themselves in the West. Wilder's descriptions in *Little House in the Big Woods* of churning butter, making bullets, and butchering a hog focus on everyday frontier occupations; in *Little House on the Prairie*, Pa and Ma engage in what they hope will be permanent and life-changing endeavors.

And yet ultimately the family has to abandon this dream, and leave behind the little house they worked so hard to create. The detailed descriptions of the hard work and even suffering the family has endured to create the little house underscores all they have lost. Readers share this loss more keenly and directly because, in effect, they worked alongside the family to build that little house on the prairie. At the end of the book, when the covered wagon stands in front of the house, "all ready to load in the morning," readers sense with Laura that something is very wrong and very sad.[50]

Failure and Loss

The West also serves as the overriding theme in *Little House on the Prairie*. The novel explores how European Americans settled the West, using one very specific fictional family in a timeless historical past to illustrate that idea. Wilder's authentic voice and her believable characters enhance this theme, and give the book a kind of historic authority. As I'll discuss in the next chapter, this has been both a blessing and a curse for Wilder's literary legacy. Generations of readers have come to view *Little House on the Prairie* as either a definitive account of how the West was won, or a damning indictment of how it was seized.

Yet the book is fundamentally about failure and how to accept loss. The Ingalls family may represent archetypal American pioneers, but their dream of building a lasting home in "Indian country" crumbles. Despite their courage and accomplishments, Laura and her family don't succeed in the West, at least not this time. They abandon their little house on the prairie: "Pa stood a moment in the doorway and looked all around inside; he looked at the bedstead and the fireplace and the glass windows. Then he closed the door carefully, leaving the latch-string out. . . . He climbed to his place beside Ma, gathered the reins into his own hands, and chirruped to Pet and Patty."[51]

Of course, the family doesn't abandon its dream of a new life in the West. They are simply "Going Out," the title of the book's last chapter. They will continue their search for a new life somewhere else, somewhere farther West, where, as the lyrics of the song that ends the book suggest, "Daily and nightly I'll wander with thee."[52]

Their decision to leave "Indian country," however, isn't easy. Laura is frightened by the anger that sparks Pa's decision to pull out. "His face was very red and his eyes were like blue fire."[53] Still, Laura knows Pa is right. He tells the family, "There's no great loss without some small gain," and when Ma says, "A whole year gone, Charles," he responds with optimism: "We have all the time there is."[54] The family faces failure with a unique combination of stoicism and optimism, characteristics Wilder will explore more fully in later books.

Frontier Neighborliness

The Ingalls family begin and end their sojourn in "Indian country" alone on the prairie, and Pa builds most of the little house there by himself. Perhaps because these images are so strong, popular culture has embraced the idea that Wilder's books showcase self-reliance. But throughout *Little House on the Prairie*, Wilder balances the virtues of self-sufficiency against the need for neighborly cooperation. This theme—that essential balance between the individual and the community—reappears throughout the Little House books. In Wilder's American West, survival itself can depend on having reliable, generous, and capable neighbors.

This theme makes its first appearance in a slightly different form in *Little House in the Big Woods*, where the extended family shares responsibilities for such labor-intensive chores as butchering hogs, harvesting maple sap, and threshing wheat. In *Little House on the Prairie*, the focus shifts from an extended family to a community of pioneers. In Wilder's West, neighbors look out for each other in times of need and crisis.

Pa engages the assistance of Mr. Edwards to help finish the cabin, and Mr. Edwards lends Pa nails for the roof. Pa and Mr. Scott dig a well together. And without the care of Dr. Tan and Mrs. Scott, the Ingalls family might have died from malaria. While Wilder's pioneers are fiercely independent, they also depend on each other for their very lives. Pa explains this essential balance between self-reliance and dependency in a conversation with Ma: "I've never been beholden to any man yet, and I never will be. But neighborliness is another matter."[55] In the American West, neighborliness is essential.

In *Little House on the Prairie*, however, it isn't essential to admire or even agree with your neighbors. The Scotts, as depicted in the book, don't share the Ingalls family's values (more about this later), but when Pa hears a scream coming from the direction of their cabin, he rushes away to provide assistance. Tolerance, Wilder implies, is an essential part of frontier neighborliness.

At the end of *Little House on the Prairie*, Wilder includes two details that reinforce this theme. The first is very subtle: As Pa closes the door of their little house for the last time, he leaves the latch string out, thinking that someone might need to shelter there someday. It's an act of frontier neighborliness, a courtesy from one pioneer to another. Then in the final chapter of the book, the family comes across a man, a woman, and a covered wagon with "no horses . . . hitched to it."[56] Horse thieves have stolen the couple's horses. The settlers are stranded. Pa offers to give them a ride to Independence, but they refuse, unwilling to leave their wagon, unable to accept wise neighborly counsel from one pioneer to another. "Whatever will become of them?" Ma asks, and Pa, in another act of frontier neighborliness, answers that he'll tell soldiers stationed at nearby Independence about the couple's plight.[57]

Still, as Pa drives away, Laura watches "that lonely wagon until it was only a small lump on the prairie. Then it was a speck. Then it was gone."[58] In refusing to accept Pa's offer, the couple in that stranded wagon risk oblivion on the prairie, just what the Ingalls family had faced in the beginning of the novel at that flooded creek. What saved the Ingalls family at the ford, of course, was Pa's skill and daring. The couple stuck at that horseless wagon are what Pa calls "tenderfeet," lacking the wisdom to accept help when it's offered.[59] It takes more than self-reliance to survive in Wilder's American West. In fact, knowing when to accept help is an essential survival skill on the frontier.

Going West, Going Out

Little House on the Prairie opens with the chapter "Going West," and ends with the chapter "Going Out." At first glance, it may appear then that the book shares a circular structure with *Little House in the Big Woods*. The family is essentially back where they started, in a covered wagon. But like *Farmer Boy*, *Little House on the Prairie* actually has a linear structure. The family isn't going back, they're going onward and out—out west, to be exact. Despite the family's failure to establish a home in "Indian country," despite the sadness Laura feels on her last night in their little house there, her spirits revive once she's on the move again: "Laura felt excited inside. You never know what will happen next, nor where you'll be tomorrow, when you are traveling in a covered wagon."[60]

Years before, in "Pioneer Girl," Wilder recalled her joy at "once more driving into the west," as the family left Burr Oak, Iowa, for Minnesota: "Oh those sunrises by the light of which we ate our breakfasts; those sunsets into which we drove looking for a good camping place!"[61] That spirit—the wonder of moving west—gives *Little House on the Prairie* its forward motion, and provides momentum for the next book as well as the rest of the series. In the book's last scene, Laura and her family camp out under the stars and watch the sun go down, "far away in the west."[62] The quest for a fresh start and a new home continues.

Little House and Beyond

When *Little House on the Prairie* was published in 1935, reviews were very good and sales were brisk. Without question, Wilder was now writing a series of books that would continue to follow Laura Ingalls and her family as they move west. Ida Louise Raymond at Harper & Brothers encouraged Wilder to let the next book "shape itself" in her mind.[63] By 1937, before her fourth Little House book was published, Wilder had emerged as something of a celebrity in children's literature. She was invited to deliver a keynote speech at the Detroit Book Fair.

But in the decades ahead, *Little House on the Prairie* would spark controversy and condemnation. As one Osage critic observed, the fictional Ingalls family were "illegal squatters on Osage land. [Wilder] left that detail out of her 1935 children's book, *Little House on the Prairie*, as well as any mention of ongoing outrages—including killings, burnings, beatings, horse thefts, and grave robberies—committed by white settlers, such as Charles Ingalls, against Osages living in villages not more than a mile or two away from the Ingalls' little house."[64]

By the late twentieth century a growing number of critics no longer praised *Little House on the Prairie* as an iconic glimpse into the pioneer experience; they perceived it as an unforgivably racist depiction of American history.

7

Little House on the Prairie, Part Two

The Rise and Fall of a Children's Classic

THE ORIGINAL EDITION OF *LITTLE HOUSE ON THE PRAIRIE*, published in 1935 and illustrated by Helen Sewell, featured only one image of a Native American: a child on horseback with the caption, "The little Indians did not have to wear clothes."[1] The book's setting in "Indian territory"—the Osage Diminished Reserve in southeastern Kansas—initially captivated young readers, and when a new edition of the entire Little House series was published in 1953, with illustrations by Garth Williams, *Little House on the Prairie* featured ten drawings with Native American subjects. It also included an illustration of the only African American character in the series.

But even before this new edition was released, Wilder's depiction of Native Americans in the book had disturbed at least one reader. In 1952 Ursula Nordstrom, Wilder's editor at Harper & Brothers, received a letter pointing to an offensive sentence in the opening chapter of *Little House on the Prairie*: "There the wild animals wandered and fed as though they were in a pasture that stretched much farther than a man could see, and there were no people. Only Indians lived there."[2]

"There were no people. Only Indians."

Nordstrom agreed that the line was offensive and suggested changing the text in the upcoming 1953 edition; Wilder felt the same way. "You are perfectly right about the fault in *Little House on the Prairie* and have my permission to make the correction you suggest. It was a stupid blunder of mine. Of course Indians are people and I did not mean to imply that they are not."[3]

The change was made and appears in current editions of the book. The following year, in 1954, the American Library Association (ALA) created the Wilder Medal to honor Laura Ingalls Wilder and subsequent writers or illustrators who made "a distinguished, creative, sustained contribution to children's books."[4] But the controversy swirling around *Little House on the Prairie* gained momentum in the late twentieth century. Now in the twenty-first century, Wilder's entire body of work has been denounced for its "anti-Native and anti-Black sentiments."[5]

IN 2006 I BUMPED INTO AN ACQUAINTANCE AT A PUBLIC library event. She was a children's book librarian who had served on several Newbery Medal committees. "What are you working on now?" she asked. Her face fell when I described my latest project, a biography of Laura Ingalls Wilder. "Hasn't everything already been said about her?" she replied. I perceived disapproval in her voice, and before I could say anything more, she quickly moved away. Laura Ingalls Wilder, even in 2006, wasn't a worthy topic.

It came as no surprise then that in 2018, the American Library Association decided to strip Wilder's name from the medal created in her honor. As early as 1995, a member of the ALA's Newbery Medal committee noted, "Let's face it, no story about a pioneer boy in the West has a hope of winning a prize today, especially if he doesn't have a 1990's consciousness about how his home was taken from the Indians."[6] She added that the committee probably wouldn't deem Wilder's work worthy of Newbery consideration because it was culturally insensitive to contemporary readers.

Is Wilder's work insensitive? Was Laura Ingalls Wilder a racist?

Little House on the Prairie rests squarely in the center of this controversy. Much of the book's action centers around the tension between the Osage people in "Indian country" and white settlers occupying Osage land. The abhorrent phrase, "The only good Indian is a dead Indian," appears not once but twice in the novel. Simply based on the frequency of the line, Wilder certainly appears to be a racist.

But Wilder's work, despite its straightforward and simple prose, is nuanced and complex. Her vision of the American West and its central historical conflict—the clash between Native peoples and the white settlers who prevailed—is direct, painful, and unflinchingly honest. It reflects prevailing nineteenth-century attitudes with a realism that is often uncomfortable, perplexing, and offensive today. Yet delving deeply into Wilder's text—exploring character, context, and historical perspective—reveals that *Little House on the Prairie* holds a mirror up to the twenty-first century. We can see contemporary social, racial, and cultural prejudices reflected back at us.

A Novel of Ambiguities

As Wilder's breakout book in the series, *Little House on the Prairie* illustrates the ambiguity and complexity of Wilder's view of the frontier. She explores this inherent complexity through the eyes of Laura, a six-year-old who doesn't understand the conventions of her parents' world. Like young readers themselves, Laura is often baffled by what she sees and hears from the people she encounters in "Indian country," even from her own family.

When Ma reveals not just her fear but her dislike of Indians, Laura asks, "What did we come to their country for, if you don't like them?"[7] And as the story deepens, as it becomes clear to Laura that the Indians will lose their land because settlers like her family are living there, she becomes more confused. Why must the Indians move West? she wonders. Why does the government make them move?

Neither Ma nor Pa provides Laura with a satisfactory answer. Finally, Laura says to Pa, "I thought this was Indian Territory. Won't it make the Indians mad to have to—." Pa silences Laura before she can finish her question, and by extension, silences the questions that inevitably arise in the minds of readers.[8] Wilder leaves this issue open to discussion, a question young readers can pursue as Laura can't.

Pa does address at least part of the complexity of the historic confrontation between cultures in the American West, and emerges with, for the nineteenth century, an enlightened view: "He figured that Indians would be as peaceable as anybody else if they were left alone. On the other hand, they had been moved west so many times that they naturally hated white folks."[9]

Manifest Destiny

Still, readers can't ignore Wilder's larger thematic purpose in *Little House on the Prairie* and the remaining Little House books: to illustrate through the lives of one fictional family the concept of Manifest Destiny—the nineteenth-century conviction that American citizens were destined to fill the continent from east to west and tame the frontier as well as the Native people who lived there. As one of the least enlightened characters in *Little House on the Prairie*—Mrs. Scott—points out, "Treaties or no treaties, the land belongs to the folks that'll farm it. That's only common sense."[10] Although Pa disagrees with the Scott family's attitudes about Indians, he too embraces this idea: the land belongs to the folks that will farm it. "White people are going to settle all this country," he tells Laura, "and we get the best land because we get here first and take our pick."[11]

But Pa and Laura do so with sadness and regret. Both believe in the humanity of the people whose land they've seized, and they recognize, at least on an emotional level, that white settlers are undermining the very spirit and freedom the American West represents. At the end of *Little House on the Prairie*, Laura watches as the Indians leave Indian Territory, and she has one of those inspired moments of observation that makes the Little House books so timeless: Laura sits "a long time on the doorstep, looking into the empty west where the Indians had gone. She seemed still to see waving feathers and black eyes and to hear the sound of ponies' feet."[12]

A Deeper Truth

Wilder uses the language of her childhood in *Little House on the Prairie*: "papoose," "tomahawk," "half-breed," "red skins," "white people," and that searing, racist phrase at the heart of the ALA's decision to strip Wilder's name from the lifetime achievement medal. Her vocabulary authentically represents mainstream attitudes of the world in which she grew up, and reflects her commitment to realism in historical fiction for young readers—a decision not to sugarcoat the past.

But she balances that realism with a deeper truth, illustrated by an episode toward the end of the novel. Pa relentlessly hunts a panther until "one day in the woods he met an Indian. They stood in the wet, cold woods and looked at each other," unable to speak "because they did not know each other's words. But the Indian pointed to the panther's tracks, and he made motions with his gun to show Pa that he had killed the panther."[13]

The unnamed Indian emerges as a hero, a man even more skilled than Pa at hunting and tracking, a man who is—like Pa—a dedicated father. "Laura asked if a panther would carry off a little papoose and kill and eat her, too, and Pa said yes. Probably that was why the Indian had killed the panther."[14]

Detractors of *Little House on the Prairie* rarely mention this scene, although it establishes a universal bond, a commonality between the two cultures. They are united by their love of family and its survival in the West. The scene is also unusual in the Little House series because it is one of only four in which Pa is indebted to someone else for the protection of his family. *Little House on the Prairie*, as we'll soon see, contains another example. The pattern is repeated in *By the Shores of Silver Lake* when Big Jerry, described as a French and Indian "half-breed," arrives in the nick of time to protect the family from a lone desperado as they cross the Dakota prairie for the first time.[15] And in *The Long Winter* Pa is indebted to Almanzo and Royal Wilder for their seed wheat, which saves the family from starvation.[16] It's significant, I think, that in two of these four episodes, the Ingalls family is indebted to Native American men.

Indians in the House

It is also significant that Wilder writes that the Indians who visit the Ingallses' little house on the Osage Diminished Reserve had a "horribly bad smell," were "dirty and scowling and mean," and had "glittering" eyes like a snake's.[17] On their own, these lines are undeniably racist, unpardonable, and reprehensible. But these lines are largely pulled out of context, and the sweeping criticisms usually leveled against *Little House on the Prairie* frequently ignore the novel's narrative voice, its underlying emotional atmosphere, and the historical realism at work in these scenes. The descriptions where these lines—and others like them—appear in *Little House on the Prairie* relate primarily to four encounters the Ingalls family have with Osage men who visit the little house and sometimes come inside. To Ma and her girls, these visitations feel like a home invasion. Fear is the underlying emotion in all these scenes. In "Indians in the House," the first of these encounters, six-year-old Laura begins "to shake all over," and when she gazes into one of the Osage men's eyes, her heart jumps "into her throat" and chokes "her with its pounding."[18]

Laura's fear is sparked by a fundamental cultural divide, a failure to understand or appreciate a different culture and the fear and prejudice that come with this failure. The most offensive scenes in *Little House on the Prairie* showcase this misunderstanding, this cultural clash. Laura, for example, wrinkles her nose and thinks the Osage men "smell awful."[19] Their faces are "bold and fierce and terrible."[20] They wear nothing but "fresh skunk skins."[21] Laura's reaction is sparked by these sensory details, a believable reaction from a young child, especially one whose prejudices reflect the prevailing attitudes of nineteenth-century society.

In this first encounter, as well as the third, Pa is away, heightening not only Laura and Mary's fear but Ma's. After the Osage men leave in "Indians in the House," Ma sits trembling on the bed and hugs the girls tight. She looks "sick."[22] Later, Ma tells Pa when he returns home, "Oh Charles! I was afraid!"[23] Ma is often singled out for criticism for her racist behavior in these scenes, and yet on close examination, she behaves responsibly, even courageously, given her deep-seated fears and prejudices. In "Indians in the House," she offers the men freshly baked cornbread. She doesn't object when they take Pa's tobacco. And when Laura tells Pa the Osage men smelled "awful," Ma provides a correction. The smell came from "the skunk skins they wore," she reminds Laura, not from the men themselves.[24] A slight distinction, perhaps, but an important one. The worst and most racist line in *Little House on the Prairie* is sometimes attributed to Ma, and yet no one in the Ingalls family says, "The only good Indian is a dead Indian" (more about this later). Ma does, however, sympathize with Jack the bulldog, who "hated Indians." Still, after admitting her prejudice, she almost immediately serves dinner to Pa and an unexpected Osage visitor.

In all but one of these encounters, Pa attempts to enlighten Ma and the girls with a more tolerant view of Native Americans. He bridges the cultural divide, at least from a nineteenth-century perspective. Pa is, of course, Laura's mentor and, as such, provides a guiding light for young readers as well. He tells the family, "We don't want to make enemies of any Indians." The "main thing," he adds later, "is to be on good terms" with them.[25] After an unexpected visit from another Osage man, Pa reassures the family again. Their visitor, Pa says, was "perfectly friendly." "If we treat them [the Osage people] well . . . , we won't have any trouble."[26] Throughout these controversial scenes, Wilder casts the prejudice and fear she remembered from this period in her life against Pa's more progressive ideas. She remains true to the historical period and to the historical record—at least from a white settler's perspective.

Rising Tension

Toward the end of "The Tall Indian," Wilder records two more detailed encounters with the Osages. Within the context of the novel, both reflect the rising tensions between settlers and Native people in "Indian territory." In the first, Jack blocks the "tall Indian's" path outside the Ingallses' cabin. The Osage man "lifted his gun and pointed it straight at Jack." Pa intervenes, dragging Jack out of the way, and "the Indian rode on, along the trail." Pa admits this was "a darned close call," then adds, "Well, it's his path. An Indian trail, long before we came."[27]

Later in the chapter, winter has set in. The nights are "freezing cold."[28] Pa has laid up a stash of wolf, fox, beaver, muskrat, and mink furs, which he plans to trade for seeds and a plow in the spring. While he's away, a pair of Osage men once again enter the Ingallses' house. Wilder writes, "Those Indians were dirty and scowling and mean. They acted as if the house belonged to them."[29] This isn't an enlightened or balanced description of Native Americans. What's implied, however, is that they are hungry and desperate.

They look though Ma's cupboards and take all the cornbread along with Pa's tobacco pouch. One of the men picks up Pa's "bundle of furs," then drops it by the door. The two men leave and Ma hugs Laura and Mary close. Laura feels Ma's heart racing. Once again, fear is the primary underlying emotion in the scene. And this time when Pa returns, he doesn't reassure or attempt to enlighten the family as he does in previous encounters. Instead, "he looked sober" and offers up one of the family's favorite platitudes, one that appears in later Little House books to dispel existential fear: "He said that all was well that ended well."[30]

Historical Perspectives

From a historical perspective, this brief fictional scene bears a haunting resemblance to the situation that prompted the Dakota War of 1862, and as we'll see, *Little House on the Prairie* refers directly to this conflict. Motivated by treaty violations, suspended annuity payments, federal government corruption, and famine, a group of Santee Dakota men killed five white settlers on a farm in Minnesota. The region exploded into all-out war. During the six-week conflict, between four and six hundred white settlers were killed. The number of Santee deaths remains unknown. But on December 6, 1862, thirty-eight Santee men were publicly hanged in Mankato, Minnesota, for their alleged participation in the conflict, and the Santee people were forcibly moved to a reservation in Dakota Territory. These events occurred just seven years before Charles Ingalls moved his family to the Osage Diminished Reserve.

In the late 1860s and early 1870s, when the Ingalls family lived on the reserve, the Osage nation "was on the edge of extinction."[31] During the Civil War, the federal government had suspended annuity payments to the Osages, and as the war deepened on the western frontier, so had their hunger and hardship. After the war, as white settlers swarmed into "Indian territory," they destroyed Osage crops, stole their horses, and seized their land. The Osages were "on the verge of starvation."[32] They rightfully viewed white settlers as trespassers, and began to take what they needed from them.

The parallels to events leading up to the Dakota War of 1862 are striking. In a history of Kansas, published just eleven years after the real Ingalls family left, author William G. Cutler wrote that during the late 1860s and early 1870s, life on the Osage Diminished Reserve was fraught with "serious difficulties between the races."[33]

In 1870, in a report to the superintendent of Indian Affairs, Osage Indian agent Isaac Gibson wrote that the Osages "could massacre the inhabitants of this valley in a few hours; and if they should be driven to do so . . . , I would not be surprised."[34] After reading this report, the superintendent concluded Gibson was right. If the Osage people and settlers continued to live side by side on the reserve, he noted, "war may result therefrom."[35]

Wilder's characters in *Little House on the Prairie* reflect this historical tension, including the fear of what Agent Gibson characterized as a potential for "massacre." At the end of the chapter "Indians in the House," Pa learns that Laura and Mary had considered unleashing Jack on their Osage visitors. In a "terrible voice," Pa warns the girls that if they had done so, "there would have been trouble. Bad trouble. Do you understand?"[36] And toward the end of the novel, Wilder directly links this fear to settlers' memories of the Dakota War in Minnesota. In this scene, the Ingallses' neighbors, Mr. Scott and Mr. Edwards, are convinced that Osage men had set a raging prairie fire "on purpose to burn out the white settlers."[37] Pa quickly discounts this idea, but Mr. Scott, who has been depicted throughout the novel as an unreliable and unenlightened neighbor, disagrees, then utters the novel's most offensive line, "The only good Indian is a dead Indian."[38] Pa disagrees, reassuring both Mr. Scott and Mr. Edwards that the Osages are "sworn to peace among themselves . . . and they're thinking about hunting the buffalo. So it's not likely they'll start on the warpath against us."[39]

Pa's more reasoned response prevails, and as the chapter ends, Mr. Scott refers to his wife, who in a previous chapter has also expressed the book's most racist sentiment. He tells Pa, "Anyway, I'll be glad to tell Mrs. Scott what you say. She can't get the Minnesota massacres out of her head."[40]

In both episodes that include the book's most repellent racial slur, Wilder mentions the "Minnesota massacre." Mrs. Scott's "Pa and brothers" were directly involved in the Dakota War, where, according to Mrs. Scott, her family and other settlers "stopped" the Santee "only fifteen miles west of us."[41] The Scotts are not likeable characters, and their attitudes are at odds with Pa's, who Wilder clearly views as heroic. But what we would now consider hate speech from the Scotts is linked to an existential fear: another "massacre." This fear of violence and retribution, based on the Dakota War of 1862, doesn't excuse the racist portrayals or dialogue in *Little House on the Prairie*, but it is emotionally true to the book's historical time and place.

Wilder didn't inflate the fear and panic her fictional settlers experience in *Little House on the Prairie* as some critics maintain; those feelings were real and reflect the tenor of the time. She did rearrange the sequence of events in the novel, placing the "Indian War-Cry" chapter toward the end of the book. In fact, the rising tensions the chapter describes occurred in 1870, the year before the real Ingalls family left "Indian territory." Writing fiction gave Wilder the freedom to restructure the historical record to tell a more compelling story. But the emotional underpinnings of the chapter—and the novel—are historical.[42]

Doctoring All the Settlers

Before the publication of *Pioneer Girl: The Annotated Autobiography*, I fielded an inquiry from a concerned reader: Did Laura Ingalls Wilder give the African American doctor in *Little House on the Prairie* an inherently racist name—Dr. Tan? He is, after all, the only African American character to appear in the Little House series, and as Wilder writes in the book, "He was so very black."[43]

Dr. George Tann was a very real person; Wilder simply misspelled his name in the novel. His role as a fictional character is small but pivotal: he saves the lives of the entire family when they're stricken with "fever 'n' ague," probably malaria. The episode provides the fourth example in the Little House series in which Pa must rely on someone else to protect his family from harm. In fact, Dr. Tann not only treated the real Ingalls family for malaria, but he attended Caroline Ingalls for the birth of Caroline Celestia—Baby Carrie, born August 3, 1870, in Indian Territory.[44]

Wilder has been criticized for not including more African Americans in her novels. But with the exception of *Farmer Boy*, written from her husband's perspective, her fiction didn't venture far from her own experiences. True, she fictionalized her memories, adding new scenes and even characters, but these were consistent with her direct experiences. As she wrote about Dr. Tan in *Pioneer Girl*, "I had never seen a colored person before."[45] Her interactions with people of color were rare throughout her lifetime, in large measure because she and her husband lived in parts of the country where few African Americans had settled. Hers was a very segregated world. Wright County, Missouri, where she and her husband lived from 1894 until their deaths—his in 1949, hers in 1957—was very white.[46]

In *Little House on the Prairie*, Wilder's depiction of Dr. Tan is unfiltered, not only because her main character is so very young but because Laura is delirious: "She lay burning up and . . . heard the voices jabbering again, and the slow voice drawling, and she opened her eyes and saw a big, black face close above her."[47]

Within the pages of *Little House on the Prairie*, Dr. Tan emerges as a hero. Even Jack likes him (by contrast, Jack later trees the beloved Mr. Edwards on a woodpile). And Laura confesses that she "would have been afraid of him [Dr. Tan] if she had not liked him so much." So does the rest of the family. "They all wanted him to stay longer," but Dr. Tan must "hurry away." He is busy caring for "all the settlers, up and down the creek."[48]

Wilder's depiction of Dr. Tan is at once consistent with her own personal experience and true to what a character from that place and time would have encountered. It is an honest representation from a northern, white, nineteenth-century child's perspective. But a closer reading takes us deeper into the history of the region. Wilder writes in *Little House on the Prairie* that Dr. Tan "was doctoring all the sick settlers" nearby.[49] In how many border state communities shortly after the Civil War would an African American doctor have been welcome?

Probably very few.

But Eastern Kansas had been a focus for the abolitionist movement before the Civil War. Abolitionist John Brown, for example, arrived in Kansas in the mid-1850s, and such towns as Lawrence and Manhattan were founded by abolitionists. Violence between abolitionists from Kansas and slaveholders from Missouri predated the American Civil War by almost a decade. As for settlement in Montgomery County, Kansas, where *Little House on the Prairie* takes place, one of the first settlers in "Indian territory" was "a colored man named Lewis Scott, who settled in the southeastern part of the county in February, 1867," not quite two years after the end of the Civil War.[50] Had the Ingalls family stayed in Kansas, as the real Dr. Tann ultimately chose to do, Wilder's experiences with African Americans could well have been more extensive and diverse. When Wilder and her young family traveled through Topeka, Kansas, in 1894 on their way to Missouri, she observed, "There are a great many colored people in & around the city."[51]

Wilder considered herself a "Yankee woman," a background that put her at odds with the culture she encountered briefly in Florida in 1891: "We went to live in the piney woods of Florida, where the trees always murmur, where the butterflies are enormous, where plants that eat insects grow in moist places, and alligators inhabit the slowly moving waters of the rivers. But at that time and in that place, a Yankee woman was more of a curiosity than any of these."[52]

The term "Yankee woman" would have held a significant meaning for Wilder. Although Charles Ingalls didn't serve in the military during the Civil War, other family members did volunteer with Union forces. Two of his brothers enlisted, and possibly his brother George, who makes an appearance in *Little House in the Big Woods* as a wild bugler with a slightly wicked reputation. Caroline Ingalls's brother Joseph Quiner fought for the Union and died from wounds sustained at the Battle of Shiloh in 1862.

Charles and Caroline Ingalls were members of the Congregational Church movement, which had its roots in New England and took a progressive stance on social reform, including women's rights and abolitionism.[53] The family's dedication to the church's progressive ideas is a common thread linking several of the later Little House novels.

Different Times

So where does this leave us? Is *Little House on the Prairie* a racist book? Is it irrelevant? And was the ALA correct in saying that the "anti-Native and anti-Black sentiments in her work" undermine its literary value? Do we simply live in a different time?

Well, of course we do.

But living in a "different time" shouldn't mean that we automatically relegate any work of literature from "a different time" to the trash heap. Historical perspective gives us wisdom, understanding, knowledge, and insight—not just into the past but into the present and future.

And can we say that the fictional Mr. Scott's declaration—"The only good Indian is a dead Indian"—is significantly different, for example, than twenty-first-century pronouncements against immigrants? A common thread links the world Wilder depicts in *Little House on the Prairie* to contemporary issues of racism and prejudice young readers encounter in their daily lives. Pretending racism didn't exist in our history is no way to prepare young readers for the racism we must continue to combat now. Consider, for example, the shift of white supremacist ideology from the fringes of American culture into the mainstream.

Given its historical and literary context, *Little House on the Prairie* exhibits a rare sensitivity to the issue of racism in the American West, exposing rather than ignoring its role in the pioneer experience. But Wilder's work doesn't provide easy answers. Her depiction of the Ingalls family's sojourn in Indian territory is raw, painful, complex, and unresolved—just as the issue of racism remains unresolved today. And while it's tempting to think children's books *should* provide a reassuring answer to this issue, that they should shield young readers from the ugly realities of life—past and present—this approach to children's literature is fundamentally deceptive. Madeleine L'Engle observed that "what the storyteller does is to look at the world with all of its brokenness and all of its problems and write a story. I do not believe that we need to protect our children from language which they already know, from the horrors of the world which they already know. I think we owe it to be honest with them."[54]

Racism is embedded in American history and American culture. To withhold this history from young readers is fundamentally dishonest. Books like *Little House on the Prairie* allow children to explore the brokenness of the past and consider its impact on the present. L'Engle also observed that children "are still brave. They still have courage," and can examine raw, difficult, and complex issues "with open minds."[55] They have a kind of courage that we adults too often lack or have forgotten we once possessed.

8

On the Banks of Plum Creek

The Model for a Perfect Juvenile

IN EARLY 1933 WILDER SUGGESTED SELLING THE ROCK HOUSE, in which she'd written "Pioneer Girl" and the subsequent Little House books. Lane agreed "heartily."[1] Certainly the grim financial realities that had settled over Rocky Ridge Farm during the deepening days of the Great Depression influenced Wilder's suggestion and Lane's endorsement of it. But the professional tension between mother and daughter, which had been building for months, must have been an equally persuasive argument in favor of selling the Rock House. Implied in Wilder's suggestion: She and Almanzo would move back into the Rocky Ridge farmhouse they had built and designed together; Lane would leave the Ozarks behind. After all, at Rocky Ridge Farm Lane had long felt cut off from the literary mainstream. She had a lingering and fundamental loathing for the Ozarks. It was a "mean, poor, dull brown country."[2]

But as Wilder worked on *Little House on the Prairie* and Lane edited it, the tension between mother and daughter eased. They apparently began to realize that Wilder's "Pioneer Girl" manuscript could serve as a creative springboard for them both. Lane even considered writing her own sweeping historical series based, in part, on material from "Pioneer Girl." In her diary, she outlined her plans to write "an American novel in many volumes, an enormous canvas, covering horizontally a continent."[3] *Let the Hurricane Roar* would be the first novel in this series.

But Lane abandoned the idea within six months: "Worked on scheme of novel until overwhelmed with discouragement."[4] Instead, perhaps with Wilder's blessing, Lane used episodes from "Pioneer Girl" as the foundation for several short stories, published in such national magazines as the *Saturday Evening Post* and the *Ladies Home Journal*.[5] By 1935, with the publication of *Little House on the Prairie*, it was clear that Wilder—not Lane—would write that American novel in many volumes. It was also clear by then, despite the editorial bond cementing mother and daughter, that Lane's experiment to live and write at Rocky Ridge Farm was, at last, no longer sustainable. Still, Lane wasn't quite ready to leave Missouri behind.

She received a commission to write a history of the state of Missouri, and moved to Columbia, home of the University of Missouri, where she would have better access to the historical documents and materials needed to write the book. She lived in Columbia's Tiger Hotel, named for the university's athletic teams. Meanwhile, Wilder and Almanzo moved back into the Rocky Ridge farmhouse in 1936.[6] She began work on her next Little House book.

Despite the miles that now separated them, Wilder and Lane continued to work together, writing letters back and forth between the farmhouse at Rocky Ridge and Lane's rooms at the Tiger Hotel. The editorial correspondence between the two women provides insights into how they may have worked together on the first three Little House books, as well as the editorial partnership that emerged during the writing and editing of *On the Banks of Plum Creek*.

This new book was a different kind of novel—for Wilder and for her characters. It marked another turning point in her career—and not simply because it was the first Little House book to receive Newbery recognition (it was an Honor Book in 1938)—but because with it, Wilder set another literary standard in American children's literature. Wilder's editor, Ida Louise Raymond at Harper & Brothers, recommended *On the Banks of Plum Creek* "to dozens of authors as the model for a perfect juvenile [novel]."[7]

MOST YOUNG READERS OF *ON THE BANKS OF PLUM CREEK* think of this book as the story with the "house in the ground," that almost magical, fairytale place described in such lyrical detail. All around the dugout door, "green vines were growing out of the grassy bank, and they were full of flowers. Red and blue and purple and rosy-pink and white and striped flowers all had throats wide open as if they were singing glory to the morning."[8]

Older readers, however, remember this novel for a totally different reason: The "glittering cloud" that appears midway in the book and changes the fictional family's entire world—physically, emotionally, and economically: "The cloud was hailing grasshoppers. The cloud *was* grasshoppers. . . . The rasping whirring of their wings filled the whole air and they hit the ground and the house with the noise of a hailstorm."[9]

Whether it's the house in the ground or the glittering cloud that readers remember, *On the Banks of Plum Creek* is a rich and unusually complex novel. Wilder gives this book a more focused plot; deepens the characters' personalities, motivations, and conflicts; and centers the novel around an unconventional theme for juvenile fiction of the period. At the same time, she also introduces a new, overarching theme for the series, which she would expand and explore throughout the remaining Little House books. As the surviving editorial correspondence reveals, Wilder trusted her own creative instincts on this book, sometimes contradicting, correcting, or simply ignoring Lane's suggestions. Did Wilder's creative self-confidence emerge as she wrote *On the Banks of Plum Creek* or is this the way she'd always responded to Lane's editorial advice? Did the physical distance that separated Wilder and Lane during the writing of this book contribute to its brilliance? It's impossible to know. But *On the Banks of Plum Creek* showcases Wilder's creative ingenuity and her ability to tackle and resolve the daunting challenges the novel posed.

False Hopes, Dashed Dreams

From its inception, Wilder knew precisely what *On the Banks of Plum Creek* was about. It would explore how the West creates false hopes, how the promise of rich soil and a ripening field of wheat can inspire a false sense of security. "The idea is that On the B. of P.C. was safety, and then look what happened," Wilder wrote Lane; "enter the grasshoppers."[10] That cloud of grasshoppers and its consequences rob the Ingalls family of their dreams, and ultimately sends them moving west again—into the next novel. This central plot and its overriding theme are grim, an unusual approach in children's literature in the 1930s. Yet Wilder pursued her vision for the book strategically, laying its foundation right from the beginning.

In the opening pages of *On the Banks of Plum Creek*, Pa tells the family, "We're safe enough, all right. Nothing can happen here."[11] His statement, however, not only seems to challenge fate, but it defies what storytelling is all about. Because in a story—any story—something *must* happen. It's an implicit pact with readers. So careful readers know intuitively that Pa's initial assessment of life along Plum Creek is wrong, that something will happen to dash his dreams of safety, security, and prosperity. But we can't yet guess what that will be.

In the same scene, Wilder makes another observation about this new country in which the family finds itself, and it also seems to foreshadow something unexpected and menacing. This new western landscape is too safe, too tame:

> They all sat quiet, looking across Plum Creek and the willows, watching the sun sink far away in the west, far away over the prairie lands.
>
> At last Ma drew a long breath. "It is all so tame and peaceful," she said. "There will be no wolves or Indians howling at night. I haven't felt so safe and at rest since I don't know when."[12]

Their new home is a different kind of place, a different kind of West; its dangers will be different too, perhaps unimaginable.

Even in chapters with a lighthearted focus, the family's rosy hopes for the future find their way into scene after scene. In the "Straw-Stack," a playful chapter where Laura and Mary "fly" off the top of a golden stack of straw, the promise of a bountiful wheat harvest looms in the background. Pa says, "Next year, we'll have a crop of wheat that will amount to something!"[13] In the next chapter, ominously titled "Grasshopper Weather," the family's dreams are grander, more specific: "Every day the velvety brown-dark patch of ploughed land grew bigger. It ate up the silvery-gold stubble field beyond the hay-stacks. It spread over the prairie waves. It was going to be a very big wheat-field, and when some day Pa cut the wheat, he and Ma and Laura and Mary would have everything they could think of."[14] As the chapter draws to a close, the weather turns unseasonably warm for late November. Pa doesn't know what to make of it, and tells Ma that their neighbor, Mr. Nelson, who is considered an old-timer in the area, calls it "grasshopper weather."[15] This ominous observation subtly increases the novel's underlying tension, and Wilder keeps the pressure building in chapter after chapter, simultaneously threading the central themes of false expectations and financial insecurity through its pages.

Wilder uses character, dialogue, and vivid details to reinforce these ideas. In the book's opening pages, she dramatizes the family's poverty and their quest for financial security when Ma realizes she and her girls will have to live in that house in the ground: "Oh, Charles! . . . A dugout. We've never had to live in a dugout yet."[16] For her, this move west to Plum Creek represents a lowering of standards, a heartbreaking kind of economic and cultural poverty she hadn't envisioned for the family. The Ingalls family's fortunes have sunk so low they have to live underground.

Pa counters with the dreams he has for their new life: "It's only till I harvest the first wheat crop. . . . Then you'll have a fine house and I'll have horses and maybe even a buggy."[17] As the scene unfolds, Pa pulls Laura—and by extension, the rest of the family—into his dream: "A good crop of wheat will bring us more money than we've ever had, Laura."[18]

Yet the family can't escape the realities poverty brings. Pa hires out with the Nelsons to earn extra money; he can't afford to work exclusively on his own farm. Even with this extra cash, he doesn't have enough to spare for a new pair of boots. Pa's old ones are "cracked clear across the toes."[19] The girls feel the impact of the family's slide into poverty too. When Laura and Mary go to school for the first time, they are barefooted, and their dresses, which they've outgrown, are too short. The family can't afford new ones. Boys in the schoolyard ridicule their appearance and call them "long-legged snipes."[20]

The novel's tone shifts as the family's financial outlook appears to improve. As spring ripens into summer, the wheat field beckons with promise: "Each tiny sprout was so thin you could hardly see it," but "a faint green mist" covers the brown field. "Everyone was so happy that night because the wheat was a good stand."[21] Yet Wilder is actually escalating the tension here, another masterful plot development.

Trusting in the promise of that good stand of wheat, Pa builds the family a new house, with store-bought luxuries: "boughten shingles," "shining-clear glass windows," "boughten doors," "boughten hinges," "boughten locks with keys," and a "shiny-black cookstove."[22] Laura is in awe of all these luxuries. "There was nothing more that a house could possibly have."[23] This wonderful house is far grander, far more extravagant than the humble cabin Pa had built for the family in Indian Territory. But he hasn't *bought* any of these grand, extravagant building supplies that make the house such a marvel. As he explains to Ma, "We'll pay for it when we sell the wheat."[24] Young readers may not grasp the implication here, but older readers do. Pa has put the family at risk.

At the end of the chapter titled "The Wonderful House," Wilder includes another ominous description, one that pairs the new house with the ripening wheat: "The wheat-field was a silky, shimmering green rippling over a curve of the prairie. Its sides were straight and its corners square, and all around it the wild prairie grasses looked coarser and darker green. Laura looked back at the wonderful house. In the sunshine on the knoll, its sawed-lumber walls and roof were as golden as a straw-stack."[25] The promise of the wheat field is a shimmering illusion; the new house might as well be built of straw.

The Glittering Cloud

Midway through *On the Banks of Plum Creek*, plot and theme unite in an unforgettable chapter, "The Glittering Cloud." The wheat is almost ready to harvest and Pa looks at it every day. On a hot, dry Saturday morning, Laura goes with Pa to look at the wheat: "It was almost as tall as Pa. He lifted her onto his shoulder so that she could see over the heavy, bending tops. The field was greeny gold"—the color of greenbacks, the color of gold coins. Pa's hopes for the future seem poised for fulfillment. By next week, Pa tells the family, the wheat will be ready for harvesting: "He had never seen such a crop. There were forty bushels to the acre, and wheat was a dollar a bushel. They were rich now. . . . Now they could have anything they wanted."[26]

And then, in the next paragraph, disaster strikes, although initially Laura and her family don't understand what's happening. Wilder masterfully draws out the suspense. It builds slowly, centering on what appears to be a mysterious change in the weather that, for a few moments, masks what is coming.

> [Laura] . . . sat facing the open door and the sunshine streaming through it. Something seemed to dim the sunshine. Laura rubbed her eyes and looked again. The sunshine really was dim. It grew dimmer until there was no sunshine.
>
> "I do believe a storm is coming up," said Ma.[27]

That storm, of course, is that glittering cloud of grasshoppers, a plague of biblical proportions, a threat far worse to the family's economic future or survival than the wolves and Indians Ma associated with their precarious existence in Indian Territory. Wilder's description, written from Laura's point-of-view, is vivid and terrifying:

> There was no wind. The grasses were still and the hot air did not stir, but the edge of the cloud came on across the sky faster than wind. . . . Then huge brown grasshoppers were hitting the ground all around her, hitting her head and her face and her arms. They came thudding down like hail. . . .
>
> Laura tried to beat them off. Their claws clung to her skin and her dress. They looked at her with bulging eyes, turning their heads this way and that. . . . Grasshoppers covered the ground, there was not one bare bit to step on. Laura had to step on grasshoppers and they smashed squirming and slimy under her feet.[28]

But this is not the real terror that descends on the family as that glittering cloud strikes. Laura hears an ominous sound, "one big sound made of tiny nips and snips and gnawings." Pa hears it too. He dashes "out the back door" and runs "toward the wheat-field."[29]

Despite his heroic efforts to save the wheat, it is already too late.

Pa tells Caroline, "The wheat is falling now. They're [the grasshoppers] cutting it off like a scythe. And eating it, straw and all."[30] He sits down at the table and covers his face with his hands, a defeated man. The scene is grim, but the disappointment deepens in the next chapter when Pa discovers that the field is now "honeycombed" with grasshopper eggs.

> "We've got no more chance of making a crop next year than we have of flying," Pa said. "When those eggs hatch, there won't be a green thing left in this part of the world."
>
> "Oh, Charles!" Ma said. "What will we do?"
>
> Pa slumped down on a bench and said, "I don't know."[31]

The rest of *On the Banks of Plum Creek*—its second half—explores how the family finds its way through the dark days ahead, an ambitious and creatively challenging storyline.

Unique Personalities and Desires

While the grasshopper plague in *On the Banks of Plum Creek* reads like a nineteenth-century adaptation of one of the ten plagues of Egypt in the book of Exodus, Wilder's characterizations of the Ingalls family are clearly grounded in reality. Pa, Ma, Mary, and Laura shed their mythic underpinnings here and emerge as more ordinary people facing extraordinary circumstances. The book explores their dreams and aspirations, and how these fully developed characters face hardship and disappointment.

Since Wilder filters the novel's actions exclusively through Laura's point-of-view, these more realistic characterizations reflect Laura's increasing maturity, her ability to see and understand the world around her with more discernment and understanding. Laura is seven when *On the Banks of Plum Creek* opens. She is "a big girl," Wilder writes in the opening chapter, "too big to cry," even when Pa swaps Pet and Patty for the property on Plum Creek.[32] But Wilder's more lifelike depictions of her characters may also reflect her own increasing commitment to realism, to portraying the past she remembered with greater emotional clarity. Furthermore, because she depicts her characters in *On the Banks of Plum Creek* as less mythic and more real, the epic tragedy they experience feels even greater and more immediate, an approach that would resonate with readers growing up in the Great Depression. The crisis the fictional Ingalls family faces in the novel mirrors the experiences of Dust Bowl families in the 1930s.

Literary realism in American fiction developed in the mid- to late nineteenth century and endeavored to depict settings, events, and characters accurately, truthfully, and believably. Fiction, according to this tradition, should be a reflection of reality, focusing on the everyday, the commonplace, the ordinary. Wilder had already introduced this tradition into American fiction for young readers. But in *On the Banks of Plum Creek*, she deepened her commitment to it, strengthening the humanity and individuality of her main characters.

Ma, for example, emerges in this novel as a more clearly defined individual, a pioneer woman with aspirations for herself and her family. As the novel unfolds, readers learn that Ma values a "tame and peaceful" existence that would offer her girls opportunities the West hasn't yet been able to provide—in education, religious instruction, or even social interaction with other children.[33] In fact, Ma's preference for a tame and peaceful existence seems diametrically opposed to Pa's ongoing quest for freedom and wilderness. Wilder distills the differences between the two when Ma says, "Oh, Charles! A dugout."

In *On the Banks of Plum Creek*, Ma is also more critical of Pa, which at once increases the tension in the novel and makes her marriage to Charles Ingalls seem more believable and equitable. "A dugout is snug and cosy," Ma says to Pa. "But I do feel like an animal penned up for winter."[34] She can't fully embrace the life she's been forced to accept, living in a house cut out of sod. Later in the novel, she even questions Pa's obsession with the wheat crop. She tells him, "I declare . . . , you're working that ground to death and killing yourself."[35]

When Pa not only builds the family a new house but presents Ma with a new cookstove, the scene is more satisfying *because* of the underlying tension between them. His longing for wide open spaces appears to have given way to her desire for stability and culture. But the subtle tension between them continues. Even as

Pa has worked to fulfill Ma's dreams, he has gone into debt to build the house and all it represents. To allay her fears, he urges Ma to "look through that glass [window] at the wheat-field!"[36] The view, however, provides little comfort. Until the wheat is harvested, the debt remains.

When the unforeseeable crisis comes, Ma stands by Pa, steadying his despair: "Never mind, Charles," she tells him. "We've been through hard times before."[37] But to get the family through those hard times, Ma is forced to assume Pa's traditional roles, fighting a prairie fire that threatens their home and taking care of the family's livestock during a four-day blizzard. She steps into his stable-boots, though "her feet were lost in them."[38]

As for Pa, he too appears less mythic and more human in *On the Banks of Plum Creek*. When faced with ruin after the grasshopper invasion, Pa's reaction isn't heroic; it's heartbreaking. He's been robbed of his dreams and his livelihood. Just as Wilder distilled Ma's initial disappointment in that one line about the dugout, she takes a similar approach to characterize Pa's despair after the grasshoppers destroy the wheat: "He put his elbows on the table and hid his face with his hands."[39] Pa is, at least in that moment, a defeated man, and despite the optimism that returns to him by the end of the scene, his only alternative to hold the family together is to abandon it—and go east in search of work. Here, Wilder's characterization of Pa—the emotional realism she gives him—enhances the drama, tension, and pathos of the scene. His despair becomes real. The West has failed him, and for the first and only time in the Little House series, Pa goes east.

Wilder's depiction of Mary and Laura is equally detailed and realistic, more three-dimensional than in the previous Little House books. Sometimes Wilder draws the distinction between Laura and Mary with a clever turn of phrase: "Mary was so scared that she could not move. Laura was so scared that she jumped right off the rock."[40] In the chapter "Grasshopper Weather," Wilder uses dialogue to illustrate the girls' distinct personalities and the growing rivalry between them:

> "I declare, you eat more plums than you pick up," Mary said.

> "I don't either any such thing," Laura contradicted. "I pick up every plum I eat."
>
> "You know very well what I mean," Mary said, crossly. "You just play around while I work."[41]

The way Laura and Mary speak—their conversation's vocabulary, rhythm, and pacing—illustrates their essential differences and brings their characters to life.

This characterization is certainly consistent with their depictions in the preceding books, but in *On the Banks of Plum Creek*, Wilder finds a fuller and more compelling expression of the two sisters, their personalities, and the tension between them. Perhaps the most vivid example occurs when the girls encounter Nellie Oleson, the Little House character readers love to hate:

> "My goodness!" Mary said. "I couldn't be as mean as that Nellie Oleson."
>
> Laura thought: "I could. I could be meaner to her than she is to us, if Ma and Pa would let me."[42]

As for Laura herself, there's no doubt she is the main character in *On the Banks of Plum Creek*. All the action in the book is expressed directly through her point-of-view, as it was in *Little House on the Prairie*. But in this book, Wilder signals a significant change in Laura's character and in the series itself. *On the Banks of Plum Creek* traces not just the Ingalls family's experiences in the West; it showcases Laura's increasing maturity and the independence that comes with growing up, a theme Wilder expands in the remaining Little House books.

Wilder subtly introduces this theme in the opening pages of *On the Banks of Plum Creek*. After Ma and Pa decide that Plum Creek is a safe place, where nothing can happen, Laura seems to intuitively sense that the safety and security her parents feel along Plum Creek is an illusion: "Laura lay in bed and listened to the water talking and the willows whispering. She would rather sleep outdoors, even if she heard wolves, than be so safe in this house dug under the ground."[43] These lines mark a significant shift in her character. For the first time in the Little House books, Laura questions her parents' view of the world.

Growing Up and Apart

On the Banks of Plum Creek introduces Laura to a world beyond her family. She goes to school for the first time, makes new friends and a lasting enemy, attends Sunday school, and begins to grow apart from her family, including Pa:

> Laura was snug in Pa's arm. His beard softly tickled her cheek. . . . After a while she said, "Pa."
>
> "What little half-pint?" Pa's voice asked against her hair.
>
> "I think I like wolves better than cattle," she said.
>
> "Cattle are more useful, Laura," Pa said.
>
> She thought about that a while. Then she said, "Anyway, I like wolves better." She was not contradicting; she was only saying what she thought.[44]

Pa assumes a new role in *On the Banks of Plum Creek*. He is no longer the hero at the center of the action; instead, he becomes Laura's mentor. She learns from him, respects him, admires him, but questions and sometimes disagrees with him. The action in this novel—and the rest of the Little House books—centers on Laura. Pa plays second fiddle to her.

His new role emerges in Wilder's last extended Little House description of a pioneer craft—building a fish-trap along the creek. Laura helps Pa build it, but the chapter devoted to its construction is less about the process and more about this new relationship between Laura and Pa: "He sat on his heels and Laura sat on hers and they waited [for the fish to swim into the trap]. The creek poured and splashed, always the same and always changing."[45] The phrase "always the same and always changing" applies to Laura and Pa's relationship as well as to the creek. Though Pa and Laura will always be father and daughter, the dynamics of their relationship are changing and always will—because Laura is growing up and away from Pa.

Then the scene takes an unexpected turn, shifting away from Laura and Pa's shared appreciation of nature to an earnest discussion about her future. Pa encourages Laura to go to school, an idea she's resisted. Pa tells her, "It isn't everybody that gets a chance to learn to read and write and cipher. Your ma was a school-teacher when we met, and when she came West with me I promised that our girls would have a chance to get book learning. . . . You're almost eight years old now, and Mary going on nine, and it's time you begun. Be thankful you've got that chance, Laura."[46] Despite her lingering reluctance, Laura takes Pa's advice. She agrees to go to school, a step that ultimately takes her farther away from Pa and the love they share of all that is wild and free.

On the Banks of Plum Creek also focuses on Laura's quest to understand herself and the world around her more fully. In the pivotal chapter appropriately titled "The Footbridge," Laura ventures out alone on the bridge after the creek has flooded, and the experience teaches her an unexpected lesson about herself—and the natural world she has always loved.

The footbridge is nothing more than a plank across Plum Creek, and although Laura knows the creek is running high, she is beguiled by its foaming "white bubbles" and "joyful noise." Laura takes off her shoes and stockings, then ventures out on the plank. But she wants more; she wants "to be really in the roaring, joyous creek." First, she stretches out face-down on the footbridge; then, clasping her hands on the plank, she rolls into the water. "In that very instant, she knew the creek was not playing. It was strong and terrible. It seized her whole body and pulled it under the plank."[47] She clings desperately to the bridge, struggling to keep her head above water.

> The water was pulling her and it was pushing too. It was trying to drag her head under the plank. . . .
>
> No one knew where she was. No one could hear her if she screamed for help. The water roared loud and tugged at her, stronger and stronger. . . . It was cold. The coldness soaked into her.
>
> This was not like wolves or cattle. The creek was not alive. It was only strong and terrible and never stopping. It would pull her down and whirl her away, rolling and tossing like a willow branch. It would not care.[48]

Laura, of course, manages to escape, and Ma hopes the incident will teach Laura a lesson. Laura has been "very naughty," Ma says, "and I think you knew it all the time. But I can't punish you. I can't even scold you. You came near being drowned."[49]

If Wilder had ended the scene here—with a predictable moral

lesson about obeying one's parents—it would have taken the more conventional direction most children's books of the period followed (and that most people casually acquainted with the Little House books even now expect from them). Laura herself would have been a more conventional heroine. But the scene isn't about obedience, and what Laura learns from the experience makes her an unconventional, even timeless main character. The key to understanding the scene is in the line "it would not care." The creek, indeed the entire West, may be beautiful and wild, but it is ultimately unyielding, sometimes deadly, and completely beyond human control. Laura recognizes this truth for the first time: "The creek would go down. It would be a gentle, pleasant place to play in again. But nobody could make it do that. Nobody could make it do anything. Laura knew now that there were things stronger than anybody." Her revelation, however, doesn't stop there. She applies this discovery directly to herself: "But the creek had not got her. It had not made her scream and it could not make her cry."[50] Laura is a very tough and irrepressible little girl. She is unrepentant, a character who has grit in a world that is sometimes dark, dangerous, and uncontrollable.

Throughout the remaining Little House books, Wilder frequently paints a dark and sometimes ambivalent portrait of the natural world and the West, peopled with sometimes dark and ambiguous characters.[51] While Laura will grow and change throughout the last four books of the Little House series, her fundamental courage and grit will come to define her.

The fictional Laura Ingalls perseveres, making unconventional and unapologetic choices that set her apart from more traditional literary heroines of the 1930s and early 1940s. "Boys love adventure, girls, sentiment," observed American educator and psychologist G. Stanley Hall in 1908.[52] His assumptions about children's literary preferences held true throughout the early twentieth century: "Many authors insisted on making their girls good and domestic and dull (if a heroine were allowed some freedom to roam outside the house, she soon regretted it or grew up, whichever came first)."[53]

Wilder's work, however, followed in the tradition of Louisa May Alcott's *Little Women*. The fictional Laura breaks with convention. She doesn't fear adventure and she doesn't regret placing herself in danger. Instead, she learns from the experience on the footbridge; it makes her tougher, stronger, more resilient. She doesn't regret the freedom to roam outside the house.

Editorial Compromises

Although "The Footbridge" is a pivotal episode in the Little House series, the editorial correspondence between Wilder and Lane reveals that the chapter was a source of disagreement between the two. The correspondence also reveals how they worked to find a satisfying solution to the creative dilemma it posed and to others in *On the Banks of Plum Creek*.

Wilder's original vision for the chapter sprang from "Pioneer Girl." Ma becomes desperately ill during the spring freshet, and Pa, who dared not leave her side, sends Laura out across the flooded footbridge to ask their neighbor to go for the doctor. Pa, Wilder writes in *Pioneer Girl*, "must have forgotten about the high water." "When I saw the creek, it terrified me for the footbridge was standing away out in the middle of the stream, with yellow, foamy water running on both sides and just over the top of it. I didn't want to go on, but Pa had told me to go and Ma was awfully sick, so I waded in."[54] As the water reaches her knees, Laura hears Mr. Nelson warning her to turn back. She yells Pa's message to him and he goes for the doctor, who arrives the next day. Ma recovers and the flood waters in the creek recede.

Wilder included a similar episode in her original draft for *On the Banks of Plum Creek*, placing it after the grasshoppers' initial invasion, Pa's absence when working the wheat harvests back east, and the tumbleweed fire that threatens their home while Pa is away. After reading the rough draft, Lane wrote Wilder, "I am doubtful about Ma's illness. It is such a wretched miserable time, and in that kind of nasty grasshopper atmosphere. I think the grasshoppers are enough." In other words, Lane worried that the book would be too dark, too gritty for young readers, if the scene remained. She added that "there are plenty of hardships and dangers" already in the book. Wilder didn't need to add another one. But, Lane observed, "the part about the creek is a pity to leave out."[55]

Wilder disagreed with Lane's general assessment because she felt the footbridge episode illustrated dramatic differences between the 1870s and the 1930s. She wrote Lane, "It was nothing for a Dr to be 40 miles away and no auto, would make a great impression on children. . . . I think if you can better leave it." She also felt the scene illustrated how in her own childhood, she and Mary had been left on their own, "and no one thought of its being wrong."[56] And in a later letter Wilder observed, "But children weren't raised to be helpless cowards in those days."[57]

Ultimately, Wilder and Lane reached an editorial compromise. Ma's illness was cut from the final draft of *On the Banks of Plum Creek*, but Laura's confrontation with the creek remained, in a different context and placed *before* the glittering cloud of grasshoppers descend on Plum Creek. It became a scene about character, not misery.

As the surviving correspondence reveals, Lane and Wilder engaged in several disagreements over dialogue, plot, and character as their editorial work on the novel progressed. Lane, for example, seemed unable to grasp the geography of Plum Creek. "Get these [Ozark] hills and our gorge [at Rocky Ridge Farm] out of your mind," Wilder told Lane.[58] Wilder mapped out diagrams of the town, complete with the schoolhouse, church, railroad tracks, and shops, to help Lane better visualize the setting. Wilder did the same thing for the farm on Plum Creek.

Lane remained an unusually aggressive editor, but her editorial observations often pushed Wilder to do better work and to think consistently about such issues as voice and point-of-view. The scene toward the end of *On the Banks of Plum Creek*—when Ma cares for the livestock while Pa is missing during the long blizzard—proved especially challenging for her.

In the original draft, Wilder abandoned Laura's third-person limited point-of-view to convey the scene from Ma's perspective. As we'll see later, Wilder used this approach strategically in subsequent Little House books, but Lane felt it wasn't effective in *On the Banks of Plum Creek*. She suggested that Laura do the chores *with* Ma. Wilder initially agreed, but then the working writer in her took over. Logistically, it didn't make sense for Laura to do the chores with Ma. Laura was too small to reach the clothesline that guided them through the blizzard to the stable—and more importantly, Ma would never agree to endanger one of her girls in this way. From Wilder's perspective, it was a question of character. "It would be something Ma would never do to let Laura go out in it." Still, Wilder was stumped. She wrote Lane, "Seeing the inside of that stable and how Ma did the chores seems rather necessary to the interest of the whole thing. But how? I'm beat!"[59]

In a letter, probably just a few days later, Wilder floated another idea. Maybe the scene could be rearranged. Ma and Laura could go to the stable together before the blizzard hit, although this new arrangement would sacrifice "the storm striking so unexpectedly." Much of the drama would be lost. Then a new idea took hold:

> It might be that Laura could follow Ma into the barn and doing the chores, with her imagination, having seen Pa do the chores she would know how they would be done and how the animals would act.
>
> She would know how Ma would cling to the rope with one hand all the way and how she would shut the stable door carefully.[60]

This is exactly how the scene unfolds in the published version of *On the Banks of Plum Creek*: "Laura ran to the darkened window, but she could not see Ma. She could see nothing but the whirling whiteness swishing against the glass. . . . Ma would go step by step, holding tight to the clothes-line. She would come to the post and go on, blind in the hard snow whirling and scratching her cheeks. Laura tried to think slowly, one step at a time, till now, surely Ma bumped against the stable door."[61] The scene unfolds from Laura's point-of-view, but she imagines the episode so vividly that she and—by extension—Wilder's readers see Ma's every step, every move. Wilder at once maintains her third-person limited narrative through Laura—and moves beyond it.

This is a brilliant solution to a tricky issue of craft, and it illustrates the complementary creative and editorial strengths Wilder and Lane brought to the Little House books. Lane could identify technical problems—voice, point-of-view, plot. But Wilder, with a deeper understanding of her characters and their motivations, was able to find creative solutions that maintained the integrity of those characters and their stories.

A Different Creative Path

On September 24, 1936, Wilder submitted the finished manuscript to her literary agent George Bye, and *On the Banks of Plum Creek* was published the next year. To mark the book's publication, she was invited to speak at the Detroit Book Fair. Wilder was, by 1937, a rising literary star in American children's literature.

Certainly, *On the Banks of Plum Creek* had broken new ground in juvenile fiction. Its introduction of darker themes and the realistic depiction of its main characters influenced authors of what we now call middle grade fiction in the decades ahead. It paved the way for such Newbery classics as Esther Forbes's *Johnny Tremain*, published in 1943, and Scott O'Dell's *Island of the Blue Dolphins*, published in 1960. Historical fiction for young readers was free to explore darker, more complicated, unconventional themes with darker, more complicated, unconventional characters. Now authors, editors, educators, librarians, parents, and young readers take this freedom for granted. Virtually no subject is too dark, complicated, or unconventional for middle grade fiction to explore.

Wilder, who had turned seventy in 1937, could have continued to produce model juvenile fiction like *On the Banks of Plum Creek*. Perhaps that's precisely what her editor at Harper & Brothers expected; Lane herself encouraged her mother to continue to write for this audience. Instead, Wilder chose a different creative path, one that would help establish an entirely new category of books for young readers. She would delve into the more "adult stuff" in her fictional characters' lives because she intuitively felt her readers would not only understand it, they would demand it.[62] Her strongest, most innovative work was yet to come.

9

By the Shores of Silver Lake

A Creative Leap of Faith

BY 1937 WILDER AND LANE HAD MADE PEACE WITH THE "PIONEER Girl" manuscript. They recognized that it could fuel both their careers, and together they embarked on their next novels. Lane abandoned work on her history of Missouri, traded her suite at Columbia's Tiger Hotel for lodgings in New York City's Grosvenor Hotel and plunged into her second pioneer novel, *Free Land*. This time, however, she worked directly with her mother on the manuscript.[1]

This was a unique editorial collaboration, both women lifting sometimes not just the same scenes from "Pioneer Girl" but often characters, descriptions, and even dialogue. These were subjects they openly discussed with each another. "You remember the old saying that 'A man who won't steal from the R.R.Co. isn't honest,'" Wilder wrote Lane. "I can't use [it] in a child's story, but you could use it if you have a place for it."[2] And Lane decided to use it. In *Free Land*, a shopkeeper proclaims, "Hell, a man that won't steal from a railroad ain't honest."[3]

Free Land was published as a serial in the *Saturday Evening Post* during the spring of 1938 and in book form later that same year by Longmans, Green. The book introduced adult readers to a character named Halfbreed Jack. He gallops into the sunset, riding "in the Indian way" without a saddle, his pony "gaudily bridled." Lane's main character, a fictionalized version of Almanzo Wilder, watches as Halfbreed Jack rides away, knowing he "would never forget that fluid motion of free redskin and free animal together."[4]

The following year, in *By the Shores of Silver Lake*, Wilder introduced her readers to a character named Big Jerry, who is "a half-breed, French and Indian," and who also rides into the sunset on a saddleless pony: "The horse was free, he could go where he wanted to go, and he wanted to go with Big Jerry. . . . The horse and the man moved together as if they were one."[5] Clearly, Wilder and Lane were comfortable with their interpretations of the same "Pioneer Girl" material. Yet *By the Shores of Silver Lake* posed new challenges for Wilder—and for the editorial partnership she'd forged with her daughter. And initially their visions for this novel clashed.

THE FIRST HURDLE WAS CHRONOLOGICAL. *ON THE BANKS OF Plum Creek* had provided an abbreviated fictionalized account of Wilder's life in Minnesota. The novel ends with Pa's safe return at Christmastime in their wonderful house: "Everything was so good. Grasshoppers were gone, and next year Pa could harvest the wheat."[6] But the real Ingalls family, devastated by the grasshopper plague in southwestern Minnesota, had sold the Plum Creek farm, moved east to Iowa (where they briefly ran a hotel), and then, after failing there, returned to Minnesota, where they lived in town—not on Plum Creek. Tragedy struck the real family twice during those years. A son, born in Walnut Grove, Minnesota, died as the family moved to Iowa: Charles Frederick Ingalls—the family called him "Freddy"—was just nine months old when, as Wilder records in *Pioneer Girl*, "one awful day he straightened out his little body and was dead."[7] Not quite two years later, Mary "was taken suddenly sick"—and as Wilder recalls in *Pioneer Girl*, the family feared for Mary's life. She then suffered a stroke, and doctors told the family that "the nerves of her eyes had the worst of the stroke and were dying." Mary was twelve. "The last thing Mary ever saw was the bright blue of Grace's eyes."[8]

Lane initially felt Wilder should depict elements of the family's history in Iowa and their return to Minnesota in the novel that would become *By the Shores of Silver Lake*. Wilder disagreed. She argued that the family's journey east to Iowa and then back to Minnesota was ". . . a story in itself, but it does not belong in the picture I am making of the [fictional] family."[9] Wilder believed the fictional family should always move west; to abandon that westward movement would undermine a central theme she had established in the previous books.

Lane was also concerned about the juvenile market and its expectations following the success of *On the Banks of Plum Creek*. At the end of that novel, Laura was poised on the brink of adolescence. And then there was the question of Mary's blindness. An adolescent main character with a blind sister didn't strike Lane as age-appropriate ingredients for another juvenile publishing success.

So how would Wilder bridge the gap between her real family's history and her fictional family's ongoing saga? How would she deal with a main character growing too old for traditional juvenile literature of the late 1930s? And what would Wilder do about Mary's blindness?

Wilder, perhaps tapping into on her own pioneering spirit, took a creative leap, and in the process, made literary history. Again.

Grown Up

From the beginning of *By the Shores of Silver Lake*, Wilder signals that something dramatic has shifted in her fictional world. The tone is somber, sad, and by extension, more mature:

> Laura was washing the dishes one morning when old Jack, lying in the sunshine on the doorstep, growled to tell her that someone was coming. She looked out, and saw a buggy crossing the gravelly ford of Plum Creek.
>
> "Ma," she said, "it's a strange woman coming."
>
> Ma sighed. She was ashamed of the untidy house, and so was Laura. But Ma was too weak and Laura was too tired and they were too sad to care very much.[10]

Without using the cliché "time passed," Wilder communicates clearly here that Laura is older, much older than she was at the end of *On the Banks of Plum Creek*. She's doing housework. Jack is "old." But something more dramatic and serious is at play here too. The fact that the house is untidy, that Ma is weak, that Laura is tired—this too signals a major change in what readers would expect from the fictional family. Laura speaks and moves with an air of responsibility, and for the first time in the series, Ma seems to depend on Laura.

Wilder reinforces this shift in the book's second chapter, titled "Grown Up." After Jack dies and when Pa drives away from Plum Creek with that strange woman in the buggy, Laura is alone with "only emptiness to turn to."[11] She must learn to rely on herself. This new maturity signals a new theme in the Little House series. The story of *By the Shores of Silver Lake*—and those that follow—will explore how Laura comes of age, how she will transition from childhood to adulthood. The final lines in the book's second chapter make this perfectly clear: "Laura knew that she was not a little girl any more. Now she was alone; she must take care of herself. When you must do that, then you do it and you are grown up. Laura was not very big, but she was almost thirteen years old, and no one was there to depend on." As the family prepares to move west again, Laura must assume new responsibilities and face new challenges, including to "somehow" help Ma get "Mary and the little girls" safely into Dakota Territory "by train."[12]

By the Shores of Silver Lake is undoubtedly a Little House novel with a new theme at its heart. The book also represents a major shift in Wilder's vision of the West, which she ultimately links to Laura's transitions from childhood to adolescence to young womanhood. For its time, *By the Shores of Silver Lake* was groundbreaking and helped establish a major genre we take for granted in the twenty-first century. In 1939, when the book was published, the Young Adult category didn't exist.

Outliers in American Fiction

Little Women was published in 1868 and is now considered the first American Young Adult novel. Its title was significant, a recognition of the transition between childhood and adulthood. The title characters aren't little girls, nor are they fully formed women. And as the book unfolds, the characters discover who they are. They come of age; they realize their futures.[13] The book's publication date is also important—1868, just three years after the end of the American Civil War. Until that time, "people were simply considered either children or adults."[14] Adolescence hadn't yet been recognized as a separate and essential phase of life.

Little Women was unexpectedly and extremely popular. It was unlike any prior American novel for young readers. As author Anne Boyd Rioux observes, "The novel immediately draws the reader in with four young voices, each expressing her own wishes and desires, and hinting at her unique personality."[15] It delighted readers and reviewers alike. Yet despite its popularity, *Little Women* didn't create a new genre for young adult readers. Nineteenth-century authors didn't immediately begin writing novels about young characters with unique personalities, voicing their wishes and desires as they transitioned from children to young women and men.

Except for Mark Twain.

The Adventures of Huckleberry Finn, published in 1884, is another milestone in Young Adult American fiction. Huck's voice was unique and unprecedented. The book's themes were weighty and important: a boy on the threshold of manhood, struggling with mainstream society's racism and acceptance of slavery. Like many young adult characters from the late twentieth and twenty-first centuries, Huck is an outsider, struggling to understand his place in society. He breaks free of the influence of his abusive father and begins a journey on which he is positioned to succeed or—as he often does—fail. And finally, like many of today's Young Adult titles, *The Adventures of Huckleberry Finn* sparked controversy—not initially because of its perceived racism but because of what many considered its seamy, unsavory cast of characters and their seamy, unsavory behaviors. As Louisa May Alcott noted, "If Mr. Clemens cannot think of something better to tell our pure-minded lads and lasses, he had better stop writing for them."[16]

As the twentieth century dawned, books for young readers remained essentially "juveniles": picture books, as well as fiction and nonfiction for an audience we now designate as middle grade readers.[17] *Little Women* and *The Adventures of Huckleberry Finn* were outliers in American fiction. They belonged to a genre that didn't yet exist.

Canadian author L. M. Montgomery published *Anne of Green Gables* in 1907, a book now considered a classic Young Adult novel. But it was originally aimed at adult readers. In the 1920s, however, critics began to reclassify Montgomery's work. According to her biographer, by 1937 Montgomery had become "increasingly annoyed that her books were now being marketed primarily as children's books, although they were written for a general audience."[18] Montgomery went to her grave believing this reassessment had forever undermined her literary legacy.

In a passage from *Old Home Town*, Lane hints at her own experience as an adolescent, searching for a more satisfying reading alternative than the conventional juvenile books she grew up with in the late nineteenth and early twentieth centuries. "We, in our teens, read the funny papers," says her narrator. "Elsie Dinsmore, Jo March and her sisters, and The Five Little Peppers, had been replaced by the Katzenjammer Kids, Buster Brown, Maud the Mule, and the Newly Weds. All through the week we discussed them, they gave us our nicknames and our slang."[19]

It isn't hard to imagine that Lane herself and her teen "chums" outgrew the pious and didactic Elsie Dinsmore novels and the rags-to-riches Five Little Peppers series.[20] But did she and her chums really find a satisfying alternative to conventional juvenile fiction in the Sunday newspaper comics, or did Lane invent this memory for the benefit of her fictional characters in *Old Home Town*? It's impossible to know, of course. But Lane's observation underscores the absence of compelling fiction for young adults at the dawn of the twentieth century.

Still, it's puzzling that Lane lumps Jo March and her sisters into the same category as Elsie Dinsmore and the Five Little Peppers. It's possible that in 1935, when Lane wrote the introduction to *Old Home Town*, she didn't fully recognize *Little Women*'s originality or its revolutionary literary influence. The book had become a classic by then. Furthermore, later editions of *Little Women* featured illustrations that made Alcott's characters appear more conventional, even Elsie Dinsmore–esque. A popular late nineteenth-century edition, one Lane herself might have read, was extensively edited, "mainly to get rid of slang and colloquialisms, clean up the grammar, and make the whole sound more genteel and proper."[21] Still, the surviving editorial correspondence between Lane and her mother reveals that Lane never fully appreciated the literary merits of children's book writers (she once characterized her mother's work as "small fry" to their literary agent) nor did she seem to recognize Wilder's originality or her revolutionary approach in *By the Shores of Silver Lake*.[22]

As for American publishers, it's not entirely surprising that they didn't initially recognize a potential market for young adult or teen readers until the mid-twentieth century. Despite growing awareness since the 1860s of that distinct transitional state between childhood and adulthood, American psychology itself didn't recognize this concept until 1904, with the publication of G. Stanley Hall's *Adolescence: Its Psychology*. Natalie Babbit, Newbery medalist and author of *Tuck Everlasting*, observed, "The category *teenager* itself is a new one, of course. It made its first appearance during the Second World War and was created partly by parents, partly by manufacturers, and partly by Frank Sinatra."[23]

Adult Stuff

When Wilder began writing *By the Shores of Silver Lake* in 1937, the teen market for music, clothing, and books hadn't yet crystalized. It isn't surprising, then, that Lane believed her mother's Little House books should remain firmly entrenched with younger readers. Although Lane's correspondence on this subject no longer survives, it's clear that she not only believed *By the Shores of Silver Lake* should remain squarely in the established juvenile or middle grade genre, but to do so, she suggested that Wilder switch main characters in this novel. Wilder vehemently disagreed: "We cant [*sic*] spoil the story by making it childish! We cant [*sic*] change heroines in the middle of the stream and use Carrie in place of Laura," she wrote.[24]

For Lane, however, the issue wasn't simply about the *age* of the main character in *By the Shores of Silver Lake*. It was about the character's growing awareness of her own maturity, of approaching adulthood and its new responsibilities. Despite her daughter's misgivings, Wilder believed these elements were vital to her new novel. "I don't see how we can spare what you call adult stuff for that makes the story," Wilder argued. "It was there and Laura knew and understood it." Wilder seemed to instinctively recognize that a new market and a new genre were taking shape. "I believe children who have read the other books will demand this one, and that they will understand and love it."[25]

A Touch of Tragedy

One other pivotal issue that divided Wilder and Lane on this new Little House book was the central tragedy that forever changed the lives of both the real and the fictional Ingalls family: Mary's blindness.[26] Lane believed it had no place in *By the Shores of Silver Lake*, or the future Little House books Wilder already envisioned. But Wilder again trusted her characters, their stories, and her audience: "I can't take Mary along in the story as she should be if she were not blind. . . . A touch of tragedy makes the story truer to life and showing the way we took it illustrates the spirit of the frontier."[27] Without Mary's blindness, Laura's character wouldn't be forced to see and describe the world for her sister. She would never evolve into the character Wilder felt compelled to create: an observant and unconventional young woman in love with the natural world and committed to fulfilling her obligations to her sister and family.

But crafting a novel with these considerations for this new audience was another matter. Once Wilder had convinced Lane that Laura should remain the main character in *By the Shores of Silver Lake*, and that the adult stuff should also remain, Wilder still had to puzzle out how to make this new kind of book work. Where should the novel begin? How would it fit into the chronology of the previous Little House books? And how much detail should she include about Mary's illness and subsequent blindness? Wilder and Lane agreed that the success of the entire novel would hinge on the opening chapter. It had to be flawless. And the chapter had to accomplish an almost insurmountable number of objectives: it had to launch an older, more mature Laura; establish a more mature tone; transition chronologically and thematically from the previous book into the unfolding action of the new one; introduce readers to a new member of the Ingalls family; address Mary's illness and blindness; propel readers into an entirely new storyline; and do all this in a compelling, interesting way to keep readers turning the pages.

An Editorial Compromise

As we've already seen, the opening lines in *By the Shores of Silver Lake* seem effortlessly masterful and direct. Yet Wilder and Lane initially disagreed on where the novel should begin. Wilder argued to start in the middle of the action. Her original manuscript begins, "A woman holding a small child on her arm and a small girl by the hand walked across the depot platform to the one passenger car at the end of the tail. Two larger girls hand in hand followed her."[28]

In this draft, the opening lines don't center on Laura's limited third-person point-of-view. Instead, this is a more cinematic perspective. It reads like a screenplay; in your mind's eye, you can visualize the scene. In fact, Wilder didn't move into Laura's perspective until the second page of this draft. This change in perspective was perhaps a strategic creative decision on Wilder's part. It allowed her to gloss over the historical fact that her family had moved from their Plum Creek farmhouse to Iowa, then back to Minnesota and into a house in town. It avoided inconvenient specifics.

When Lane read these opening lines, she objected. "It is not written from *Laura's* viewpoint. I think your lead should be Aunt Docia driving up unexpectedly to the house on the banks of Plum Creek."[29] Initially, Wilder wasn't convinced. She believed Lane's approach would "take the interest of the reader back to Plum Creek, instead of ahead with curiosity to what lies ahead [in the story]." Furthermore, Wilder believed Lane's idea "would begin the story with a recital of discouragement and calamities."[30]

Yet Lane persisted. She maintained that readers needed a clear transition between *On the Banks of Plum Creek* and *By the Shores of Silver Lake*. If Wilder insisted on skipping over those years the real family spent in Iowa and then back in Walnut Grove, why not place the fictional family on the Plum Creek farm, at that wonderful Plum Creek house? The transition would be smoother.

On the surface, it appears that Lane won this editorial argument. The novel begins at the Plum Creek house as Aunt Docia, the "strange woman alone in a buggy," drives up. But in fact, it's something of an editorial compromise—and a brilliant one. As Lane advised, the transition between *On the Banks of Plum Creek* and *By the Shores of Silver Lake* is as smooth as a fictional chronology of this kind can be. Not only does the book open on the Plum Creek farm, but it weaves essential details about the past into the unfolding action. As soon as Ma knows a stranger is headed toward the house, she asks Laura what they can possibly serve for a "company dinner." The previous two years are dispatched in a pair of revealing paragraphs:

> There was bread and molasses, and potatoes. That was all. This was springtime, too early for garden vegetables; the cow was dry and the hens had not yet begun to lay their summer's eggs. Only a few fish were left in Plum Creek. Even the little cottontail rabbits had been hunted until they were scarce.
>
> Pa did not like a country so old and worn out that the hunting was poor. He wanted to go west and take a homestead, but Ma did not want to leave the settled country. And there was no money. Pa had made only two poor wheat crops since the grasshoppers came; he had barely been able to keep out of debt, and now there was the doctor's bill.[31]

But as Wilder advocated, the chapter doesn't linger on calamity and discouragement. The stranger turns out to be lovely Aunt Docia, and she arrives with an irresistible job offer for Pa: a clerical position with the new railroad being constructed out west in Dakota Territory. Best of all, the job will pay fifty dollars a month. The fictional family's bright future immediately dispels the dark clouds of its past. Laura and her family are about to move west again.[32]

Still Brave and Patient

As for Mary's blindness, Wilder also deals with it squarely and succinctly in the first chapter. She doesn't pull any punches with her readers. Just four paragraphs into the novel, Wilder reveals that Mary is blind. But rather than provide the details of Mary's illness as Wilder does in *Pioneer Girl*, she explains it away quickly. Its literary cause: scarlet fever. It "had settled into Mary's eyes" and now "she could not see even the brightest light any more."[33]

When Wilder wrote *By the Shores of Silver Lake*, the precise cause of Mary's blindness wasn't entirely clear. In *Pioneer Girl*, Wilder recalls that Pa had consulted two local doctors about Mary's condition, and the senior of the two had concluded that the nerves in her eyes "were dying, that nothing could be done."[34] In 1937 Wilder and Lane corresponded about Mary's illness, trying to place it in perspective for the novel. Wilder struggled to remember precisely what the doctors had concluded: "Mary had ~~spinal mengitis~~ some sort of spinal sickness. I am not sure the Dr. named it."[35] In 2013 medical researchers concluded that Mary's blindness was likely the result of viral meningoencephalitis.[36]

So why did Wilder settle on scarlet fever? A clue exists in one letter from Lane. After finally agreeing with her mother's decision that Mary's blindness was essential to the novel, Lane outlined a possible scenario: "Times have been hard, Grace has been born, Jack has died, Mary has had—scarlet fever, was it?—between Plum Creek and this volume."[37] So, perhaps because it was such a historically deadly disease, and after exhausting the possibilities for the real cause of Mary's blindness, Wilder concluded—at Lane's suggestion—that scarlet fever was a swift, clear, and believable explanation. Readers were familiar with scarlet fever; after all, it had led to the death of Beth March in *Little Women*.[38]

In *By the Shores of Silver Lake*, Wilder doesn't describe Mary's illness in detail. Instead, she lingers on the family's response to it—and Mary's courage in accepting her fate. "She was still patient and brave."[39] This strategy reinforces the strength of Mary's character, and simultaneously encourages readers to admire rather than pity her. In the 1930s, Wilder's depiction of Mary as a disabled character in fiction for young readers was groundbreaking. In the late nineteenth and early twentieth centuries such characters—if they appeared at all in books for young (or adult) readers—were usually presented as victims of their own goodness, unnaturally sweet and ethereal, too noble for a base and insensitive world. Think Little Eva in *Uncle Tom's Cabin* or Beth March in *Little Women*. Their virtues, while embraced by nineteenth-century readers, haven't aged especially well with a contemporary audience. Mary, however, remains uniquely herself, despite her illness and subsequent blindness. She may be disabled, her life may be forever changed, but she does not withdraw from the world, and as we'll see later, her observations are often sharp, pragmatic, and grounded in reality.

At Times, Completely Grown Up

Mary's eyes remain a beautiful blue, but she can "never look through them again to tell Laura what she was thinking without saying a word." Yet the bond between the two sisters is strengthened rather than weakened by Mary's blindness. Pa facilitates this new bond. He tells Laura "that she must be eyes for Mary."[40] So in one creative stroke, Wilder unites the two sisters but also endows Laura with gifts of observation that will shape, define, and ultimately determine who she will become. Furthermore, this plot development also illustrates Wilder's nuanced understanding of character. She doesn't let Mary take over the story in the opening pages of the book, a challenge when writing about such a tragedy. Readers remain grounded in Laura's point-of-view, never losing sight of the fact that the novel belongs to her. It is her story and no one else's.

Wilder's seemingly intuitive sense of character and story is also what makes *By the Shores of Silver Lake* a successful Young Adult novel. Other than *Little Women*, perhaps, Wilder didn't have a model or pattern for how a young adult main character should behave. Instead, she relied on her own intuition and memory. As she explained to Lane, the Laura of this novel is "at times, completely grown up and again just a child."[41] Wilder understood the essential contradictions of adolescence.

By the Shores of Silver Lake is essentially about change and maturity, signaled in the opening chapter by the arrival of Aunt Docia and followed by Jack's death. But throughout the book, Wilder includes scenes that underscore Laura's changing and evolving self. The chapter "The Black Ponies" illustrates Laura's lingering attraction to childhood when she takes her wild ride on Jean's pony: "Her hair came unbraided and her throat grew hoarse from laughing and screeching, and her legs were scratched from running through the sharp grass and trying to leap onto her pony while it was running."[42] But earlier in this chapter, Laura and her cousin Lena face a sobering truth about themselves when they take Aunt Docia's washing to a homesteader's wife and learn her thirteen-year-old daughter—Lizzie—got married the previous day:

> "She was only a little older than I am," said Laura, and Lena said, "I'm a year older than she was."
>
> Then Lena tossed her curly black head. "She's a silly! Now she can't ever have any more good times."
>
> Laura said soberly, "No, she can't play any more now. . . ."

After a while Lena said she supposed that Lizzie did not have to work any harder than before. "Anyway, now she's doing her own work in her own house, and she'll have babies."

"Well," Laura said, "I'd like my own house and I like babies, and I wouldn't mind the work, but I don't want to be so responsible. I'd rather let Ma be responsible for a long time yet."[43]

Both girls realize that childhood is slipping away and that new responsibilities are ahead for them *if* they follow a conventional path. Laura's wild ride on the black ponies, which follows this conversation about the homesteader's daughter, can also be read as a rejection of convention and a form of rebellion.

The conversation about Lizzie and marriage seems to provoke Laura into one more act of rebellion. Earlier in the scene, as the two girls drive out to the homesteader's claim shanty, Lena takes the reins because "Pa never let Laura drive his horses." He believes Laura isn't "strong enough to hold them if they ran away."[44] Still, Laura wishes she could drive, and after Laura and Lena discuss Lizzie's marriage, Laura asks to take the reins. "She wanted to forget growing up." The moment the lines pass from Lena's hands to Laura's, the ponies break into a gallop and test every ounce of Laura's strength. But Laura relishes the challenge. It's an act of defiance and freedom, a measure of both her physical and emotional strength: "Laura braced her feet and hung onto the lines with all her might . . . and yelled, 'Yi, yi, yi, yip-ee!'"[45]

Laura is doing what she wants to do, and in this scene, she begins to assume control of her own life. While she may sometimes continue to act like a child, Laura is an almost-teenager, expressing herself in her own way, testing and defying her parents' expectations for her. She does so without regret.

Facing Down the Wolf

In later chapters in *By the Shores of Silver Lake*, however, Laura assumes more responsibility for herself and her family, evolving into the adult she will become. Midway through the book, for example, Laura faces down a buffalo wolf on a wintry moonlit night on Silver Lake. The scene bristles with a kind of naturalistic magic. The wolf looks straight at Laura as the wind "stirred his fur and the moonlight seemed to run in and out of it."[46]

But Laura isn't alone with the wolf in this chapter. She's running and sliding on Silver Lake's ice with her timid little sister Carrie, who is "almost afraid" of being outdoors in the nighttime cold—even before Laura spots the wolf.[47] Conscious not only of her own safety but of Carrie's too, Laura takes charge and leads Carrie safely home. Laura is the brave, responsible adult in this scene. She acts with the same maturity and self-possession that Ma exhibited with Laura years before, when the bear slipped into the barnyard in the Big Woods.

Laura not only does the right thing in this episode—protecting herself and Carrie—but she also faces downs haunting memories from her childhood. In *Little House in the Big Woods* and *Little House on the Prairie*, Laura is both frightened and fascinated by the wolves she sees at night through the windows of her family's little houses. In those scenes, Pa and Jack protect Laura from the wolves and the danger they represent. In *By the Shores of Silver Lake*, nothing stands between Laura and that lone buffalo wolf except a short stretch of ice. She must rely on herself alone to escape danger.

The experience forges a connection between Laura and the buffalo wolf. When Pa observes that the wolf and his mate were "pretty nearly the last buffalo wolves that'll ever be seen in this part of the country," Laura mourns their loss. "Oh, Pa," she says, "the poor wolves."[48] An essential part of Laura's childhood is gone. But an essential part of the West, embodied by the buffalo wolves, has also gone, and perhaps Laura mourns this even more. Throughout the remaining Little House books, Wilder will depict the taming of the West not as an inherent virtue but as a haunting and inevitable outcome of the American pioneer experience.

The West Begins

Although the fictional Ingalls family has always lived on the frontier, for Wilder the West, the *real* West, is Dakota Territory. In *By the Shores of Silver Lake*, she gives a pivotal chapter the title "The West Begins," and all the remaining Little House books unfold in this real West. A haunting passage in this chapter reflects what the West—Dakota Territory—means to Wilder and her characters:

"All morning Pa drove steadily along the dim wagon track, and nothing changed. The farther they went into the west, the smaller they seemed, and the less they seemed to be going anywhere. . . . Laura thought they might go on forever, yet always be in this same changeless place, that would not even know they were there."[49] As we've seen in Wilder's previous Little House books, the natural world is indifferent to the human condition. But this West, this new West of Dakota Territory, is vast and seemingly endless. It's a different frontier, even for experienced pioneers like the Ingalls family. Laura asks:

> "Pa . . . , when you find the homestead, will it be like the one we had in Indian Territory?"
>
> Pa thought before he answered. "No," he said finally. "This is different country. I can't tell you how, exactly, but this prairie is different. It feels different."
>
> "That's likely enough," Ma said sensibly. "We're west of Minnesota, and north of Indian Territory, so naturally the flowers and grasses are not the same."
>
> But that was not what Pa and Laura meant. There was really almost no difference in the flowers and grasses. But there was something else here that was not anywhere else. It was an enormous stillness that made you feel still. And when you were still, you could feel great stillness coming closer.[50]

The stillness is ominous, overwhelming, chilling—characteristics that Wilder explores in her next Little House book. But in *By the Shores of Silver Lake*, this vast, still frontier is filling up with people who hope to tame it. Throughout the chapter "The West Begins," Wilder creates an undercurrent of sadness and loss in her descriptions of this wild, seemingly untamable frontier, where they drive on and on, "never seeing a house or any sign of people, never seeing anything but grass and sky."[51] But Laura recognizes what she believes might be "old Indian trails and buffalo paths" and "large depressions, straight-sided and flat-bottomed, that had been buffalo wallows." When Laura points them out, Pa tells her it isn't likely she'll ever see a buffalo in Dakota Territory. He tells her that not long ago "vast herds of thousands of buffaloes had grazed over this country. They had been the Indians' cattle, and white men had slaughtered all of them."[52]

Part of this loss is bound up with the railroad, which Wilder views with a mix of disdain and admiration. For Wilder, the railroad is a necessary evil, a corrupt institution on which pioneers in this vast western landscape have to rely, including even Pa himself. The railroad as an institution is so corrupt that it triggers even more corruption: horse thieving, riots, larceny (even involving Laura's extended family). Initially, as we've seen in her correspondence with Lane, Wilder was reluctant to depict corporate corruption (and the pioneers' response to it) in a book for young readers—even the older readers she envisioned for *By the Shores of Silver Lake*. And yet it became an essential theme of the book. When Uncle Hi helps himself to railroad company supplies, Pa is sympathetic. "It wasn't stealing," he tells Caroline. "Hi hasn't got away with any more than's due him. . . . The company cheated him there [at the camp on the Sioux], and he's got even here. That's all there is to it."[53]

Yet for Wilder, railroads also represent progress and change. After Laura's first brief railroad journey, she is elated and knows now "what Pa meant when he spoke of the wonderful times they were living in. There had never been such wonders in the whole history of the world."[54] In fact, Wilder devotes a lengthy chapter to the railroad's construction. Its title is "The Wonderful Afternoon," and in correspondence to Lane, Wilder admitted that she created a fictional scenario in this chapter so readers could see the railroad's construction directly through Laura's eyes. "I stretched a point when I had Laura go with Pa to see the work [on the railroad]. I never did," Wilder wrote.[55] "I did it," she added, "to have Laura see it first hand and get her reaction."[56]

Laura's reaction to the railroad is important. It showcases the inherent contrast of Dakota Territory. Its landscape is overwhelming, as seemingly endless and untamable as an ocean. Yet the men and women pouring into this new West not only seek to tame it but to transform its landscape and the future itself. At the end of the wonderful afternoon, Laura is inspired by all she's seen—the men and horses moving together so seamlessly to build something out of nothing that she "could almost sing the tune to which they moved."[57] Their efforts spark Laura's imagination: "There was no railroad there now, but someday the long steel tracks would lie level on the fills and through the cuts, and trains would come roaring, steaming and smoking with speed. The tracks and the trains were not there now, but Laura could see them almost as if they were."[58] Yet Laura mourns these changes even as she embraces them. For her, there's a part of this new West that will forever remain untamed and free—and it stirs Laura's imagination even more deeply than the railroad.

Parallel Paths

In perhaps the most memorable and iconic moment in *By the Shores of Silver Lake*, Laura attempts to describe a fleeting experience that somehow, for her, transcends time. The "half-breed, French and Indian" Big Jerry and his "snow-white horse" appear seemingly out of nowhere in time to save the Ingalls family from a desperado who has been trailing them. Big Jerry and his horse are "beside the wagon only a moment. Then away they went in the smoothest, prettiest run, down into a little hollow and up and away, straight into the blazing round sun on the far edge of the west." Laura "lets out her breath."

> "Oh, Mary! The snow-white horse and the tall, brown man, with such a black head and a bright red shirt! The brown prairie all around—and they rode right into the sun as it was going down. They'll go on in the sun around the world."
>
> Mary thought a moment. Then she said, "Laura, you know he couldn't ride into the sun. He's just riding along on the ground like anybody."
>
> But Laura did not feel that she had told a lie. What she had said was true too. Somehow that moment when the beautiful, free pony and the wild man rode into the sun would last forever.[59]

As we've already discussed, Lane used this image too—but in her *Free Land* it lacks the resonance and depth it takes on in *By the Shores of Silver Lake*. For Wilder—and by extension, Laura—the scene represents the real West: a Native American man riding a wild, white horse forever into the sun. And yet this is a vanishing image, one that Laura and her family along with dozens of other families like theirs will displace. By the end of *By the Shores of Silver Lake*, not only is the railroad taking shape but so is the town of De Smet, as thousands of people overrun Dakota Territory. While *By the Shores of Silver Lake* is Laura's introduction to the real West, it is simultaneously her farewell to it, just as the book signals the beginning of Laura's farewell to childhood.

Laura and the West are on parallel paths. Will civilization tame the West? Will approaching womanhood tame Laura Ingalls?

What She Had Said Was True

Laura's attempt to convey something more in her description of Big Jerry than "a man riding along the ground like anybody," is one of Wilder's hints that Laura in the Little House series will grow up to be the Laura Ingalls Wilder who writes it. In *By the Shores of Silver Lake*, readers begin to see Laura as a storyteller. She has the vision to see beyond everyday reality to a larger, more universal truth—the truth of a storyteller. Mary's vision, by contrast, is limited not by her blindness but by her practicality. She perceives the world in a sensible, literal way. Still, Laura's emerging gifts of observation and description are bound up with Mary's blindness. It has forced this new occupation on Laura—to be Mary's eyes, to describe the world for an audience unable to see what she does.

Wilder uses simple, concrete vocabulary to relay Laura's descriptive powers to readers. Unlike Lane, who often resorted to abstract vocabulary in her fiction, Wilder appears to have instinctively understood the lyricism and strength of clean, uncluttered prose. Another passage in *By the Shores of Silver Lake* illustrates how Wilder capitalizes on a direct, straightforward style to convey Laura's growing awareness that her own imagination can spark something deep, true, and intangible:

> "The road pushes against the grassy land and breaks off short. And that's the end of it," said Laura.
>
> "It can't be," Mary objected. "The road goes all the way to Silver Lake."
>
> "I know it does," Laura answered.
>
> "Well, then I don't think you ought to say things like that,"

> Mary told her gently. "We should always be careful to say exactly what we mean."
>
> "I was saying what I meant," Laura protested. But she could not explain. There were so many ways of seeing things and so many ways of saying them.[60]

Laura's description hints at the vast mystery of storytelling—"so many ways of seeing things and so many ways of saying them." And that mystery is as vast and as rich as the West itself.

A Shift in Style and Tone

By the Shores of Silver Lake helped establish many of the conventions we now associate with Young Adult fiction: adolescent protagonists finding their way in a confusing and sometimes dangerous world; confronting more adult situations; accepting new responsibilities; considering their own futures and the inevitable questions about physical maturity, sexuality, and romance; discovering their own unique identities; questioning social, political, and cultural conventions; coming of age. By today's standards in Young Adult literature, the challenges Laura faces in *By the Shores of Silver Lake* may seem quaint and old-fashioned. But in 1939, Wilder's work was innovative. In fact, the category she pioneered in this book wouldn't be fully recognized until a year after her death, when the American Library Association officially adopted the term "Young Adult" in 1958.

But Harper & Brothers recognized that the style and tone of *By the Shores of Silver Lake* set it apart from Wilder's previous work, and modified the book's format to reflect a shift to older readers. Wilder's previous Little House books had been slightly oversized, an almost square shape—seven inches wide, eight and a half inches tall—and featured a slightly oversized font. The format for *By the Shores of Silver Lake*, on the other hand, corresponded to the dimensions of a traditional adult book of the period. In a telegraph to Lane, literary agent George Bye explained: "HARPERS WANT TO PUBLISH YOUR MOTHERS BOOK IN NOVEL SIZE FORMAT AS OLDER CHILDREN WONT BUY SQUARISH BOOKS."[61]

So, like Lane's *Free Land*, *By the Shores of Silver Lake*'s hardcover edition was leaner, more rectangular; its text was set with a slightly smaller font. Its size and shape made *By the Shores of Silver Lake* look like a book for adults, despite its cover design and interior illustrations.[62] The book's more adult format matched the "adult stuff" depicted inside.

Pinning Up Her Hair

In *Pioneer Girl*, Wilder writes that she first "pinned up" her hair and began wearing long dresses while Ma and Pa worked in the railroad camp on Silver Lake. Her "long braids," which hung down her back, got in the way as she helped Ma serve meals to the men in the camp. "So there I was," Wilder remembers, "a young lady with long dresses and hair done up."[63] The fictional Laura Ingalls of *By the Shores of Silver Lake* doesn't grow up quite so quickly. She remains, as Wilder described her to Lane, "at times, completely grown up and again just a child." A short scene near the end of *By the Shores of Silver Lake* illustrates this dichotomy perfectly. When Laura discovers that the "whole enormous prairie" is "a green carpet flowered with spring blossoms," she flings herself "on the flowery grass" and rolls "like a colt." Then suddenly, she remembers herself—her responsibilities, even her appearance. She realizes that now there's "a green stain on her calico" dress and that "she should be helping Ma" with the morning chores.[64] Laura hurries home. She is no longer a child, and yet she's not quite a woman yet.

Like the West, Laura's future at the end of *By the Shores of Silver Lake* is unknowable. But readers understand that Laura and her family have already been changed by their experiences in this very new and different frontier. The railroad and the new town rising up around it have transformed the landscape, just as they've also transformed Laura and her family. Their quest for the promised land has ended. The fictional family lives in a new shanty on their homestead claim near the Big Slough and Pa even owns a building in town.[65] Prosperity seems in their grasp at last.

Yet readers also sense that more transformations are ahead—for the West, and for Laura herself. In another scene near the end of the novel, Laura is once more doing dishes, just as she had in the opening chapter. She carries the dishpan to the back door and flings the dirty water away, far over the grass where tomorrow's sun would dry it. The first stars were pricking through the pale sky. A few lights twinkled yellow in the little town, but the whole great plain of the earth was shadowy. There was hardly a wind, but the air moved and whispered to itself in the grasses. Laura almost knew what it said. Lonely and wild and eternal were land and water and sky and the air blowing.

"The buffalo are gone," Laura thought. "And now we're homesteaders."[66]

The novel has come full circle. Laura is once again washing dishes, just as she had in the first chapter when that unexpected visitor arrived. But the first chapter's opening recital of discouragement and calamities have given way to a bittersweet ending, a perfect note on which to end a Young Adult novel.

But Wilder's next book would stretch the conventions of this category even further, test her own creative vision as never before, and ultimately showcase her artistry. She was about to produce a masterpiece.

10

The Long Winter, Part One

Imaginative Iron

IN 1940 WILDER'S LITERARY AGENT GEORGE BYE WROTE Wilder to tell her that he had sat up until two o'clock in the morning, reading the manuscript for *The Long Winter*, and then had trouble going to sleep, "for thinking of the plight of the Ingalls family and that awful winter."[1] The book was published later in 1940 to critical acclaim. The reviewer for the *New York Herald Tribune* observed, "For sheer gallantry, the story can't be beat. It puts iron into the imagination."[2]

Over eighty years later, the *New York Herald Tribune*'s review still holds up. *The Long Winter* is a story that can't be beat. It is the book I most admire in the series—for its artistry, structure, and power. That imaginative iron. But I didn't always feel this way about *The Long Winter*.

When I first read the book, as a ten-year-old, I assumed Wilder's descriptions of blizzards were exaggerated in the same way my family exaggerated their stories about Ozark tornadoes, copperhead snakes, and those giant catfish that inevitably got away. I couldn't quite believe in the novel's "whirling winds" and "swirling whiteness."[3]

My initial response to *The Long Winter* shifted when I moved to Vermillion, South Dakota, and experienced my first prairie blizzard. It stretched over two days. I was safe and warm in my apartment, but a driver, stranded on a highway somewhere between Sioux Falls, South Dakota, and Sioux City, Iowa, had panicked and left his car. His body was found not far from it—after the whirling wind and swirling whiteness had relented. That's when I knew that *The Long Winter* wasn't hyperbole. It was real, as real as fiction can be. And as I began to write fiction myself, I also realized that *The Long Winter* is Wilder's masterpiece, a novel with an almost flawless structure, unforgettable characters, a powerful yet menacing setting, and a masterful voice that unites these other narrative elements to create a seamless, artistic whole. And while the book explores the Ingalls family's struggle to fight off starvation and cold, it also gives new depth and resonance to themes Wilder believed were essential to the Little House books: Laura's evolving maturity, the cruel indifference of the natural world, the unflinching courage of some pioneers and the mindlessness of others, and ultimately their dependence on one another to survive.

Reading *The Long Winter* now, the book feels effortless. Like E. B. White's *Charlotte's Web, The Long Winter* has the rhythm, the perfect pitch of a classic. And yet for Wilder, writing the book proved to be an extremely challenging process. She observed that "it is rather a dark picture, not so much sweetness and light as the other books."[4] And Wilder confessed to George Bye that "it has been rather trying, living it all over again as I did in the writing of it, and I am glad it is finished."[5]

WILDER NOT ONLY FOUND IT TRYING TO RELIVE "THE HARD Winter"—the book's working title—she found it technically challenging to write.[6] In *By the Shores of Silver Lake*, Wilder had taken a groundbreaking creative leap: writing for the yet unrecognized young adult audience. When her thoughts turned to writing the next Little House book in 1938, she didn't yet know if her creative gamble had paid off, but she remained committed to her new audience. *The Long Winter* would continue to explore young adult themes through Laura's eyes. But the book would be unlike any of the previous Little House books. Its central conflict would be survival. Would Laura and her family outlast the Hard Winter before they ran out of food and fuel?

With such a grim theme, setting, and situation, Wilder grappled with issues of craft as never before. How would she build a dynamic plot to sustain reader interest? How could she introduce new characters to Laura's world when Laura herself would be a prisoner in her own home for much of the novel? How would she illustrate Laura's maturing character in such a claustrophobic, existential setting? And what about the novel's voice? How could Wilder possibly convey the fear and terror of that relentless winter? And yet *The Long Winter* is her most seamless novel. All the essential elements of craft form one solid piece of imaginative iron. For Wilder, this process began with two essential elements: plot and character.

The Necessary Thread

By 1938 Wilder had decided on the subject of her next novel—the Hard Winter of 1880–81—but felt as blocked by its intensity as the railroads had been almost sixty years before, when "storms followed storms so quickly that the railroad track could not be kept open."[7] She wrote Lane: "I can't seem to find a plot, or a pattern as you call it. There seems to be nothing to it only the struggle to live through the winter, until spring comes. This is of course all they did. But is it strong enough, or can it be made strong enough to supply the necessary thread running all through the book." Wilder went on in the letter to outline various plot possibilities for her new novel, but she came back to the same sticking point, unsatisfied with her own preliminary ideas: "But where is the plot in Hard Winter?"[8]

Lane offered several ideas, including a plot that sprang directly from "Pioneer Girl." During the Hard Winter, the real Ingalls family had shared their home in the raw, new town of De Smet with a young couple—George and Maggie Masters—whose families had essentially banished them to Dakota Territory when it became clear the wife's pregnancy predated their marriage. Charles and Caroline Ingalls took the young couple in when no one else would. In fact, Caroline assisted in the birth of Maggie's baby. It was born in the Ingallses' home.[9] Lane recognized that the intrinsic drama in this situation could create a wealth of interesting plot points for her mother's new book.

Wilder agreed that the presence of George and Maggie Masters could add tension and conflict to the novel. She told Lane that "George paid Maggie's board while he was working. Afterward he paid nothing."[10] Furthermore, George refused to help Pa with chores during that long, hard winter. This situation—extra mouths to feed and a freeloader unwilling to share the burden of work—might have tempted other writers, struggling to find the necessary thread through a challenging novel. But Wilder rejected Lane's suggestion. The focus was wrong. The additional characters and the conflict they brought to the story would obscure the novel's survival theme.

Lane offered another idea. If not George and Maggie Masters, why not let Robert and Ella Boast move in with the fictional family for the winter? The Boasts, Lane argued, had been introduced to readers in *By the Shores of Silver Lake*, and they would certainly enliven the plot of this new book. Wilder rejected this suggestion too. With her usual insight into character, she argued that bringing the Boasts into the plot would weaken the novel. The Boasts were generous, hardworking people. Mrs. Boast would not sit idly in a "chair by the fire," and Mr. Boast "would help haul hay and he would help twist it. He would help grind wheat." Wilder concluded, "The point of the situation would be blunted."[11] The fictional family must be alone.

Wilder's instincts were right. By isolating Laura and her family during the Hard Winter, their struggle to survive would be more heroic, more mythic. But their isolation also made finding the necessary thread all the more challenging. Still, Wilder had successfully employed the theme of mythic isolation before—in her first Little House book, *Little House in the Big Woods*. In that novel, Wilder had structured a very loose plot around a year in the life of her characters, whose stories play out against the isolation of the dark, wild, and dangerous Big Woods of Wisconsin. Ultimately, Wilder and Lane realized that this idea—with modification—could also work for *The Long Winter*. It could provide the necessary thread.

A Strategic Beginning

Wilder's initial plan was to plot her new novel around the fictional family's struggle to survive from autumn to spring. "I am beginning Hard Winter as you suggested," Wilder wrote Lane, "with the strangeness of the geese not stopping at the lake."[12] And indeed, readers of *The Long Winter* find just such a passage when Pa tells the family: "Something's queer. Not a goose nor a duck on the lake.

None in the slough. Not one in sight. They are flying high above the clouds, flying fast. I could hear them calling. Caroline, every kind of bird is going south."[13]

But this passage isn't from the novel's first chapter; it appears toward the end of the third. At some point, Wilder recognized that an abbreviated story arc—from fall to spring—shortchanged her survival theme and weakened the mythic atmosphere she envisioned for *The Long Winter.* Instead, Wilder extended the novel's story line, plotting pivotal scenes from summer through the following spring. *The Long Winter* opens in a hay field on a hot summer day:

> The sky was high and quivering with heat over a shimmering prairie. Half-way down to sunset, the sun blazed as hotly as at noon. The wind was scorching hot. . . .
>
> Laura drew up a pailful of water from the well at the edge of the Big Slough. She rinsed the brown jug till it was cool to her hand. Then she filled it with the fresh, cool water, corked it tightly, and started with it to the hayfield.[14]

This opening scene is at once masterful and strategic. Given the book's title—*The Long Winter*—readers immediately sense the contrast between a hot summer day and the long, cold future Laura can't begin to imagine as she takes Pa a jug of cool, fresh water. It's a satisfying and intriguing contrast.

Laura, with Ma's permission, then goes to work the next day in that hot hay field, helping Pa make hay. Wilder emphasizes the heat throughout this chapter, further underscoring the contrast with the novel's title. A hot wind blows under a hot sun as Laura tramples loose hay in the hayrack. She feels the heat keenly. "Her face and her neck were wet with sweat and sweat trickled down her back."[15] Wilder pairs heat with hay, foreshadowing the role the harvested hay will play later in the novel. It is a subtle but brilliant pairing.

Toward the end of the first chapter, Wilder provides the first hint of conflict and lays the foundation for the Hard Winter ahead. Laura finds a muskrat house in the Big Slough, and after examining it Pa makes an unsettling prediction: "We're going to have a long winter." As he explains to Laura, "The colder the winter will be, the thicker the muskrats build the walls of their houses. . . . I never saw a heavier-built muskrats' house than that one." Initially, Laura can't imagine the possibility of "ice and snow and cruel cold," not while the sun is "blazing, burning on her shoulders."[16] Still, Laura wonders why muskrats can sense the coming of a long, hard winter when people can't. Pa's quick reply—"we got to take care of ourselves"—hints at the isolation and challenge that lies ahead for the Ingalls family.[17]

Yet Pa's answer doesn't completely satisfy Laura, and as the chapter ends, she's haunted by a realization that goes to the heart of the novel: "The muskrats had a warm, thick-walled house to keep out the cold and snow," but the claim shanty, where the family plans to spend the winter, is "built of thin boards that had shrunk in the summer heat till the narrow battens hardly covered the wide cracks in the walls. Boards and tar-paper were not very snug shelter against a hard winter."[18] The chapter ends here—with Laura's uneasy realization and deeper understanding of not just the natural world but her family's precarious place in it.

Throughout the rest of the novel, Wilder builds one conflict on top of the next, ratcheting up the tension and suspense, and in the process creates a seamless structure that hinges on dramatic plot points: A rare October blizzard; a warning from a wise Native American man that prompts the Ingalls family to move into town; a sudden blizzard that strikes while Laura, Carrie, and their classmates are at school; a cluster of blizzards that blocks the trains; dwindling supplies of food and fuel; the ultimate threat of starvation and freezing to death. This greatest threat—a threat to the family's existence itself—comes, as it should, toward the end of the book. When readers finally get to the chapter "It Can't Beat Us," it's clear that unless something almost miraculous happens, Laura and her family will die before the Hard Winter loosens its grip. Then something miraculous—and heroic—does happen (more about this in the next chapter).

The novel resolves itself with quick, falling action in the last two chapters as Laura and the family wait for supply trains to arrive and finally celebrate Christmas in May. The novel's closing lines bring the story to a satisfying conclusion: "And as they sang, the fear and suffering of the long winter seemed to rise like a dark cloud and float away on the music. Spring had come. The sun was shining and warm, the winds were soft and the green grass was growing."[19] The fictional family has gone from light into ever-deepening darkness and emerged on the other side—at the end of *The Long Winter*—into springtime and light.

But a masterful plot doesn't necessarily translate to a masterful novel. *The Long Winter*'s imaginative iron extends to its characters—old and new—who move the action forward and give the plot its life. In *Little House in the Big Woods*, Wilder used an ensemble cast of characters, centering on Pa, to set the book's mythic structure in motion. In *The Long Winter*, Laura is at its center, and her deepening awareness and responsibilities as a young adult heighten the tension and ongoing drama as the action unfolds.

Breaking with Convention

In *The Long Winter*, Laura becomes less and less a child and more and more a young woman. Her decision to help Pa make hay in the opening chapter signals this shift. She's eager to embrace new responsibilities. She's also unafraid to break nineteenth-century social conventions. Working in the fields, for example, isn't an accepted role for a young lady, even in the West. As Ma points out, only "foreign women" worked in the fields. "Ma and her girls were Americans, above doing men's work." Still, Ma can't deny that Laura's idea will solve Pa's dilemma; it's the family's only way to "get this haying done" before winter sets in.[20] So Laura works in the fields, shouldering a man's traditional task. She takes pride in this work, though her "arms ached and her back ached and her legs ached" and at night "she ached all over so badly that tears swelled out of her eyes, but she did not tell anyone."[21]

Ultimately, Laura's decision to help Pa harvest the hay also saves their lives. When the trains stop running and the town runs out of coal, Pa hauls the hay he and Laura stacked on the family's claim back into town. That ready supply of hay becomes the family's lifeline. Pa and Laura twist the hay into "hard sticks," which make a "quick, hot fire" against the Hard Winter's cold and dark.[22] Laura's willingness to break established conventions not only deepens her character, it helps keep her family alive throughout *The Long Winter*.

Reasoning as an Adult

Throughout the novel Wilder further showcases Laura's increasing understanding of the adult world and her attempts to navigate it. When a sudden blizzard strikes during the school day, for example, Laura immediately understands the danger and carefully weighs the alternatives—to go or stay behind. The decision is fraught with life-and-death consequences: "It was not safe to leave the schoolhouse and it was not safe to stay there."[23] Yet only Laura appears to realize this. Miss Garland, the schoolteacher, and the rest of Laura's classmates are new to the West. Only Laura and Carrie have seen and survived a prairie blizzard before, and Carrie is too young to act on that knowledge. Laura feels responsible for the safety of the entire school, but before she can act another newcomer to the West, Mr. Foster, stumbles into the schoolhouse and offers to lead everyone to safety.[24] A pair of misguided adults then lead Laura, Carrie, and their classmates into the blinding, beating, whirling snow.

Laura's indecision in the schoolhouse, her inability to speak and tell Miss Garland what to do, allows Wilder to create a more dramatic scene and heightens the ongoing tension in the chapter. It is also a believable representation of a young adult character, torn between her own understanding of the world and adult authority. Despite her hesitation to advise Miss Garland, Laura has assessed the situation in the schoolhouse more responsibly than the adults in this scene. As is often the case in Young Adult literature, adolescent characters frequently understand their worlds better than the adults in their lives.

An Introspective Young Adult

The schoolhouse blizzard chapter illustrates another important turning point in Wilder's depiction of Laura as a young adult protagonist. She becomes more introspective. Throughout *The Long Winter*, Laura contemplates her own identity, her place in an adult world, and her responsibilities to herself and her family. In part, this emphasis on introspection is created by the realities of the Hard Winter itself. As Laura struggles to get herself and Carrie safely home during the schoolhouse blizzard, for example, the storm makes even speech virtually impossible. Laura is forced inside herself as never before: "The winds struck her this way and that. She could not see nor breathe. . . . She tried to think."[25]

Throughout this dramatic chapter, Wilder focuses on Laura's inner turmoil—her sense of overwhelming sibling responsibility balanced against a grim assessment of the consequences if she fails. "If they were lost on the prairie," Laura tells herself as she and her classmates struggle to find their way home, "they would freeze to death. But perhaps they were already lost."[26] Cap Garland, another new character introduced in this pivotal chapter, breaks away from the group and heads off in another direction. Laura is tempted to follow, yet doesn't trust herself enough to break away from Miss Garland and Mr. Foster. Her inner turmoil is excruciating. Has she made the right decision? Are the adults wrong? Is Cap Garland—an impulsive student she barely knows—right?

At this point in the chapter, Laura's thoughts take a darker turn, and Wilder reveals her character's fatalistic frame of mind. Laura remembers what happened to Pa on Plum Creek, when he weathered a three-day blizzard by curling up under a snow bank and surviving on the girls' Christmas candy. Yet Laura has no illusions about her chances—and Carrie's—if they are lost in this "whirling whiteness." No "creek banks" offer shelter on the "bare prairie." Their only hope: to huddle under the snow like sheep lost in a blizzard. "Some of them had lived," she tells herself. "Perhaps people could do that, too."[27]

Laura remains that gritty, persistent character Wilder depicted in *On the Banks of Plum Creek*, the little girl refusing to cry as she clings to the footbridge while the flooded creek surges around her. But in *The Long Winter*, Laura bears the responsibility for her sister's life as well as her own. She looks death squarely in the eye and determines to struggle for life with Carrie for as long as they can.

Fate, of course, intervenes. Laura bumps into the wall of a building, yells for the others "with all her might," and together they make their way down Main Street, using building walls to guide them. Everyone makes it safely home. But Laura is haunted by the randomness of fate, the thought that if she hadn't fallen behind the rest of the group, if she "had been only a few steps nearer the others, they would all have been lost."[28] These are dark but perhaps inevitable thoughts for a teenager, and Wilder doesn't dwell on them—at least, not here. As the chapter ends, Wilder lightens the mood. Surrounded by her family, sipping "hot, sweet, ginger tea," Laura thinks, "This must be a little bit like heaven, where . . . the storm could not touch them."[29]

But as the Hard Winter tightens its grip, Laura begins to understand that even indoors, surrounded by Pa, Ma, Mary, Carrie, and Grace, the storm *can* touch them. The Hard Winter is the most dangerous and relentless threat to the family's existence that Laura has known. She lies awake one night, unable to sleep, her most frightening memories from childhood reawakened by the howling winds of yet another blizzard. Her past weaves itself into the present in a kind of waking nightmare. The wind

> sounded like the pack of wolves howling around the little house on the prairie long ago, when she was small and Pa had carried her in his arms. And there was the deeper howl of the great wolf that she and Carrie had met on the bank of Silver Lake.
>
> She started trembling, when she heard the scream of the panther in the creek bed, in Indian territory. . . . Now she heard the Indian war whoops when the Indians were dancing their war dances through the horrible nights by the Verdigris river.
>
> The war whoops died away. . . . But she knew she heard only the voices of the blizzard winds. She pulled the bedcovers over her head and covered her eyes tightly to shut out the sounds, but still she heard them.[30]

Laura can't escape this adversary. Because she is older, because she understands more of the adult world than she did as a little girl in "Indian territory," she realizes her family is powerless against such a relentless force. When she learns the blizzards have overpowered even the railroad and trains won't run again until spring, Laura mentally takes stock of the family's dwindling supplies: "There was half a bushel of wheat that they could grind to make flour, and there were the few potatoes, but nothing more to eat until the train came. The wheat and the potatoes were not enough."[31]

Much of *The Long Winter* centers on such moments of stark introspection. They signal Laura's maturity, her ability to think independently, to see beyond Ma and Pa's attempts to screen their children from what appears to be the inevitable outcome of this long, hard winter. In one of the novel's most memorable passages, Wilder describes a new fear that has seized Laura's imagination as one blizzard after another strikes home:

> She lay still and small in the dark, and all around her the black darkness of night, that had always been restful and kind to her, was now a horror. . . . "I am not afraid of the dark," she said to herself over and over, but she felt that the dark would catch her with claws and teeth if it could hear her move or breathe. Inside the walls, under the roof where the nails were clumps of frost, even under the covers where she huddled, the dark was crouched and listening.

It is not just the dark that Laura fears; it is the darkness of hunger and cold, the darkness of death, waiting to catch her with claws and teeth. It waits not only for Laura but for the whole family. And although "daytimes were not so bad as the nights," because the dark is "thinner then," Laura knows that even Pa, for all his courage and all his knowledge of the natural world, can't vanquish the dark as it crouches and listens and waits.[32]

A Waning Influence

Wilder deepens her depiction of Laura's new maturity by diminishing the influence Pa has over her. Throughout *The Long Winter*, Wilder presents Pa as a more vulnerable, less invincible character—and usually this characterization appears directly through Laura's eyes. Pa remains courageous and inventive, hauling hay for fuel between blizzards, shoveling out the railroad tracks at Volga fifty miles away, and talking down a price-gouging merchant when the townspeople are starving (more about this scene later). But for the first time in the Little House books, Laura recognizes Pa's limitations, even his frailties: "He was hungry. His eyes looked eagerly at the brown bread and the steaming potatoes when he came [inside] from struggling along . . . in the storm."[33]

Toward the end of the novel, Pa reaches a breaking point as another blizzard strikes: He shakes his fist at the northwest and shouts, "Howl! Blast you! howl! We're all here safe! You can't get at us! You've tried all winter but we'll beat you yet. We'll be right here when spring comes!" When he regains his composure, Pa looks down at his hands, "cracked and stiffened" from twisting hay for hours every day in the freezing lean-to. He tells the family, "I wouldn't mind so much if I could only play the fiddle." "In all the hard times before," Laura thinks, "Pa had made music for them all. Now no one could make music for him."[34]

This scene is also a turning point for Laura. She feels compelled "to do something" for Pa, to ease his suffering. She begins to sing the "Song of the Freed Men," and eventually the whole family joins in. The lyrics are rousing, full of hope: "We're all here, we're all here / Do thy-self-a no harm."[35] In that moment, Laura reverses roles with Pa. She lifts the family's spirits and provides them with at least a temporary path out of darkness and despair. As the scene ends, "the storm raged outside, screaming and hammering at walls and window, but they were safely sheltered . . . in the warmth of the hay fire [and] went on singing."[36] Laura has taken responsibility not just for Pa but for the entire family, and in so doing, she is beginning to outgrow him. Pa's influence over Laura's thoughts, actions, and emotions begins to wane. His role as her mentor is fading.

This relationship between a young protagonist and her mentor is yet another characteristic of Young Adult fiction. In order to grow and change in coming-of-age novels, adolescent main characters have to ultimately face their futures alone, working through the challenges and conflicts that come their way. Laura begins this inevitable journey toward independence in *The Long Winter*.

Wilder further emphasizes Pa's diminished role in Laura's life by introducing two male characters whose courage and heroism assume mythic proportions. One of these characters is so important that Wilder not only gives him a starring role but relays crucial scenes in the novel from his point-of-view. On the surface, this switch in point-of-view might appear to weaken Laura's position as the book's strong and often fierce protagonist. But the male characters underscore her transition from child to young woman. Laura is going on fourteen when *The Long Winter* opens, a time when, realistically, she would begin to have a growing awareness of the opposite sex and the physical changes in her own body. What better way to showcase Laura's evolving maturity than through new friendships with young men?

A Smart Boy

Laura meets Cap Garland on the first day of school, and he immediately captures her attention. She admires the way he leaps to catch a ball midair. Cap is "tall and quick," moving as "beautifully as a cat." His hair is "sun-bleached almost white." He has blue eyes, and when he sees Laura, "a flashing grin lighted up his whole face and he threw the ball to her."[37] Instinctively, Laura makes "a running leap" and catches the ball. Most of the boys in the schoolyard complain, "Girls don't play ball," but Cap admires Laura's athleticism. "She's as good as any of us!" he shouts.[38] The two form an immediate bond.

Cap's role in *The Long Winter* is so important that the chapter devoted to the schoolhouse blizzard is titled "Cap Garland." As Pa reveals at the end of that chapter, Cap had found his way to Fuller's Hardware Store and raised the alarm. Thanks to Cap, Pa is armed with winter gear and ready to launch a search for the girls when Laura and Carrie return home. He's "a smart boy," Pa says, implying that Cap's a worthy acquaintance for Laura.[39]

As If He Had Known Her

The other heroic young man in *The Long Winter* first appears in the book's second chapter, when Laura and Carrie are lost in the Big Slough. The girls come across a "strange wagon," its rack piled high with "an enormous load of hay." There, they find a "strange man" and a boy. Laura notices the boy right away. He's lying on his stomach with "his chin on his hands and his feet in the air," high atop that load of hay. He has "black hair and blue eyes and his face and his arms were sunburned brown."[40]

The boy calls down to Laura, and intuitively seems to know

who she is. His gaze makes her uncomfortable, so much so that she wants to "turn and run back into hiding" in the Big Slough. But Laura holds her ground and as the boy continues to look at her, she realizes who he is—by the horses hitched to the wagon: "She had seen those beautiful brown horses before, their haunches gleaming in the sun and the black manes glossy on their glossy necks. They were the Wilder boys' horses. The man and the boy must be the Wilder brothers." The boy directs Laura to where Pa is cutting hay in the Big Slough, but "his blue eyes twinkled down at her as if he had known her a long time."[41]

Their meeting seems fated, auspicious. The boy, in a careless, off-hand way, saves Laura and Carrie from the fate of "the children near Brookings, lost in the prairie grass."[42] But Wilder hints that there's something more, something deeper yet to be explored between Laura and this boy. He looks at her as if he had known her a long time. Something undefinable, something intangible binds Laura to this boy.

There's also an undercurrent of sensuality in the scene—the boy, lying on his stomach on top of a load of hay, his dark hair, his sunburned arms. And then—the horses. Those beautiful brown creatures with their gleaming haunches and glossy black manes. Throughout the rest of the Little House series, Laura's impressions of the Wilder boy—Manzo, as he's identified in this scene—are bound up with his horsemanship and all it represents: his physicality, his daring, his skill, his strength.

In *By the Shores of Silver Lake*, Laura's ride on the black pony signals her independence from parental constraints. But the scene also reveals an undercurrent of physical awareness and sensuality, something new in Laura's life. When the pony breaks into a run, "everything" smooths "into the smoothest rippling motion. This motion went through the pony and through Laura and kept them sailing over waves in rushing air. . . . She and the pony were going too fast but they were going like music."[43] It isn't surprising, then, that in *The Long Winter* Laura finds the Wilder boy's association with horses—and its fascinating but dangerous implications—more unsettling than Cap Garland's catlike athleticism. But Wilder doesn't linger on Laura's intriguing first meeting with the Wilder boy in *The Long Winter*. After Laura observes that his blue eyes are twinkling down at her in that provoking way, she thanks him "primly" and walks away to find Pa.[44]

Wilder had actually lived this scene. Its bare outlines appear in "Pioneer Girl," including a less dramatic rendering of Almanzo's lingering look. As Wilder and Carrie pass by the Wilder brothers' hay wagon, Almanzo "scrambled out from under the hay and looked at us. . . . I had never seen him before."[45] Yet initially Wilder wasn't sure how to introduce Almanzo's character in *The Long Winter*. She knew readers were eager for that first meeting between Laura and Almanzo. As she wrote Lane, "They all seem wildly interested and want to know how, where and when Laura met Almanzo."[46]

One of her early inclinations for *The Long Winter* was to place both Almanzo and Cap Garland in the schoolhouse blizzard scene. As Wilder explained to Lane, "Laura and Almanzo are to meet when the blizzard closes the school. . . . I don't know how it will work out, but I'm going to have Laura go with Almanzo to town."[47] Wilder, of course, abandoned this idea, and settled on the hayfield episode, a richer and more satisfying alternative. The facts of her life, in this case, made a better story than the fictional scenario she had envisioned.

The hayfield scene could also serve a larger thematic purpose. Bringing the fictional Laura and Almanzo together out on the prairie rather than in town reinforces their connection to the land and to the West. They are young adults working the land for their families and, in the opening chapters of *The Long Winter*, performing the same task: stacking hay. They are already in unison.

Nerve and Muscle

The fictional Laura Ingalls's first glimpse of the Wilder boy, however, isn't in *The Long Winter*. It occurs near the end of *By the Shores of Silver Lake*. In the chapter "Moving Day," Almanzo makes a brief but dramatic appearance along with his beautiful team of Morgans. Laura sees the horses on the open prairie and admires their "flowing black manes and tails" as they trot "side by side in harness." She exclaims, "What beautiful horses!" and watches "them as long as she could." Laura eventually realizes that a young man is driving the wagon the horses are pulling. Pa tells her: "Those are the Wilder boys. . . . Almanzo's driving, and that's his brother Royal with him. They've . . . got the finest horses in this whole country." Wilder ends the scene with a kind of literary wink, almost daring readers to guess Laura's future. "With all her heart Laura wished for such horses. She supposed she would never have them." But with her sun bonnet flying back in the wind, Laura thinks "of riding behind such big fast horses."[48] She does precisely that in the last two Little House books.

In *The Long Winter*, Wilder makes a subtle shift in Laura's perception of Almanzo Wilder. He's no longer the "young man" of *By the Shores of Silver Lake*; he's simply "a boy." Like Laura in *The Long Winter*, he's a teenager, a nineteen-year-old eager to take on the responsibilities of an adult. Yet when Wilder first met Almanzo in 1880, he was twenty-three. She was thirteen.

Why did Wilder recast Almanzo as a teenager on the brink of manhood in *The Long Winter*? No editorial correspondence remains to explain her decision, but perhaps she worried the ten-year age difference in her principal characters might alienate some readers—or perhaps even her editor at Harper & Brothers. But Wilder also uses Almanzo's fictional age as a way to define his character and his commitment to homesteading in the West. In *The Long Winter*, Almanzo's age is "a secret because he had taken a homestead claim, and according to the law, a man must be twenty-one years old to do that." Wilder tells readers that Almanzo doesn't "consider" that he's breaking the law; instead, he's simply ambitious and self-confident. He has decided that since "the Government wanted this land settled," then it should be willing to "give a farm to any man who had the nerve and muscle to come out here and break the sod and stick to the job till it was done."[49] The fictional Almanzo's youthful ambition and determination to make good on a homestead claim underscore his courage and heroism. It also makes him a more appealing character for young adult readers. He's willing to break meaningless rules. He's a bit of a rebel, as unconventional in his own way as Laura is in hers.

Like Cap, Almanzo is respected by other men in De Smet, including Pa. In a memorable scene that unfolds in Harthorn's store, Almanzo is part of a group of men who have gathered there to share news and conduct business. Wilder herself is also conducting a little business in this chapter, shifting point-of-view away from

Laura and giving readers a glimpse into the masculine world that Pa and Almanzo inhabit. In this scene, a Native American man enters the store and makes an ominous prediction about the coming winter. Pa, Royal, and Almanzo take the warning seriously. They unanimously decide to move into town for the winter from their homestead claims. The scene adds tension and mystery to the novel, as well as confirming Almanzo's acquaintance with Pa and the other men in town. Almanzo is part of their circle.

But the chapter does something more. Wilder writes virtually the entire "Indian Warning" chapter in third-person objective, a detached voice reporting on the scene directly as it unfolds. The action centers entirely on the men in the store but doesn't linger on their thoughts or emotions: "One afternoon a little crowd of men gathered in Harthorn's store in town. The trains, which had been stopped by the blizzard, were running again, and men had come in to town from their claims to buy some groceries and hear the news."[50] Laura is completely absent from the unfolding action, and Wilder doesn't return to her point-of-view until briefly at the chapter's end. Why make this dramatic shift? Why is this writerly piece of business important?

The chapter functions as a transitional scene. Its new perspective prepares readers for an even bigger shift in point-of-view later in the novel, one that centers entirely on Almanzo and signals the central role he will assume throughout the rest of the Little House series. But this shift in point-of-view also showcases how Wilder moves her characters into new emotional territory and simultaneously plunges readers directly into the danger, despair, and desperation that form the imaginative iron of *The Long Winter*. As we'll see in the next chapter, the novel's artistry and experimentation are unique to Wilder's Little House books.

14. Wilder's writing desk in her tiny office in the farmhouse at Rocky Ridge Farm. Photo by Dan Rowland.

15. Wilder's studio portrait used to publicize her appearance at the Detroit Book Fair, 1937. Courtesy of Laura Ingalls Wilder Home Association, Mansfield, Missouri.

THE SATURDAY EVENING POST

Founded A°D' 1728 by Benj. Franklin

Volume 210 | 5c. THE COPY | PHILADELPHIA, PA., SEPTEMBER 11, 1937 | $2.00 By Subscription (52 issues) | Number 11

The Cutter Stopped by the Kitchen Door and Jenny Tried to Get Out of It. She Fell, But Her Mother Ran to Her

HOME OVER SATURDAY

By ROSE WILDER LANE

JENNY would not be sixteen years old until December, but old Claus Oleson did not know that. He set out from Lone Tree at dawn, and through the white-hot August day, while his oxen trudged the twenty miles to Horace, he thought about the young ladies there. Old Claus always took time to make up his mind, and his judgment was good. In his part of the country it had more force than the law.

He camped by the lumberyard that night, and next morning, in his belted blouse and boots, he tramped into Judge Boles' general store and offered to give Jenny the fall term of Lone Tree district school. It was a four months' term, paying fifteen dollars a month and found.

Jenny's father knew what he should say, but the words stuck in his throat. He set a foot on a nail keg and leaned on his knee, tugging at his beard.

The men of Horace showed what they thought of him when they re-elected him justice of the peace year after year. Jeremiah Boles had been in the Territory before the railroad; he had put up the first building in Horace; he had led in organizing the county and the Congregational church. In the Hard Winter he had done more than anyone else to keep the starving settlers alive. He was a hard worker; he farmed his homestead, he carpentered and butchered and ran the store with his wife's help, and neither of them wasted a cheese-paring. But times were hard. He was barely able to clothe his family for the winter; they would have to burn twisted hay because he could not buy coal. If Jenny earned sixty dollars, he could make out to meet the interest on the homestead mortgage.

He conquered temptation and brought out the fact that Jenny was not sixteen. By law, a teacher must be sixteen years old.

Old Claus Oleson was stopped only for a moment. He had seen Jenny grow up. On last day of school, he had heard her recite the whole of American history, giving every event in proper order and sketching with colored chalks on the blackboard while she talked, so that the whole continent with its mountains and rivers, its battlefields and States and Territories, grew to its great completeness before their eyes.

16. Lane's short story "Home over Saturday," based on an episode in *Pioneer Girl* and published in the *Saturday Evening Post*. Herbert Hoover Presidential Library.

17. Ursula Nordstrom, Laura Ingalls Wilder's final editor at Harper & Brothers. Used by permission of HarperCollins Publishers.

18. *By the Shores of Silver Lake*, Wilder's groundbreaking Young Adult novel, 1939. Used by permission of HarperCollins Publishers.

19. Wilder at home with her Little House books, 1949. © Springfield Leader and Press—USA TODAY NETWORK.

20. Wilder and Almanzo (on the porch) at their Rocky Ridge farmhouse, possibly the last photograph of Almanzo before his death, May 1949. © Springfield Leader and Press—USA TODAY NETWORK.

21. Helen Sewell and Mildred Boyle's depiction of the old Native American man in *The Long Winter*, 1940. Used by permission of HarperCollins Publishers.

22. Garth Williams's depiction of the old Native American man in *The Long Winter*, 1953. Used by permission of HarperCollins Publishers.

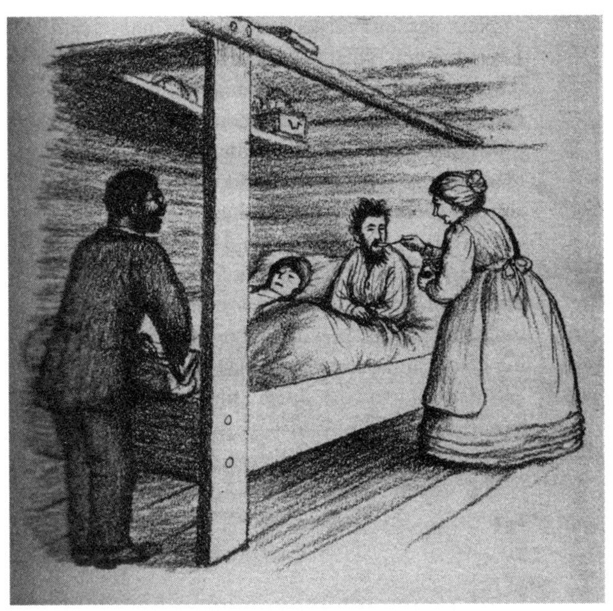

23. Garth Williams's depiction of Dr. Tan in "Fever 'n' Ague" for *Little House on the Prairie*, 1953. Used by permission of HarperCollins Publishers.

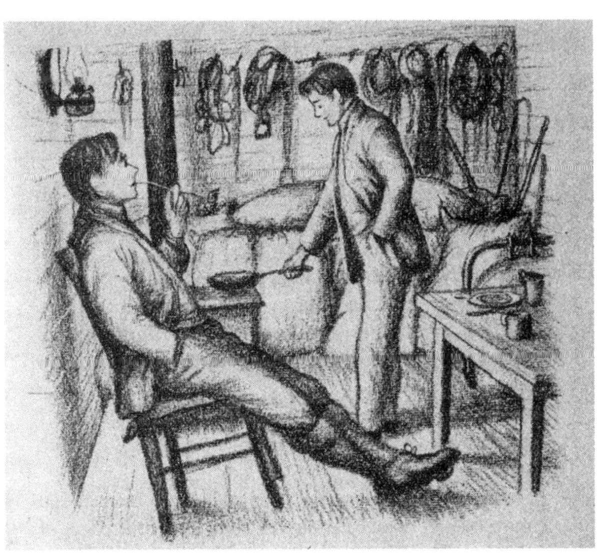

24. Garth Williams's depiction of Almanzo making pancakes in "Three Days Blizzard" for *The Long Winter*, 1953. Used by permission of HarperCollins Publishers.

25. Garth Williams's illustration for the dramatic butcher knife scene in *These Happy Golden Years*. Used by permission of HarperCollins Publishers.

"Just stopped to tell you your wheels are going round," he said and with a wave of his hand toward the barn, he ran to his wagon climbed in and drove on down the road. His face was so black with dust that he looked like a negro and he was gone before they recognized him as the man who had bought the homestead.

[illegible] laughed hysterically. "Your wheels are going around," she said. "What did he mean?"

She and Manly went into the kitchen and looked from the window toward the barn and then they knew.

Between the house and barn, the wagon with the big hayrack on it had been left standing. The wind had lifted it turned it over and it had dropped bottom side up. The wagon rested on the rack underneath leaving [illegible]

in the wind.

There was only a cold bite to eat at noon for no one felt like eating and it was not safe to light a fire.

About one o'clock Laura insisted that she could smell fire and that there was a prairie fire near but no smoke could be seen through the clouds of dust.

The wind always rises with a fire and on the prairie the wind many times is blowing strongly enough to carry flame from the fire and light the grass ahead of the burning so that the fire travels faster than the grass burns.

Once Manly and Peter raced toward a fire trying to save a large haystack that stood between it and them.

They ran their horses heads up to the stack and jumped off just as a blown flame lit the opposite end of the haystack.

Each had a wet grain sack to fight the fire. They scrambled up the stack and slid down the end scraping the fire off and putting it out at the ground after it had been set back a little way from the end of the stack. They [illegible] down each side as a back fire and the main fire raced by and on leaving the haystack with [illegible]

The horses had stood heads against the stack [illegible]

26. Wilder's original manuscript for *The First Four Years*. Herbert Hoover Presidential Library.

27. Laura Ingalls Wilder at Rocky Ridge Farm in 1954, the year the American Library Association awarded her a literary legacy medal created in her honor. Courtesy of Laura Ingalls Wilder Home Association, Mansfield, Missouri.

11

The Long Winter, Part Two

A Sustained Artistic Force

IN 1932, EIGHT YEARS BEFORE *THE LONG WINTER* WAS PUBlished, Rose Wilder Lane sent her agent George Bye a synopsis for a new novel she proposed to write. Its working title was "The Hard Winter." She told Bye, "There was a lot of fun through it all. Everybody starved but nobody died."[1]

Lane's project didn't go anywhere, and by the time she chose to write about the Hard Winter of 1880–81 in her novel *Free Land*, she had tempered her approach to the subject somewhat. After her main characters experience a swift series of fall blizzards, Lane interrupts her action to tell readers: "That was the beginning of the Hard Winter. No such weather has been known since then. At the time, men spoke as if that country intended to drive out or kill the settlers who had come into it. They never felt that the blizzard quit. It paused only to gather strength for greater violence."[2] Lane's phrasing in *Free Land* is reminiscent of Wilder's description of the Hard Winter in "Pioneer Girl," but even so, Wilder's phrasing is more immediate, more personal. She describes the Hard Winter as "a malignant power of destruction . . . wreaking havoc as long as possible, then pausing for breath to go on with the work. Or as Pa forcibly put it, 'The blizzard just let go to spit on its hands.'"[3] For Wilder, the Hard Winter was a tangible adversary, a force with a character all its own, a villain who spit on his hands and then, with relish, plunged back into his villainous work.

In *The Long Winter*, Wilder takes this personification to a new level. One blizzard after another becomes simply one Blizzard, one sweeping, giant storm with powers of wind, cold, snow, and even darkness, intent on scouring out life itself. The Blizzard becomes not just Laura's adversary but everyone's. It inspires nobility and heroism in some of Wilder's characters, incompetence, greed, fear, and frustration in others.

Lane initially felt her mother's approach to *The Long Winter* lacked emotional resonance and drama. Wilder defended her characterization as being more emotionally true to the period and to her characters themselves. "You know," she explained to Lane, "a person can not live at a high pitch of emotion. The feelings become dulled by a natural unconscious effort at self-preservation." Wilder called this "the stoicism of the people."[4] Lane eventually agreed with her mother's approach in *The Long Winter*, a restrained approach that integrates setting, character, and voice and in the process strengthens the novel's imaginative iron.

Wilder herself recognized that the novel painted "rather a dark picture, not so much sweetness and light as the other books," something that must have troubled Harper & Brothers.[5] It troubled them enough that they changed the novel's working title from "The Hard Winter" to *The Long Winter*, and they chose a cozy illustration for the dust jacket of the Ingalls family gathered around a glowing stove as Pa played his fiddle. By this time Lane was convinced that Wilder's depiction was both realistic and forceful. She wrote George Bye, "My mother has written a book about the Hard Winter, and I think an attempt to conceal that fact from the book's reader is worse than futile. . . . My god, if THE HARD WINTER as a title is too depressing, what is the book?"[6]

TO ACHIEVE THE SWEEPING, RELENTLESS, AND EXISTENTIAL force Wilder envisioned for *The Long Winter*, she made a striking creative decision: Laura's experiences and impressions of the Hard Winter weren't enough. The narrative field of vision had to be bigger, more expansive, more inclusive. Readers needed to experience the Hard Winter through other characters and other voices to fully comprehend all that was at stake for Laura, her family, and "the lost and lonely houses, each one alone and blind and cowering in the fury of the storm."[7] These additional voices, including the storm's itself, intensify the novel's impact and heighten its artistry.

A Cinematic Transition

Ten chapters into *The Long Winter*, Wilder takes the novel in its new direction. As the Ingalls family settles in to endure a three days' blizzard, Laura breathes on the icy front room window to form a peephole, hoping for a glimpse of the town. Instead, she sees nothing but blank, swirling snow. She can't even see across the street to Fuller's Hardware, "where Pa had gone to sit by the stove and talk with the other men."[8]

In the next paragraph, the chapter makes a sudden and cinematic transition—away from Laura and her family and into the back room of Royal Wilder's feed store several storefronts away. It's as if a movie camera is pulling away from Laura, giving viewers—readers actually—a sweeping view through the blizzard and up the street, then pivoting and moving inside a different home for a glimpse into the lives of a different pioneer family: "Up the street, past Couse's Hardware store and the Beardsley Hotel and Barker's grocery, Royal Wilder's feed store was dark and cold. But the back room, where he and Almanzo were batching, was warm and cosy and Almanzo was frying pancakes."[9] The rest of the chapter unfolds from Almanzo's point-of-view, providing insights into his age, character, and aspirations. This is where Wilder presents Almanzo's backstory, at once updating established Little House readers with what's happened to Almanzo since they first met him in *Farmer Boy* and introducing new readers to his character.

But this shift signals something more strategic. It allows Wilder to introduce not just Almanzo but a cast of secondary male characters who advance the novel's plot, reinforce its themes, and illustrate the destructive power of the Hard Winter itself. In fact, the Hard Winter becomes a central character in the novel, a powerful, menacing antagonist that drives the story's action, threatening and transforming its characters. *The Long Winter* is a sustained artistic force "with wild voices and an unnatural light of its own."[10]

His Own Man

As Wilder's literary camera zooms in on the back room in Royal Wilder's feed store in the chapter "Three Days' Blizzard," it settles on an unconventional scene in a frontier novel: a young man—Almanzo—making pancakes. He is unapologetic about taking on traditional women's work. Since he and Royal "had come West to take up homestead claims, they had to cook or starve." Readers learn his pancakes are even better than their mother's, light and fluffy with plenty of molasses. Sure of himself, unafraid of stereotypes, Almanzo is his own man. He is "handy at anything."[11] As we've already seen, these qualities make him worthy of Laura, who is equally unafraid of stereotypes and handy at almost anything.

Wilder's shift in point-of-view, however, does much more than reintroduce an older and unconventional Almanzo Wilder to Little House readers. It showcases the artistry she brings to *The Long Winter*. The scene in the feed store, and later chapters when she again shifts point-of-view from Laura to Almanzo, illustrate her mastery of details and how she uses them to at once advance the plot and reveal essential qualities about her characters. In the chapter titled "Seed Wheat," Wilder returns to the back room in the feed store. This time Almanzo is making a false wall to hide and protect his precious seed wheat, which he hopes to plant on his homestead claim in the spring:

> He had taken saddles, harness, and clothes from the end wall and piled them on the bed. He had pushed the table against the cupboard and in the cleared space he had set a chair for a sawhorse.
>
> He had set a frame of two-by-fours a foot from the end wall. Now he was sawing boards one by one and nailing them to the frame. The rasping of the saw and the hammering were hardly louder than the blizzard's noise.[12]

Saddles and harnesses. The sawhorse. A frame of two-by-fours. But it's not just the visual details that bring this masculine scene to life, it's also the *sounds*—the rasping and hammering—which Wilder links to the underlying tension that pulses through the entire novel: the storm's relentless and shrieking winds. A paragraph later, there's a satisfying payoff to all these details as Almanzo hoists a "one-hundred twenty-five-pound sack" of seed wheat and pours it behind the false wall he's just constructed.[13] These details reveal Almanzo's strength and inventiveness.

The scene's mastery extends to Almanzo's and Royal's dialogue.

Their vocabulary and the rhythm of their speech are different from Laura's or even Pa's and radically different from Mary's or Ma's. Their dialogue is rougher around the edges, tougher, more masculine:

> "I figure she'll hold it all," he [Almanzo] said to Royal who sat whittling by the stove. "When I build all the way up so the bin won't show."
>
> "It's your funeral," said Royal. "It's your wheat."
>
> "You bet your life it's my wheat!" Almanzo replied. "And it's going into my ground, come spring."[14]

Almanzo's voice—and Royal's—are distinctive. The two young men emerge as strong-willed and capable characters with their own stories to tell, their own unique roles to play in the novel.

But Wilder's focus on the Wilders—and Almanzo, in particular—fulfills another creative objective in *The Long Winter*. She uses his perspective to give readers a more direct and disinterested portrait of the Ingalls family's struggle for survival. Wilder wrote Lane that during the Hard Winter, "we were shorter of food than any one."[15] But within the context of the novel, the fictional family—and certainly Laura herself, confined indoors for most of the winter—couldn't have known this. Nor would she have recognized the gradual physical toll their lack of food has exacted on them. But Almanzo would. He's an outsider, who sees Pa sporadically throughout the winter. From Almanzo we get a brief but riveting description of Pa, a description Laura's character could not have credibly delivered. Almanzo tells Royal, "I think there's folks in this town that are starving. . . . Take Ingalls, there's six in his family. You notice his eyes and how thin he was?"[16]

Almanzo is haunted by the desperation he sees in Charles Ingalls's eyes, and it triggers the heroic climax of the book, action that will conclusively establish Almanzo's generosity and heroism. In one masterful stroke, Wilder integrates character with plot but also simultaneously paints a vivid portrait of the Ingalls family's suffering. Her spotlight on Almanzo doesn't exclude Laura and her family. Instead, it expands and illuminates it.

A New, Masculine World

The same is true of the less admirable characters Wilder introduces in this new masculine world of *The Long Winter*. They don't entirely shift focus away from Laura and her family. Instead, they expand readers' vision of Laura's world, and provide contrast to the more noble qualities embraced by the Ingalls family. Mr. Foster, as we've already seen, is inept, an inexperienced and overconfident pioneer who almost costs Laura, Carrie, and their classmates their lives during the schoolhouse blizzard. He returns later in the novel and fires too soon into a herd of antelope, scattering the herd and costing the town a much-needed supply of venison. He also nearly costs Almanzo his beautiful Morgan mare, loaned to Mr. Foster for the hunt. Spooked by her clumsy rider, Lady bolts. Almanzo then sets out across the snowy landscape under a threatening sky to recapture her. Mr. Foster's incompetence in this episode reinforces Almanzo's generosity and foreshadows his heroism toward the end of the book. Mr. Foster isn't simply an extraneous character; he's a strategic one.

So too is Mr. Loftus. As we'll see later, he finances Almanzo and Cap's heroic mission in *The Long Winter*. But he also supports one of Wilder's secondary themes in the book. Although its central theme is survival, focusing on the Ingalls family's singular courage, Wilder returns to an idea she's explored before. While pioneers may aspire to ideas of independence and self-sufficiency, they often need each other to survive. In *The Long Winter*, Pa relies on Almanzo's generosity to sell pailfuls of his seed wheat for twenty-five cents a pail. Without it, the Ingalls family wouldn't have survived the winter. Nor would the family have survived if townspeople hadn't banded together against Mr. Loftus, a price-gouging merchant.

In a dramatic confrontation toward the end of the book, Pa, Almanzo, Cap, and even Mr. Loftus's competitor, Mr. Harthorn, convince Mr. Loftus to sell his wheat at cost. Pa then makes a further suggestion, reinforcing the idea of pioneer interdependence and cooperation on the frontier: "What do you say we all get together and kind of ration it [the wheat] out, on a basis of how much our families need to last through till spring?" The men take Pa's advice, and it "seemed that there was wheat enough to keep every family going for eight to ten weeks."[17]

The scene—and Mr. Loftus's character—bolster additional strategic objectives. Almanzo confirms the price-gouging charges against Mr. Loftus, then suggests that "Mr. Ingalls engineer" the protest, solidifying the friendship and understanding the two men share—and hinting at a deeper connection between them in the future.[18] The episode, written from a third-person objective point-of-view, also gives readers a glimpse of Pa near the end of the Hard Winter, chiseled into a fierce essence by cold and hunger. He is "tall and thin," his face "shrunken to hollows and jutting cheekbones." But his eyes still "glittered bright."[19] When the negotiations with Mr. Loftus succeed, Wilder shifts back to Almanzo's point-of-view and again readers see Pa through Almanzo's eyes, confirming the toll the Hard Winter has exacted. As Pa lifts his two-bushel sack of wheat, "Almanzo noticed the he did not swing it onto his shoulder as a man naturally would. 'That's quite a load to handle,' Almanzo said, and helped him lift and balance it. He would have carried it across the street for him, but a man does not like to admit that he cannot carry a hundred and twenty-five pounds."[20] The moment is at once heartbreaking and tender. Mr. Loftus may be a disreputable character, but his greed gives readers fresh insight into all that Pa has lost during the Hard Winter and all that Almanzo will eventually gain. The scene further signals that Pa's influence over Laura is weakening as Almanzo's is about to increase.

And then there's the railroad superintendent, who appears indirectly in the novel through a colorful story Pa relates. The superintendent, angry that trains aren't running in Dakota Territory because of incessant blizzards, arrives in Tracy, Minnesota, where the line west into Dakota Territory begins. He steps out of his "special [railroad] car" in his "city clothes and his gloves and his fur-lined coat" with orders to clear the tracks of snow. He is from the East, self-assured and overly confident. He tells the railroad crew in Tracy, "I'll show you how to keep those trains running."[21] He fails, of course, in a splendid send-up complete with snow, ice, and steam. Pa explains the superintendent's failure this way: "Well, he's an Easterner. It takes patience and perseverance to contend with things out here in the West."[22]

But the superintendent's failure represents more than the misplaced arrogance of easterners. He is a manifestation of the railroad and its technology, a technology that fails and puts citizens of De Smet—and all the railroad towns along the line—at risk. Even seasoned pioneers like Pa have come to depend upon the railroad, and it has given them all a false sense of security. In *The Long Winter*, the railroad—and modern technology—prove to be no match for the uncontrollable, sweeping power of the West.

The Very Old Indian

Another character in *The Long Winter* also reinforces the idea that civilization and its technologies are no match for the natural forces of the West. The "very old Indian," who appears only in the chapter "Indian Warning," embodies this theme.[23] As we've seen, a group of men has gathered in Harthorn's store, which in itself represents the values and aspirations the settlers have brought with them to the West. The store is stocked with farm supplies and implements, including a plow; groceries such as salt pork; even a cracker barrel. Perhaps more importantly, the store is a news source where men gather to share ideas and information. As the Native American man enters, the store goes suddenly silent. The scene bristles with tension, surprise, and anxiety.

For Wilder, the Native American man represents the untamed West and knowledge that comes from generational experience of living close to the land, knowledge that seems almost intuitive. Her detailed description of the old man takes on a mythic quality, as mythic as the West itself: "His brown face was carved in deep wrinkles and shriveled on the bones, but he stood tall and straight. . . . His eyes were bright and sharp."[24] The man delivers an enigmatic warning, and only Pa exchanges a word with him. When the Indian leaves, the men inside the store are confused, unsure of what the warning means. But Pa, because of his inherent affinity with the West, explains: "The Indian meant that every seventh winter was a hard winter and that at the end of three times seven years came the hardest winter of all. He had come to tell the white men that this coming winter was a twenty-first winter, that there would be seven months of blizzards."[25]

While the men in Harthorn's store aren't quite sure how to respond to the old man's message, it feels ominous. Everyone is "sober" after he leaves, and as we've seen, Pa, Almanzo, and Royal take the old man's message to heart.[26] They decide to move into town for the winter.

To many contemporary readers, this scene may appear as a dated and patronizing portrayal of a Native American man. He speaks in what seems to be a stereotypical, clichéd dialect, using such phrases as "heap big snow," and punctuates his broken English by holding up "four fingers, then three fingers" to indicate seven months of blizzard.[27] But before rushing to condemn Wilder's reliance on what appears now to be "Hollywood Injun English," linguist Beverly Olson Flanigan's warning appears apt: "We have to be careful to distinguish reality from stereotype. . . . Historical novels may represent the language of the past credibly or otherwise."[28]

The scene in *The Long Winter* is semi-autobiographical, drawn from a brief episode in *Pioneer Girl.* Wilder recalled that just after the October blizzard of 1880, "an old Indian passing through town" warned the citizens of De Smet that a "terrible winter was coming" and it would bring "heap big snow."[29] In *The Long Winter*, Wilder fictionalizes the scene, embellishing the old Indian man's warning and placing Pa in the middle of the action. As we've discussed, Wilder had an ear for dialogue and believed that it should reflect a character's background and essential qualities. In this scene, did Wilder resort to stereotypical dialogue or did she depict the old man's warning credibly?

In the twenty-first century, it's difficult to untangle stereotypical Native American dialogue from historical reality, in part because some of the most pervasive stereotypes are rooted in linguistic history. Their origins are embedded in American Indian pidgin English, a subject that is not only complex but layered with cultural and racial implications. Its interpretation by scholars has shifted over the last sixty years, but in its most classic definition, American Indian pidgin is described as a contact language "in which a pidginized variety of English served in contacts between Indians and Whites." This form of communication "was used by both groups in the contact situation" and was "not merely broken

English used by Indians alone." Historical attributions documenting this form of communication date back to the mid-seventeenth century in North America.[30]

Like all languages, American Indian pidgin English evolved. Vocabulary from one Native American nation was borrowed by both whites and Native Americans from different tribal groups, and spread across the continent.[31] So too did a form of literary American Indian pidgin, which began to take shape in the nineteenth century, perhaps most memorably in James Fennimore Cooper's Leatherstocking Tales.[32] Other writers followed suit, and Native American dialogue, sometimes credibly based on American Indian pidgin and sometimes not, found its way into literary and popular works of fiction, dime novels, comics, radio programs, films, and finally television shows. In this context, the idea of a contact language, spoken by whites and Native Americans alike, was lost and Hollywood Injun English took root. In programs like *The Lone Ranger*, for example, Tonto continued to speak pidgin, the Lone Ranger himself did not.

The nineteenth century, however, also produced nonfiction narratives depicting conversations between whites and Native Americans that appear to reinforce the existence of a more or less standardized American Indian pidgin English. One of the most relevant to *The Long Winter* is Fanny Kelly's *Narrative of My Captivity among the Sioux Indians*, published in 1871. The events in Kelly's narrative took place during the spring and summer of 1864, when she was taken captive by "an overwhelming force of hostile Sioux . . . resulting in my capture." Throughout Kelly's account, she reports that her captors communicated with her "partly in words and partly by signs," a description that corresponds to Wilder's depiction of the old Indian man in *The Long Winter*. Kelly's narrative also includes a conversation in which Ottawa, "a war chief of the Ogalalla band of the Sioux nation," uses the word "heap" to convey "very." He introduces himself to Kelly and her party as a "heap good Indian."[33] The old Indian man in *The Long Winter* and *Pioneer Girl* uses "heap" in exactly the same way.[34]

Although the events in Kelly's narrative took place sixteen years before the Hard Winter on which Wilder based her novel, the two works draw from the same linguistic well. They focus on Sioux

(Lakota, Nakota, or Dakota) characters from the same geographic region during a period when Native Americans and whites lived essentially segregated lives in an uneasy and sometimes adversarial coexistence. They relied on a form of pidgin to communicate. In *Observations on the American Indian, 1895–1901*, Hamlin Garland noted that even at the dawn of the twentieth century, Native Americans living on reservations throughout the West still spoke a "Pigen English."[35]

So where does this leave us? Did Wilder build the dialogue of "Indian Warning" from Hollywood Injun English or did she rely on her own memories of American Indian pidgin English? The question is impossible to answer with any certainty in part because she left no notes or correspondence on the subject and in part because she so seamlessly blended fact with fiction throughout the Little House books. Still, if Wilder was influenced by traditions other than her own experiences in the American West, Hollywood probably wasn't one of them.

She wrote the original "Pioneer Girl" episode about the "old Indian passing through town" in 1930 or early 1931, just a few years after the first talking motion pictures were released in the 1920s.[36] Given Wilder's age and her lifestyle in rural Wright County, Missouri, it's unlikely that she was influenced by Hollywood's early depictions of Native American speech. Even when she came to write *The Long Winter* in 1940, her influences would have been grounded in the nineteenth-century literary traditions of Cooper and his contemporaries, not the Hollywood stereotypes most of us bring to the chapter "Indian Warning." Still, these stereotypes have become so pervasive that now in the twenty-first century they dominate our perceptions of Wilder's scene in Hawthorn's store and, for many, color their response to Wilder herself.

Wilder's depiction of the very old Indian in *The Long Winter* illustrates a historical reality that many modern readers may not fully appreciate: that in 1880 very few Dakota, Lakota, or Nakota men of her character's age would have spoken fluent English.[37] During treaty negotiations with the United States throughout the 1870s, for example, Indigenous leaders were usually forced to rely on interpreters, who themselves often had a vested interest in promoting favorable terms for the United States. Language was an enormous barrier. In the late 1890s, Hamlin Garland relied on an interpreter when visiting the Standing Rock Reservation to research the life of Lakota leader Sitting Bull and interview reservation elders who had known him.[38] So despite Wilder's reliance on what appears to us now as Hollywood Injun English, it's clear that she attempted in "Indian Warning" to illustrate this barrier. The two cultures not only don't understand each other; they don't speak the same language. Only Pa, perhaps because of his experience in "Indian territory," understands the Indian's warning.

And perhaps more importantly, Wilder emphasizes Pa's respect for the old man and his insight. She creates an unspoken bond between the two, despite their fundamental cultural differences. Pa not only understands the old man's warning, he acts on it—by moving the family into town. That warning saves the fictional family's lives. They wouldn't otherwise have survived the Hard Winter in their claim shanty out beyond the Big Slough. In his own way, the old man is as heroic as Big Jerry in *By the Shores of Silver Lake*. Both appear at just the right moment, both offer invaluable assistance to Laura and her family, and both ride "away toward the west."[39]

For Daily Bread

Wilder's decisions to shift perspectives in *The Long Winter* and to more directly depict male characters in the novel—both flawed and heroic—also serves a very practical structural purpose: it allows her to drop readers directly into the action of the novel's most suspenseful and climactic chapters, a sequence that, from the beginning, Wilder believed was essential to the novel. As she wrote Lane, "Manly did go after the wheat to feed the town. . . . He got it before everyone went hungry." By writing from Almanzo's point-of-view earlier in *The Long Winter*, and introducing what Wilder felt was his essential "kindness and helpfulness," she lays the narrative foundation for *The Long Winter*'s satisfying climax and resolution.[40] It spans four chapters, including the dramatic "For Daily Bread."

Based on nothing but a vague rumor, Almanzo has enlisted Cap Garland's help to find a homesteader with seed wheat twenty miles south of town. Together they set out with their horses and sleds on a bright, subzero morning across the treacherous, snow-covered Big Slough. As the chapter unfolds, they struggle against the elements, against time, and against distance to find and deliver a load of seed wheat for the starving families of De Smet. Wilder integrates all the creative tools at her disposal—plot, character, dialogue, voice, and point-of-view—to create a masterful chapter.

The stakes couldn't be higher. Once the two young men are out on the open prairie, Almanzo knows "they should turn back," but he doesn't want to return to "the hungry town" with "an empty sled."[41] Cap agrees: "Never give up till you're licked!" The town's need for food demands they risk their very lives. So they continue their quest, searching "the white land from west to east . . . for a wisp of smoke from what might be that homesteader's shanty with its cache of seed wheat."[42]

As shadows deepen, Almanzo and Cap spot a thin trace of smoke in the distance—the homesteader's shanty—and the rumor proves true: the homesteader indeed has plenty of seed wheat. But they face an unexpected challenge. The homesteader—Mr. Anderson—is unmoved by Almanzo's arguments that in town "women and children" must have "something to eat or they'll starve to death."[43] Mr. Anderson's response: "Nobody's responsible for other folks that haven't got enough forethought to take care of themselves."[44]

Again, Wilder's physical descriptions reinforce her characters' actions and dialogue. She chooses a few vivid, telling details to bring the scene to life, without impeding the forward movement of the chapter. Mr. Anderson's hair is long and his "unshaven beard" has grown up to his cheekbones. His shanty is primitive, home to a man without any attachments, except to the land itself: "The one room's low ceiling was made of poles covered with hay and sagging under the weight of snow. The walls were sods."[45]

Dialogue—a business transaction between desperate men—carries the action through the rest of this scene. As Anderson continues to hold out, Almanzo and Cap grasp at one argument after another. Almanzo offers Anderson "eighteen cents a bushel above market price." Anderson refuses. Cap reminds Anderson that farming in Dakota Territory is a risky business. Why turn down a handsome profit now when "hailstorm's liable to hit it, or grasshoppers"? As a last resort, Almanzo offers Anderson forty-three cents a bushel above market price, and lays "a stack of bills on the table." Anderson's greed gets the better of him, and he agrees to sell "around sixty bushels at that price."[46]

Sealing the deal, however, doesn't resolve the chapter, and the tension continues to mount. Almanzo and Cap know Anderson's mind is still "quivering in the balance."[47] So despite his invitation for them to stay the night, they quickly pack the wheat on their sleds and head back to town in the dark and cold.

Will the next blizzard hold off long enough for Almanzo and Cap to haul sixty bushels of wheat and make it safely back to town? As the chapter closes, Wilder once again pits her characters against the malignant power of the West: "Stars shone in the sky overhead and in the south and the east, but low in the north and west the sky was black. And the blackness rose, blotting out the stars above it one by one."[48]

The writing throughout the chapter is spare and vigorous, yet lyrical. Wilder at her best. The rhythm of the dialogue between Almanzo and Cap is fast, clipped, exactly what you'd expect from two young men in a cold, bleak, and potentially deadly environment. As the chapter narrows to its close, they share this exchange, followed by a perfect one-line paragraph:

> "We're in for it, I guess," Cap said.
>
> "We must be nearly there," Almanzo answered . . . and moved on ahead. Cap followed, he and the sled a bulky shadow moving over the dim whiteness of snow.
>
> Before them in the sky, star after star went out as the black cloud rose.[49]

Breathing Spell

Although the chapter "For Daily Bread" belongs to Almanzo and Cap, Wilder frames it with a pair of chapters that center on Laura's perceptions. In "Breathing Spell" Wilder not only lays the foundation for Almanzo and Cap's heroic quest, she reveals its essential hopelessness—through Laura's perspective. Pa comes home from the drugstore with news that "Almanzo Wilder and Cap Garland are going after the wheat south of town." Mr. Loftus has put up the money Almanzo and Cap might need "to buy all [the wheat] that they can haul," a promising development. But it's tempered by the source of the rumor about that homesteader and his wheat: Mr. Foster, the least reliable man in town. Pa tells the family that no one—not even Foster—knows the homesteader's name, how far he lives from town, where his claim might be, or if he actually has any wheat. The entire family knows then that Almanzo's and Cap's lives are at stake and that their quest is virtually impossible. Pa says, "They may make it all right. . . . So long as this clear weather holds." Then he adds, "If they do make it . . . we'll have wheat enough to last us til spring."[50]

Almanzo and Cap are the town's last hope for survival. But this dire reality remains unspoken. Pa trusts his family to read between the lines; Wilder trusts her readers to do the same. The implied consequences are all the more powerful because they're left unsaid. And as the chapter ends, Laura is jolted awake in the night as yet another powerful blizzard strikes the town. She is both fearful and relieved: "The blizzard would let nobody start out tomorrow to look for wheat."[51] When readers turn the page, that blizzard has suddenly subsided, and now Almanzo is awake in the night, about to begin his epic journey. The transition between chapters and between characters is seamless, smooth, and yet suspenseful.

The Last Mile

Wilder makes a similar transition when she returns to Laura's point-of-view from Almanzo's. When readers last glimpse Almanzo and Cap in the chapter "For Daily Bread," their fate remains uncertain: "There was still the neck of Big Slough to cross. . . . They could see only a little way by the paleness of the snow and the faint starshine."[52]

Their fate also remains uncertain for Laura as the chapter "Four Days' Blizzard" opens. Wilder shifts back in time—so that readers relive that day when Almanzo and Cap are out on the open prairie, but this time from Laura's point-of-view: "All day, while Laura turned the coffee mill and twisted hay, she remembered that Cap Garland and the younger Wilder brother were driving across the trackless snow-fields, going in search of wheat to bring to the town." Later when Laura and Mary go outside for a rare breath of fresh air, Laura continues to look to the northwest, "dreading to see the low-lying rim of darkness that was the sure sign of a coming blizzard." Mary feels a cold sense of dread too. She says, "The sunshine is too cold. Do you see the cloud?"[53] Laura responds to Mary's question with another one of her writerly observations, a description that isn't factual but is at once imaginative and true—a storyteller's deeper, more expressive truth:

> "There is no cloud," Laura assured her. "But I don't like the weather. The air feels savage, somehow."
>
> "The air is only air," Mary replied. "You mean it is cold."
>
> "I don't either mean it's cold. I mean it's savage!" Laura snapped.[54]

Wilder's strategy in this chapter, traveling back twenty-four hours in time, heightens the novel's suspense, and intensifies the simultaneous feelings of hope and dread she inspires in her characters—and her readers.

In this heightened state of anxiety for Almanzo, Cap, and the fate of the entire town, Laura sees the Hard Winter as an adversary. It is a savage character—ruthless, merciless, relentless—bent on destruction. Later in this chapter, Laura thinks of the storm "truly like a great beast worrying the house, shaking it, growling and snarling and whining and roaring at the trembling walls that stood against it."[55]

At the end of this chapter, the family runs out of wheat. "This is the last, Charles," Ma tells Pa. And as night falls and the blizzard finally blows itself out, Carrie says, "I hope Cap Garland and young Mr. Wilder are somewhere safe." Laura hopes so too, "but she knew that saying so would not make any difference."[56] Laura's despair sustains the tension into the next chapter, titled "The Last Mile." There, readers finally learn that Almanzo and Cap have survived—and so will the town. In a "whirl of snow," they pull up in front of Mr. Loftus's store and deliver their precious cargo.[57] But Wilder has successfully sustained this heightened level of suspense over four chapters, effectively switching point-of-view to propel the action forward and deepen her depiction of Laura's and Almanzo's characters. Yet the real mastery of these chapters—and the entire novel—is Wilder's all-encompassing voice, which simultaneously captures the unyielding malice of the natural world and her characters' responses to it.

The Wind Was Something Alive

Wilder's account of the Hard Winter covers several pages in *Pioneer Girl*, but she personifies the severe weather—giving it a human quality—in just two lines, where she characterizes it as a "malignant power of destruction" that paused "for breath to go on with its work."[58] In *The Long Winter*, however, Wilder takes this personification to a new level. The Hard Winter itself becomes a character in the novel. "Sometimes in the night, half-awake and cold, Laura half-dreamed that the roof was scoured thin. Horribly the great blizzard, large as the sky, bent over it and scoured with an enormous invisible cloth, round and round on the paper-thin roof, till a hole wore through and squealing, chuckling, laughing a deep Ha! Ha! the blizzard whirled in."[59] In previous Little House books, Wilder depicts the natural world as indifferent, unconcerned with human activity. But in *The Long Winter*, Laura and Pa sense something darker, as if nature itself seems bent on destroying human life. Throughout the novel, Laura suffers from nightmares, images of cold and wind and death, vivid dreams packed with terrifying images: "In the night Laura dreamed that Pa was playing the wild storm-tune on his fiddle and when she screamed to him to stop, the tune was a blinding blizzard swirling around her and it had frozen her to solid ice."[60]

The Hard Winter as a character ultimately moves from Laura's nightmares into her waking dreams: "The storm was always there, outside the wall, waiting, sometimes, then pouncing, shaking the house, roaring, snarling, and screaming in rage."[61] As the novel moves into its darkest and most hopeless scenes—when Laura twists hay or mills the family's dwindling supply of wheat in the coffee grinder—reality *becomes* a waking nightmare:

> In the morning Laura got out of bed into the cold. She dressed downstairs by the fire that Pa had kindled before he went to the stable. They ate their coarse brown bread. Then all day long she and Ma and Mary ground wheat and twisted hay as fast as they

> could. The fire must not go out; it was very cold. They ate some coarse brown bread. Then Laura crawled into the cold bed and shivered until she got warm enough to sleep.
>
> Next morning she got out of bed into the cold. . . . But she did not ever feel awake. She felt beaten by the cold and the storms. She knew she was dull and stupid but she could not wake up.[62]

This dreamlike quality pervades the entire book. Chapter after chapter ends as Laura drifts off to sleep, listening to the wind howl, or worrying about their dwindling supply of food and fuel. In the earlier chapters of *The Long Winter*, this dreamy quality seems almost benign. But in the closing chapters, Wilder depicts a waking nightmare world that is numbing, dull, and disorienting. Even Pa's attempt to read from his big green book sends Laura into a waking nightmare:

> Laura tried to listen but she felt stupid and numb. Pa's voice slid away into the ceaseless noises of the storm. She felt that the blizzard must stop before she could do anything, before she could even listen or think, but it would never stop. It had been blowing forever.
>
> She was tired. She was tired of the cold and the dark, tired of brown bread and potatoes, tired of twisting hay and grinding wheat, filling the stove and washing dishes and making beds and going to sleep and waking up. She was tired of the blizzard winds. There was no tune in them any more, only a confusion of sound beating on her ears.[63]

The trancelike reality through which the fictional Ingalls family moves in *The Long Winter* is unique to this book, and it appears to be a deliberate stylistic device, a technique that brings readers closer to the emotional and physical experiences of starvation and freezing to death. A dreamy, trancelike state is a symptom often associated with both.

This trancelike state affects the whole family, even pragmatists like Ma and Mary. When Laura tells Ma, "I don't know what's the matter with me! I can't think," Ma replies:

"It's this storm. I believe we are all half-asleep. . . . We must stop listening to it."

Everything was very slow. Mary asked after a while, "How can we stop listening to it?"[64]

This dreamlike quality makes the family's experiences more immediate and tangible. It communicates the feelings of cold and hunger in a credible, compelling way. But it also gives *The Long Winter* its creative and narrative strength. *The Long Winter* is Wilder's masterwork, a powerful artistic achievement.

It Can't Beat Us

Wilder ultimately resolves *The Long Winter* with a shift in the natural world itself. Overnight, the Hard Winter gives way to spring: "Sometime in the night Laura heard the wind. It was still blowing furiously but there were no voices, no howls or shrieks in it. . . . She listened as hard as she could. She uncovered her ear to listen and the cold did not bite her cheek. The dark was warmer." Laura recognizes the sound of the spring Chinook wind, and she "blissfully" stretches "out in bed" and puts "both arms on top of the quilts" to luxuriate in the warmer air.[65] This is another masterful touch. Even at the end of *The Long Winter*, the natural world—the West—maintains its control over its inhabitants. Despite Almanzo and Cap's heroism, Laura's endurance, and the Ingalls family's unflinching will to survive, the West continues to shape the novel's action.

It takes weeks for the trains to come through. The tracks are blocked with blown sod and packed snow. Pa works with other men to clear the tracks west of town, where a work train has been stranded for months. When he comes home at the end of the day, his hands shake from fatigue. By then, their supply of Almanzo and Cap's seed wheat flour is almost gone, and Ma parcels out the family's last biscuits—the largest one for Pa, the smallest for Baby Grace. Then finally the trains begin to run again, supplies trickle in, and ultimately Laura and her family celebrate Christmas in May with the arrival by train of their Christmas barrel from the East.

In the remaining Little House books, the natural world continues to exert some control over the lives of Wilder's characters, but its power recedes as the West submits to civilization—more people, more commerce, more culture, more reliable technologies. Its essential wildness remains, but its threat to human life is diminished. Wilder's West is no longer the frontier. It has been tamed. As for Laura, it's clear that at the end of *The Long Winter*, she isn't a child anymore. She's a young woman who has survived a harrowing experience and emerged on the other side transformed. Will she, like the West, submit to the changes ahead? Or will she find new ways to interpret what it means to be a young woman, coming of age in Dakota Territory?

12

Little Town on the Prairie

A Classic Coming-of-Age Novel

IN JUNE 1939 WILDER AND ALMANZO PLANNED TO RETURN to South Dakota and attend Old Settlers Day in De Smet. Three days before their departure, Wilder wrote Lane and outlined their itinerary—a few days in De Smet, followed by a drive west across the state to Keystone in the Black Hills to visit Carrie—now Carrie Swanzey, recently widowed. Wilder was seventy-two, Almanzo eighty-two.[1]

Traveling cross-country by motorcar in the late 1930s was a daunting experience, especially for a pair of senior citizens, and Wilder's thoughts turned to practical matters should something untoward happen along the way. In the same letter, she left Lane with instructions on where to find the key to the safety deposit box, where valuables were stored, and where she'd left her notes for the last Little House book. They were "in a large envelope, marked Pioneer Girl in one of the tills of my old writing desk in the little study off the stairs," Wilder explained. "You could write the last book from them and finish the series if you had to do so."[2]

The "notes" referred to in this letter may have been a five-page outline titled "Prairie Girl." It was written on tablet paper, and loosely divided into fifteen sections or chapters with such headings as "4th of July," "School," "Lyceum on Saturday nights," and "Spring on the Homestead." Beside each heading, Wilder listed the plot points she envisioned for each chapter. She titled the outline's final chapter "One Saturday Night" and specified four plot points: "A long drive. Barnum walks through town for the first time with

Laura driving. Home in the starlight. Manly has the ring." From here, the outline digressed in format and included a descriptive passage for what Wilder then imagined would be the final scene in the Little House series:

> The horses stand quietly, beside the claim shanty, within the hollow square of young cottonwoods. There is no light in the windows but the music of Pa's fiddle floats softly out. Laura's voice joins it singing just above her breath—"In the starlight, in the starlight we will wander gay and free, for there's nothing in the daylight half so dear to you and me"—
>
> "And while we wait," Manly whispered, "I will build us a little house on the tree claim where the trees will shelter it as they grow."
>
> The End

Then Wilder added and circled the phrase "Or words to this effect." At the bottom of the page, she noted, "I am sure this will spread into more chapters as it is written. This is just a tentative draft."[3]

THE OUTLINE FOR WILDER'S LAST LITTLE HOUSE BOOK APPEARS to have grown out of a series of editorial letters she exchanged with Lane in 1938, as Wilder worked on *The Long Winter*. Already her thoughts had turned to chronology—how the fictional Laura's timeline in the final Little House book would correspond to events in her own life. Wilder believed her fictional counterpart's age in this book was essential to its plot since Laura would not only begin to earn her own living teaching school but would accept a proposal of marriage. In March 1938 Wilder wrote Lane, "Let the book end with the engagement . . . I don't know how else to handle the last book for the children will keep track of Laura's age."[4]

That same year, Wilder also strategized about which secondary characters should take the stage for a final appearance in "Prairie Girl." She planned to reintroduce readers to Nellie Oleson, who would become a fictional stand-in for Wilder's real teenage rivals in De Smet, Jennie Masters and Stella Gilbert because "their characters were alike."[5] Wilder also planned to introduce new characters, including her Uncle Tom, who had been among "that first party of white men in the Black Hills." When Lane suggested switching

Uncle Tom for "wild man" Uncle George, who had made a brief appearance in *Little House in the Big Woods*, Wilder reminded her daughter, "Unfortunately, we have used real names in these books and must stick closer to facts than otherwise we would need to do."[6]

The Literary Trail Goes Cold

Wilder returned safely home to Rocky Ridge Farm with Almanzo after their road trip through South Dakota in 1939, but from that point on, "Prairie Girl"'s trail goes cold: no editorial letters survive between Wilder and Lane after that point—none that reveal how "Prairie Girl" became *Little Town on the Prairie*, or how Wilder decided to create two books and not one from her initial five-page outline. Did Wilder and Lane stop communicating about these books? Did Wilder simply entrust her rough manuscripts to Lane's editorial discretion? Had Wilder grown too old, too tired of writing, revising, and making editorial decisions? These questions are impossible to answer with any certainty.

It's possible, of course, that Wilder and Lane's editorial correspondence about the last two books may have been lost or destroyed. As William Anderson observes in *The Selected Letters of Laura Ingalls Wilder*, after Wilder's death in 1957, Lane burned "handfuls of papers" in the farmhouse fireplace at Rocky Ridge Farm. He adds that while "little of the correspondence that Rose sent home after 1939 now survives," her "letters had continued unabated."[7]

By early 1940, when Wilder began writing her final novels in the Little House series, Lane had settled into a two-story farmhouse in Connecticut, which she had purchased in 1938. Wilder remained in the farmhouse at Rocky Ridge. It seems likely that they would have continued to correspond about the last Little House books, given the geographic distance that separated them, as well as the editorial ones. It's also hard to imagine that Wilder would have relinquished editorial control, given the pronounced ideas she'd expressed through the late 1930s about how the series should end. In fact, in 1940 she described her writing process in very active terms: "The way I work is a mixture of remembering, inspiration, and just plain plugging. . . . Sometimes I can't sleep for trying to place the right word in the right place and again I will wake with a perfectly turned phrase in my mind, to be remembered and written down the next day."[8] Still, the existing manuscript for *Little Town on the Prairie* is significantly different from the published version, suggesting that Lane made extensive revisions and additions to the novel, fleshing it out, giving it more structure, and deepening its themes.

Regardless of how *Little Town on the Prairie* came together, it is a classic example of a Young Adult coming-of-age novel. Laura assumes her place in a larger world. She learns to be a citizen in a more civilized, less threatening West. The novel's voice, though more mature, is consistent with the deceptively simple yet lyrical style Wilder perfected in the previous Little House books. Laura remains Laura. Only older. More independent. Contemplating her future—and curious about life beyond her family circle.

In 1940 Ursula Nordstrom became Wilder's editor at Harper & Brothers. After reading the manuscript for *Little Town on the Prairie* for the first time in 1941, she wrote Wilder that the book "seems to me to be absolutely perfect. Sincerely, it is beautiful. When Nellie Oleson came into the school I almost wept with pleasure and anticipation."[9]

An Important Transition

Little Town on the Prairie opens with a question from Pa: "How would you like to work in town, Laura?"[10] This simple question signals another major shift in the fictional Ingalls family's life and in Laura's maturity. Never before had "life in town" appealed to the family—other than offering a place to worship or to educate the girls, or as a refuge from the Hard Winter.

Yet in *Little Town on the Prairie* the archetypal pioneer patriarch—Charles Ingalls—looks toward town as a place of opportunity for the daughter who, like himself, has always had an affinity for the wild, untamed spaces of the West. His question to Laura also signals an important transition in Wilder's scheme for the Little House books. The family, like the West itself, is well on its way to becoming "settled." They have established their home in the West and now must find their places within a newly formed and settled community. As Wilder observed in her Detroit Book Fair speech, "I realized that I had seen and lived it all—the successive phases of the frontier," from the first solitary frontiersmen to the founding of permanent towns. Her Little House novels would be shaped by this transition, moving from the frontier to the "agricultural settlements [that] had taken its place."[11]

For Laura, this evolution—from frontier to community—is entwined with an added complication. She herself is beginning to transition out of adolescence. As *Little Town on the Prairie* opens, she is "going on fifteen years old," facing inevitable new experiences that will lead her away from the relative isolation and protection of her family.[12] Pa's question—"How would you like to work in town?"—immediately brings Laura's situation into sharp focus. She isn't a little girl anymore, and not only must Laura accept more mature responsibilities and challenges, she must find her way in an entirely new and alien setting. The frontier is now a little town, and it will shape the young woman Laura chooses to be. As Laura moves through the book, the town will force her to make new discoveries and new decisions. Along the way, all the standard Young Adult coming-of-age themes will surface: achieving emotional independence from parents and adult authority figures; accepting the physical changes in a maturing, adolescent body; choosing an occupation; developing a personal sense of morality; preparing for sex, marriage, and parenthood; and becoming part of a larger community.

As *Little Town on the Prairie* opens, however, Laura is reluctant to accept change—within herself or in the world around her. She "thought of the town, and of the homestead claim where they were all so busy and happy . . . and she did not want anything changed. She did not want to work in town."[13] Laura prefers to linger on what remains of the familiar frontier—her family's homestead claim—and continue to live life as she always has: out on the open prairie, and within the supportive circle of her family.

Laura's new dilemma unfolds over just a two-page opening chapter titled "Surprise," and it creates instant conflict, another essential characteristic of a coming-of-age novel. It's an unusual opening for a Little House book, but so is what follows: three chapters of flashback, focusing on Laura's contentment with life on the homestead claim and revealing all she'll give up if she accepts Pa's challenge.

A Kind of Under-Rhythm

Wilder's previous Little House books contain very little exposition or background information for readers, even when significant changes have occurred within the Ingalls family between books. In *By the Shores of Silver Lake*, for example, Wilder quickly moves through major transitions in Laura's life since readers last saw her in the previous novel: Mary's illness and blindness, the family's subsequent financial crisis, and the birth of Baby Grace. Wilder relays all this information in the first two pages, and on page three she tells readers that two years have passed.

But in *Little Town on the Prairie*, Wilder takes over thirty pages to deliver Laura's answer to Pa's question in the book's opening line—and all of those pages are flashback. Why does Wilder essentially stop the forward action of this novel to linger on a short slice of Laura's life—the spring and early summer after the Hard Winter? Why so much flashback?

The existing original manuscript for *Little Town on the Prairie* doesn't include this long flashback; instead, an abbreviated section opens with Laura's happiness out on the homestead claim, and closely parallels Wilder's depiction of similar events in *Pioneer Girl*. This suggests that perhaps the flashback structure was Lane's editorial idea. She consistently argued that her mother's central weakness as a novelist was structure. "What you haven't developed," Lane wrote Wilder in 1937, "is structure, a kind of under-rhythm in the whole body of the writing and a 'pointing up' here and there."[14]

The multichapter flashback in *Little Town on the Prairie*—following on the heels of Pa's provocative opening line—certainly provides under-rhythm and pointing up. This structural approach, unique in the Little House series, immediately dramatizes Laura's internal conflict: the pull of childhood against new responsibilities and the contrast between a simple country life and the complex, varied world of life in town. Laura wants "nothing more than just being outdoors," and feels "she never could get enough sunshine soaked into her bones" after the Hard Winter.[15] But she is too old to follow Pa as he plows the prairie sod, playing as Carrie and Grace do "in the fresh, clean-smelling dirt."[16]

Instead, Laura must assume more adult responsibilities—milking Ellen the cow, tending her calf, working in the garden. She embraces her chores wholeheartedly, reveling in the beauty of the West. And yet an undercurrent of tension remains. The West is changing: "People were coming from the East now, to settle all over the prairie. . . . Every few days a wagon went by, driven by strangers."[17] Laura is changing too, although she doesn't yet realize it.

Introspection, Revelation, and Transformation

The novel's flashback structure also serves another purpose: by lingering on Laura's contentment with country life, it slows down the forward action of the novel, and like *The Long Winter*, gives this older, more mature Laura moments of introspection and revelation. These moments will ultimately lead to transformation.

In a pivotal scene with Mary in the novel's second chapter, Laura launches into a struggle that will carry her through the rest of *Little Town on the Prairie*: her quest to understand goodness and embrace it:

> "You used to try all the time to be good," Laura said. "And you always were good. It made me so mad sometimes, I wanted to slap you. But now you are good without even trying."
>
> Mary stopped still. "Oh, Laura, how awful! Do you ever want to slap me now?"
>
> "No, never," Laura answered honestly.
>
> "You honestly don't? You aren't just being gentle to me because I'm blind?"
>
> "No! Really and honestly, no, Mary. I hardly think about your being blind. I—I'm just glad you're my sister. I wish I could be like you. But I guess I never can be," Laura sighed. "I don't know how you can be so good."[18]

This struggle for inner goodness sets the stage for Laura's very adult decision later in the book to set aside her own desires and, instead, teach school to help pay for Mary's college expenses. Laura is moving toward a new and personal sense of duty and morality, a hallmark of coming-of-age novels.

Little Town on the Prairie's flashback chapters reveal transformations within the fictional family as well. Pa buys a plow, plants corn, and begins to transform the claim shanty into a house with three rooms. Laura believes these developments mean "better times" are coming for her family at last.[19] Yet Pa's actions signal another major shift in the final Little House books. From the opening pages of *Little House in the Big Woods*, Laura and Pa have shared a deep bond with wild, untamed spaces. Now Pa introduces Laura to a new experience: life in town.

This shift—away from the beauty and isolation of the open prairie and into a bustling, thriving community—further loosens Pa's mentoring influence over Laura. He becomes essentially a secondary character in this novel. What's interesting here, however, is that Pa's character transitions along with Laura's. The town ultimately shapes them both. Pa evolves from a ground-breaking pioneer to a leading citizen in a prosperous small town. He serves on the school board, is a leader in the church, and helps organize programs for the town's literary society. As *Little Town on the Prairie* opens, he spends much of his time not on the homestead claim but in De Smet, working as a carpenter, laying the foundation for the new church. He works from seven o'clock in the morning until "half past six," earning fifteen dollars a week, a sum that fuels dreams of lasting prosperity for the Ingalls household.[20]

The final chapter in the flashback sequence is titled "The Happy Days," and not surprisingly, during this brief, blissful period of hope and contentment, Laura finds "perfect satisfaction" in every passing day.[21] But as J. R. R. Tolkien observes in *The Hobbit*, "Things that are good to have and days that are good to spend are soon told about and not much to listen to."[22] Without conflict, a novel has nowhere to go, and its characters are unable to grow. So Laura's idyll comes to an abrupt end on the last page, in the last line of that last flashback chapter when Wilder repeats Pa's provocative question that opens the novel: "How would you like to work in town?"[23]

Yet the shadow of conflict Pa's question casts over the flashback chapters in *Little Town on the Prairie* creates narrative tension between Wilder's fictional characters and her readers. They sense that Laura's happiness will soon be shattered, and turn the page to find out what will happen next—will Laura accept Pa's challenge, will she relinquish her perfect satisfaction with life on the prairie and accept adult responsibilities in town? As the flashback chapters end, Laura and the West itself exist in a transient yet pivotal literary moment before civilization transforms them both. Life on the prairie is filled with sweetness and hope, suspended in a kind of timeless certainty: "In all that satisfaction, perhaps the best part was knowing that tomorrow would be today, the same and yet a little different from all other days, as this one had been."[24]

And then *Little Town on the Prairie* really begins. Laura leaves her idyllic country life behind and begins a new and seemingly unwelcome adventure in town, an experience that will forever change and shape her.

Working as a Hired Girl

The first hurdle Laura faces, however, isn't whether she'll accept the job in town. It's whether the job Pa has in mind is appropriate for her. Nineteenth-century employment opportunities for women were limited, and even more so for teenaged girls in booming frontier towns, where the only imaginable job was "working as a hired girl in a hotel."[25] Even before Laura can ask Pa for more details about the job, Ma jumps to this conclusion and objects: "No, Charles, I won't have Laura working out in a hotel among all kinds of strangers." Pa quickly dismisses this idea: "No girl of ours'll do that, not while I'm alive and kicking."[26] He then explains that Laura would work making buttonholes in a new dry goods establishment.

Yet Wilder herself had worked as a hired girl in a hotel among all kinds of strangers, and at a much younger age than her fictional counterpart. Wilder was nine going on ten when she began working at the Masters Hotel in Burr Oak, Iowa, and later she went to work again as a hired girl in a hotel, this time in Walnut Grove, Minnesota. As we've previously discussed, Wilder excluded her real-life experiences as a preteen town girl from the Little House series. They formed, she observed, "a story in itself" and did "not belong in the picture I am making of the [fictional Ingalls] family."[27]

Was Wilder's decision to introduce Laura to town life late in the Little House series a conscious thematic or plot-related decision? It certainly enhances the drama of Laura's experiences in *Little*

Town on the Prairie, and solidifies the book's coming-of-age focus. What is clear, however, is that Laura's childhood in the Little House series is much more sheltered than Wilder's own. It could be that Wilder recognized her young readers themselves led more sheltered lives—even during the Great Depression—than she had. She certainly was conscious of whether the stories she presented in the Little House series were appropriate or "responsible for putting in a book for children."[28] But perhaps more importantly, if Laura had gone to work at nine or ten in the Little House series, it would have revealed Pa's failure to adequately provide for his family—and perhaps that was Wilder's primary concern: to strengthen Pa's character rather than shelter Laura's.

In the context of *Little Town on the Prairie*, Laura's job offer reflects not only her maturity and her desire to help finance Mary's college education, it illustrates the spirit of progress and ingenuity sweeping through town. Pa tells the family that this new dry goods establishment is built around a "new idea," and will serve a valuable and growing market—all those men who "are batching on their claims" and "haven't got womenfolks to do their sewing." The icing on the cake: the owner of this establishment, a Mr. Clancy, even has a sewing machine. Although Laura will do only "hand sewing" for Mr. Clancy, she'll work for a business that employs the latest technology.[29] This detail—the sewing machine—wins even Ma over.

None of these arguments, however, impress Laura. She makes her decision based on details introduced in the flashback chapters: the question of attaining goodness combined with the family's desire to send Mary to the College for the Blind in distant Vinton, Iowa. While working in the garden before Pa arrives with news about Mr. Clancy's offer, Laura looks up at the "snowy piles of huge summer clouds" and feels blessed. She has "so much," while Mary sees "only darkness."[30] Laura vows then that she will "work so hard" at her studies that "surely she could teach school as soon as she was sixteen years old" and apply her earnings to Mary's college fund.[31] When Pa tells Laura how much she'd make working in Mr. Clancy's dry goods establishment—twenty-five cents a day "with a good dinner"—she quickly does the math in her head. Laura concludes that if she's able to work throughout the summer, "she might earn fifteen dollars, maybe even twenty, to help send Mary to college." This is an offer Laura can't refuse. While she doesn't want to give up her satisfying life on the homestead claim and work in town "among strangers," she nevertheless sacrifices her own desires for Mary's welfare and for the family's.[32] This is Laura's first step toward finding goodness.

Yet in making this sacrifice, Laura is simultaneously charting a new and independent course for herself. Throughout the rest of the novel and into the final Little House book, Laura becomes a more autonomous, more worldly young woman. New experiences separate her from her family. Laura even keeps secrets from Pa—starting on that very first day of work in town.

Bringing Home Good Wages

In Mr. Clancy's shop, Laura is exposed to what we now call a dysfunctional family. The "good dinner" she was promised as part of her compensation becomes an ordeal as Mr. and Mrs. Clancy and her mother, Mrs. White, quarrel "at the top of their voices," while eating "heartily." The experience is disorienting, and Laura can't tell "whether Mr. Clancy was quarreling with his wife or her mother, nor whether they were quarreling with him or with each other." Laura only knows that "they seemed so angry that she was afraid they would strike each other."[33]

As for the work itself, it is grueling. Laura bastes one shirt after another, "driving the needle" as fast as her hands can move "along the seams." She sits next to the sewing machine, which makes an enormous racket. Its sound buzzes "in her head."[34] Her shoulders and neck ache. Laura wants "desperately to be somewhere else."[35] Yet when Pa comes to fetch her home, she doesn't reveal the misery of that first day:

> "How did you like your first day of working for pay Half-Pint?" Pa asked her. "You make out all right?"
>
> "I think so," she answered. "Mrs. White spoke well of my buttonholes."[36]

Day after day, Laura continues to work in town, confiding nothing to her family about her misery at Mr. Clancy's establishment, sustained by her hope of helping to send Mary to college, and by the "pleasure" of bringing home "good wages" to Ma every Saturday night.[37] Laura relies more and more on herself and her own instincts to see her through—and relies less and less on her parents.

The town itself begins to transform her. Laura still thinks of the town as a "sore on the beautiful, wild prairie." The town smells of dust and smoke "and a fatty odor of cooking." But the longer she works in town, the more she begins to accept and even enjoy it. The town even sharpens Laura's powers of observation, a necessary skill for a budding writer. She especially enjoys "seeing strangers go by."[38]

After only six weeks, the "spring rush" for handmade shirts ebbs, and Laura's employment ends. She has earned only nine dollars, not nearly enough to make a significant difference in Mary's college fund. And while Laura knows "how good it would be to stay at home again, to help with the housework and do the chores and work in the garden," she comes away from her first job feeling "cast out, and hollow inside."[39] Laura has had her first taste of freedom as a young adult—and longs for more.

Moving in New Directions

That's not to say that Laura's relationship with her family weakens in *Little Town on the Prairie*. It doesn't. But it does move in new directions. Pa's influence, as we've already seen, diminishes. Mary's, on the other hand, increases. Not only does she become a model of goodness for Laura, Mary becomes her soul mate. Both are on the threshold of womanhood; their childhood ties with their parents weaken. So too do their childhood rivalries. Laura and Mary confide in each other, taking long walks together across the open prairie, discussing their futures, their hopes and dreams. They take one last walk on the night before Mary leaves for college, and Laura is so moved that she does something she has rarely done in previous Little House books: she chokes back tears. "Then suddenly," Wilder writes, "they felt as if she [Mary] were going away forever. The years ahead of them were empty and frightening."[40]

After "a minute," Laura clears her throat and resumes her familiar role of being Mary's eyes. She tells her sister, "The sun has gone through the white clouds. It is a huge, pulsing ball of liquid fire. The clouds above it are scarlet and crimson and gold and purple, and the great sweeps of cloud over the whole sky are burning flames." Rather than contradict Laura's dramatic description, as Mary does in previous Little House novels, she says, "It seems to me I can feel their light on my face."[41] Mary accepts Laura's artistry and is moved by it. She is Laura's first appreciative audience and helps set her sister on the path toward discovering her future as a writer.

In *Little Town on the Prairie*, Laura also forms a tighter bond with her sister Carrie, and like her deepening relationship with Mary, it illustrates Laura's quest for goodness—and its limits. Just as she was in *The Long Winter*, Laura is fiercely protective of Carrie, who is "pale and still spindly, and always tired."[42] But in a series of extended scenes in the middle of *Little Town on the Prairie*, Laura's defense of Carrie's vulnerabilities unfolds publicly—in the classroom—and with implications reaching far beyond the two sisters.

Laura is outraged as Miss Wilder, the incompetent new schoolteacher and Almanzo's older sister, sets out to humiliate and persecute Carrie in front of their classmates. As the situation escalates, Laura struggles to control her temper, but how can goodness prevail against an authority figure who is not only unfair but "mean and cruel?"[43] In an unforgettable scene, Laura shoulders Carrie's punishment and allows fury to take complete "possession of her."[44] When Miss Wilder sends both girls home from school—"a punishment worse than whipping with a whip"—Laura continues to defend her sister, this time against Ma and Pa. "They won't blame you, this isn't your fault," Laura tells Carrie. "It's my fault."[45]

As a member of the school board, Pa must publicly side with Miss Wilder. Now Laura is at odds with two authority figures, including one she deeply loves and respects. This is a situation most young readers will recognize, and Wilder never veers from their perspective. Despite a stern warning from Pa, Laura remains unrepentant, and in a revealing passage, she obeys Pa in form only, remaining true to herself and her developing sense of right and wrong. Laura "still felt a burning resentment against Miss Wilder's cruel unfairness to Carrie. She wanted to get even with her. Outside, she was shining clean with good behavior, but she made not the least effort to be truly good on the inside."[46]

The implication here is that achieving goodness is a complicated business. It is not simply a static state of being; it is an ever-changing whirlwind of difficult and sometimes ambiguous choices. Laura discovers that "being good" is governed not simply by resolve, especially when confronted by people who seem completely unmoored from even the most basic definition of goodness. Laura is "dumbfounded," for example, when Miss Wilder tells school board members a blatant lie, blaming Laura "for all the trouble in this school."[47]

In the end, although Laura is gently chastised by both Ma and Pa for the role she has played in the schoolhouse trouble, her loyalty to Carrie and her opinion of Miss Wilder are vindicated. At the end of the fall term, Miss Wilder gives up teaching and goes east for the winter, never to return to a De Smet classroom. And Laura has remained true to herself. She is a loyal and caring sister, quick-tempered, strong, and fierce. Laura's interpretation of goodness is uniquely her own.

One other family relationship in the novel moves in an entirely new direction: Laura's connection to Ma. Although Laura grows away from her parents in this novel—creating a social life with friends of her own, making plans for a future away from her family—she nevertheless forges a more mature bond with Ma. Laura sometimes playfully, sometimes seriously engages Ma in discussions that revolve around the physical changes that occur in teenage girls and their inevitable new interests: in appearance, in clothes, in boys. Ma understands these things as Pa cannot.

In *Little Town on the Prairie*, readers learn that Laura now wears corsets. Like sunbonnets, Laura's corsets are "a sad affliction to her," but the question of having a good figure brings Laura and Ma closer together—almost.[48] Ma tells Laura she should wear her corsets all night, as Mary does. "What your figure will be, goodness knows," Ma tells Laura. "When I was married, your Pa could span my waist with his two hands." Laura's quick response: "He can't now. . . . And he seems to like you." Ma tells Laura not to be "saucy," and yet both seem to enjoy this playful, new, more adult relationship. Ma's cheeks flush "pink and she could not help smiling."[49]

Perhaps the most poignant scene between Laura and Ma occurs toward the end of *Little Town on the Prairie* when Laura asks Ma about teaching school.

> "How many terms of school did you teach, Ma?"
>
> "Two," said Ma.
>
> "What happened then?" Laura asked.
>
> "I met your Pa," Ma answered.
>
> "Oh," Laura said. Hopefully she thought that she might meet somebody. Maybe, after all, she would not have to be a schoolteacher always.[50]

Even the prospect of marriage doesn't seem as frightening now to Laura as it did when she and Lena discussed the homesteaders' daughter who had married at thirteen in *By the Shores of Silver Lake*. Of course, it isn't just Ma who has dispelled Laura's dread of marriage. The change has come within Laura herself as she embraces the idea of the woman she will become. But Laura's friends have helped with this evolution too. So has her sworn enemy, the "prim and prissy" Nellie Oleson.[51]

Friends and Enemies

On the first day of school, Laura renews her friendships with Mary Power and Minnie Johnson. Laura also befriends the new girl in school—Ida Brown, the adopted daughter of Reverend and Mrs. Brown. These three—Mary, Minnie, and Ida—form the core of Laura's new social circle. When Laura and her family move into town for the winter, the four girls grow even closer. Together, they share in the town's latest teen fads: autograph albums, name cards, and especially fashion, which plays a central role throughout the last two books in the Little House series.

Throughout *Little Town on the Prairie*, Wilder devotes paragraphs describing dresses and hats, buttons and trims, beginning with the best dress Ma makes for Mary before she leaves for college: "It was brown cashmere, lined with brown cambric. Small brown buttons buttoned it down the front and on either side of the buttons and around the bottom Ma had trimmed it with a narrow, shirred strip of brown-and-blue plaid, with red threads and golden threads running through it. A high collar of the plaid was sewed on, and Ma held in her hand a gathered length of white machine-made lace. The lace was to be fitted inside the collar, so that it would fall a little over the top."[52]

To some readers, these lengthy descriptions may seem frivolous. Yet Wilder taps into universal adolescent yearnings, bridging the fashion gap between late nineteenth-century hoop skirts, the pleated skirts and bobby socks her adolescent readers were wearing in the early 1940s, and the unimaginable styles generations of readers would desire in the future. Almost seventy years later, Suzanne Collins tapped into this same young adult preoccupation in the Hunger Games novels, which include detailed descriptions of elaborate Capitol fashions. Fashion is a timeless form of adolescent self-expression, something Wilder clearly understood, and it becomes an important part of Laura's life as she transitions toward womanhood.

In fact, on that first day of school in *Little Town on the Prairie* another new girl catches Laura's eye, and Wilder includes a lengthy description of what she's wearing: "a fawn-colored dress made with a polonaise. Deep pleated ruffles were around the bottom of the skirt, around her neck, and falling from the edges of the wide sleeves. At her throat was a full jabot of lace." The girl in that fashionable fawn-colored dress is Laura's old enemy, Nellie Oleson. But her beautiful clothes don't mask her real nature, and Laura recognizes her immediately: "Nellie's nose was still held high and sniffing, her small eyes were still set close to it, and her mouth was prim and prissy."[53] Nellie quickly bonds with the odious Miss Wilder, who also dresses beautifully, and together they ensnare Laura in the unfolding schoolhouse crisis we've already discussed.

Nellie's schemes, however, aren't limited to the schoolhouse and they ultimately awaken Laura's interest in friendships beyond those with Ida, Mary Power, and Minnie. When a handsome pair of horses pulling a "shining new buggy" drives past the schoolhouse at recess, Minnie observes, "I bet that's what Nellie's scheming about."[54] The driver—a "grown-up man"—raises his hat as he passes by, though Laura, entranced by the horses, doesn't notice. The driver is Almanzo, of course, and Minnie, Mary Power, and Ida seem to realize before Laura does that Nellie is "setting her cap for him."[55]

Laura is horrified—not so much by Nellie's scheme to "get a ride behind" Almanzo's Morgans but by her own realization that she herself has "often thought that if Miss Wilder liked her, she might someday take her riding behind them."[56] Laura's moral superiority evaporates, and the schoolhouse crisis is suddenly bound up not just with an old childhood rivalry but with sexual attraction.

How Could She Prevent Such Thoughts

In *Little Town on the Prairie* and, as we'll see in *These Happy Golden Years*, Wilder uses Almanzo's horses as a metaphor for Laura's sexual awakening. Laura tells Ida, Minnie, and Mary Power that his horses "are just like poetry," and despite her shame at realizing she might be "as horrid as Nellie Oleson," Laura is determined to ride in Almanzo's buggy. "How could she prevent such thoughts, when those horses were so beautiful and the buggy so swift?"[57]

Almanzo, however, isn't the only young man in Laura's growing social circle. Cap Garland returns: "His smile still flashed quick as lightning and warmer than sunshine."[58] Nellie calls him "Cappie," and she smiles "up into his face with a look that Laura had never seen before."[59] When Cap tries to offer Mary Power a piece of candy, Nellie inserts herself between them and takes a piece for herself. Laura realizes she and her friends are caught up in something new—a kind of sexual competition: "Angrily Laura wondered, Must a girl like Nellie be able to grab what she wants? It was not only the candy."[60]

And other young men provide Laura with new adolescent experiences: Minnie's brother Arthur, Fred Gilbert, and Ben Woodworth, who hosts the town's first teen birthday party. His guests—boys and girls together—play drop-the-handkerchief, blind-man's-bluff, and a new game where a "burning tingle" (an electrical charge) flashes through their "clasped hands."[61] Laura and her friends have become a kind of human telegraph wire, united by a "queer" feeling and the wonder not just at this new technology but the "electricity" that jolts through them all, causing the boys to yell and the girls to scream. It's a rare moment of nineteenth-century physical contact between the sexes in the Little House series, and it transforms Ben's guests: "The party had made such a jolly friendliness among the big girls and boys that now at recess and noon on stormy days they gathered around the stove, talking and joking."[62]

But the electricity between Laura and Almanzo remains a primary focus of *Little Town on the Prairie*. In the last half of the book, the two finally have a meaningful conversation as they exchange name cards. He explains the origins of his unusual name and for the first time, Laura really *sees* Almanzo—not just his horses: "His hair was not black, as she had thought. It was dark brown, and his eyes were such a dark blue that they did not look pale in his darkly tanned face. He had a steady, dependable, yet light-hearted look."[63] The name card fad may have finally brought Laura and Almanzo together, but readers sense something deeper has occurred, something transformational. It is Laura's first step toward courtship, a thread that runs through the remainder of *Little Town on the Prairie* and into the final Little House book.

Madcap Days

In *Little Town on the Prairie*, the town itself matures alongside Laura. Despite a spring blizzard that strikes late in the novel, the West is virtually tamed. In fact, the last half of the book focuses almost exclusively on the town and how Laura interacts with it. One community event follows another—from the Ladies' Aid Society sociable to the Friday night "Literaries," which include a variety of programs, "each more exciting than the last."[64] Chapter titles reflect how life has changed for Laura and her family now that the little town is thriving: "The Whirl of Gaiety," "The Birthday Party," "Madcap Days," and "The School Exhibition."

The chapter "Madcap Days," however, contains a scene contemporary readers find not simply disturbing but racist: a blackface minstrel show in which Pa participates. The performance is the culmination of the season's Literaries, a night, as Ma puts it, that comes along "once in a lifetime."[65] Why did Wilder include this episode in the novel? Why didn't her editor at Harper & Brothers suggest cutting it from the manuscript? And does the scene strengthen the charge that Wilder herself was a racist?

Wilder's intention for the scene seems to have been to illustrate how sophisticated and cultured De Smet had become: "The famous minstrel shows in New York surely could not be better than that minstrel show [in De Smet] had been."[66] As difficult as it is for us to accept now, minstrel shows were a popular form of entertainment during the nineteenth and early twentieth centuries, sometimes embraced by otherwise enlightened audiences, including Abraham Lincoln.[67]

In *Pioneer Girl*, Wilder mentions a "vaudavill [*sic*] sketch," which was given "by some men blacked up as negro minstrels." But the "star performer" of this show was Gerald Fuller, not Pa.[68] The real Charles Ingalls apparently wasn't part of the performance. Wilder gives him a starring role in *Little Town on the Prairie*'s fictionalized version to showcase Pa's playfulness, his musicality, and his showmanship. When the minstrel show comes to an end, everyone in the audience is "weak from excitement," and eager to discover who the performers were.[69] Pa's participation puts Laura—and by extension, Wilder's readers—more directly into the scene, which from a creative point-of-view strengthens the episode. From a contemporary perspective, however, it's problematic, disturbing, and offensive.

Should the scene now be stricken from *Little Town on the Prairie*? Certainly the book wouldn't suffer from its absence. It isn't integral to the plot, to Laura's character development, or to the novel's underlying themes. Yet erasing a controversial, racially invested scene from the novel feels dishonest, and censors a disturbing aspect of nineteenth- and early twentieth-century American life: that "a white man blacking up with burnt cork was common in those days," so common, as Jeanine Basinger writes in *The Movie Musical*, such entertainers as Al Jolson and (by extension) many authors and editors "didn't think about whether it was racially offensive or not."[70] From Wilder's perspective, writing in the early 1940s, a blackface minstrel show was not only part of her personal experience, it was part of a larger American experience that extended from New York's theaters in the East to a remote frontier town in the West.

The original version of *Little Town on the Prairie*, published in 1941 and illustrated by Helen Sewell and Mildred Boyle, doesn't include an illustration of this scene, as does the iconic Garth Williams edition, published twelve years later. But the original published version of the novel contains additional lyrics from the song "The Skidmore Guard," which were cut from the 1953 edition with Wilder's approval. Apparently, editor Ursula Nordstrom found those lyrics more racially charged than Williams's illustration and suggested trimming them. Literary perceptions were beginning to change even then.[71]

Still, the question remains: Should *Little Town on the Prairie* be shelved now because of this scene? Or should the scene simply be deleted from the book? When a posthumous Wilder manuscript came to light in 1969, Wilder's editor Ursula Nordstrom resisted the idea of making "judicious" editorial changes. "I think we just better not," she wrote. "I would hate like hell to tamper with this."[72] Rewriting literary works—tampering with them after an author's death—is a form of censorship, which, like racism itself, is dangerous and objectionable. In an essay titled "My Young Mind Was Disturbed by a Book: It Changed My Life," author Viet Thanh Nguyen argues that "by banning books, we also ban difficult dialogues and disagreements, which children are perfectly capable of having and which are crucial to a democracy." He suggests that parents should discuss classic works of literature in context, pointing out elements of racism that make their way into these books. "These are not always easy conversations," he observes. "And perhaps that's the real reason some people want to ban books that raise complicated issues: They implicate and discomfort adults, not the children."[73]

Wilder's Little House books certainly raise complicated issues. And while everything about Wilder's blackface episode in *Little Town on the Prairie* feels wrong, it reflects a period in American history when blackface was culturally accepted, a history children should thoughtfully examine and discuss now. Wilder wanted her readers to be entertained by her Little House books, but she also wanted them to think about the past, to understand it more clearly, and, as she herself put it, "to know what is behind the things they see—what it is that made America as they know it."[74] Perceptions have changed in the eight decades since Wilder wrote *Little Town on the Prairie*, but the book remains relevant, in part because of the weighty, difficult, and meaningful discussions it can inspire.

Politics and Religion

Wilder includes two other significant events in *Little Town on the Prairie* that showcase Laura's growing sense of community and shape her outlook as a young adult: the Fourth of July celebration at the beginning of the novel and the revival meeting at its end. Politics and religion bookend the novel, and though these topics are still virtually off-limits in mainstream Young Adult fiction now, *Little Town on the Prairie* addresses them directly, recognizing their influence on adolescents and how they ultimately come to view the world.

Wilder had always envisioned a Fourth of July chapter for this novel. In fact, it was the first chapter she listed on her outline, which included these very specific plot points:

Reading of Declaration Speeches
Singing "When you hear the first whippoorwill"
Picnic dinner, firecrackers, peanuts
Horse races, footraces, dancing on platform
Lemonade in a barrel, dipped with dipper[75]

Many of these plot points found their way into both the rough draft and the published version of *Little Town on the Prairie*. Yet there are pronounced differences between the two, leading many scholars to suggest that Lane heavily rewrote the "Fourth of July" chapter. As we've discussed, the textual evidence for *Little Town on the Prairie* is incomplete and no editorial correspondence survives. Still, a number of Wilder scholars have interpreted the additions in the published chapter not merely as imaginative elaborations but as Lane's (and by extension, her mother's) attempts to indoctrinate young readers against Franklin Roosevelt's New Deal.[76] In particular, they maintain that the lengthy Fourth of July speech, which appears in the published version but not the novel's rough draft, reflects ideas Lane would later develop in her political treatise, *Discovery of Freedom*. It was published in 1943, and is now regarded as one of the foundational texts of American libertarianism.

In *Little Town on the Prairie*, the Fourth of July speaker tells the audience, "Every man Jack of us [is] a free and independent citizen of God's country, the only country on earth where a man is free and independent." He maintains, "Most of us are out here trying to pull ourselves up by our own boot straps" and will fight "the despots of Europe" any time they "try to step on America's toes."[77] Biographer William Holtz skirts the libertarian indoctrination issue but argues both that Lane wrote the Fourth of July speech in

Little Town on the Prairie and that it raises "Laura to her moment of political illumination."[78]

Yet the lengthy quotations from the Declaration of Independence and the published version of the "Fourth of July" speech bring the chapter's unfolding action to a dead stop. From a creative point-of-view, they weaken the chapter—at least for young readers. *Little Town on the Prairie* was the first Little House book I read, and as a ten-year-old I skipped over those pages devoted to the Declaration of Independence and the speech about the despots of Europe. I was eager to get back to Laura—and the lemonade and horse races yet to come. Still, even with what may be Lane's additions to this chapter, the political or patriotic messages in the novel were, in fact, not unusual in books for young readers during the 1930s and 1940s. Patriotic themes appeared frequently in books, movies, radio programs, and even popular songs as the country endured the Great Depression and watched on the sidelines as Europe plunged into war.

Patriotic themes and declarations course through Carol Ryrie Brink's *Caddie Woodlawn*, a Newbery Award winner in 1936. Early in the novel, Caddie's father proclaims, "God created all men free and equal . . . and men themselves must come to understand the truth at last!"[79] His declaration could be a paraphrase from the speech in *Little Town on the Prairie*: "Every man Jack of us [is] a free and independent citizen of God's country." Similar themes appear in Florence Crannell Means's 1931 *A Candle in the Mist: A Story for Girls*, and in Esther Forbes's *Johnny Tremain*, another Newbery Medal winner, published in 1943. They also appear sporadically in Bobbs-Merrill's ubiquitous biographical series, the Childhood of Famous Americans, also published during the 1940s. If Lane hadn't gone on to publish *The Discovery of Freedom*, it's unlikely that the Fourth of July chapter in *Little Town on the Prairie* would be interpreted as it so often is now—as an overtly political episode with Libertarian overtones.

Regardless of its contemporary interpretations, the Fourth of July speech attempts to reinforce an essential theme in the novel: a young adult's relationship to community. The episode places Laura squarely in the middle of a thriving, growing town. And while she realizes, after hearing the speech, that like all Americans she "will have to obey" her own conscience and "make" herself "good," she also recognizes that she is part of something much bigger.[80] Never had she "been in such a crowd before."[81] She's swept into the Fourth of July festivities, sampling lemonade and watching Almanzo's Morgans win an exciting horse race. Laura is at once an individual and part of a larger community, wanting "to yell and to laugh and to cry" with the crowd as it surges around Almanzo and his Morgans as they cross the finish line.[82]

Toward the end of *Little Town on the Prairie*, the novel depicts yet another aspect of community. It shifts from patriotism to religion, from a soul-stirring political speech to a soul-stirring sermon. Laura is inspired and challenged by the Fourth of July celebration; she's repulsed by the sermon.

The church Pa helped build in the opening chapters of *Little Town on the Prairie* is finished, and becomes a community center for school as well as church activities. The minister is Ida Brown's father, Reverend Brown, who Wilder identifies as being a distant relative of abolitionist John Brown. "His eyes glared, his white mustache and his whiskers bobbed, and his big hands waved and clawed and clenched into fists pounding the pulpit and shaking in air." To Laura, he looks "like the picture of John Brown in her history book, come alive."[83]

Laura and the whole Ingalls family find Reverend Brown distasteful, despite his family connection to a legendary abolitionist. And as a budding writer, Laura amuses herself "by changing his sentences in her mind, to improve their grammar."[84] During a revival meeting, however, Laura is deeply shaken by the manipulative power Reverend Brown wields: "Chills ran up Laura's spine and over her scalp. She seemed to feel something rising from all the people, something dark and frightening that grew and grew under that thrashing voice. . . . For one horrible instant Laura imagined that Reverend Brown was the Devil. His eyes had fires in them." This is a rare glimpse into evil in the Little House series, and that it appears in the guise of religion may surprise contemporary readers. But it is a powerful scene and reflects a young adult's critical view of the world around her, a refusal to be manipulated or swept away by the sheer force of a magnetic personality spewing a calculated and emotionally charged message. The scene also seems especially relevant now in the twenty-first century, when huge segments of the American public willingly fall victim to manipulative misinformation and outright lies—words that "no longer make sense, that aren't sentences, only dreadful words."[85]

Implied in the scene, however, is not only the strength of Laura's character but the integrity of her upbringing. As one person after another goes forward in response to Reverend Brown's message and as others press toward the pulpit to "wrestle for their souls," Pa, "in a low voice," says, "Come, let's go." The entire family quietly walks back up the aisle, "the open door ahead" a "refuge for their eyes."[86]

This upbringing hinges on love and parental support but also on education, a theme that runs through the entire Little House series. In *Little Town on the Prairie*, the family has made sacrifices to ensure an education for Mary; Ma, as a former schoolteacher, provides informed guidance to her children throughout the novel; Pa is on the school board; and by the time Laura senses "something dark and frightening" in Reverend Brown's powers of manipulation, she is "at the head of the class in all her studies" and thriving under the supervision of a new schoolmaster.[87] A loving family and a good education have armed Laura to recognize the danger in Reverend Brown's brand of persuasion and reject it.

Nothing Would Ever Happen

Despite Laura's deepening maturity, Wilder never loses sight of the angst at the heart of adolescence. Throughout *Little Town on the Prairie*, Laura continues to struggle with herself, with conflicted feelings about her appearance, with the complexities of friendship, with uncertainty about her future. During the family's first Christmas without Mary, for example, Laura is bored and unhappy, almost unable to "bear it all." She believes "nothing would ever happen but going to school and going home, lessons at school and lessons at home. Tomorrow would be the same as today."[88] Laura feels her friends at school are "better dressed" than she is, and that "the more she fussed about her appearance the more dissatisfying it was."[89] As for the future, she worries about the prospect of teaching school, frets about growing up, and sometimes longs to be a little girl again. One line in the book sums up the uncertainties of adolescence perfectly: "She did not know what she wanted, but she knew she could not have it, whatever it was."[90] This depiction heightens the emotional realism of *Little Town on the Prairie*, and strengthens the bond between Laura and Wilder's young readers.

A Cliffhanger Ending

Still, the focus of the book is Laura's coming-of-age, and the final chapters of the novel propel her forward toward new, more adult experiences. And while Laura's world seems to shift suddenly in the last three chapters, the ending feels almost inevitable and organic. Laura's character is ready for these changes. She has pushed herself throughout the novel to excel at school—for her own sake, for Mary's, and for the family's. As her sixteenth birthday approaches—the date she will qualify to teach school—Laura "suddenly knew . . . she must stay in the house and study. . . . If she did not, perhaps next spring she could not get a teacher's certificate, and Mary might have to leave college."[91]

Because Laura has worked so hard, it comes as no surprise when Mr. Owen, Laura's inspiring schoolteacher, chooses her, along with Ida, to "recite the whole of American history, from memory" for the school exhibition.[92] But as she prepares for it, something else shifts in Laura's life, something the novel has been building toward from that Fourth of July horse race, through her rivalry with Nellie Oleson, to the moment she exchanges name cards with Almanzo Wilder: he walks her home from community events, beginning the night of Reverend Brown's troubling revival meeting. As Laura follows Ma and Pa up the aisle at church that night, she hears a voice asking, "May I see you home?" His hand stays "on her arm and he walked beside her through the door."[93]

It's a tender and romantic moment—the touch of his arm on hers, the protection he offers from the unruly church crowd. Laura savors "the faint scent of cigar smoke" rising from his overcoat and decides it's a "more dashing scent" than the "homelike" smell of Pa's pipe. The scene is also funny. Ma is "petrified" when she looks over her shoulder and sees Laura and Almanzo together. Carrie is "wide-eyed," and Laura can't think of anything to say to him.[94] But their courtship has begun.

Almanzo is also in the audience for the School Exhibition, which draws such a large crowd it has to be moved from the schoolhouse to the church. Thematically, the young adult elements in the novel come together in this scene as Laura moves to the platform to deliver her solo part of the evening's program: her scholastic diligence, her commitment to her family, her independence, her interest in fashion, her sense of her place in the community and the world beyond. She steadies her voice and stands in front of the entire town, looking poised in "her blue cashmere held grandly out by the hoops, with Ma's pearl pin" clasped to the lace at her throat.[95] When Laura finishes, "a loud crash of applause" almost makes her "jump out of her skin."[96] Ma and Pa are proud of Laura's performance, and Almanzo is waiting at the church door to help Laura into her coat. And perhaps best of all, he offers to take her sleighing behind his beautiful team of Morgans in a new cutter after Christmas. The world seems suddenly bright and full of possibilities.

But Wilder has one more card to play in *Little Town on the Prairie*—and it's a dramatic one. Laura's performance at the school exhibition leads directly to her first teaching job—an offer from a homesteader twelve miles south to teach at a small community school. Laura's dreaded yet anticipated career as a schoolteacher is set to begin—away from her family and just as her romance is about to blossom. At fifteen, two months shy of her sixteenth birthday, Laura passes her teaching exam, receives her teaching certificate, and accepts the homesteader's offer to teach at his school and board with his family.[97]

Little Town on the Prairie begins and ends as Laura accepts employment. But teaching school and living away from home are far bigger challenges, with higher stakes than making buttonholes in Mr. Clancy's dry goods store. Laura has come of age, despite her youth. When the novel ends, Pa congratulates Laura on all she has accomplished, but his voice "has a hollow sound" because "now Laura was going away." She turns to Pa, and for that one last pivotal moment, he assumes his familiar role as mentor. "Oh, Pa, do you think I—I *can* teach school?" Laura asks. He replies, "I do, Laura. . . . I am sure of it."[98]

The novel's ending is a cliff-hanger, worthy of Charles Dickens himself. Will Laura succeed? Will she make it on her own? And what about Almanzo Wilder, his magnificent horses, and their date to speed over the snow in cold, sunny air? It's the perfect ending to a Young Adult coming-of-age novel, and it leaves readers waiting for Laura's next and perhaps biggest adventure in the Little House series.

13

These Happy Golden Years, Part One

A Knife in the Dark

WHEN *PIONEER GIRL: THE ANNOTATED AUTOBIOGRAPHY* WAS published in 2014, headlines proclaimed it as grittier, edgier than Wilder's wholesome and uncomplicated Little House books. Parents across the country, whose impressions of the novels had apparently been shaped by this publicity or perhaps by their own memories of the television series, began to read the Little House books to their very young children—only to be shocked and sometimes outraged by the adult material in Wilder's last four books. One scene in particular consistently alarmed parents with five-, six-, and seven-year-olds: Mrs. Brewster and her butcher knife in *These Happy Golden Years*. Parents sent me emails complaining about it; one reporter even called to express his outrage that such a potentially violent scene had found its way into a book for young children.

ALTHOUGH WILDER BEGAN WRITING FOR WHAT'S NOW IDENtified as a young adult audience with *By the Shores of Silver Lake*, her role in pioneering the genre, as we've discussed, has largely been forgotten. In the twenty-first century, her entire body of work is often viewed as a sunny, cheery, easy-to-read series written for very young readers. Wilder's clear, conversational style and concrete vocabulary contribute to this misperception. But her seemingly simple style masks the richness and complexity of her novels. In the first four Little House books, this is like candy to young readers, who skim right over passages containing unexpected depth about poverty, loss, and even failure. But in *These Happy Golden*

Years, Wilder's style gives her darker themes and images more immediacy, impact, and power. It's impossible to skim lightly or unfeelingly over a chapter as harrowing as "Knife in the Dark."

Pushing the Boundary Too Far

In 1942, after reviewing the manuscript for *These Happy Golden Years*, Ursula Nordstrom, Wilder's editor at Harper & Brothers, believed Wilder had pushed the boundaries of juvenile fiction too far. Literary agent George Bye wrote Wilder that Miss Nordstrom is "suggesting that Mrs. Brewster's butcher knife incident be cut out."[1] She believed the scene was too dark, too frightening, for Wilder's readers, who at the time were living through World War II.

To be sure, the scene was unprecedented in American juvenile fiction. But Wilder stood firm. While she had compromised with Nordstrom on the title for *The Long Winter* two years before, Wilder felt the episode in *These Happy Golden Years* was essential. Not only was it autobiographical, but it marked an important turning point in the life of Wilder's fictional counterpart. For the Laura of the Little House books, her life takes a dramatic shift because of that butcher knife. It severs Laura from childhood.

So the scene remained.

In 1943 *These Happy Golden Years* was published with that controversial chapter, "A Knife in the Dark." Perhaps to Nordstrom's surprise, it resonated with young readers. They understood and appreciated the chapter's bleak and unnerving drama. Ten years later, under Nordstrom's editorial direction, the new 1953 edition of *These Happy Golden Years* even featured a full-page illustration of Mrs. Brewster and the butcher knife by Garth Williams. The original 1943 edition had left the depiction of the scene entirely up to its readers' imaginations.

But the dark, edgy material in *These Happy Golden Years* isn't restricted to just that one chapter. The entire first half of the novel is dark and edgy. Wilder's mastery of setting, character, and plot combine to produce what was in 1943 a revolutionary new direction in the emerging category of Young Adult fiction. And it opened the door for the meaty, thoughtful, and often disturbing themes we now associate with the genre.

Inexperience, Isolation, and Insignificance

As *These Happy Golden Years* opens, Laura sits next to Pa in his bobsled on a cold, clear Sunday afternoon. Their destination is the Brewster settlement, twelve miles away. Laura is about to begin her career as a schoolteacher there the next day. The tone is anything but optimistic. Instead, Wilder emphasizes Laura's inexperience, her youth, and her misgivings about teaching school and living among strangers: "She did not really know how to do it. She never had taught school, and she was not sixteen years old yet. Even for fifteen she was small; and now she felt very small." Wilder uses setting to further underscore Laura's feelings of isolation and insignificance: "The slightly rolling, snowy land lay empty all around. The high, thin sky was empty overhead. Laura did not look back, but she knew that the town was miles behind her now; it was only a small dark blot on the empty prairie whiteness."[2] This long, cold, essentially silent drive is Laura's farewell to childhood, her transition into a new life as a young woman. The scene bristles with tension, longing, and sadness. The future is unknowable, as bleak and as empty as the wintry horizon ahead. Already Laura is homesick, but with characteristic grit, she doesn't look back.

This moment is significant to Pa as well as Laura. She's letting go of childhood, but he's letting go of his little girl. As he sits "looking ahead into the distance," Wilder makes a one-paragraph shift in point-of-view—to Pa. He intuitively knows how Laura feels, and at last breaks the silence, speaking "as if he were answering her dread of tomorrow."[3] What follows is a brief, restrained pep talk. For the last time in the Little House series, Pa assumes his role as Laura's mentor. He reminds her, "You've never failed yet at anything you tried to do," and tells her that "success gets to be a habit, like anything else a fellow keeps doing."[4] There's a strained moment of laughter as Pa reminds Laura of "how little and scared and funny she had been . . . so long ago," and one last heartfelt piece of advice—to think first and "speak afterward."[5] But the inevitable changes ahead, punctuated by the unrelenting cold, prove too much even for Pa. Silence descends again.

Wilder layers yet more dread over the scene when the Brewster settlement comes into view: "At last she saw a house ahead. Very small at first, it grew larger as they came nearer to it. Half a mile away there was another, smaller one, and far beyond it, another. Then still another appeared. Four houses; that was all. They were far apart and small on the white prairie."[6] In this bleak, inhospitable setting, Laura will not only be essentially alone, she'll be physically isolated, cut off from the rest of the world. Her parting with Pa is swift and unsentimental. Although his eyes smile "encouragement to her," Laura knows she's on her own: "Twelve miles was too far to drive often; she would not see him again for two months."[7]

More and More Dreadful

When Laura steps inside the Brewster claim shanty, Wilder takes the novel into even darker territory. Laura's first evening in her new surroundings is raw and unsettling. After supper, Laura tries to strike up a conversation with Mrs. Brewster, but "she did not answer. The silence grew more and more dreadful. Laura felt her face grow burning hot. She went on wiping the dishes blindly. When they were done, Mrs. Brewster threw out the dishwater and hung the pan on its nail. She sat in the rocking chair and rocked idly, while Johnny [the Brewsters' toddler] crawled under the stove and dragged the cat out by its tail. The cat scratched him and he bawled. Mrs. Brewster went on rocking."[8]

The Brewster family is far more dysfunctional than the quarrelsome Clancy household in *Little Town on the Prairie*. There's no humor in Laura's scenes with the Brewsters, no light or hope, only bitterness and dread. Mr. Brewster's attempts to make Laura feel welcome or comfortable are ineffective, negated by his wife's rage. When he attempts to explain to Laura why the family eats only two meals a day, his wife cuts him off:

> "Whose fault is it, I'd like to know!" Mrs. Brewster blazed out. "As if I didn't do enough, slaving from morning to night in this . . ."
>
> Mr. Brewster raised his voice. "I only meant the days are so short . . ."
>
> "Then say what you mean!" Mrs. Brewster slammed the high chair to the table, snatched the little boy and sat him in it, hard.[9]

The image of isolated, angry, or fragile pioneer women struggling to maintain their sanity in claim shanties or sod houses on the Great Plains is a recurring image in early twentieth-century American literature. One of the most notable examples is the character of Beret, who follows her husband into Dakota Territory in O. E. Rolvaag's *Giants in the Earth: A Saga of the Prairie* and is seized by the realization that the "formless prairie had no heart that beat, no waves that sang, no soul that could be touched." Beret is a tragic and haunted woman, tortured by "the dreadful nature of the fate that had overtaken her."[10]

Like Willa Cather and Bess Streeter Aldrich, Wilder, for the most part, attempts to counterbalance this image in the Little House books. Ma is a sometimes-reluctant pioneer woman, for example, but she is also capable, resilient, and courageous. For Wilder, it's women like Ma who ultimately shape the West. Mrs. Brewster in *These Happy Golden Years* is Ma's antithesis, a woman temperamentally ill-equipped to live in the West. In fact, the entire Brewster family provides a bleak contrast to the pioneer values of the fictional Ingalls family. As Laura struggles to cope with her new environment at the Brewsters', she looks out from their miserable claim shanty at the prairie beyond and imagines herself back home: "Ma was getting supper now; Carrie was home from school; they were laughing and talking with Grace. Pa would come in, and swing Grace up in his arms as he used to lift Laura when she was little."[11] But during that first week with the Brewsters, Laura can't imagine away the unpleasant experience of living in the Brewster household. It is utterly joyless.

Wilder heightens Laura's anxiety with tangible physical discomfort. Her bed in the Brewsters' home is a narrow sofa "with a curved wooden back and one end curved up."[12] Laura struggles though the night "not to fall off" of it.[13] What's worse: the sofa is just inches away from the Brewsters' bed. A pair of "brown calico curtains" on a string that "could be pulled together to hide the sofa" provides Laura with just a thin layer of privacy at night.[14] She can't escape the oppressive wretchedness of living in the Brewsters' home. "Before Laura could hurry into bed in the cold dark, Mrs. Brewster began to quarrel with him [Mr. Brewster]. Laura tried not to hear. She pulled the quilt over her head and pressed her ear tight against the pillow, but she could not help hearing. She knew then that Mrs. Brewster wanted her to hear."[15] This is deeply disturbing material loaded with undertones of sexual tension: Laura shares a bedroom with a married couple. The situation is menacing today, and it was even more so in 1943, before readers had grown accustomed to the subjects Young Adult novels tackle now: physical and verbal abuse, dysfunctional families, sex, violence, and suicide.

Louisa May Alcott and Mark Twain, whose books launched the Young Adult category in the late nineteenth century, touched on such subjects, but lightly or indirectly. In *Little Women*, Alcott uses the poverty of the Hummel family as an important plot point but never takes readers directly into their lives. Twain's *Huckleberry Finn* certainly includes dark and unsettling material—racism, alcoholism, physical abuse, and violence—but it's tempered by humor and Huck's incomparable voice. In *These Happy Golden Years*, Wilder places Laura directly into the Brewsters' dysfunctional family. Like Laura, readers can't escape the misery Mrs. Brewster inflicts.

One Day at a Time

Wilder's first three chapters of *These Happy Golden Years* are claustrophobic. Laura—and by extension, Wilder's readers—are trapped in the Brewster settlement. Laura's only escape isn't an escape at all: teaching school. As she prepares for her first day, her circumstances are grim: "Teaching school can not possibly be as bad as staying in that house with Mrs. Brewster. Anyway, it cannot be worse."[16]

Teaching school, as we'll see in the next chapter, ultimately proves far more satisfying than Laura imagines, but in the opening chapters of *These Happy Golden Years*, Laura seems destined to fail. Not only is she inexperienced, but the minute she steps foot into the grim, cold, and primitive schoolhouse, Laura realizes she's at a physical disadvantage: Three of her five students are taller than she is. And Clarence, who proves to be her most troublesome student, is even older than Laura. How will she be able to maintain discipline in the classroom? Will her students respect her?

Throughout these first three chapters of *These Happy Golden Years*, Wilder uses verbs to reinforce Laura's hopeless existence at the Brewster settlement. Laura shivers, dreads, and trudges, while

Mrs. Brewster blazes, slams, and quarrels. Even the Brewsters' son Johnny crawls, drags, and screams. Mr. Brewster is usually silent, moving carefully through the house. But his silence and reticence enable his wife's disturbing behavior and underscore the tension between them. As for Laura's students, they spell, recite, and write, but they do so slowly, defiantly, inattentively. This simple, concrete vocabulary deepens the sense of hopelessness and despair throughout the novel's opening chapters. At one point, Laura feels she can't go on, then recognizes that she is "whimpering" and is ashamed of herself. Her grit, once again, sees her through: "The sun was setting, and tomorrow it would rise; everything must go on."[17]

At the end of Laura's first week at the Brewster settlement, Wilder ratchets up the tension even more. The day is cold and stormy. As Laura tries to concentrate on her students, her mind wanders. She listens "to the wind, afraid that its sound" will "signal a blizzard's howl," and wonders, "How am I going to get through the time till Monday," trapped inside that miserable house with the miserable Brewsters.[18] Then the scene shifts unexpectedly. The wind carries a "strangely silvery sound." Laura and her five students listen as the sound grows "clearer, almost like music," and suddenly "the whole air filled with a chiming of little bells. Sleigh bells!"[19]

It's Almanzo Wilder, appearing like a frontier version of a knight in shining armor, to whisk Laura away from her misery. It's a magical literary moment, full of hope and wonder and tremendous relief.

Vivid, Dark, and Hopeless

Yet Wilder isn't interested in telling a frontier fairytale—at least, not yet. Although Almanzo braves bitter cold and snow for Laura weekend after weekend, he doesn't actually rescue her. That's because Laura is determined to finish her two-month contract, come what may. While her weekends at home with her family provide temporary escape, they also intensify Laura's misery: Sunday after Sunday, she has to face five more days of sleeping in the Brewsters' bedroom on their narrow sofa, eating in their increasingly squalid kitchen, and enduring the "smolder" of "Mrs. Brewster's silence."[20] Laura tells Carrie, "Do you ever think how lucky we are to have a home like this?" And Carrie is surprised. To her eyes their home isn't remarkable. Upstairs "there was nothing to be seen but the two beds, the three boxes under the eaves where they kept their things, and the underside of the shingles."[21] But to Laura home has "never looked so beautiful."[22]

Chapter titles signal Laura's ongoing emotional conflict: "A Stiff Upper Lip" and "Managing." All the while, the Brewster family continues to disintegrate: "Mrs. Brewster let the housework go. She did not sweep out the snow that Mr. Brewster tracked in; it melted and made puddles with the ashes around the stove. She did not make their bed nor even spread it up. Twice a day she cooked potatoes and salt pork and put them on the table. The rest of the time she sat brooding. She did not even comb her hair."[23] Wilder's depiction of Laura's circumstances in *These Happy Golden Years* is vivid, dark, and hopeless, an unconventional portrayal in a book for young readers of the 1940s. But Laura's situation grows even more dire.

As the weeks go by, life in the Brewster household takes a physical as well as emotional toll on Laura. Ma is convinced that Laura isn't sleeping well and worries that she's losing weight. Pa even suggests that Laura could break her teacher's contract: "You know, Laura," he says, "you don't *have* to finish the term. If anything worries you too much, you can always come home."[24]

Modern readers may be puzzled by Laura's determination to stay—and her refusal to tell Ma and Pa how wretched her life has become at the Brewsters'. Laura tells Ma, for example, that she has "plenty" to eat, though it "doesn't taste like home cooking." And Laura tells Pa that she can't possibly quit. "I wouldn't get another [teacher's] certificate."[25] She is determined to hold on, to take responsibility for herself and the commitments she has made to the Brewster school, no matter how difficult. Perhaps more importantly, Laura comes to a very mature, very adult conclusion about Mrs. Brewster: "She isn't mad at *me*, she's only quarreling about me because she wants to quarrel."[26]

Wilder uses the dark, disturbing Brewster household to showcase Laura's maturity, her break with childhood. Her strength and resolve reflect her emotional growth, a theme consistent with previous Little House books. Laura may be homesick, but she refuses to shirk adult responsibilities, even as the Brewster household spins more dangerously out of control. Laura navigates her own path through an uncommonly, almost unimaginably difficult situation.

But another situation, related to Laura's life with the Brewsters, isn't as easy to navigate, and it adds to the tension in the opening chapters of *These Happy Golden Years*: What to do about Almanzo Wilder?

Teacher's Beau

When Almanzo Wilder appears at the end of Laura's first week of teaching school, she is surprised and grateful but unsure of how to interpret his attentions. Clarence, Laura's most precocious student, identifies Almanzo as "Teacher's beau."[27] So do Laura's friends in town. Laura doesn't see it that way. "It isn't like that at all. He came for me as a favor to Pa." But her friend Mary Power isn't convinced. "He must think a lot of your Pa!"[28]

Despite the inclement weather and the layers of clothing Laura wears as protection against the cold, the long drives with Almanzo between the Brewster settlement and De Smet are romantic, even intimate. He takes her hand to help her into the cutter, then tucks "furry, warm buffalo skins, lined with flannel . . . snugly around her."[29] The cutter itself enhances their intimacy. It's "only five feet long, and twenty-six inches wide at the bottom." As Almanzo explains, "Makes it snugger to ride in." Laura finds the experience exhilarating. "It's like flying!" she observes.[30] By nineteenth-century standards, these long, unchaperoned sleigh rides introduce Laura to unconventional physical intimacy with a very eligible young man.

On the one hand, Wilder uses these scenes between Laura and Almanzo to illustrate the almost intuitive understanding that develops between them. He is clearly devoted to Laura and immediately grasps, as no one else around her does, how wretched conditions are within the Brewster household. When he stops at the Brewster house on their first ride together, he glances inside, where "Johnny was screaming angrily again." As Laura emerges from the doorway, satchel in hand for the weekend, she sees Almanzo looking at the house "with disgust."[31] On a later Sunday drive from

De Smet back to the Brewster settlement, he tells Laura, "I've got an idea it's pretty tough, staying at Brewster's."[32]

On the other hand, Wilder builds emotional tension with these scenes, tensions that add yet another layer of struggle to Laura's life. When Almanzo tells Laura he thinks staying at Brewster's must be tough, she acknowledges only that she gets homesick and thanks him for "driving so far to take me home." Almanzo replies, "It's a pleasure," but Laura sees "no pleasure for him in that long, cold drive."[33] She's puzzled by his attention, unsure of how to respond, uncomfortable with the expectations that might arise from their growing intimacy.

She's also embarrassed. When Clarence yells, "Teacher's beau's here!" Laura is mortified: "Almanzo Wilder must have heard. He could not help hearing. Laura did not know how she could face him. . . . How could she tell him that she had given Clarence no reason to say such a thing?" What's worse, Almanzo appears amused by Clarence's comment. It seems to Laura that Almanzo is "smiling" as he tucks her into the cutter. Laura can "hardly look at him," and decides it's "better to say nothing of Clarence" or his comment.[34]

In the opening chapters of *These Happy Golden Years*, Laura undeniably needs Almanzo. She needs the escape only he can provide from the privations of living and working at the Brewster settlement. "Being at home every Saturday raised her spirits and gave her courage for another week."[35] Yet Laura has an independent spirit, and always has. How can she justify this dependence to herself? And is it fair to Almanzo? What does he expect from his attentions to her? For Laura, these questions relate to her ongoing pursuit of "goodness," a theme, as we've discussed, that Wilder introduced in *Little Town on the Prairie*. Here, however, the question of her goodness, of choosing the right path, is complicated by the question of survival. Without Almanzo's help, can Laura endure life with the Brewsters? She agonizes over this question: "Laura felt guilty. She had not expected him to make that long drive every week. She hoped he did not think that she was expecting him to do it. Surely, he was not thinking of . . . well, of maybe being her beau?"[36] Laura struggles with this dilemma and finally decides her own emotional survival is less important than following her conscience. As much as she needs his help, "it was not fair to take so much from Almanzo Wilder."[37]

A Knife in the Dark

Wilder uses these parallel struggles—Laura's unhappiness with the Brewsters and the implications of her dependence on Almanzo—to create a physical and emotional crisis, one that will propel Laura through the rest of *These Happy Golden Years*. It begins when Laura summons her courage to speak honestly and directly to Almanzo. As they near the Brewster house on a sparkling cold Sunday afternoon, she tells him: "I am going with you only because I want to get home. When I am home to stay, I will not go out with you any more. So now you know, and if you want to save yourself these long, cold drives, you can."[38]

But the moment she speaks her mind, Laura regrets it: "The words sounded horrid to her as she said them. They were abrupt and rude and hateful. At the same time, a dreadful realization swept over her, of what it would mean if Almanzo did not come for her again. She would have to spend Saturdays and Sundays with Mrs. Brewster." What's worse, there's no time to call her declaration back. Before pulling away from the Brewsters' door, Almanzo simply says, "I see." To "keep her spirits from sinking," Laura reminds herself that surely the worst is behind her. She has "only three weeks more" with the Brewsters, and then she can go home.[39]

The weather turns even more bitterly cold, and on Thursday morning, Laura wakes to find "the quilt frozen stiff around her nose as she slept," and Mr. Brewster, as the head of the school board, cancels school for the day. Laura is marooned inside the house with the Brewsters for "a long, wretched day."[40] She makes her bed, does the dishes, and spends the day studying her own schoolbooks, not wanting to fall behind her classmates in De Smet while she's away teaching school. When Laura tries to talk to Mrs. Brewster, "there was something menacing in Mrs. Brewster's silence." Laura goes to bed that night hoping "desperately" that, despite the extreme cold, school will resume in the morning.[41]

A scream wakes Laura in the middle of the night, and what follows is that scene that carved out new territory for Young Adult American fiction.

> Laura sat straight up. Moonlight was streaming over her bed from the window. Mrs. Brewster screamed again, a wild sound without words that made Laura's scalp crinkle.
>
> "Take the knife back to the kitchen," Mr. Brewster said.
>
> Laura peeped through the crack between the curtains. The moonlight shone through the calico, and thinned the darkness so that Laura saw Mrs. Brewster standing there. Her long white flannel nightgown trailed to the floor and her black hair fell loose over her shoulders. In her upraised hand she held the butcher knife. Laura had never been so terribly frightened.
>
> "If I can't go home one way, I can another," said Mrs. Brewster.[42]

For first-time readers, the scene seems unimaginably frightening and dangerous. It explodes on the page. Yet it effectively fuses elements Wilder has introduced earlier in *These Happy Golden Years*: Mrs. Brewster's mental instability and volatile temper, Mr. Brewster's guarded passivity, the sexual tension lying just below the surface, and its unsettling proximity to Laura. The scene is inevitable, essential, and Wilder was right to maintain it, despite Ursula Nordstrom's initial editorial disapproval.

Within a few short paragraphs, Mr. Brewster diffuses the immediate danger. Although Laura senses he is ready to spring into action, Mr. Brewster remains in bed, true to his characteristic passivity, and calmly convinces his wife to put away the knife. She takes it to the kitchen and then, unarmed, slips back into bed with Mr. Brewster. But the impact of that knife in the dark remains—on Laura and Wilder's readers.

Throughout the Little House books, Laura and her family have faced down one danger or another—wolves, bears, panthers, the relentless Hard Winter. But in this scene, Laura confronts mortal danger alone, and far from home. She is "terribly frightened. She dared not sleep. Suppose she woke to see Mrs. Brewster standing over her with that knife?"[43] Yet Laura also controls her fear. Huddled under the quilt on the Brewsters' narrow couch, she stares at the calico curtains, listening for sounds of movement on the other side, and waits for the dawn. Wilder's portrayal of Laura's emotional turmoil is gripping, menacing, and suspenseful. But it also illustrates Laura's maturity and self-control. It is a revelation of character.

What's more: Wilder hasn't lost sight of the other complication in Laura's life—Almanzo Wilder. As Laura teaches school on that bitterly cold Friday, fighting to stay awake after a sleepless night, struggling to keep herself and her students warm inside the frigid schoolhouse, she again wrestles with her fear to spend another night in Mrs. Brewster's bedroom: "She knew that she must not be afraid. . . . Very likely, nothing would happen. . . . But she had never wanted so much to go home." Laura's thoughts turn to Almanzo—and her declaration on the previous Sunday. She doesn't regret her honesty with him, but she regrets its timing: "It had been right to tell Almanzo Wilder the truth, but she wished that she had not done it so soon."[44]

As this chapter winds down, Wilder uses vivid, concrete details to enhance Laura's fear, isolation, and regret. The temperature plummets. Laura's students wear their overcoats and take turns studying by the stove to keep warm. Blowing snow drifts through the cracks in the schoolhouse walls. The food freezes in their dinner pails before lunchtime. "Every moment the wind blew stronger, and colder."[45] The suspense mounts. Should Laura dismiss school early? What will she find at the Brewster house when she returns? Will Mrs. Brewster take out that knife again, and threaten Laura with it?

And then suddenly, Laura hears sleigh bells, and Clarence shouts, "That Wilder's a bigger fool than I thought he was to come out in this weather!"[46]

Readers rejoice at Almanzo's timely return, but Laura hasn't, in fact, escaped mortal danger. She's about to face an even more deadly foe than that knife in the dark: the relentless power of the West. It's another brilliant plot twist that amplifies Laura's misery in the Brewster home and her ongoing struggle to understand Almanzo's motivations.

A Cold Ride

When I first read *These Happy Golden Years* as a ten-year-old, I didn't fully appreciate the tremendous risk Laura takes when Almanzo arrives at the schoolhouse door on that bitterly cold Friday afternoon. Like Laura, I was swept up in her escape. What could be more dangerous, more potentially deadly than Mrs. Brewster and her butcher knife? Who could be more unselfish, more heroic than Almanzo Wilder? And as a ten-year-old, I'd never experienced extreme subzero temperatures. So when Wilder writes that Almanzo braves extreme cold to go after Laura in the chapter "A Cold Ride," I didn't quite grasp the implications of her description: the mercury in the thermometer "was all down in the bulb, below forty."[47] Nor did I fully appreciate Mr. Brewster's observation. "It's not safe," he tells Laura, suggesting that Almanzo "put up here for the night." And I must have skimmed over the question Almanzo puts to Laura: "Think you'd better risk it?"[48]

And, of course, Laura does.

On the surface, Laura's decision is a thoroughly believable young adult decision—impulsive, emotional, and perhaps even reckless. Which is why, when I first read *These Happy Golden Years*, I didn't give it a second thought. Driving away from the perceived danger of Mrs. Brewster in forty-below weather seemed to me then entirely logical. And, of course, it makes for a good story, one that appeals to adolescent readers. But as an adult, I realize now that Wilder isn't simply creating a suspenseful and exciting scene; she is reinforcing the depths of Laura's misery with the Brewsters. After all, Laura is already a seasoned, tough pioneer. She's lived in the West almost all her life and knows how to read its weather. Just as she instantly recognized the danger of the schoolhouse blizzard in *The Long Winter*, Laura knows the danger she places herself in on that twelve-mile, subzero ride back to De Smet. She knowingly chooses to risk freezing to death rather than spend another sleepless night in the Brewsters' bedroom. And in so doing she entrusts her life to Almanzo and his team. This is a major turning point for Laura and a major turning point in *These Happy Golden Years*.

The chapter "A Cold Ride" begins with a description of Laura's preparation for this ride home. She slips on another flannel petticoat, pulls another pair of "woolen stockings" over her shoes, doubles her thick woolen veil and wraps it "twice around her face and hood," then crosses a muffler around her throat and chest. Finally, she buttons "her coat over all."[49] In the cutter, Almanzo has layered horse blankets over the seat and a lantern burns near Laura's feet to keep them warm. These preparations reinforce the danger ahead.

But the drive back to town is even more perilous than Laura could have imagined: "The cold was piercing through the buffalo robes. It crept through Laura's wool coat and woolen dress, through all her flannel petticoats and the two pairs of woolen stockings drawn over the folded legs of her warm flannel union suit. In spite of the heat from the lantern, her feet and her legs grew cold. Her clenched jaws ached, and two sharp little aches began at her temples."[50] It's so cold that Almanzo has to stop "every couple of miles" to thaw the horses' frozen breath from their noses.[51] As for Almanzo himself, "his breath froze white on the fur and along the muffler's edge," and he drives "with one hand, keeping the other under the robes, and often changing so that neither hand would freeze."[52]

As the ride continues, Laura begins to grow "more used to the cold," and the "sound of the wind and the bells and the cutter's runners on the snow all blended into one monotonous sound, rather pleasant."[53] Almanzo instinctively senses this new danger. "Don't go to sleep. You hear me?" he tells her. Laura understands the warning. Living on the frontier all her life, she knows that "if you go to sleep in such cold, you freeze to death." But the urge to sleep "kept coming over her in long, warm waves."[54]

This scene, however, isn't simply about Laura's need to escape the Brewsters. It's also about Almanzo's heroism and his determination to keep Laura alive. His voice saves her. His repeated question "All right?" prevents her from surrendering to the comfort of sleep and death.[55] When they finally arrive in town, Almanzo, ever vigilant for the safety of his precious cargo, pulls up at the back door of the Ingallses' house in town, where "the wind was not so strong."[56] Ma and then Pa come to the door. Together, they help Laura as she stumbles safely into the kitchen. Almanzo and his team dash away, but he has proved himself worthy of Laura.

Pa, however, recognizes the tremendous risk Laura has taken. He tells her, "You took a long chance, Laura. . . . It was forty below zero when that crazy fellow started, and the thermometer froze soon afterward. It has been steadily growing colder ever since; there's no telling how cold it is now." Laura answers with a "shaky laugh" and a familiar Ingalls family cliché: "All's well that ends well, Pa."[57]

And for Laura, it has ended well. In facing down death by freezing, in forming a life-and-death partnership with Almanzo, Laura finds she can cope with the Brewster household. "Everything was still all wrong there," but now Laura simply marks off the days on her notebook.[58] While she remains sleep-deprived, Laura is more determined than ever to finish out her term at the Brewster school. What's more, she tells no one about that knife in the dark. She doesn't tell Ma and Pa because "if they knew, they would not let her go back, and she must finish her school."[59]

The shared experience of that cold ride also creates more intimacy between Laura and Almanzo. On one of their last rides to the Brewsters', Laura asks Almanzo about his horses, and he tells her about his childhood in New York, about his colt Starlight, and his family's move to Minnesota. It is one of their first lengthy conversations together. The time passes "so quickly" that Laura is "surprised to see the Brewsters' ahead." Her heart sinks, and Almanzo intuitively responds. "What makes you so quiet, so sudden?" Laura tells him, "I was wishing we were going in the other direction." Almanzo slows the horses, and Laura knows "that somehow he understood how she dreaded going into that house."[60]

A Tie That Binds

The chapters "A Knife in the Dark" and "A Cold Ride" are dramatic and suspenseful. They are also autobiographical. In *Pioneer Girl*, Wilder writes that her attachment to Almanzo was formed, in large part, because they "had been through blizzards, near-murder and danger of death together and those things do create 'a tie that binds.'"[61] Yet Wilder made a subtle but strategic shift when she jumped from autobiography in *Pioneer Girl* to fiction in *These Happy Golden Years*: she rearranged plot points. In *Pioneer Girl*, the real Laura Ingalls took that extremely cold ride in subzero temperatures with Almanzo *before* Mrs. Brewster wielded her butcher knife. Why is this switch important?

As Wilder had learned from Lane, novels—and even chapters—need that "necessary thread" not only to pull readers through a story from one page to the next but to give its characters motivation, conflict, and emotional depth.[62] By placing "Knife in the Dark" immediately after Laura dismisses Almanzo and *before* "The Cold Ride," Wilder heightens Laura's anguish—and her urgent need to escape the Brewster household. At the same time, this switch makes the "tie that binds" Laura to Almanzo even stronger. He appears when she needs him most, and because her situation is so dire, she's willing to risk that long, cold ride home. This sequence in *These Happy Golden Years* is perfectly plotted.

Yet Wilder's decision to load and then resolve so many big and dramatic plot points in the first half of *These Happy Golden Years* is creatively risky. Tension and conflict sustain the action of a novel, so if characters resolve major conflicts too early or too easily, readers lose interest. The necessary thread disappears long before the final chapters. But Wilder's creative risk in *These Happy Golden Years*—as calculated and as daring, in its own way, as her characters' cold ride home—pays off. True, Laura is safely home, and Almanzo has proved himself worthy, but Wilder then introduces an even bigger conflict, a bigger element of suspense. Will Laura accept Almanzo's attentions? Will he become her beau? And will they have a future together?

From Darkness, Light

Laura's misery in the Brewster household ultimately leads her toward a fulfilling profession, a lively romance, and an entirely new life. She is forever changed by the experience of living in an abusive household but emerges stronger and more self-sufficient. And as we'll see in the next chapter, the atmosphere in *These Happy Golden Years* shifts from darkness to light.

By taking Laura—and the novel's first-generation readers of the 1940s—into darker fictional territory, Wilder expanded the boundaries of the emerging Young Adult genre. But she didn't leave Laura or her readers trapped in that dysfunctional space, something especially important in the early 1940s, as the world endured the devastation of World War II. Instead, Wilder provided a roadmap for hope. As Laura permanently leaves the Brewster settlement behind, her heart "is so light" that she feels "like singing with the sleigh bells" while Almanzo and his horses speed her "home to stay."[63]

14

These Happy Golden Years, Part Two

A Happy Ending

NO EDITORIAL CORRESPONDENCE SURVIVES TO INDICATE HOW Wilder and Lane worked together on *These Happy Golden Years*, making it impossible to know conclusively how the published version took shape. What concepts and ideas did Wilder view as essential? How much editorial influence did Lane exert over it? But what is clear is that during the early 1940s, Lane's interest in producing fiction was waning. Even in the late 1920s she had struggled with her failure to grasp the elusive artistic challenges of writing a novel. She wrote, "Heaven knows that everything there is to know about a novel coincides precisely with what I don't know about it. It isn't only a question of technique; I don't know the feel of a novel. . . . I don't know what a novel is when I meet it."[1] So perhaps it isn't surprising that by the late 1930s, Lane seemed far more interested in politics—and nonfiction. She remained vehemently opposed to President Franklin Roosevelt's New Deal, and believed that if war broke out in Europe, the president would drag the United States into the conflict. Her political ideas took shape in essays and articles published during the late 1930s and early 1940s.

Did the march toward World War II affect the writing of *These Happy Golden Years*? Again, it's impossible to know with any certainty. We do know that both Wilder and Lane supported the Ludlow Amendment to the Constitution, circulating in the late 1930s, which would have required a national referendum on any congressional declaration of war unless the United States was directly attacked or invaded. Lane testified before the Senate Judiciary Committee in support of the amendment, and continued to press for an isolationist stance on World War II until the bombing of Pearl Harbor on December 7, 1941. In 1943, the same year *These Happy Golden Years* was published, Lane released *Discovery of Freedom*, a book that, in part, launched the American Libertarian movement. Wilder's response to the coming of the war is less easy to track. She shared her daughter's distrust of Roosevelt, writing, "Hitler's word is about as good as Roosevelt's, isn't it?" But then added: "I am worried though, for between dictators and Communism, what chance has a simple republic?"[2]

World War II certainly influenced the work of other prominent authors who, like Wilder, wrote historical fiction set in the American West. For example, Bess Streeter Aldrich's biographer notes that in 1941 Aldrich initially felt "unable to write historical fiction" because of the war, and yet she nevertheless completed her last historical novel, *The Lieutenant's Lady*, in 1942.[3] As an insightful editor pointed out to Aldrich, "People [now] more than ever, will turn for relaxation and at least temporary inner peace, to read of the past."[4]

Perhaps a similar understanding of the reading public propelled Wilder forward during this period. Her age may have also been a factor. She was seventy-six when *These Happy Golden Years* was published. Her baby sister Grace Dow had died almost two years earlier, in 1941, at the age of sixty-four. In a letter to one of her readers, Wilder wrote, "There are only sister Carrie and myself left of our family now."[5] Wilder, however, seemed determined to finish her Little House series and, despite this novel's dark opening chapters, to give it the happy ending she had promised her readers years earlier when she told them "all good novels" should end "happily."[6]

IN 1942 WILDER SENT THE MANUSCRIPT OF *THESE HAPPY Golden Years* to her agent, George Bye. "This children's story is now complete in eight volumes," she wrote.[7] The following year, when the novel was published, Bye pronounced it beautiful and accepted it as the last book in the series "with great reluctance."[8]

Like Wilder's young readers, Bye wished the series "would never come to an end."[9]

In the 1960s, as a young reader then myself, I thought the book was beautiful too. *These Happy Golden Years* was my favorite book in the Little House series. Laura's ambition to become a writer emerged (at least for me) just as clearly as Jo's in *Little Women*, and Laura's courtship and marriage to Almanzo were far more exciting than Jo's with the stodgy Professor Bhaer. And then there were Laura's experiences teaching school, her beautiful hats, but perhaps best of all, her still untamed spirit and strength—jumping into Almanzo's cutter seconds before the colts dashed out onto the open prairie, something no "man in town except Cap Garland" would do.[10] When I finished reading *These Happy Golden Years* for the first time, I hoped I would be as fearless and unconventional as Laura when I was eighteen. And while I wanted Laura's story to continue, I was also perfectly satisfied with the way the book—and the entire series—ended.

Now all these decades later, I've come to realize that *These Happy Golden Years* achieves something final series novels rarely do: a satisfying ending, one that wraps all the threads of an extended narrative together while simultaneously telling a strong, compelling story as a stand-alone novel. Its voice is consistent with the previous Little House books, and while its main character (Laura) is older and more mature, she is somehow still herself—another rare artistic achievement in a final series novel.

But the book's artistic achievements don't end there. *These Happy Golden Years* is a landmark Young Adult novel, forging into new territory in 1943. In addition to opening the door for the disturbing, more adult themes we now associate with Young Adult fiction, it was also one of the first Young Adult romances or courtship novels. And while the intimacy between Laura and Almanzo may seem tame by today's standards, it was new in the early 1940s.

Courtship and Marriage

It seems only natural now, after decades of readers have grown up with the Little House books, that Wilder would finish the series with Laura's courtship and marriage. Even in the emerging Young Adult category in the 1940s, there was already a solid precedent for romance and marriage plot lines. A notable example is Florence Crannell Means's three-book series, published in the 1930s. Its heroine is Janey Grant, whose family moves from Wisconsin to Minnesota to Colorado during the 1870s. The parallels between Janey's fictional world and Laura's are striking. Both the Grant and Ingalls families battle poverty, grasshoppers, prairie fires, and blizzards. Like Laura, Janey becomes a schoolteacher, aspires to become a writer, and in the last book in the series, *A Bowlful of Stars*, published in 1934, she is courted by two suitors. But the novel's primary plot focuses more on Janey's adventures and misadventures in Colorado gold country than on romance and courtship.

By the 1920s and early 1930s, young adult readers were drawn to L. M. Montgomery's novels, most notably *Anne of Green Gables*, which was published in 1908. Anne's relationship with Gilbert Blythe transforms and deepens into romance and marriage by the end of the Green Gables series. But Montgomery wrote these books for adults, not, as we've previously discussed, young adult readers.

What's now considered the first Young Adult romance, Maureen Daly's *Seventeenth Summer*, was published in 1942, just a year before *These Happy Golden Years*. But like Montgomery, Daly intended *Seventeenth Summer* for adult readers. "I would like, at this late date [1994]," said Daly, "to explain that *Seventeenth Summer*, in my intention and at the time of publication, was considered a full adult novel and was published and reviewed as such."[11] In the late 1930s and early 1940s, publishers hadn't fully recognized that young adult readers were interested in novels that focused on courtship and romance.

Of course, the very first American Young Adult novel, Louisa May Alcott's *Little Women*, features three marriages: Meg marries Laurie's devoted tutor, Amy marries Laurie, and Jo marries Professor Bhaer. Yet romance itself isn't exactly a major theme in *Little Women*. John Brooke's bumbling courtship of Meg is more comedic than romantic. In fact, Alcott devotes more time to Meg's life as a newlywed than to her courtship. As for Laurie and Amy, their romance happens offstage, while they're both in Europe. Alcott doesn't explore their romance; instead, they appear as a married couple toward the end of the book. And Jo's decision to marry the professor has disappointed readers for over 150 years.

Wilder's approach to courtship and marriage in *These Happy Golden Years* is fundamentally different from all of her predecessors' books. There's nothing fussy or paternal, for example, about Almanzo Wilder. He may be older than Laura, but he's also dashing, courageous, even slightly dangerous. He is the town's most eligible bachelor. Unlike Professor Bhaer, Almanzo is a distinctly romantic character, and Laura's response to him, as she progresses through the middle and final chapters of *These Happy Golden Years*, isn't about becoming a dutiful or responsible wife like the March girls or, as we'll see, about pursuing an all-consuming first love as Daly's heroine does in *Seventeenth Summer*. Nor does Wilder's approach align with Crannell's depiction of frontier romance in *A Bowlful of Stars*. Courtship in *These Happy Golden Years* is about falling in love and finding a soul mate, concepts more consistent with adult romances of the 1930s and 1940s—and L. M. Montgomery's later adult novels (for example, *The Blue Castle*, published in 1926). Still, like Jo March , Laura doesn't embrace courtship or romance easily. And for Wilder, this character trait posed a significant creative challenge: how to believably move Laura from romantic reluctance to acceptance, and still remain true to the essence of her character?

It Isn't Like That at All

As we've seen in previous Little House books, Laura comes to the idea of courtship and romance reluctantly. In *By the Shores of Silver Lake*, Laura and Lena find the idea of marriage unappealing, and Laura is surprised and confused by the attention she receives from Almanzo in *Little Town on the Prairie*. Even when Almanzo begins to drive her home from the Brewster school, Laura refuses to admit that he's her beau. As she tells her friend Mary Power, "It isn't like that at all."[12] And in that brutally honest conversation Laura has with Almanzo before the butcher knife episode, she tells him directly that she has no romantic interest in him whatsoever: "When I am home to stay, I will not go out with you any more."[13] Indeed, after Laura has finished her term at the Brewster school, she seems to stand firm in her resolve. It appears that Wilder has written herself into a box. What could possibly change Laura's attitude toward romance and courtship?

Wilder's solution to this creative dilemma hinges, once again, on her perceptive insights into character, and her understanding of young adults—their longing for companionship and need for acceptance. Not that young adults necessarily realize this about themselves; Laura certainly doesn't. Back home with her family in De Smet, for example, Laura feels contented and "happier than Christmas."[14] Yet, just a few short paragraphs later, Laura's heart jumps at the sound of sleigh bells speeding by, and when she looks out the window, she sees her friends flashing past in sleighs and cutters. "Two by two they went gaily by, laughing and singing with the chiming bells. No one remembered Laura. She had been away so long that everyone forgot her."[15]

The emotional transition here is swift but believable. Laura doesn't want to be left behind. "She tried not to mind being forgotten and left out. She tried not to hear the sleigh bells and the laughter, but more and more she felt she could not bear it."[16] In this small, transitional literary moment, Wilder begins to open Laura's heart to Almanzo:

> Suddenly, a ringing of bells stopped at the door! Before Pa could look up from his paper, Laura had the door open, and there stood Prince and Lady with the little cutter, and Almanzo stood beside it smiling.
>
> "Would you like to go sleigh riding?" he asked.
>
> "Oh, yes!" Laura answered.[17]

As they speed away in his cutter, it dawns on Laura that she's doing what she vowed she would never do. She bursts out laughing. "What's so funny?" Almanzo asks. "It's a joke on me," Laura replies. "I didn't intend to go with you any more but I forgot."[18]

This episode signals Laura's deepening understanding of herself and her unconscious attraction to Almanzo. Her experience at the Brewster settlement has changed her. But so has Almanzo's devotion. He understands Laura better than she knows. "Why did you come?" she asks him, a reference to her declaration that she'd never go out with him again. He tells her, "I thought maybe you'd change your mind after you watched the crowd go by."[19]

Yet Almanzo still hasn't won Laura. Although she looks forward to the "pleasant" Sunday afternoon "sleigh ride parties" with him, she still isn't interested in romance. Laura remains the Laura readers have always admired—independent, unconventional, scholarly, devoted to her family and eager to earn wages again to help with Mary's college expenses. Laura is content to be free of romantic entanglements. She resumes her place at the head of the class at school; works as a seamstress on Saturdays for the town's new dressmaker, Mrs. McKee; and enjoys quiet evenings at home with her family. Laura believes that "Nothing anywhere could be better than being at home with the home folks."[20]

In subsequent chapters of *These Happy Golden Years*, Wilder creates more plot points that spring from this fundamental understanding of Laura's character. Almanzo must win Laura on her terms, and even though he rarely appears directly in the next four chapters, Laura—and Wilder's readers—never lose sight of him. An undercurrent of romantic tension simmers through chapters that seem inherently unromantic: "Holding Down a Claim," "Mary Comes Home," "Summer Days." It's a masterful approach, one that reinforces the inevitability of this romance yet sustains its suspense.

In the chapter "Holding Down a Claim," for example, Laura has this exchange with Mrs. McKee:

> "It would be pleasanter for you to be riding in Wilder's buggy."
>
> "I likely won't do that any more," Laura remarked. "Someone else will be in my place before I go back. . . ."
>
> "Don't worry," Mrs. McKee told her. "An old bachelor doesn't pay so much attention to a girl unless he's serious. You will marry him yet."
>
> "Oh, no!" Laura said. "No indeed I won't! I wouldn't leave home to marry anybody."[21]

When Mary returns from college for the summer, she asks Laura, "Where's that Wilder boy, that Ma wrote me about? It seems like he'd be around sometime." Laura dismisses Mary's question by saying, "I think he is too busy on his claim. Everybody is busy." Still, Laura has a growing awareness that not only are townsfolk and neighbors talking about a possible relationship between herself and Almanzo, now her family is curious about it too. And suddenly, Laura discovers she feels "shy" talking about Almanzo.[22]

The final turning point—moving Laura from romantic reluctance to acceptance—comes midway through *These Happy Golden Years*. It is wintertime again. A year has passed since Laura taught at the Brewster school, and one Sunday afternoon Cap Garland knocks on the door at the Ingalls house in town. He asks Laura, "Would you like a sleigh ride behind the colts?"[23] Laura's heart sinks. To her surprise, she discovers that Cap no longer holds any attraction for her. Instead, her thoughts turn immediately to . . . Almanzo.

But how should she respond to Cap? Should she say yes to his invitation, and deny what's in her heart, or should she decline and risk exposing feelings for Almanzo that, until now, she hasn't openly admitted even to herself? This split second of inner turmoil is another subtle but brilliant creative brushstroke. Wilder eliminates Cap as a possible romantic rival for Almanzo while simultaneously revealing Laura's sudden recognition that she cares for him. This pivotal moment covers just two paragraphs but reveals more than pages of emotional description or inner dialogue could convey. It also reinforces the spontaneity and spark of romance, which is often indescribable.

Before Laura has to commit herself, Cap tells her, "Wilder asked me to ask you, because the colts won't stand. He'll be by here in a minute and pick you up, if you'd like to go."

Now Laura doesn't hesitate. "Yes, I would! . . . I'll be ready."[24]

But she's ready not just for this next sleigh ride; Laura is ready now for the adventure of courtship.

A Modern Courtship

When Laura accepts Almanzo's attentions, however, she does so on her own terms. She doesn't abandon the qualities that have defined her throughout the Little House series. She remains impulsive, independent, unwilling to be confined by the conventions of courtship. Almanzo seems to understand this about her; Laura can be herself with him. And in this sense, their courtship, despite its nineteenth-century trappings, feels modern.

Throughout the last half of the novel, for example, Laura continues to demonstrate the physical courage and determination she exhibits in earlier Little House books. Once again, Wilder uses Almanzo's horses—his mastery and Laura's attraction to them—as a metaphor for the romance, passion, and understanding Laura and Almanzo share. When he comes calling, driving a wild, unbroken team of horses—Barnum and Skip—Laura is quick to join him, although she's dressed in her good brown poplin worn over a wide set of hoops and petticoats. As she approaches the buggy, Barnum rears "straight up on his hind legs."[25] The buggy springs away, and Almanzo has to circle the house, leaving Laura behind. When the buggy almost stops by the door again, Laura leaps into the buggy, hoopskirts and all. Ma tells Laura, "I am afraid to have you ride behind those horses." Pa takes a more measured stance. "Does seem like Wilder is trying to get you killed. But I'd say you are enjoying it from the way your eyes are shining."[26]

Laura may have accepted courtship, but hers is an unconventional one. She remains at heart an athletic tomboy, dratting her hoop skirts and leaping safely "between the wheels" into a barely stationary buggy.[27] She retains the spirit of the pioneer girl she was in *On the Banks of Plum Creek*, who fiercely clings to the footbridge as the cold, flooded creek soaks into her—never screaming or crying or giving in to the ruthless power of the West.

Even when Laura finally accepts Almanzo's proposal, she remains playful, independent, and slightly willful:

> "I was wondering if you would like an engagement ring."
>
> "That would depend on who offered it to me," Laura told him.
>
> "If I should?" Almanzo asked.
>
> "Then it would depend on the ring," Laura answered, and drew her hand away.[28]

When she accepts Almanzo's engagement ring on the next page, he promises to build Laura "a little house in the grove on the tree claim. It will have to be a little house. Do you mind?" Wilder gives Laura the perfect response—for the novel and for the series: "I have always lived in little houses. I like them."[29]

Fireworks Flash

While the relationship that develops between Laura and Almanzo feels modern, their courtship itself seems tame and relatively passionless to modern readers of Young Adult fiction. Since the late 1980s, Young Adult novels have become more sexually direct and explicit. John Greene's *Looking for Alaska*, for example, includes a very candid description of oral sex. By contrast, Almanzo doesn't even kiss Laura when he proposes. He waits until Laura invites him to kiss her.

Wilder's approach, however, wasn't unusual in the 1940s. Mainstream American publishers in the early twentieth century expected even authors writing for adult readers to largely ignore the physicality of their characters—or to write discreetly about it. One reason *Gone with the Wind* was so popular in 1936 was because its author, Margaret Mitchell, found a way to write about sexual attraction in what, for the period, seemed candid, persuasive, and passionate. Although now the book is often considered a Young Adult novel, Mitchell wrote it for adult readers.

In the twenty-first century, it's hard to imagine a world where writers were unable to openly describe their characters' sexual feelings, but when Wilder wrote *These Happy Golden Years*, only a handful of literary authors were experimenting with sexual content—and exclusively for adults. Romance itself—as both plot and theme—was considered adult subject matter.

Yet Laura and Almanzo's courtship in *These Happy Golden Years* isn't without passion. It's just that their passion appears indirectly in the novel. As we've already discussed, his horses radiate sexual energy. In scene after scene, Laura is drawn to their strength, beauty, and even danger. In *These Happy Golden Years*, however, Wilder extends Laura's attraction to Almanzo himself. Only he can master those horses; only he has the physical prowess to control them. As Pa tells Laura, "That young fellow missed his vocation; he ought to be a lion tamer. Those horses are wilder than hawks."[30]

When Laura is with Almanzo, she shares directly in this very physical experience. As he and Laura take their first sleigh ride together up Main Street, Prince and Lady whisk them out to the open prairie "around in a circle to the north, and back again, and again."[31] Laura is so happy that she feels like singing. Later in the novel, Almanzo passes her the reins to the wild and virtually uncontrollable Barnum. Laura's "arms took the force of Barnum's pull; his strength flowed up the lines with the thrill she had felt before." As the scene comes to an end, Laura feels "a little dizzy, from the excitement." All the while, Almanzo is sitting close beside her in the buggy, speaking in a "low tone."[32] Toward the end of *These Happy Golden Years*, Ma tells Laura, "Sometimes I think it is the horses you care for, more than their master." And Laura's shaky reply: "I couldn't have one without the other."[33]

As the novel progresses, Wilder subtly increases the intimacy between Laura and Almanzo. For example, the chapter "The Cream-Colored Hat," which appears toward the end of *These Happy Golden Years*, is about much more than that hat. Granted, the hat is beautiful, embellished with three perfectly shaded ostrich feathers. It fits perfectly "under the mass of Laura's braided hair."[34] She wears the hat for the first time on a Sunday afternoon buggy ride with Almanzo.

Wilder layers the scene with familiar Little House elements—the beauty of the prairie landscape, the unpredictability of the West—but gives them a distinctly romantic spin: "Instead of being white with blowing snow, the prairie was many shades of soft green, but the wind still blew. It came from the south and was warm; it blew the wild grass and the grain in the fields; it blew the horses' manes and tails streaming behind them; it blew the fringes of the lap robe that was tucked in tightly to protect Laura's delicate lawn dress. And it blew the lovely, cream-colored ostrich feathers off Laura's hat."[35] Laura catches the feathers before they blow away, and Almanzo puts them in his pocket so she won't lose them. It's a small moment, perhaps, but it reveals the intimacy between the two. In the late nineteenth century, a young woman wouldn't entrust something as personal, as intimate as the feathers from her hat to just any young man. And Almanzo accepts them without surprise or question. They are clearly a couple, bound together by something deep, unspoken, and personal.

But the scene doesn't end here. Laura and Almanzo drive back into town for the Fourth of July celebration, and they watch from his buggy, "well outside the crowd." As fireworks flash, the horses rear and leap. They "come down running," and Almanzo swings them out and around in a "wide circle," again and again: "After each explosion of beauty against the darkness, Almanzo drove the circle, always bringing Barnum and Skip around in time to face the next rush and blossom of fire. Not until the last shower of sparks had faded did Almanzo and Laura drive away."[36] The scene reads like a frontier version of the fireworks scene in Alfred Hitchcock's *To Catch a Thief*, where Cary Grant and the beautiful Grace Kelly essentially seduce each other off-camera. As for the feathers from Laura's hat, they remain safely in Almanzo's pocket until he hands them back to her as the chapter ends.

A close reading of *These Happy Golden Years* reveals that Wilder's depiction of Laura and Almanzo's courtship isn't entirely antiquated or passionless. And like Wilder, many contemporary authors for young adult and adult readers continue to write indirectly or metaphorically about love, passion, and their characters' sexual feelings. In this context, the romance at the heart of *These Happy Golden Years* is timeless.

Grit, Talent, and Persistence

More importantly, perhaps, Wilder's depiction of romance and courtship, despite its sexual restraint, is refreshingly modern. Laura, for example, doesn't define herself by the young man who's courting her, as does Angie Morrow in Maureen Daley's *Seventeenth Summer*: "It's funny what a boy can do. One day you're nobody and the next day you're the girl that some fellow goes with. Going with a boy gives you a new identity."[37]

Laura doesn't feel that Almanzo changes her identity. Throughout their courtship in *These Happy Golden Years*, she pursues other interests. Her independence defines her, not romance. As central as the romance theme is to *These Happy Golden Years*, Laura's quest to establish herself as a successful schoolteacher is equally important.

Wilder devotes several chapters to the challenges Laura faces in the classroom and her struggle to overcome them. Initially, as we've seen, her struggles seem insurmountable. Not only is Laura an inexperienced schoolteacher, she's physically tiny. Three students at the Brewster school are taller than she is, and Clarence, her most troublesome student, is even older than Laura. He defies her at every turn. After two weeks of teaching, Laura is convinced that she is failing, unable to maintain discipline in the classroom. Her thoughts center on finishing her first term as a schoolteacher and surviving the trauma of the Brewster household, not entirely on Almanzo Wilder.

Ultimately, Laura proves herself to be a fine schoolteacher, who is able to inspire and maintain order in the classroom. Even on the day after the butcher knife incident, when Laura is clearly distraught, her students behave admirably. They've learned discipline and diligence from her. They study by the stove in their coats to keep warm as snow blows "through the schoolroom's walls" and their lunches freeze in their dinner pails. It cheers "Laura to see how well every pupil behaved."[38]

Laura's first term as a schoolteacher ends successfully, but she's determined to continue her education when the term is over. In fact, the value of education is an essential thread that runs through *These Happy Golden Years*. It's woven into Laura's determination to be a better teacher and, as we'll see, into her unspoken ambition to become a writer. Her commitment to education—for her students and for herself—marks her growth and maturity as a young woman. Her romance with Almanzo is secondary to this achievement.[39]

Laura goes on to teach at two other schools.[40] Although she initially dreaded to be a teacher, she discovers the work is challenging and satisfying. It actually makes her "happy." Best of all, her students are "as good as gold, and eager and quick to learn."[41]

Laura savors her independence, her new maturity—and she has achieved it herself, through grit and perseverance, talent and hard work. By the end of *These Happy Golden Years*, Laura has become an accomplished and independent young woman.

Ambition

Throughout the Little House series, Wilder plants intriguing conversations or scenes that hint at a future Laura may have as a writer. In *These Happy Golden Years*, Wilder includes two more. They cement the connection readers have already made between the fictional Laura Ingalls of the Little House books and the real Laura Ingalls Wilder who wrote them. These scenes, appearing as they do in the last Little House book, bring this thread of Wilder's novels to a satisfying conclusion, the first of many thematic threads that are woven into the fabric of *These Happy Golden Years*.

The first of these writerly scenes occurs just after Laura has completed her first term as a schoolteacher at the Brewster school.

She happily returns to De Smet as a student herself, and after weeks of independent study at the Brewster settlement, is relieved to discover that she is "still sailing at the head of the class with flying colors."[42] Her delight, however, is soon crushed. At recess, she learns that her class has been assigned to write a composition about ambition. Laura panics. "She had never written a composition, and now she must do in a few minutes what others had been working on since yesterday."[43] Laura's own ambition, however, drives her to tackle the assignment. With five minutes to spare before class begins, Laura writes quickly, efficiently, and instinctively. When she reads her composition aloud to Mr. Owen, her beloved schoolteacher, he is surprised by the quality of her writing and tells her, "You should write more."[44]

As we've already discussed, this scene is autobiographical, but in the context of the novel, this fictional account is pivotal. As the scene ends, Laura feels not only "confident" that "with steady work she would keep her place at the head of her classes," but more importantly, she looks "forward to happily writing more compositions." In other words, Laura has begun to find her voice as a writer, and while Laura maintains she knows "nothing about ambition," she is, indeed, ambitious. In becoming a successful schoolteacher, impressing Mr. Owen with her composition, and maintaining her place at the head of the class, Laura has already demonstrated an essential idea from her own composition: "Without an ambition to excel others and to surpass one's self there would be no superior merit. To win anything, we must have the ambition to do so."[45] Readers of *These Happy Golden Years* sense that Laura's ambition will sustain her beyond the pages of the Little House books, and that she will happily continue to write.

Later in *These Happy Golden Years*, Wilder adds one final grace note to her fictional counterpart's ambition to write. When Mary returns from college for the summer, she and Laura walk together across the prairie while the wild roses are in bloom. Mary confides:

> "I am planning to write a book some day. . . ." Then she laughed. "But I planned to teach school, and you are doing that for me, so maybe you will write a book."

> "I write a book?" Laura hooted. She said blithely. "I'm going to be an old maid schoolteacher, like Miss Wilder. Write your own book!"[46]

Yet readers know Mary's prediction is right. In this moment, the fictional Laura Ingalls and the real Laura Ingalls Wilder seem to merge. The author's past becomes her character's unspoken future. In this passage, reality and fiction become virtually indistinguishable.

Everything Changes

This conversation between Laura and Mary illustrates how capably Wilder resolves her characters' stories, their ongoing conflicts, and the overriding thematic issues at the center of the Little House books in *These Happy Golden Years*. Later in the novel, Laura and Mary share their last scene together. Mary remains the proper, more conventional older sister; Laura is ever the unconventional one. During church services, a kitten being chased by a dog takes refuge under Laura's hoop skirts, and she can barely suppress her laughter. Afterward Mary, in characteristic fashion, tells Laura, "Will you never learn to behave yourself properly in church?" Laura's answer? "No, Mary, I never will. . . . You might as well give me up as a hopeless case."[47] In this scene, Laura is eighteen and engaged to marry Almanzo, but her response to Mary is consistent with the little girl she had been in *Little House on the Prairie* and *On the Banks of Plum Creek*.

But a few paragraphs later it's clear that Laura and Mary have nevertheless evolved as Little House characters. Their relationship has deepened despite the fundamental differences in their personalities. They take a final walk together "to the top of the low hill" on the family's claim at sunset. Mary tells Laura, "I never see things so well with anyone else."[48] The girls are at peace with one another. They have forged an unbreakable bond, and yet from this moment forward, both realize that nothing between them will be the same. They gaze out at the prairie together, imagining a future landscape of cottonwoods, box elders, maples, and willows, planted on tree claims like Almanzo's. Mary says, "It will be strange to see those prairies wooded." Laura's response captures the essence of the scene: "Everything changes," she says.[49] This final scene between the two sisters is moving and eloquent.

This evolution in character applies to Pa as well. In *These Happy Golden Years*, his restless, westering spirit remains, but it has been tempered by age and by Ma's vision for the family:

> "I would like to go West," he told Ma one day. "A fellow doesn't have room to breathe here any more."
>
> "Oh, Charles! No room, with all this great prairie around you?" Ma said. "I was so tired of being dragged from pillar to post, and I thought we were settled here."
>
> "Well, I guess we are, Caroline. Don't fret. It's just that my wandering foot gets to itching."[50]

Ma has prevailed. The Ingalls family will set down lasting roots in Dakota Territory, where Pa will live out his life. Still, Wilder ends the scene with a bittersweet paragraph that binds Laura and Pa together, uniting them one last time in their fundamental love of the wild, untamed West: "Laura knew how he felt for she saw the look in his blue eyes as he gazed over the rolling prairie westward from the open door where he stood. He must stay in a settled country for the sake of them all."[51]

Everything has changed and yet nothing has changed. Wilder's archetypal pioneer family has found a permanent home in the West, but that restless spirit to move on, to dream of something better just beyond the horizon remains unquenched. Now, however, it must find new expression—not in westward movement but in guarded optimism. As Laura tells Mary, "What good times we had when we were little. . . . But maybe the times that are coming will be even better. You never know."[52]

As for the West—at least that slice where the Ingalls family has put down roots—it too has changed in *These Happy Golden Years*. On long buggy rides with Almanzo, Laura continues to admire the wild expanse of the West. But even as far away as Lake Henry, they observe new claim shanties, some with "a stable" or "a field of broken sod nearby." As Almanzo tells Laura, "This country is settling up fast."[53]

Still, the West remains unpredictable and dangerous. A summer storm almost overtakes Laura and Almanzo one afternoon, and for an instant the uncontrollable power of the West returns: "Almost overhead now, the tumbling, swirling clouds changed from black to a terrifying greenish-purple. . . . No horses, however fast they ran, could outrun the speed of those clouds. Green-purple, they rolled in the sky above the helpless prairie, and reached toward it playfully as a cat's paw tormenting a mouse."[54] Laura and Almanzo escape the storm, but other settlers do not. At the end of the chapter "Summer Storm," Pa tells Ma, "It's a queer country out here. . . . Strange things happen." Ma agrees, and says, "I'm thankful that so far they don't happen to us."[55]

So the West itself is changed and yet unchanged. Life in the West may be settled but is never staid. Even as the curtain closes on the Ingalls family, their life in the West promises more adventure, more unpredictability. Their pioneer story is resolved and yet unresolved, a perfect solution as the Little House saga draws to a close.

A Liberating Spirit

In the final chapters of *These Happy Golden Years*, the courtship theme once again moves center stage. But Wilder's conclusion of the courtship story, at its heart, isn't strictly about romance. It's once again about character: Laura's—and Almanzo's. Their romance blossoms because both are unconventional, both have been shaped by the West and its liberating spirit. In a masterful stroke, Wilder also inserts Nellie Oleson into the courtship story. Her return toward the end of *These Happy Golden Years* resolves the rivalry between the two girls (who are now young women) and provides tension, contrast, and even humor as Laura and Almanzo edge closer toward a lasting commitment.

Throughout the Little House series, Nellie has always represented everything Laura is not. In *On the Banks of Plum Creek*, Nellie is a town girl who brags about her New York connections. Her parents are prosperous merchants, providing Nellie and her brother with fashionable clothes, beautiful books, and wonderful toys. Nellie is pampered, prim, and selfish. Laura, on the other hand, is a country girl. Her parents can't begin to provide all the luxuries Nellie enjoys, and by the end of the novel, Laura and her family have lost almost everything they own to that glittering cloud of grasshoppers. The girls become instant and lasting rivals.

When Nellie returns in *Little Town on the Prairie*, the Olesons' and Ingallses' fortunes have reversed. The Ingalls not only have a homestead claim, they have a house in town. Pa is one of the town's leading citizens. Nellie's family, on the other hand, moved west because they lost their store and everything they owned in Minnesota. Nellie continues to dress well, but her clothes come out of a charity barrel. She's now a poor "country girl," living "on a claim north of town."[56] This reversal of fortune is enormously satisfying for Laura. She "supposed she should be sorry for Nellie, but she wasn't. She wished that Nellie Oleson had stayed in Plum Creek."[57]

Wilder's readers are glad she didn't.

The clash between Nellie and Laura, however, is more than just about childhood rivalry. It's a clash between the conventional East and the unconventional West. It's a question of character. Who would win the most eligible bachelor in town? Whose values will prevail? Nellie's conventional approach, where a girl sets her cap for the man of her choice while appearing dainty and helpless? Or Laura's unconventional path, showcasing her independence, strength, and intelligence?

Wilder sets the stage for this final showdown midway through *These Happy Golden Years*. Laura glimpses the Oleson homestead on a buggy ride with Almanzo. She "had not seen Nellie Oleson's home before, and she felt a little sorry for her; the shanty was so small, standing among the wild grass in the wind."[58] But the very next Sunday afternoon, there's Nellie—sitting beside Almanzo in his buggy when he stops at the Ingalls homestead to take Laura for a ride. Laura is "stupefied" by this development but lets Almanzo help her into the buggy, and then, they're off![59] What follows is one of the funniest scenes in the Little House series.

Nellie talks continuously: "She admired the buggy; she exclaimed over the colts; she praised Almanzo's driving; she gushed about Laura's clothes." Everything, Nellie says, is "just utterly too-too!"[60]

And Laura's reaction? Her "head ached; her ears rang with the continuous babble, and she was furious. Almanzo seemed to be enjoying the drive. At least, he looked as though he were being amused."[61]

Laura soon finds the perfect resolution to this rivalry. When Nellie appears with Almanzo the following week, Laura uses his horses—those wild, still untamed colts, Barnum and Skip—to her advantage:

> Laura bent to tuck the dust robe more closely in at her feet, and as she straightened up again, she carelessly let the end of the robe flutter out on the strong prairie wind. The colts left the ground in one leap and ran.
>
> Nellie screamed and screamed, clutching at Almanzo's arm, which he very much needed to use just then. Laura quietly tucked down the end of the lap robe and sat on it.
>
> When it was no longer flapping behind them, the colts soon quieted and went on in their well-trained trot.[62]

This is a solution only a character as unconventional and perceptive as Laura could envision, and it reflects not only her intuitive understanding of Almanzo but of the West itself—and what its spirit means to them both. Nellie is suitably frightened, and her response underscores the sectional clash rippling below the surface of this longstanding rivalry. "Oh, I never understand these western horses. New York horses are quiet."[63] On the following Sunday, Almanzo appears without Nellie, and Laura learns that Nellie was never a rival for his affections. In "disgust," Almanzo tells Laura, "She is afraid of horses."[64] Not long thereafter, Nellie retreats from the field. She goes back to New York, where she belongs.

Haste to the Wedding

Of course, Almanzo himself is from New York. On that last buggy ride with Nellie, Laura listens as Nellie talks "as though she knew" New York well. Laura senses that Almanzo sees through all this mindless chatter; he knows more about New York than Nellie does.[65] But Laura also recognizes that like Pa, Almanzo is a pioneer, a man of the West. He is capable and courageous. He defines his life on his own terms, unfettered by traditional expectations. And Almanzo appears to admire Laura because she too is fearless in the face of convention. "You're independent, aren't you?" he asks Laura. She immediately answers, "Yes."[66]

Yet even with the prospect of marriage ahead, Laura retains her own identity and her thirst for independence. She refuses to submit to conventional marriage vows, and perhaps just as significantly, Almanzo doesn't expect her to.

> "Almanzo, I must ask you something. Do you want me to promise to obey you?"
>
> Soberly he answered, "Of course not. I know it is in the wedding ceremony, but it is only something that women say. I never knew one that did it, nor any decent man that would want her to."
>
> "Well, I am not going to say I will obey you," said Laura.[67]

She adds, "I do not think I could obey anybody against my better judgment," and Almanzo responds, "I'd never expect you to."[68] Theirs will be a modern marriage of equals.

Their wedding itself is unconventional. It is a rushed and simple affair to avoid interference from Almanzo's bossy sister, Eliza Jane. Even Laura's wedding dress reflects a break with tradition: she chooses a black cashmere. It's a new dress, one that she and Ma have made together, the kind of dress every married woman "should have." It's practical and handsome but not traditionally "pretty" or appropriate for a bride.[69] Ma worries, "Married in black, you'll wish yourself back." Ultimately Laura convinces Ma, who concedes, "I don't suppose there's any truth in these old sayings."[70]

And perhaps even more importantly, Laura gains Pa's support—not just for her choice of a wedding dress but also for the simplicity of the wedding itself: "I think it is a sensible thing to do. You and Almanzo show good judgment."[71] So Laura has the blessing of her mentor and guide, even as she's about to begin an entirely new life away from him.

Laura and Almanzo are married at the home of Reverend Brown, who agrees not to use the word "obey" in the ceremony.[72] They start their life together in the final Little House chapter, appropriately titled "Little Gray Home in the West."

All That Has Happened Since

While Laura's story ends with marriage, it doesn't feel as if she has conformed, or buckled to convention. Throughout *These Happy Golden Years*, Laura has made mature and emotionally satisfying choices that remain consistent with the independent, pioneer spirit of her childhood in the earlier Little House books. As the novel ends, readers sense that Laura is about to begin another adventure, and yet one that is informed by her past, represented by the echo of Pa's fiddle and the lines of a bittersweet song, lines that suggest not just the passing of Laura's childhood but perhaps those of Wilder's readers as well:

> Golden years are passing by
> These happy, golden years.[73]

It is a satisfying ending for the novel, a satisfying ending for the Little House series. And it resonated with readers and critics alike during the final years of World War II and beyond. In 1944 *These Happy Golden Years* was named a Newbery Honor Book, the fifth Little House book to receive this distinction. But the praise that meant the most to Wilder came from her only surviving sister: "Sister Carrie writes me that after she read the book it seemed that she was back in those times again and all that had happened since was a dream."[74]

15

The First Four Years

Unraveling a Literary Mystery

WILDER WROTE HER LITERARY AGENT GEORGE BYE IN MAY 1943 that "a story keeps stirring around in my mind and if it pesters me enough I may write it down and send it to you sometime in the future."[1]

She didn't.

Instead, she decided to "spend what is left of my life in living, not writing about it."[2]

Wilder died at the age of ninety on February 10, 1957. Lane died eleven years later on October 30, 1968, at the age of eighty-one. Apparently, both women felt that *These Happy Golden Years* served as a satisfying ending to the Little House series. But the story doesn't end here.

In 1969 Ursula Nordstrom, Wilder's editor at Harper & Brothers, received astonishing news. "The young man [Roger Lea MacBride] who inherited all the assets of Laura Ingalls Wilder's daughter, Rose Wilder Lane, came in a few days ago and dropped the casual remark that there is a NINTH WILDER MANUSCRIPT, written after *These Happy Golden Years*." Nordstrom was thrilled but perplexed: "I asked why in mercy's name we had never been given it and he explained that it covers the first year of married life for Laura and Almanzo and that there is a faint air of slight disillusion in it, which Laura's daughter thought not suited for the feeling of the 8 published books."[3]

That "faint air of slight disillusion" indeed proved problematical.

Later that same year, Nordstrom observed, "I think Rose Wilder Lane's grandson [Roger Lea MacBride] . . . would let us do some judicious editing [of the ninth Little House book], but I think we just better not. . . . I would hate like hell to tamper with this."[4]

By the time Nordstrom received a typewritten copy of the manuscript, however, it had already been tampered with—by Roger Lea MacBride himself. His secretary created the typewritten copy of the manuscript from Wilder's original, but he authorized changes that went beyond corrections of spelling and punctuation. He cut several lines (and sometimes whole paragraphs) from Wilder's original manuscript and even changed characters' names (more about this later). The book was published as *The First Four Years* in 1971, and marketed as the final installment in the Little House series.

Garth Williams was enlisted to illustrate this new Wilder novel, and his illustrations convey the same warmth and optimism that he brought to the revised edition of the Little House books in 1953. But even Williams's artwork couldn't dispel the disappointment many readers felt as they read *The First Four Years*. They found a new and different Laura in its pages.

THE LAURA WHO MARRIES ALMANZO WILDER IN *THESE HAPPY Golden Years* embraces life on the prairie, admires his skills as a farmer, and looks forward to their new life together with optimism and an open heart. By contrast, the Laura in *The First Four Years* is shrewd, calculating, and critical. She seems motivated by financial security, not by the joy of frontier life or the promise of farming a homestead claim. And her beau in *The First Four Years* has an entirely different name—Manly. She tells him that "a farmer never has any money" and complains that "a farm is such a hard place for a woman. There are so many chores for her to do."[5]

This unappealing, joyless Laura marries Manly reluctantly, questioning his love of the land and belief in farming: "I don't want to marry a farmer. I have always said I never would. I do wish you'd do something else."[6] She sounds more like Nellie Oleson than the Laura Ingalls of the Little House books, who treasures her chores on Pa's homestead claim and finds "perfect satisfaction" as part of a hardworking farm family.[7] In fact, the entire premise of *The First Four Years* hinges on this different Laura's aversion to farming. Before she accepts his marriage proposal, she forces Manly to pledge that if he doesn't succeed as a farmer in three years, he'll quit "and do anything" Laura wants him to do.[8]

She Lost Interest in Revising

How could Laura Ingalls Wilder have written this book as a sequel to *These Happy Golden Years*? In an introduction to *The First Four Years*, MacBride offered the following explanation: "My own guess is that she wrote this one [*The First Four Years*] in the late 1940's and that after Almanzo died [in 1949], she lost interest in revising and completing it for publication. Because she didn't do so, there is a difference from the earlier books in the way the story is told."[9]

As a teen reader of *The First Four Years*, I'd already read and reread Wilder's entire series. The previous Little House books flowed seamlessly in and out of each other. But not *The First Four Years*. It felt as if someone else had written the book, someone who hadn't read *These Happy Golden Years*—or any of the books that came before. MacBride's explanation didn't address what for me, even then, seemed like its most glaring and obvious discrepancy: Almanzo's name. Why would Laura Ingalls Wilder change his name in this last book? It made absolutely no sense, especially since nothing in *The First Four Years* addressed this change. He's simply "Manly."

In the decades since the 1970s, critics, scholars, and biographers have focused on the single phrase in MacBride's introduction that indirectly addresses the *First Four Years*' unsettling and inexplicably un–Little House voice, style, and tone: "She lost interest in revising." By the 1990s, this phrase had taken on a new interpretation: *The First Four Years* didn't measure up to the other Little House books because Lane hadn't rewritten it. Clearly, Lane and not Wilder was the real creative genius behind the Little House books. Without Lane's editorial brilliance, all the Little House books would surely have read like *The First Four Years*. "It was in considering this posthumous volume," writes Lane biographer William Holtz, "that I began to understand the source of the special power of the earlier [Little House] books. . . . The art of the book [*The First Four Years*] does not persuade. And it does not persuade because it is the only book by Laura Ingalls Wilder that did not pass under the shaping hand of Rose Wilder Lane."[10]

On the surface this interpretation of the Little House books seems persuasive. And yet it discounts Wilder's own commitment to character development, theme, and continuity in the Little House books, as evidenced by the editorial letters she exchanged with Lane throughout the 1930s. In August 1938, for example, she discussed not just a possible cast of characters for what became the last two Little House books but her rationale for her decisions: "As Laura grows up and moves on she must leave people behind and make new friends. . . . We have five principal characters who go all the way [through the previous Little House books] counting Almanzo. That is enough to carry the story."[11]

"Counting Almanzo"—not Manly.

Wilder knew her main characters' names and wasn't inclined to change them.

In the same letter, she voices her concern about continuity and accuracy in the Little House books: "Unfortunately we have used real names in these books and must stick closer to facts than otherwise we would need to do."[12] Wilder was well aware that in writing a series of novels, she had to bring consistency to her characters and their stories. She was far from oblivious to glaring inconsistencies in her work.

Wilder's editorial letters contradict the idea that she was nothing but an amateur with a "commonplace mind and a commonplace style," who simply allowed her daughter to have "her way with" the Little House manuscripts.[13] Yet if Wilder wrote *The First Four Years* in the 1940s as a sequel to *These Happy Golden Years*, why did she abandon the continuity she'd passionately defended in the earlier books? Why did Wilder take such a radically different approach in voice and style, plot and characters in *The First Four Years*? Surely Wilder would have caught that glaring Almanzo/Manly inconsistency. *The First Four Years* seemed to be an unfathomable literary mystery.

Striking Parallels

I wrestled with these questions as a biographer, and reluctantly came to accept MacBride's theory that Wilder wrote the manuscript in the 1940s. But what eventually came to haunt me weren't the dissimilarities between *The First Four Years* and the rest of the Little House books, but the similarities between *The First Four Years* and Lane's novel *Let the Hurricane Roar*. It seemed to me that *The First Four Years* wasn't a Little House book at all; it was Wilder's attempt to write an *adult* novel—and that she had used *Let the Hurricane Roar* as a template. But the only evidence I had to support this idea was literary: the striking parallels in plot, style, voice, and theme between the two books (more about this later).

Then I went back to the original manuscript, which Wilder had titled "First Three Years." I remembered my colleague William Anderson had a vague recollection that somewhere in the manuscript, a specific date appeared on one of its pages. William Holtz hinted at something similar, maintaining that Wilder "apparently" wrote *The First Four Years* "sometime before 1937."[14] Unsure of what I would find, or where exactly in the manuscript I should look, I enlisted the help of archivists at the Herbert Hoover Presidential Library, which houses the original.

Like all of Wilder's existing manuscripts, "First Three Years" is written in pencil on ruled tablets and includes false starts, crossed-out paragraphs, marginal notes, and inserts. One of those inserts provided the clue I was looking for, and it appears to unlock the mystery of the book we now know as *The First Four Years*. This random clue suggests that, indeed, Wilder wrote "First Three Years" in the 1930s but several years before 1937, and even *before* she had envisioned a series of Little House books. And it appears to cement the link between Wilder's novel and Lane's *Let the Hurricane Roar*.

The Wind Always Rises with a Fire

The essential clue that seems to unlock this mystery appears toward the end of the original manuscript.[15] There, Wilder inserted a paragraph into the dust storm scene, which unfolds in the final section of the manuscript. The inserted paragraph is all flashback, explaining why Laura thinks the dust storm might have been triggered by a prairie fire, and detailing how Manly and Cousin Peter had previously battled a prairie fire to save a haystack. The insert begins with the line, "The wind always rises with a fire" and ends with the sentence, "The horses had stood with their heads against the stack where they could breathe without fire."[16] This addition appears to have been an afterthought, placed in the manuscript shortly after Wilder had written the dust storm scene—or perhaps even later, after she'd completed the entire draft of the novel. At any rate, she taped the inserted sheet of paper into the tablet and folded it back on itself.

As was her custom, Wilder was conservative with her writing materials, and wrote that flashback paragraph on the back of a letter she'd started and then abandoned, addressed to the Federal Land Bank in St. Louis. The aborted letter is dated "Jan. 20, 1933."[17]

January 20, 1933.

The date is significant—because in January 1933 Wilder had published just one book: *Little House in the Big Woods*. She hadn't yet embarked on the Little House series, much less envisioned the fictional Laura Ingalls of *These Happy Golden Years*. Far from being representative of Wilder's unedited Little House voice, the faint air of slight disillusion in "First Three Years" may, in fact, be her attempt to emulate her daughter's voice in *Let the Hurricane Roar*. Its publication in the fall of 1932 precipitated a painful rift between mother and daughter, and it appears to have inspired Wilder to write this manuscript.

Betrayed and Crushed

First, a quick review: the atmosphere at Rocky Ridge Farm in September 1932 was tense. Until then Wilder had no idea that *Let the Hurricane Roar* existed. Lane, as we've discussed, wrote and marketed her novel in secret. She'd lifted characters, scenes, even dialogue and description directly from Wilder's "Pioneer Girl" manuscript and had then sold *Let the Hurricane Roar* to the *Saturday Evening Post*. Lane's novel quickly achieved all that Wilder had hoped for "Pioneer Girl." *Let the Hurricane Roar* was serialized in the *Saturday Evening Post* in October and November 1932 and then was almost immediately sold again to be republished in book form by Longmans, Green in 1933.

Very little remains in the historical record to document the tension that developed between Wilder and Lane during the autumn of 1932, but Wilder must have felt betrayed and even crushed. *Let the Hurricane Roar* had essentially killed any chances "Pioneer Girl" had of publication. Her daughter's book covered much of the same material and, with its publication in both magazine and book form, would reach a sizable audience. Furthermore, Lane was already a successful and established author with longstanding connections to the publishing establishment. Her book had instant credibility; "Pioneer Girl" did not. It's also important to remember that in the fall of 1932, Wilder had no plans to write a series of books for young readers about her family's pioneering experiences in the West. She had pinned her hopes on "Pioneer Girl" to tell that story to an adult audience. Now her own daughter, behind Wilder's back, had simultaneously scooped and plagiarized her work.

To make matters worse for Wilder that September, she also learned that Harper & Brothers had rejected her second manuscript for children, "Farmer Boy." Wilder's career as a novelist seemed to be over as quickly and as unexpectedly as it had begun.

Lane, on the other hand, felt her mother resented the success of *Let the Hurricane Roar*, and even before the novel was published in the *Saturday Evening Post*, left Rocky Ridge Farm on an extended cross-country trip to New York. She didn't return home until shortly before Christmas, and even then, the tension between mother and daughter lingered. In January 1933 Lane records that Wilder's response to *Let the Hurricane Roar* was "it's all wrong."[18]

During this interval while Lane was away—from late September until December 1932—Wilder apparently wrote much of "First Three Years." As her daughter had done with *Let the Hurricane Roar*, Wilder wrote in secret, creating an entirely new manuscript, this one based on her experiences as a young wife. It picked up where "Pioneer Girl" had left off. But unlike "Pioneer Girl," which was a memoir, this new manuscript was a novel, with a different voice, different characterizations, and its own plot—in short, material that hadn't existed before and that Lane couldn't readily plunder.

Still, in her own way, Wilder borrowed heavily from *Let the Hurricane Roar*. She coopted its main premise: a pair of newlyweds striking out on their own in the American West. And she also drew heavily on its structure, theme, tone, and style. *The First Four Years*, far from reflecting Wilder's unadulterated literary voice, mirrors her daughter's. In fact, it is essentially a sequel to *Let the Hurricane Roar*.

One Inconsistency after Another

Before delving into the similarities between "First Three Years" and *Let the Hurricane Roar*, let's jump from 1932 to 1969, the year Roger Lea MacBride told Ursula Nordstrom about this "new" Wilder manuscript. At the time, the Little House books were bestsellers, and a novel about Laura and Almanzo as grown-ups would undoubtedly have instant national and international appeal. A sequel to *These Happy Golden Years* would be virtually irresistible, an immediate bestseller. There was just one problem, and it went well beyond that "faint air of slight disillusion": this newly discovered manuscript didn't read like a sequel.

Although its opening pages covered some of the same material as *These Happy Golden Years*, it presented a completely different interpretation of Laura's courtship and marriage, even of her family. And it wasn't just a question of Almanzo's new name. Page after page included one inconsistency after another. "First Three Years" didn't conform to the established Little House universe.

In the first place, Pa and Ma weren't Pa and Ma. In the novel's opening pages, they were Laura's "Father" and "Mother." The manuscript mentioned her "three sisters" but didn't give them names.[19] For example, when Laura and Manly leave her home for the wedding ceremony at the Reverend Brown's, she looks back and sees her "father, mother, and sisters" grouped "among the young trees."[20] Not Pa, Ma, Mary, Carrie, and Grace.

Furthermore, key details in the new manuscript's wedding sequence failed to conform to those in *These Happy Golden Years*. In that novel, Mary has returned to the College of the Blind before Laura and Almanzo's wedding. She isn't part of the family watching as Laura and Almanzo drive away to Reverend Brown's. The ceremony itself takes place at "ten o'clock Thursday morning."[21] In "First Three Years," Mary *is*, by implication, one of Laura's three sisters grouped by the doorway on Laura and Manly's wedding day. And their marriage ceremony takes place on a Wednesday, not on Thursday. Even an important detail about Laura's unforgettable black wedding dress has a different spin in "First Three Years": "Her wedding dress was the new black cashmere, she had thought would be so serviceable for as a married woman she should have a black dress. Ida Brown the preacher's daughter and her chum had said 'married in black you will wish yourself back.'"[22] In *These Happy Golden Years*, Ma—not Ida Brown—worries about Laura's black wedding dress.

In conversations with Roger MacBride about this ninth Wilder book, did Ursula Nordstrom express her reluctance to change the manuscript? Possibly. Because the changes in MacBride's typewritten version didn't eliminate the original's "faint air of slight disillusion." Yet it did attempt to subtly bridge the divide between *These Happy Golden Years* and "First Three Years." "Manly" remained as Laura's husband, without any explanation for the change in his name, but Laura's parents assumed their familiar Little House identities as "Ma" and "Pa." Laura's sisters became "Carrie and Grace." Any implied reference to Mary was dropped in the typewritten version. As for those contradictory details and paragraphs, they were eliminated or changed to conform to the established Little House canon. Occasional sentences or details that might disturb or confuse young readers were cut from the published text too. Then, there was the title: "First Three Years" became *The First Four Years*, a change that reflected the four-year structure of Wilder's original manuscript.

These editorial changes gave *The First Four Years* a kind of Little House gloss. In the published text, for example, Laura glances back at her family on her wedding day, and sees "Ma, Pa, and Carrie and Grace." As for Laura's wedding dress, the description in *The First Four Years* is brief and conforms to details in *These Happy Golden Years*: "Her wedding dress was the new black cashmere she had thought would be so serviceable, for a married woman should have a black dress."[23] Still, such editorial sleight of hand failed to disguise the novel's distinctive voice, structure, and characterizations. *The First Four Years* doesn't *read* like a Little House book. It reads like *Let the Hurricane Roar*.

A Mythic Template

Both *Let the Hurricane Roar* and *The First Four Years* open with swift introductions to their main characters. Lane's are simply known as Charles and Caroline; Wilder's are Manly and Laura.

Charles and Caroline are archetypal pioneers; Manly and Laura are archetypal homesteaders, representing the next generation in the West. While their circumstances are different, as are their places in American history, both couples must forge new lives together in an unpredictable, unforgiving environment.

The structural similarities between these two novels are also unmistakable, and impose a kind of mythic template over the characters and their stories. Neither *Let the Hurricane Roar* nor *The First Four Years* have traditional chapter breaks. Instead, they both unfold over four sections, moving characters through sweeps of fictional time and space. Though both books are short, their four-part structure transports readers into settings where characters endure epic hardships with courage, perseverance, and ultimately grace. Lane numbers and titles her sections: "I: Wild Plum Creek"; "II: And there remained not any green thing"; "III: In a little old sod shanty/On a claim"; "IV: Let the hurricane roar!/It will the sooner be o'er!/We'll weather the blast and land at last,/On Canaan's happy shore!" Wilder's section titles are less poetic and more practical: "The First Year"; "The Second Year"; "The Third Year"; "A Year of Grace." But they function as Lane's do, giving *The First Four Years* a four-part structure with storybook resonance.

Wilder deviates from Lane's structure in just one way: she adds a two-page prologue to *The First Four Years*, and it establishes a dreamy, impressionistic quality to the novel right from the beginning. On a soft, starry night in June, a pair of nameless "lovers" drive slowly along the banks of Silver Lake. The stars hang "luminous and low over the prairie," and the night is "sweet with the strong, dewy fragrance of the wild prairie roses that grew in masses along the way." The lovers themselves are indistinct. He is a "dark blur." She is "the white-clothed form beside him." The woman breaks into song with a "sweet contralto voice."[24] What follows are the lyrics to the song "In the Starlight."

Wilder had used the lyrics to this same song in a scene toward the end of "Pioneer Girl." So on the surface it appears that she has written overlapping scenes, that *The First Four Years*—at least, its opening pages—begins with nothing more than a fictional retelling of her own courtship and marriage. But the scenes in "Pioneer Girl" and the prologue in *The First Four Years* end quite differently.

After Laura sings "In the Starlight" in "Pioneer Girl," she accepts Manly's offer of an engagement ring and invites him to kiss her. The scene unfolds primarily with dialogue interspersed with brief descriptive passages; it has a clear resolution.[25] In *The First Four Years*, the prologue ends more enigmatically: the lovers are simply "abroad in the still, sweet" evening, savoring the quiet that comes "after the winds had hushed at sunset."[26] Wilder doesn't break the scene's emotional intensity with dialogue or even resolution. The "dark blur" and the "white-clothed form beside him" are simply archetypal lovers in an archetypal western landscape. As Lane does in the opening pages of *Let the Hurricane Roar*, Wilder sets the stage for a pair of mythic lovers who will soon marry and face a series of almost unimaginable adversities. Their struggle will ultimately be heroic.

Both Wilder and Lane, however, place the wife at the heart of this struggle for survival in the West. Caroline in *Let the Hurricane Roar* and Laura in *The First Four Years* wrestle with the choices their husbands have made for them, even as they experience universal rites of passage that have defined women's lives for millennia: separation from their families, homemaking, and childbirth. Again, the similarities between the two novels are undeniable, reinforcing the idea that Wilder used Lane's novel as a model for her own.

Parallel Journeys as Young Wives

In the opening line of Lane's novel, Charles and Caroline are married and just two pages later embark on their life in the West, leaving their families behind in the Big Woods, where they had grown up together. Initially, Caroline finds it difficult to embrace the life of a pioneer, one she hadn't envisioned for herself until Charles decides to move West. She aches for her old life with her father, mother, and sisters, but memories of home "soon ceased to hurt her, in her happiness for Charles."[27]

In the original "First Three Years," Wilder's depiction of Laura's departure with Manly on their wedding day strikes a similar tone. As Laura looks back, she sees her family waving and throwing kisses: "There was a little choke in Laura's throat." But her feelings are immediately lightened as Manly takes her hand and presses it "strongly."[28] Wilder's passage contains more warmth and intimacy than Lane's, but both exhibit a similar detachment from their characters—and create an undercurrent of tension: the young wife still longing for the security of home, the husband drawing his wife into the new life he is about to create for them.

Wilder and Lane give their characters a similar start as they begin their journeys as young wives. Caroline's parents in *Let the Hurricane Roar* give her "two blankets, two wild-goose-feather pillows," a set of cooking pots and pans, and provisions for the trek west. They also send her west with "Tennyson's poems beautifully bound in green and gilt."[29] Laura's parents, first-generation pioneers themselves, provide Laura with a "bright red-and-white checked" tablecloth, as much a symbol of home as Caroline's feather pillows.[30] Instead of provisions for a young couple's trek west, Laura's parents present their newlywed daughter with a "fawn-colored heifer," an ideal gift for a pair of young homesteaders. And by implication, "the copies of Scott's and Tennyson's poems" on the bookshelf in Laura's new home are from her family's household, not Manly's.[31] With these treasures from home, both Caroline and Laura establish themselves as homemakers.

Lane's Caroline sets up housekeeping first in a sod shanty in a railroad camp, then in a dugout on the banks of Wild Plum Creek, where in the spring Charles will plant wheat and build them a new house. The dugout proves "cozy for winter-time, cooler in the summers," and Caroline is happy there. "It is clean and neat."[32] Wilder follows a similar pattern for the first section in *The First Four Years*. Like Caroline, Laura initially delights in her new home, despite her doubts about Manly's ambition to be a farmer. She sets up housekeeping in a "bright and shining little house," on Manly's tree claim.[33] She takes "pride of possession" in the house he has provided for them.[34]

Laura's modest little house is undoubtedly far grander than Caroline's sod shanty and dugout. And on the surface Laura and Manly appear to be a more prosperous newlywed couple than Caroline and Charles. But Wilder is simply laying the foundation for the crisis to come. Manly and Laura spend money freely. He even buys her a pony, and a "beautiful all-leather saddle, tan-colored and fancy-stitched with nickel trimmings" from the Montgomery Ward's catalogue.[35] This prosperity appears to banish Laura's reservations about Manly's ambition to farm. Wilder writes, "It was a carefree, happy time, for two people thoroughly in sympathy" with each other.[36] Like Caroline in the opening pages of *Let the Hurricane Roar*, Laura is happy and "festive."[37]

Borne Away on a Wave of Pain

Another mythic rite of passage unites Wilder's and Lane's characters in their novels' opening sections: motherhood. In *Let the Hurricane Roar*, Caroline gives birth to a son. Laura, in the first section of the original "First Three Years" manuscript, learns she is pregnant. Wilder places the birth of Laura's baby in the second section of her novel but otherwise appears to follow Lane's example, devoting several paragraphs to Laura's childbirth experience. Furthermore, Wilder's depiction of childbirth is hauntingly similar to Lane's.

Lane's childbirth scene in *Let the Hurricane Roar* is original, one of a handful of episodes in the novel she *didn't* lift from the "Pioneer Girl" manuscript. Wilder's references in her memoir to the births of her younger siblings had been brief and restrained, a reflection perhaps of her upbringing. In "Pioneer Girl," for example, she recorded the birth of her baby brother, Charles Frederick, in just one sentence. When she and Mary come home from school one day, they find "a strange woman getting supper and a little brother beside Ma in bed."[38]

Lane, on the other hand, devotes over two pages to her childbirth scene in *Let the Hurricane Roar*. Caroline is alone in the dugout with Charles when her time comes. She tries "to remember all she had heard about childbirth" and conceals from her husband "how much she wanted her mother."[39] Her labor stretches over two days, and five paragraphs, culminating in this one: "Then everything became confused. Daylight and darkness were mixed. She heard shrieks and knew they were hers; she could not stop them. Even Charles was gone. There was nothing anywhere but unbearable agony. She herself was ebbing, going—a last little atom fighting, failing—."[40] Caroline's experience is so nightmarish, so traumatic, that she, at first, believes her baby is dead. Then Charles, who is sobbing, tells her, "He's all right. Oh, Caroline, Caroline—."[41] It's a melodramatic ending to the scene.

It's important to note, however, that Lane wasn't the only novelist in the late 1920s and early 1930s to depict pioneer childbirth experiences in the American West. In 1928, for example, Beth Streeter Aldrich included a pair of brief childbirth sequences in her popular novel *A Lantern in Her Hand*. Aldrich, as Lane herself would do four years later, focused on the fear and isolation women faced when their "hour had come" and their bodies were "wracked." One line from *A Lantern in Her Hand*, in particular, seems almost to foreshadow Caroline's predicament in *Let the Hurricane Roar*: "The greatest fear of all for prairie women—to be alone on the desert of grass with the pangs of childbirth upon her."[42] Still, unlike Lane's Caroline, Aldrich's pioneer doesn't give birth alone. She is assisted in her births by a neighbor, the women in her family, and a doctor who arrives just in the nick of time.

Wilder's childbirth scene in *The First Four Years* follows Lane's example, also unfolding like a nightmare as Laura moves in and out of consciousness. Gone is the reticence Wilder exhibited on this subject in "Pioneer Girl." But unlike Lane's Caroline, Wilder's Laura isn't left to give birth alone with her husband in an isolated dugout. Manly fetches Laura's mother, a neighbor, and ultimately the doctor. Despite its dreamlike structure, these important details ground the scene in reality. Gone is Lane's melodrama.

In Wilder's handwritten manuscript, Laura watches from the window as Manly drives away to fetch her mother. Laura wants to go with him, "to drive away and away even from herself if that were possible."[43] This line is important, and signals the transition into that altered physical and emotional state that inevitably comes with labor and childbirth. Unfortunately, the line doesn't appear in the published novel, perhaps because MacBride felt it was inappropriate for young readers. In fact, the childbirth scene in *The First Four Years* is among the most heavily edited in the book. For this reason, I've chosen to quote entirely from Wilder's original manuscript here.

When Manly returns, Laura takes her mother's advice and goes to bed. She drifts in and out of consciousness, awaking at one point to realize that her mother's friend, Mrs. Power, has arrived. Laura hears her say, "But we'd better have the Dr. out now I'm thinking."[44] Laura slips away again, then reawakens: "When Laura could again see and know what went on around her, her mother and Mrs. Power were standing one on each side of her bed. And was that Manly at the foot? No! Manly had gone for the Dr. Then were there two mothers and two Mrs. Powers. They seemed to be all around her."[45] This is clearly a nightmare scenario with parallels to the scene in *Let the Hurricane Roar*.

Wilder then layers her childbirth narrative with a more lyrical expression of suffering as Laura struggles to remember an old hymn, and take comfort in its lyrics:

—angel band
Come and around me stand
Oh bear me away on your snowy wings
To—

Laura's memory then fails her, and she is "borne away on a wave of pain."[46]

The song, popularly known as "Angel Band," is about the last moments before death, a summons to a band of angels to bear the dying soul away to "my immortal home."[47] This is the line Laura fails to remember, and it signals a brush with death. Laura, like Caroline in *Let the Hurricane Roar*, believes she may be dying, or as Lane puts it, "fighting, failing."

Wilder includes one other detail in this episode that gives it even more emotional resonance. The hymn is one that Laura's father—"Pa"—used to sing. This is a rare reference to Laura's father as "Pa" in the original manuscript. It gives the scene more immediacy and intimacy. Pa becomes part of Laura's angel band, a source of solace and comfort as she's borne away on waves of pain. Unfortunately, the typed manuscript that MacBride submitted to Harper & Row in 1969 included a typo in the lyrics to the hymn, which carried over into the published version of *The First Four Years*: "angel bank," instead of "angel band."[48] Still, the published version of the scene retains its original emotional integrity. As Laura faces death, she is surrounded by family: her mother at her bedside, her father in her memory, her husband hovering nearby. The moment is multigenerational.

"A gust of cold fresh air" then brings Laura back to herself, and she sees "a tall man drop his snowy overcoat by the door"—the doctor. Relief is moments away. She feels "a cloth touch her face" and smells "a keen odor." She then drifts "away into a blessed darkness" without pain.[49] Laura awakens to a baby daughter, Rose.

While Wilder's childbirth scene in *The First Four Years* certainly differs from Lane's in *Let the Hurricane Roar*, its broad outlines are identical: a very young, inexperienced mother (Caroline is seventeen; Laura is nineteen); pain conveyed through a nightmare sequence; and the mother restored to consciousness with a baby nestled beside her. In both books, the young mothers rejoice in the birth of their firstborn. For Caroline, "The baby had been born on her seventeenth birthday, like a present."[50] Laura observes that "a Rose in December was much rarer than a rose in June."[51] Their infants, however, will complicate their futures and the inevitable hardships of life in the West. Once again, Caroline and Laura seem to exist in parallel universes.

The Promise of Wealth

Like Pa in "Pioneer Girl," Charles in *Let the Hurricane Roar* plants wheat along Wild Plum Creek in the spring, and as the crop matures, it promises abundance. He tells Caroline that at harvest the wheat will bring "two thousand dollars, I tell you, if it brings us a cent." Caroline is "dazed" by the promise of such wealth.[52]

Before the wheat is harvested, Charles begins to dig the cellar for their new house, eager to move Caroline and the baby out of the dugout on Wild Plum Creek. His dreams of success multiply, his mind leaping "into the next year, and the next." He forecasts a profit of five thousand dollars the following year. Surely what he and Caroline need is more land—a tree claim! On a fiercely hot summer day, he drives into town, planning to file for more land, leaving Caroline and the baby behind. But he returns with a load of lumber and "a new, red mowing machine."[53] His haul also includes "four window sashes," four "panes of real glass," "shimmering brown silk" for Caroline, and beefsteak, candy, raisins, and "even a pound of butter and a pound of white sugar."[54] Charles has taken out a loan against his wheat crop.

Then, as the first section in *Let the Hurricane Roar* comes to a close, grasshoppers descend from the sky, the air twinkling "with their shining wings."[55] Caroline's bliss as a young wife and mother comes to a nightmarish end. Their wheat crop is "devastated": "There was nothing but bare earth to the rim of the sky. Earth, and a litter of old, dead weed stalks."[56]

Manly in *The First Four Years* also plants wheat in the spring, and as the days go by, it grows "tall and strong and green and beautiful."[57] And like Charles in *Let the Hurricane Roar*, Manly believes the wheat crop will turn an almost unimaginable profit for his young family. "'Didn't I tell you,' he said 'that everything evens up? The rich get their ice in the summer but the poor get theirs in the winter.' He laughed and Laura laughed with him. It was wonderful."[58]

And again, like Charles in *Let the Hurricane Roar*, Manly soon goes into town and comes home with farm machinery—a new binder. He takes out a loan for two hundred dollars. But before he can harvest the entire crop, a storm strikes and hailstones begin to fall, "at first scattering slowly, then falling thicker and faster while the stones were larger, some of them as large as hens' eggs."[59] The crop is ruined. "The storm lasted only twenty minutes but it left a desolate, rain-drenched and hail-battered world."[60] The line echoes Caroline's observation of the apocalyptic landscape the grasshoppers have left behind in *Let the Hurricane Roar*.

But unlike Caroline, Laura then learns something even more devastating: Manly is already five hundred dollars in debt for their bright and shining little house on the tree claim, a fact he had concealed from her when they married. Laura and Manly are now actually seven hundred dollars in debt, and to raise money to see them through the next year and pay interest on his existing loan, they must rent out their house, mortgage Manly's homestead claim, and move into a twelve-by-sixteen-foot claim shanty there.

By the end of the first section in *The First Four Years*, Laura's circumstances mirror Caroline's in *Let the Hurricane Roar*. Their stories are virtually identical.

Continuing Hardships

In Lane's novel, Caroline and Charles spend much of its second section fighting off grasshoppers only to realize the wheat can't be saved. Charles tries and fails to find work at a railroad camp twenty miles away. Ultimately he strikes out east, hoping to find work, and lands a job at an Iowa Feed Mill, earning "$30 a month."[61] Caroline is left behind with the baby in the dugout to hold down their homestead claim. As the second section of *Let the Hurricane Roar* closes, Caroline loses her nearest neighbors: "The Svensons were giving up; they were going east."[62] With winter closing in and no sign of Charles, Caroline must decide whether to go east and try to find him or hold down the claim herself.

The remaining two sections of *Let the Hurricane Roar* focus entirely on Caroline. She, at first, takes the Svensons' advice, and decides to overwinter in town. But she can't find work there, and returns to the dugout on the homestead claim. Caroline's decision to overwinter alone in an isolated dugout is unconventional. As one of the townswomen tells Caroline, "Well, of course you can't stay by yourself on a claim and winter coming on! There's not many men'll do it."[63] What's more—Caroline is pregnant again. Yet she returns to the dugout, armed with supplies for the winter and a loaded pistol for protection. The final section of *Let the Hurricane Roar* focuses on Caroline's struggle to survive Lane's version of the Hard Winter. Caroline battles cold, dark, hunger, loneliness, and even a pack of wolves.

Caroline's isolation at first appears to be original to Lane's novel. But it is based on her mother's account in "Pioneer Girl" when Pa leaves after the grasshopper invasion to find work "in the harvest fields to earn money for us to live on through the winter."[64] Ma is left behind to fend for herself with the girls. The crises Caroline faces alone with her infant son in *Let the Hurricane Roar* also were inspired by incidents in "Pioneer Girl."

On the closing pages of Lane's novel, Charles returns in the middle of a blizzard, and suddenly Caroline realizes that his dream has become her own. She looks at Baby Charles and "somehow, without quite thinking it, she felt that a light from the future was shining in the baby's face. The big white house was waiting for him, and the acres of wheat fields, the fast driving teams and swift buggies. If he remembered at all this life in the dugout, he would think of it only as a brief prelude to more spacious times."[65]

In *The First Four Years*, Laura and Manly also face continuing hardships that test their marriage and the life he hopes to create for them in the West. In fact, the last sections of the book detail a relentless series of disasters that seem implausible—even in fiction. But the events in *The First Four Years* are, for the most part, autobiographical and completely original to Wilder's novel. The challenges Laura and Manly face are ones Wilder herself had endured during the first four years of her marriage: three failed wheat crops, lost to wind and drought; diphtheria; Manly's "slight stroke of paralysis . . . from overexertion too soon after diphtheria"; more debt from the doctor bills; the birth and death of their infant son; and the loss of that shining little house on the tree claim by fire.[66]

But unlike Lane's Caroline, Laura faces these adversities together *with* Manly. After his stroke, for example, his "fingers were clumsy so that he could neither hitch up nor unhitch his team." So Laura hitches up the horses, helps him "get started," and is "on hand ready to help him unhitch" when Manly drives home.[67] Together Laura and Manly also retain some of their newlywed romance, even as young parents. When Rose is sleeping soundly after suppertime, Laura and Manly saddle their "ponies" and ride "in the moonlight."[68]

Yet Caroline and Laura continue to share experiences during the closing sections of both novels. In *Let the Hurricane Roar*, for example, Caroline has a frightening encounter between blizzards with a timber wolf: "The hair stood rough along its back. Fangs showed beneath the curling lip. . . . Its mate could not be far away."[69] Caroline worries that the wolf and its unseen mate could "scratch their way through" the walls of the barn and kill her precious heifer.[70] Safely back in the dugout, Caroline arms herself with her pistol, keeps a lamp lighted night and day, and ultimately outlasts the wolves. With the pistol in her hand, she leaves the dugout and finds "no trace of the wolves anywhere."[71] The heifer is safe inside the barn.

Laura in *The First Four Years* also has a brush with wolves that threatens her livestock on a wintery night. While Manly and Cousin Peter are away, Laura hears first "the howl of a wolf" and then "several together." She believes the wolves will attack her sheep: "Then Laura put on her coat and hood, lighted the lantern, and taking it and the dog with her, went out into the darkness and the storm."[72] Armed with a pitchfork, Laura walks the "length of the barn, flashing her lantern in every direction. . . . There was no sight nor sound of the wolves." Her sheep are unharmed. When Manly returns, he asks Laura, "What would you have done if you had found the wolves?" She replies, "Why, driven them away, of course. That's what I took the pitchfork for."[73]

The most significant parallel, however, between Caroline and Laura occurs on the final pages of *The First Four Years*. Like Caroline, Laura decides to embrace her husband's dream of living and farming in the West. Despite her ongoing doubts about farming at the end of their first three years together, Manly convinces Laura to give it one more year, a year of grace—a fourth year—to finally prove his point. And despite ongoing hardships during that year of grace, Laura is convinced: "It would be a fight to win out in this business of farming, but strangely she felt her spirit rising for the struggle."[74]

Like Caroline at the end of *Let the Hurricane Roar*, Laura envisions a brighter future for herself and her young family on the final pages of *The First Four Years*: "The incurable optimism of the farmer who throws his seed on the ground every spring, betting it and his time against the elements, seemed inextricably to blend with the creed of her pioneer forefathers that 'it is better farther on'—only instead of farther on in space, it was farther on in time, over the horizon of the years ahead instead of the far horizon of the west."[75] Wilder's ending to the *First Four Years* reads like a variation on Lane's, where Caroline feels that a "light from the future" is shining in her baby's face.

Little House Literary Characteristics

Despite its many parallels to *Let the Hurricane Roar*, *The First Four Years* features several characteristics that later came to define the Little House series. Although Wilder approaches her characters in *The First Four Years* with a detachment similar to Lane's, she includes small but revealing concrete details that add warmth and even tenderness to the book: that moment, as we've already seen, when Manly covers "Laura's hand with one of his" as they drive away from her parents' home on their wedding day is just one example of many.[76]

Another characteristic of Wilder's later Little House books:

emotional restraint underlying the warmth of her characters. As we've already seen, Lane later argued with her mother throughout their editorial collaboration on this very point. Lane believed Wilder's Little House characters should be more demonstrative, that their emotions should erupt more dramatically on the page. Wilder, however, maintained that emotional outbursts undermined the pioneer spirit she had experienced firsthand: "It seems to me we were rather inclined to be fatalistic—to just take things as they come," she wrote Lane.[77]

So Wilder's characters in *The First Four Years* are restrained. They don't deliver emotional outbursts as Charles does in *Let the Hurricane Roar*: "'Yes, give up the homestead!' He turned on her savagely. . . . 'And I'll be lucky if I can steal—that's what I said, steal!—steal my horses to get out with. Oh, you got a fine husband when you married me!'"[78] Compare this passage with the one in *The First Four Years* after Manly suffers a stroke: "From that day on there was a struggle to keep Manly's legs so that he could use them. Some days were better and again they were worse, but gradually they improved until he could go about his usual business if he was careful."[79] Even Wilder's description of the death of Laura and Manly's newborn is emotionally restrained:

> The baby was taken with spasms, and he died so quickly that the doctor was too late.
>
> To Laura, the days that followed were mercifully blurred. Her feelings were numbed and she only wanted to rest—to rest and not to think.
>
> But the work must go on.[80]

Wilder's characters in *The First Four Years* exhibit a fatalistic acceptance of tragedy. There's no place in their lives for emotional outbursts or self-pity: their work must go on.

Like the later Little House books, *The First Four Years* also demonstrates Wilder's preoccupation with the grandeur of the West. Her descriptions of the prairie are vivid, immediate, and concrete. The landscape becomes a character in its own right; its beauty moves and influences Laura in *The First Four Years*: "Laura loved to watch them [the wild geese] high against the blue of the sky, large V's and smaller V's with the leader at the point, his followers streaming behind, always in perfect V-formation. . . . There was something so wild and free about it, especially at night when the lonely, wild cry sounded through the darkness, calling, calling. It was almost irresistible. It made Laura long for wings so that she might follow."[81]

And yet, as in Wilder's later novels, nature can be a treacherous force. It is powerful, uncontrollable, and ruthless. In *The First Four Years* it wreaks havoc on Manly's dream to build a successful and profitable farm. Toward the end of the novel, the natural world even invades Laura and Manly's home: "After that they all sat in the house and let the wind blow. Their ears filled with the roar of it. Their eyes and throats smarted from the dust that was settling over the room even though the doors and windows were tightly closed."[82] For Wilder, the beauty of the West is linked to its unpredictability, its inherent wildness. Laura in *The First Four Years* feels this as well. "The plowland lay to the north of the hill out of sight from the house. Laura was glad of that. She loved the sweep of unbroken prairie with the wild grasses waving in the winds."[83]

Lane's descriptions of the West in *Let the Hurricane Roar* never achieve this intimacy or immediacy. In fact, her setting in the novel is never grounded in a real place as in Wilder's. When Lane plundered the "Pioneer Girl" manuscript, she scrambled its settings. The world Caroline and Charles inhabit is a composite of southwestern Minnesota and eastern Dakota Territory. Lane's jumbled literary landscape is perhaps one reason why Wilder believed *Let the Hurricane Roar* was fundamentally "wrong" and why she set out to write her own adult novel about newlyweds in the West.

A Fundamental Difference

The differences between Lane's *Let the Hurricane Roar* and Wilder's *The First Four Years*, however, run deeper than style, tone, or craft. They reflect a fundamental difference in how Wilder and Lane viewed the pioneer experience itself, and by extension, its relevance to their readers. While Wilder's *First Four Years* is an anthem to the inherent optimism, courage, and grit of American farmers, Lane's *Let the Hurricane Roar* focuses on individual responsibility.

It carries a direct political message to Depression-era readers, encouraging them to rely on themselves, to persevere into the future with pioneer grit and gumption. The message appears at the end of the novel's third section in a letter Caroline writes to Charles:

> We are having hard times now, but we should not dwell upon them but think of the future. It has never been easy to build up a country, but how much easier it is for us, with such great comforts and conveniences, kerosene, cookstoves, and even railroads and fast posts, then it was for our forefathers. I trust that, like our own parents, we may live to see times more prosperous than they have been in the past, and we will then reflect with satisfaction that these hard times were not in vain.[84]

Perhaps not surprisingly, then, Lane's novel focuses on the individual—Caroline—and her freedom to discover herself, her strength, and her courage. Singlehandedly, Caroline not only accepts Charles's vision of life in the West, she makes it possible for them both to achieve it. Caroline's experience as a pioneer woman serves as a metaphor for the values of the American West, where individuals with courage and persistence will find the freedom to fulfill their dreams. Caroline is an expression of Lane's emerging political views.

Wilder, on the other hand, focuses more on partnership in *The First Four Years*. Laura, despite her initial doubts about farming, becomes a full partner in Manly's homesteading enterprise. She comes to their marriage with her own money—one hundred dollars from teaching school—and invests it, first, in buying a colt, and then, as Manly suggests, in "buying half the sheep if she wanted to gamble on them."[85] The phrasing here is important—"if she wanted to gamble on them." Manly doesn't assume the money Laura brings to their marriage is automatically his; she is his partner, and has her own say in their future together. He learns, over the course of the novel, not to conceal business decisions from her, as he did when they were newlyweds, neglecting to tell her then that they were already five hundred dollars in debt.

In many ways, *The First Four Years* seems to be an expanded, fictional interpretation of ideas Wilder had explored in an article published in 1919 in *McCall's* magazine, "Whom Will You Marry?" In that article, a young woman named Elizabeth, "a banker's granddaughter," seeks advice, ostensibly from Wilder. Elizabeth asks, "Would—would you be a farmer's wife if you had the chance to live your life over again?"[86]

The article's lead is fictional, and it serves as the foundation for Wilder's discussion on the virtues not just of farming but of "farm women" as "wage earners and partners in their husband's business."[87] As a fictional character in a nonfiction piece, however, Elizabeth is clearly a forerunner of Laura in *The First Four Years*. Both young women have doubts about farming and both are reluctant to become farmers' wives. In "Whom Will You Marry?" Elizabeth's Jim is coming home from World War I and "doesn't want to go back into the bank again." Instead, he "wants to buy a farm when he comes back." Elizabeth then confesses, "I don't know whether I want to be a farmer's wife or not."[88]

Although Elizabeth comes from a banking family in the early twentieth century and Laura is a pioneer's daughter in the late nineteenth century, the young women share the same dilemma, one that Wilder believed was important. As "Whom Will You Marry?" unfolds, Wilder observes: "There must be a great many . . . who, like Elizabeth, are undecided because of their ignorance of the real conditions of life on a farm, and nothing I have ever read seems to tell the truth about these conditions."[89] So, while Wilder may have copied her daughter's general premise from *Let the Hurricane Roar*—a pair of newlyweds starting their life together in the West—she interpreted her version of that story through her own thematic lens in *The First Four Years*. Laura's pioneer story focuses on "the truth" about the farming life, and the fulfilling role it ultimately offers women who accept the challenges of full partnership with their husbands. In "Whom Will You Marry?" Wilder writes: "There is scope here for all that a woman has of intelligence and fine spirit. There is an opportunity here for the woman who will do her part in remaking a world that has been shaken to its foundations by discoveries the war has forced upon us."[90] *The First Four Years* is Wilder's fictional exploration of these ongoing opportunities for women, but this time in a world shaken to its foundations, not by war but by the Great Depression.

Working It Over into Fiction

It's tempting to read *The First Four Years* as autobiography, and assume that the real Laura Ingalls Wilder struggled with her role as a farm wife during the first years of her marriage. Yet nothing in her autobiographical columns for the *Missouri Ruralist* or in the original "Pioneer Girl" manuscript itself supports this view. And certainly there's nothing later in the Little House series to suggest that the fictional Laura Ingalls had second thoughts about marrying a farmer. At the end of *These Happy Golden Years*, Laura's heart is "full of happiness." She has no doubts about Almanzo's profession. "All was theirs; their own horses, their own cow, their own claim. The many leaves of their little trees rustled softly in the gentle breeze."[91]

The Laura of *The First Four Years* appears to have originated entirely from Wilder's imagination, a composite of Elizabeth in "Whom Will You Marry?" and a response to Lane's Caroline in *Let the Hurricane Roar*. Yet Wilder's vision for *The First Four Years* could also have been inspired by an observation Lane had made in late 1930—in a letter explaining why the *Saturday Evening Post* had rejected "Pioneer Girl." According to Lane, the *Saturday Evening Post* "said that if the same material were used as a basis for a fiction serial they'd take it like a shot. But I know you don't want to work it over into fiction."[92]

Lane had done exactly what the *Saturday Evening Post* had asked for: worked sections of "Pioneer Girl" over into fiction. That wasn't an option for Wilder in late 1932, but fictionalizing her life as a newlywed in Dakota Territory . . . that was certainly possible. Lane had shown her how in *Let the Hurricane Roar*.

But when Lane returned from her extensive travels in late 1932, feeling sick, tired, and depressed, Wilder apparently lost interest in her adult novel. Instead, as we've already seen, she eventually began to work with Lane on a revision of the "Farmer Boy" manuscript, and by March 1933, Wilder had started writing *Little House on the Prairie*, which would launch the Little House series.

Then in 1937, *The First Four Years*—at least, as a concept—

emerged from the shadows once more. Perhaps, not surprisingly, Wilder's thoughts returned to her languishing adult novel just as Lane, once again, mined the "Pioneer Girl" manuscript for another pioneer novel of her own.

A Grown-Up Story

Lane's new novel was *Free Land*, and it centers on a character—David Beaton—who is based on Almanzo Wilder. Young Nettie Peters is patterned on Wilder herself, and many of the episodes in *Free Land* are lifted directly from "Pioneer Girl." But this time around, Lane asked her parents for advice as she wrote her new novel, and both fully cooperated. Wilder herself was at work on *By the Shores of Silver Lake*, which covered much of the same material as Lane's *Free Land*. The two corresponded regularly about their works-in-progress and Wilder even suggested a specific episode for her daughter's new book: "I can't use [it] in a child's story, but you could use it if you have a place for it."[93] Lane sold *Free Land* to the *Saturday Evening Post* later in 1937, and it was published as a serial in the spring of 1938.

Lane's success with *Free Land* apparently renewed Wilder's interest in resurrecting "First Three Years." On December 13, 1937, Wilder wrote Ida Louise Raymond, her editor at Harper's, with an idea for a "story about grownups about the times I am writing of in the Little House books." She told Raymond that "for some time" she had had this story "in mind," but she wasn't sure "if it will jell."[94] Raymond was interested, and responded to Wilder's letter right away. When Lane learned of her mother's suggestion for a "grown-up story about Laura and Almanzo," she was, at best, lukewarm about the prospect: "As to your doing a[n adult] novel, there is no reason why you shouldn't if you want to, but unless by wild chance you did a best-seller, there is much more money in writing juveniles."[95] Lane then warned, "Do not take seriously anything that publishers say. They write these letters idiotically as part of a policy of cheering their authors along."[96]

Lane's reaction, however, probably had less to do with distrusting the idiotic policies of publishers and more to do with promoting her own professional interests over her mother's. She certainly wouldn't have welcomed the prospect of competing against an adult bestseller from her mother, because even by 1937, Laura Ingalls Wilder *was* writing bestsellers. Granted, they were for children, but Wilder's literary reputation was beginning to outstrip Lane's even then. And it's interesting to note that after decades of advising her mother not to expect to earn any money in children's books, Lane argued in 1937 that there was "more money in juveniles." She added that "I'd do one myself if I could get the time."[97]

Lane's letter appears to have killed Wilder's interest in pursuing a publisher for "First Three Years" in the 1930s. In fact, Wilder felt compelled to explain her reasoning for suggesting a "grown-up story" to Harper & Brothers in the first place: "I thought it might wangle a little more advertising for the L.H. books if I said I might do a grownup one. It was not a promise and if I didn't it wouldn't matter."[98]

"First Three Years" then temporarily disappears from the historical record. Wilder was, after all, working on *By the Shores of Silver Lake*, her first Young Adult novel. As we've seen, she and Lane had distinctly different views on the book, and perhaps all Wilder's creative energy flowed into that project, along with the next, *The Long Winter*. But by 1940, the subject of an adult book reappears in Wilder's correspondence, this time with her literary agent, George Bye.

In this letter, Wilder outlined the conclusion of the Little House series. "In the last book," she wrote, "Laura will be eighteen and the story will be of the courtship and wedding of Laura and Almanzo." Wilder worried that this last book "might be called adult," though she hoped "to retain the appeal" to younger readers. Then Wilder added this: "A story following the 8th book telling of what next happens is taking shape slowly in my mind, but it is to [*sic*] soon to say if it will crystalize into a completely adult novel. I can only say perhaps it may do so."[99] A draft of this adult story had already been written, of course, but it focused on Laura and Manly, not Laura and Almanzo. Wilder apparently recognized that a ninth book in the Little House series—this one for adults—would have to take a different shape than the one she'd written in the decade before as a response to *Let the Hurricane Roar*.

Her Niche as a Writer

So why didn't Wilder rewrite and reshape "First Three Years" during her lifetime? Why didn't she pursue the manuscript's publication?

These are questions that can't be answered with any certainty, but I've come to believe that Wilder ultimately recognized her literary reputation, which was always important to her, rested on her work for young readers. She had been interested in writing for children since at least 1915, when the *San Francisco Bulletin* published her series of poems for young readers, and as the years passed after the publication of *These Happy Golden Years*, it eventually became clear that she had already written the perfect ending to the Little House series.

Throughout the 1940s and until her death in 1957, "reader response to the [Little House] books was overwhelming," William Anderson writes. "Fan mail filled the Wilders' rural route mailbox with each delivery. Some days brought . . . twenty-five letters, others fifty or more pieces of mail. . . . Her dining table was usually spread with letters, stationery, and postage stamps."[100] Wilder told a reporter in 1949 that "I've always answered all my letters," which arrived at Rocky Ridge Farm "singly and in packets including those from all the boys and girls in a schoolroom." According to the reporter, young readers from around the world viewed Laura's childhood in the Little House books as "a magic time."[101] Perhaps, at last, Wilder simply recognized her niche as a children's book writer and put the adult story of Laura and Manly away without regret. The Little House series didn't need a "grown-up" book to bring the story of Laura Ingalls to a satisfying end.

But where does that leave *The First Four Years*? Should it have been published at all? Unlike "Pioneer Girl," which Wilder sought to publish in the early 1930s, "First Three Years" was a rough draft, an unpolished novel that she had abandoned. Wilder didn't revise the manuscript or submit it for review to her literary agent or editor. Clearly, she herself chose *not* to publish the book. At the end of the original manuscript, Wilder paraphrased a few lines from Edward Rowland Sill's poem "The Fool's Prayer": "But for our blunders, Lord in shame / Before the face of Heaven we fall / —oh Lord be merciful to me a fool."[102] She drew a circle around these lines, setting them off from the rest of the text. The quotation doesn't appear to be part of the novel; instead, it reads more like an editorial footnote, perhaps reflecting Wilder's final assessment of this literary experiment—that it was a foolish "blunder." There's no way to know conclusively when Wilder wrote these lines in that Fifty-Fifty tablet. But it's possible that even as early as 1933, when she and Lane resumed work on *Farmer Boy*, Wilder had already begun to lose faith in "First Three Years."

Still, Ursula Nordstrom's initial instinct back in 1969 to publish the manuscript in its original form is admirable. Wilder was an important and influential author; her newly discovered manuscript merited posthumous publication. But Roger MacBride's editorial changes and the decision to position *The First Four Years* as the final Little House book were ill-conceived and ultimately damaging. The novel's shrewd, new Laura; her initially jaded opinion of farming; and that "faint air of slight disillusion" gave the Little House series a jarring and discordant new conclusion.

In retrospect, it's puzzling that apparently no one considered publishing *The First Four Years* as a stand-alone, adult novel in 1969. Back in 1937, editor Ida Louise Raymond had done exactly that. While she responded enthusiastically to Wilder's idea for a "grown-up book," she told Wilder to submit her adult manuscript to the head of Harper & Brothers' book department, Eugene Saxton, who had published O. E. Rölvaag's *Giants in the Earth* in 1927.[103] Raymond appeared to recognize that an adult book for adult readers would need an adult editor. And it would inevitably have its own voice, plot, and cast of characters.

The First Four Years tarnished Wilder's literary reputation, in large measure *because* it was positioned as part of the Little House canon. *The First Four Years* suggested that Wilder was, at best, a careless writer (or worse, an inferior one), unable to recognize obvious inconsistencies in her Little House manuscripts. If Wilder couldn't write a satisfying sequel to *These Happy Golden Years*, how had she made the smooth, satisfying connections between the previous Little House books? Maybe she wasn't the creative genius behind the series; maybe it was Rose Wilder Lane.

The irony, of course, is that it now appears Wilder used Lane's work as a model for *The First Four Years*. Its "faint air of slight disillusion" sprang directly from *Let the Hurricane Roar*. If the art of *The First Four Years* doesn't persuade, as Lane's biographer contends, it's because Wilder's attempt at an adult novel mirrored her daughter's approach to writing fiction. Lane's editorial influence isn't absent from *The First Four Years*; it permeates it.

In a letter to Wilder in 1937, Lane told her mother, "Copying is the best way to really get down to basic study of a piece of writing." As she had often done herself, Lane advised Wilder to literally copy another author's work "from end to end."[104] It's doubtful that Wilder actually copied out *Let the Hurricane Roar* word for word or end to end back in the fall of 1932. But she evidently studied it closely.

In the same letter, Lane includes an especially haunting sentence: "As to similarity in our writing, of course. You often write lines and whole paragraphs that I feel are what I would have written or anyway wish I had."[105]

As we've seen, Lane essentially lifted lines and whole paragraphs from Wilder, placing them in her most successful and enduring novels—*Let the Hurricane Roar* and *Free Land*. Yet Lane's novels and short stories—including her work published before 1932, without the benefit of the "Pioneer Girl" manuscript—lack the brilliance and spark generations of readers and critics came to admire in Wilder's Little House books. If Lane was indeed the real creative genius in the family, where is the artistry in her own fiction? Why does the art of her novels fail to persuade?

A definitive answer to these questions is impossible. But it's clear that Wilder and Lane had distinct, even complementary editorial skills. They relied on each other throughout their writing careers.

They were a symbiotic editorial team with magical editorial chemistry, and in its own way, that is the ongoing mystery not only of *The First Four Years* but the entire body of work Wilder and Lane produced through the 1930s and into the 1940s.

Yet Wilder clearly possessed her own unique storytelling gifts and infused her Little House books with unforgettable characters, powerful settings, lyrical descriptions, and an unprecedented emotional realism. She inspired generations of readers and influenced generations of writers. Her artistry forever changed the landscape of American literature.

The Little House books are too good to be altogether lost.

A Note on Sources

REFERENCES TO WILDER'S LITTLE HOUSE NOVELS ARE excerpted from the revised editions with illustrations by Garth Williams, published in 1953, then reissued in 1971 by Harper Trophy Book for Harper & Row. Wilder's Little House novels were originally illustrated by Helen Sewell and Mildred Boyle and published by Harper & Brothers:

Little House in the Big Woods, 1932
Farmer Boy, 1933
Little House on the Prairie, 1935
On the Banks of Plum Creek, 1937
By the Shores of Silver Lake, 1939
The Long Winter, 1940
Little Town on the Prairie, 1941
These Happy Golden Years, 1943

Harper & Row, Harper Trophy, or HarperCollins published the following titles, based on Wilder's manuscripts, travel diaries, and letters, after her death in 1957:

On the Way Home, 1962
The First Four Years, 1971
West from Home, 1974
A Little House Reader, 2005
A Little House Traveler, 2006
The Selected Letters of Laura Ingalls Wilder, 2016

Other titles, also based on Wilder's manuscripts, letters, magazine articles, and newspaper columns, have also been released posthumously:

A Little House Sampler, University of Nebraska Press, 1988
Laura Ingalls Wilder, Farm Journalist, University of Missouri Press, 2007

Pioneer Girl: The Annotated Autobiography, South Dakota State Historical Society Press, 2014

Five versions of Wilder's autobiography date from 1930. None were published during Wilder's or Lane's lifetimes:

Handwritten rough draft, completed in May 1930.
Brandt & Brandt version, initial typewritten draft submitted to Lane's literary agent Carl Brandt on May 17, 1930, lightly edited by Lane.
Brandt & Brandt revised version, a leaner, more aggressively edited version of the manuscript, which includes new material, apparently inserted by Lane: a transitional, incomplete manuscript dating from August 1930.
Juvenile Pioneer Girl, a collection of "Pioneer Girl" stories for young readers, prepared by Lane apparently without Wilder's knowledge, completed August 17, 1930: the foundation for *Little House in the Big Woods*, the first Little House novel. Also known as "When Grandma Was a Little Girl."
George T. Bye version, the final, edited "Pioneer Girl" manuscript for adult readers. Completed in September 1930 and unsuccessfully marketed by Lane's new literary agent, George Bye, from 1931 through 1933. The Bye Agency returned the unsold manuscript in 1938.

The *Saturday Evening Post* originally published Lane's derivative "Pioneer Girl" novels in serial form:

Let the Hurricane Roar, October and November 1932
Free Land, March and April 1938

Longmans, Green published these novels in book form:

Let the Hurricane Roar, 1933
Free Land, 1938

Let the Hurricane Roar was reissued by Harper Trophy in 1976, eight years after Lane's death, and retitled *Young Pioneers*. The book's original main characters—Charles and Caroline—were renamed David and Molly.

Notes

Abbreviations

AJW Almanzo James Wilder

Brown Collection James Oliver Brown Collection, Rare Book and Manuscript Library, Columbia University, New York

Lane Papers Rose Wilder Lane Papers, Herbert Hoover Presidential Library, West Branch, Iowa

LIW Laura Ingalls Wilder

LIW Papers Laura Ingalls Wilder Papers, Laura Ingalls Wilder Historic Home and Museum, Mansfield, Missouri; a microfilm edition, 1894–1943, of most but not all of the collection is available: Western Historical Manuscript Collection, Ellis Library, University of Missouri, Columbia

London Correspondence Jack and Charmian London Correspondence and Papers, Utah State University Special Collections and Archives, Logan

RWL Rose Wilder Lane

Preface

1. LIW, "Detroit Book Fair Speech," 1937, p. 2, box 13, Lane Papers.
2. Meagan Flynn, "Laura Ingalls Wilder's Name Stripped from Children's Book Award over 'Little House' Depictions of Native Americans," *Washington Post*, June 6, 2018.
3. Flynn, "Laura Ingalls Wilder's Name Stripped from Children's Book Award."
4. LIW, "Detroit Book Fair Speech," 2.
5. LIW, "Detroit Book Fair Speech," 6.
6. In "Historicizing Presentism," Jeffrey R. Wilson traces the history of the term "presentism" to 1916, when it was defined as "a bias toward the present or present-day attitudes, esp. in the interpretation of history." According to Wilson the term wasn't widely used until the 1940s but "skyrocketed" to popularity in the 1980s, at about the same time the first groundswell of criticism against the Little House series began to surface. Wilson also explains, "In literary studies today . . . presentism is less a bad form of historical inquiry and more a good form of political scholarship." See Wilson, "Historicizing Presentism," sec. 1.
7. MacNicol, "Problem with Laura."

8. Nathan Heller, “The End of the English Major,” *New Yorker*, February 27, 2023, 31.
9. Heller, “End of the English Major,” 32.
10. Heller, “End of the English Major,” 34.
11. MacNicol, “Problem with Laura.”
12. Wilder, *Little House on the Prairie*, 47.
13. Petersen, *Bess Streeter Aldrich*, 5.
14. Means, *Candle in the Mist*, n.p.
15. Brink, *Caddie Woodlawn*, vi.
16. *The Simpsons* episode “Simpsons Tall Tales” (season 12, episode 21) includes a one-line reference to Laura Ingalls Wilder. Two episodes of *The Big Bang Theory* feature *Little House on the Prairie* as part of their plot lines: “The Scavenger Vortex” (season 7, episode 3) and “The Raiders Minimization” (season 7, episode 4). A one-line reference to *Little House on the Prairie* appears in *Derry Girls* (season 2, episode 1). *Northern Exposure*, which aired in the 1990s, includes a random reference to Mary Ingalls's blindness (“Duets,” season 4, episode 13).
17. Wilder, *Little House on the Prairie*, 24.
18. Wilder, *On the Banks of Plum Creek*, 156.
19. LIW to RWL, January 26, 1938, box 13, Lane Papers.

1. Ambition

1. LIW to RWL, March 32, 1937, box 13, Lane Papers.
2. Wilder, *Pioneer Girl*, 49.
3. Wilder, *Pioneer Girl*, 59.
4. Wilder, *Pioneer Girl*, 292–94.
5. Wilder, *Pioneer Girl*, 292.
6. Wilder, *Pioneer Girl*, 294.
7. Wilder, “Ambition,” original draft, LIW Papers.
8. Wilder, “Ambition,” revised draft, LIW Papers.
9. Wilder, *Pioneer Girl*, 294.
10. LIW, “Ambition,” original draft, LIW Papers.
11. Wilder, *These Happy Golden Years*, 98.
12. LIW to RWL, February 5, 1937, in Wilder, *Selected Letters*, 107.
13. Wilder, “The Difference,” in *Little House Reader*, 39.
14. Wilder, *Pioneer Girl*, 311.
15. Wilder, “So Far and Yet So Near,” in *Little House Reader*, 48.
16. Wilder, *First Four Years*, 89.
17. RWL, quoted in Wilder, *On the Way Home*, 4.
18. Wilder, *Pioneer Girl*, 234.
19. RWL, quoted in Wilder, *On the Way Home*, 3.
20. LIW, July 17, “Trip from Dakota to Mansfield Missouri,” folder 33, LIW Papers. Part of this entry is illegible on microfilm. A faded line or sentence appears between “2 o'clock” and “Camped.” The

only readable words in this line are "fear of the." The word "looks" appears toward the end of the entry with several other illegible words or scribbles.

21. Wilder, *On the Way Home*, 69.
22. LIW, July 20, "Trip From Dakota to Mansfield Missouri."
23. LIW, July 23, "Trip From Dakota to Mansfield Missouri."
24. LIW, July 23, "Trip From Dakota to Mansfield Missouri."
25. LIW, "From Missouri: Lamar, Mo., August 28, '94," *News and Leader* (De Smet), 1894.
26. LIW, August 29, "Trip From Dakota to Mansfield Missouri."
27. LIW as A. J. Wilder, "My Apple Orchard" and "The Story of Rocky Ridge Farm," quoted in Hines, *Laura Ingalls Wilder*, 20, 18.
28. RWL, "I, Rose Wilder Lane, Am the Only Truly Happy Person I Know and I Discovered the Secret of Happiness on the Day I Tried to Kill Myself," *Hearst's International/Cosmopolitan*, June 1926.
29. LIW, "Ideas for Work," 1903 and n.d., box 14, Lane Papers.
30. LIW, "Ideas for Work."
31. LIW, "Ideas for Work."
32. Wilder, *Pioneer Girl*, 185.
33. LIW, "Ideas for Work."
34. LIW, "Ideas for Work."
35. LIW, "Ideas for Work."
36. LIW, "Ideas for Work."
37. RWL in LIW, "Ideas for Work."
38. LIW to RWL, August 19, 1937, in Wilder, *Selected Letters*.
39. LIW, "Ideas for Work."
40. "Churches," Genealogy Trails History Group, Wright County, Missouri, accessed May 9, 2024, genealogytrails.com/mo/wright/history2.html#Churches.
41. LIW, "Ideas for Work."
42. LIW, "Favors the Small Farm Home," quoted in Hines, *Laura Ingalls Wilder*, 16.
43. LIW as A. J. Wilder, "The Story of Rocky Ridge Farm," 17.
44. LIW as A. J. Wilder, "The Story of Rocky Ridge Farm."
45. Brantley, "History of the *Missouri Ruralist*," 94.
46. LIW, "A Plain Beauty Talk," quoted in Hines, *Laura Ingalls Wilder*, 28.
47. LIW, "All in the Day's Work," quoted in Hines, *Laura Ingalls Wilder*, 48.
48. LIW, "What the War Means to Women," quoted in Hines, *Laura Ingalls Wilder*, 146.
49. John F. Case, "Let's Visit Mrs. Wilder," in Wilder and Lane, *Little House Sampler*, 7.
50. LIW, "A Bouquet of Wild Flowers," quoted in Hines, *Laura Ingalls Wilder*, 118.

51. LIW, "So We Moved the Spring," quoted in Hines, *Laura Ingalls Wilder*, 66.
52. LIW, "And a Woman Did It," quoted in Hines, *Laura Ingalls Wilder*, 117.
53. LIW, "If We Only Understood," quoted in Hines, *Laura Ingalls Wilder*, 129–30.
54. Wilder, *Pioneer Girl*, 295.
55. LIW, "As a Farm Woman Thinks," no. 33, quoted in Hines, *Laura Ingalls Wilder*, 312.
56. LIW, "As a Farm Woman Thinks," no. 31, quoted in Hines, *Laura Ingalls Wilder*, 309.
57. LIW to Martha Carpenter, June 22, 1924, box 14, Lane Papers.
58. LIW to Martha Carpenter.
59. RWL, "Rose Wilder Lane by Herself," *Sunset*, in Wilder and Lane, *Little House Sampler*, 12.
60. RWL to Clarence Day, June 26, 1928, box 5, Lane Papers.
61. RWL, "Rose Wilder Lane by Herself," *Sunset*, in Wilder and Lane, *Little House Sampler*, 13.
62. Charmian London to RWL, April, 28, 1918, box 10, folder 5, London Correspondence.
63. RWL to Charmian London, May 22, 1917, box 13, folder 14, London Correspondence.
64. Holtz, *Ghost in the Little House*, 66.
65. LIW, "What Makes My Country Great," quoted in Hines, *Laura Ingalls Wilder*, 297.
66. LIW to AJW, October 4, 1915, in "West from Home," Wilder, *Little House Traveler*, 242–43.

2. *Pioneer Girl*

1. RWL, diary #25 (1926–30), May 7, 1930, box 21, Laura Ingalls Wilder Series, Lane Papers.
2. RWL, diary #25, July 31, 1930, box 21, Lane Papers.
3. RWL to LIW, April 11, 1919, box 13, Lane Papers.
4. Wilder, *Pioneer Girl*, 5.
5. RWL, diary #25, May 10–17, 1930, box 21, Lane Papers.
6. Wilder once told a gathering of Sorosis Club women in Mountain Grove, Missouri, that "the only stupid thing about words is the spelling of them." Like most writers, she apparently recognized an inherent creative weakness in herself. LIW, "My Work," in Wilder and Lane, *Little House Sampler*, 179. The original of this speech appears to be lost.
7. RWL, diary #25, July 16–21, 1930, box 21, Lane Papers.
8. RWL, diary #25, October 17, 1930, box 21, Lane Papers.
9. George Bye to RWL, April 6, 1931, box 13, Lane Papers.

10. Judith Thurman, "The Little House Memoir," *New Yorker*, February 18, 2015.
11. Holtz, *Ghost in the Little House*, 65.
12. LIW to RWL, August 17, 1938, box 13, Lane Papers.
13. The chronological section breaks in the published version of *Pioneer Girl: The Annotated Autobiography* were added to help readers navigate the manuscript more easily and place Wilder's narrative into historical context.
14. John F. Case, "Let's Visit Mrs. Wilder," *Missouri Ruralist*, February 20, 1918, in Wilder and Lane, *Little House Sampler*, 11.
15. LIW, "As a Farm Woman Thinks," *Missouri Ruralist*, December 15, 1924, quoted in Hines, *Laura Ingalls Wilder*, 311.
16. LIW, "As a Farm Woman Thinks," 312.
17. RWL to LIW, April 11, 1919, box 13, Lane Papers.
18. RWL to LIW, November 1924, box 13, Lane Papers.
19. RWL to LIW, November 1924, box 13, Lane Papers.
20. Wilder, *Pioneer Girl*, 1.
21. Wilder, *Pioneer Girl*, 155.
22. Wilder, *Pioneer Girl*, 287.
23. LIW to RWL, ca. February–March 1931, folder 19, Lane Papers.
24. Lane, *Let the Hurricane Roar*, 9. Lane's main characters in this novel are named Charles and Caroline. The book was retitled *Young Pioneers* in the 1970s, and its main characters were renamed David and Molly.
25. Lane, *Let the Hurricane Roar*, 3.
26. Lane, *Let the Hurricane Roar*, 5.
27. Wilder, *Pioneer Girl*, 158.
28. Wilder, *By the Shores of Silver Lake*, 67.
29. Lane, *Let the Hurricane Roar*, 70.
30. Lane, *Free Land*, 37.
31. Wilder, *Pioneer Girl*, 1.
32. Wilder, *Pioneer Girl*, 99.
33. Wilder, *Pioneer Girl*, 78–79.
34. Lane, *Let the Hurricane Roar*, 42.
35. Lane, *Let the Hurricane Roar*, 42–43.
36. Wilder, *Pioneer Girl*, 140–41.
37. LIW to RWL, n.d. [1932], box 13, Lane Papers.
38. Lane, *Let the Hurricane Roar*, 136–37. Even this brief description of wrenching ice from a herd of cattle's eyes after a blizzard originated with "Pioneer Girl." Pa, without any emotional outburst, tears ice from the eyes of twenty-five cattle and saves their lives (Wilder, *Pioneer Girl*, 202). A similar scene appears in *The Long Winter*.
39. Lane, *Let the Hurricane Roar*, 50.
40. Wilder, *Pioneer Girl*, 112.

41. Wilder, *Pioneer Girl*, 103, 106.
42. Wilder, *Pioneer Girl*, 106.
43. Wilder, *Pioneer Girl*, 110.
44. LIW, "Pioneer Girl," Bye manuscript, p. 49, Lane Papers.
45. LIW to RWL, March 7, 1938, box 13, file 194, Lane Papers.
46. George Bye to LIW, July 25, 1941, Brown Collection.
47. George Bye to LIW, May 5, 1943, Brown Collection.
48. Graeme Lorimer to George Bye, April 15, 1932, box 1, Lane Papers.
49. George Bye to RWL, April 28, 1932, box 1, Lane Papers.

3. "When Grandma Was a Little Girl"

1. Marion Fiery to LIW, February 12, 1931, box 13, file 189, Lane Papers.
2. RWL to LIW, February 16, 1931, box 13, file 189, Lane Papers.
3. Marion Fiery to LIW, February 12, 1931, Lane Papers.
4. "When Grandma Was a Little Girl," box 14, file 214, Lane Papers.
5. RWL, diary #25, August 5, 1930, box 21, Lane Papers.
6. RWL, diary #25, August 16–17, 1930, box 21, Lane Papers.
7. Wilder's children's poems were published in a column titled "The Tuck'em In Corner" and featured such titles as "Naughty Four o'Clocks" and "Where Sunshine Fairies Go." Wilder wrote verse throughout her lifetime, both for adults and young readers, but her poetry lacks the strength, lyricism, and immediacy of her prose.
8. RWL to LIW, April 11, 1919, box 13, Lane Papers.
9. RWL, diary #37 (1931–35), February 15, 1931, box 22, Laura Ingalls Wilder Series, Lane Papers.
10. "When Grandma Was a Little Girl," 1. The only existing copy of "When Grandma Was a Little Girl" is clearly an early typewritten draft of the manuscript, complete with strike-outs and handwritten marginal notes. Most of these notes appear to be in Lane's handwriting, but one handwritten correction at the beginning of the manuscript may belong to Wilder herself. The typewritten text reads, "When Grandma was a little girl, she lived in a little gray house made of logs. The house was in the Big Woods, in Michigan." A line runs through the word "Michigan," and directly above it in ink is the word "Wisconsin."
11. Marion Fiery to LIW, March 3, 1931, box 13, file 189, Lane Papers.
12. By February 1931, the adult version of "Pioneer Girl," which Lane finished editing in September 1930, had been rejected by such prominent magazines as the *Saturday Evening Post*, the *Ladies Home Journal*, and *Good Housekeeping*.
13. RWL to LIW, February 16, 1931, Lane Papers.
14. RWL to LIW, February 16, 1931.
15. RWL to LIW, February 16, 1931.
16. Marion Fiery to LIW, February 12, 1931, Lane Papers.

17. RWL and LIW, "When Grandma Was a Little Girl," Lane Papers.
18. Lane used a similar perspective—an older woman looking back on her childhood and adolescence—in *Old Home Town*, published in 1935.
19. Kirkus, "Discovery of Laura Ingalls Wilder," 428.
20. RWL to LIW, February 16, 1931, Lane Papers.
21. RWL to LIW, February 16, 1931.
22. RWL to LIW, February 16, 1931. It's unlikely that Lane was referring here to herself and Berta Hader. Given the Haders' experience in children publishing, they would have known a six- to seven-thousand-word manuscript wasn't a picture book.
23. LIW, draft of *Little House in the Big Woods*, folder 7, LIW Papers.

4. *Little House in the Big Woods*

1. RWL to Marion Fiery, May 27, 1931, box 13, file 189, Lane Papers.
2. LIW, "Suggested Titles," 1931, box 13, file 198, Lane Papers. The list of suggested titles appears on a single, typewritten sheet of paper and includes twelve titles. Eight of the titles are crossed out by a typewriter key and are virtually unreadable. Wilder and Lane probably rejected these themselves.
3. Kirkus, "Discovery of Laura Ingalls Wilder," 428–29.
4. Marion Fiery to RWL, November 3, 1931, box 13, file 189, Lane Papers.
5. RWL to Marion Fiery, n.d. [1931], box 13, Lane Papers.
6. Virginia Kirkus to LIW, December 8, 1931, box 13, file 189, Lane Papers. Wilder received news that Harper & Brothers had accepted her manuscript on Thanksgiving Day, November 26, 1931. But the message arrived from Marion Fiery, her editor at Knopf. Lane recorded in her diary, "Marian [*sic*] wires Harpers will take mothers [*sic*] juvenile." RWL, diary #37, November 26, 1931, box 21, Lane Papers.
7. Kirkus, "Discovery of Laura Ingalls Wilder," 429.
8. Wilder, *Little House in the Big Woods*, 1.
9. Brink, *Caddie Woodlawn*, vi.
10. Wilder, *Little House in the Big Woods*, 35.
11. Wilder, *Little House in the Big Woods*, 38.
12. Wilder, *Little House in the Big Woods*, 36.
13. Wilder, *Little House in the Big Woods*, 2.
14. Wilder, *Little House in the Big Woods*, 73.
15. LIW to Marion Fiery, n.d. [1931], box 13, Lane Papers.
16. LIW to RWL, March 23, 1937, box 13, file 193, Lane Papers.
17. Wilder, *Little House in the Big Woods*, 119.
18. Wilder, *Little House in the Big Woods*, 3. A similar episode occurs in *Little House on the Prairie*. The basis for both these fictional scenes appears in *Pioneer Girl*: "One night Pa picked me up and out of bed and carried me to the window so I could see the wolves. There were so many of them all sitting in a ring around the house, with their

noses pointed up at the big, bright moon, howling as loud and long as they could." Wilder, *Little House on the Prairie*, 95–98; Wilder, *Pioneer Girl*, 5.

19. Wilder, *Little House in the Big Woods*, 144.
20. Wilder, *Little House in the Big Woods*, 238.
21. Wilder, *Little House in the Big Woods*, 1–2.
22. Wilder, *Little House in the Big Woods*, 52.
23. Wilder, *Little House in the Big Woods*, 48–49.
24. Wilder, *Little House in the Big Woods*, 131.
25. Wilder, *Little House in the Big Woods*, 52.
26. Wilder, *Little House in the Big Woods*, 111.
27. Wilder, *Little House in the Big Woods*, 113.
28. Wilder, *Little House in the Big Woods*, 110.
29. Wilder, *Little House in the Big Woods*, 104–5.
30. Wilder, *Little House in the Big Woods*, 114.
31. RWL to LIW, February 16, 1931, box 13, file 189, Lane Papers.
32. Wilder, *Little House in the Big Woods*, 238.
33. Wilder, *Little House in the Big Woods*, 184.
34. Wilder, *Pioneer Girl*, 52.
35. Wilder, *Little House in the Big Woods*, 211.
36. Wilder, *Little House in the Big Woods*, 211.
37. Wilder, *Little House in the Big Woods*, 235.
38. Wilder, *Little House in the Big Woods*, 141–42.
39. Wilder, *Little House in the Big Woods*, 141.
40. Wilder, *Little House in the Big Woods*, 181.
41. Wilder, *Little House in the Big Woods*, 182.
42. Wilder, *Little House in the Big Woods*, 183.
43. Wilder, *Little House in the Big Woods*, 167.
44. Wilder, *Little House in the Big Woods*, 36.
45. The songs and lyrics that appear in the Little House books, as well as *Pioneer Girl*, were an authentic part of Wilder's childhood. Most of the songs in *Pioneer Girl* eventually made their way into the Little House novels, although Wilder used lyrics more strategically in her fiction to enhance the action, setting, and mood she sought to create.
46. Wilder, *Little House in the Big Woods*, 237.

5. *Farmer Boy*

1. Wilder, *Farmer Boy*, 2.
2. RWL, diary #37 (1931–35), October 7, 1931, box 22, Laura Ingalls Wilder Series, Lane Papers.
3. Although *Let the Hurricane Roar* would be Lane's fourth novel, her reputation as a successful writer during the 1920s hinged on the publication of short stories and nonfiction. Her experience as a novelist was limited. In 1928 she observed, "I don't know the feel of

a novel. . . . I don't know what a novel is when I meet it." *Diverging Roads*, her first novel, published in 1918, had been autobiographical, based on her marriage and divorce from Gillette Lane. *Hill-Billy*, published in 1926, was a collection of interrelated short stories. Lane wrote *Cindy: A Romance of the Ozarks* "for money" as a serial and believed it was shallow and said "nothing worth saying." Lane's career stalled in the early 1930s; *Let the Hurricane Roar* was a creative leap for her. RWL to Clarence Day, June 26, 1928, box 5, Laura Ingalls Wilder Series, Lane Papers; RWL to Carl Brandt, April 24, 1928, quoted in Holtz, *Ghost in the Little House*, 188.

4. RWL, *Let the Hurricane Roar*, 3–4.
5. Graeme Lorimer to George Bye, April 15, 1932, box 1, file 12, Lane Papers.
6. George Bye to RWL, April 28, 1932, box 1, file 12, Lane Papers. In a letter to Wilder recapping Lorimer's reaction to "Pioneer Girl," Lane wrote that "if the same material were used as a basis for a fiction serial they'd take it like a shot. But I know you don't want to work it over into fiction." Instead, Lane had taken up that challenge herself. RWL to LIW, November 12, 1930, box 13, file 188, Lane Papers.
7. RWL, diary #37, September 6, 1932, box 22, Lane Papers. An entry from Lane's diary dated August 1, 1932, reads, "Worked on Courage now called Let the Hurricane Roar." From the context of Lane's diary, Lane's publisher, Longmans, Green, apparently requested the lyrics for the hymn in late 1932 or early 1933, before publishing the novel in book form. The line is from the hymn "The Evergreen Shore," published in 1861, lyrics by William Hunter, music by William B. Bradbury. The line "Then let the hurricane roar" is the first line of the refrain. Pa sings the chorus of this hymn in *The Long Winter* in the chapter "We'll Weather the Blast."
8. RWL, diary #37, September 16 and September 20, 1932, box 22, Lane Papers.
9. *Let the Hurricane Roar* also generated almost immediate interest from Hollywood, but to Lane's disappointment, she didn't sell the book's film rights to Hollywood during her lifetime. A made-for-television adaptation of the book was released in 1976, eight years after Lane's death. It was retitled *Young Pioneers*. RWL, diary #37, December 13, 1932, box 22, Lane Papers.
10. During this period, Lane also used material from "Pioneer Girl" as the basis for such short stories as "Long Skirts" (*Ladies Home Journal*, 1933) and "Object Matrimony" (*Saturday Evening Post*, 1934). "Long Skirts" was republished as a chapter in Lane's novel *Old Home Town* in 1935.
11. RWL, journal, January 25, 1933, box 23, Lane Papers.
12. RWL to LIW, n.d. [postcard, 1932], box 13, Lane Papers.

13. After searching for the lyrics to "Let the Hurricane Roar" for several weeks, Lane wrote that "Mother got Hurricane song from Aunt Carrie." RWL, diary #37, February 2, 1933, box 22, Lane Papers.
14. RWL, diary #37, December 7, 1932, box 22, Lane Papers.
15. RWL, diary #37, March 19, 1933, box 22, Lane Papers.
16. Louise Raymond, quoted in RWL to George Bye, March 20, 1933, box 13, Lane Papers.
17. Louise Raymond, quoted in RWL to George Bye, March 20, 1933.
18. RWL, diary #37, January 13, 1933, box 22, Lane Papers. Louise Raymond, quoted in RWL to George Bye, March 20, 1933, box 13, Lane Papers.
19. Louise Raymond, quoted in RWL to George Bye, March 20, 1933.
20. Wilder, *Farmer Boy*, 1.
21. Wilder, *Little House in the Big Woods*, 1.
22. Wilder trimmed the size of Almanzo's real family in *Farmer Boy*. In fact, James and Angeline Day Wilder had six children: Laura Ann, born in 1844; Royal Gould, born in 1847; Eliza Jane, born in 1850, Alice M., born in 1853; and Perley Day, born in 1869. Almanzo was born on February 13, 1857.
23. Wilder, *Farmer Boy*, 61.
24. Wilder, *Farmer Boy*, 50.
25. Wilder, *Farmer Boy*, 57
26. Wilder, *Farmer Boy*, 132.
27. Wilder, *Farmer Boy*, 109.
28. Wilder, *Farmer Boy*, 130.
29. Wilder, *Farmer Boy*, 5.
30. Wilder, *Farmer Boy*, 41
31. Wilder, *Farmer Boy*, 44.
32. Wilder, *Farmer Boy*, 46.
33. Wilder, *Pioneer Girl*, 101.
34. Wilder, *Farmer Boy*, 47–48.
35. Wilder, *Farmer Boy*, 370.
36. Wilder, *Farmer Boy*, 371.
37. Wilder, *Farmer Boy*, 22.
38. Wilder, *Farmer Boy*, 2–4.
39. Wilder, *Farmer Boy*, 22–23.
40. Wilder, *Farmer Boy*, 86–87.
41. Wilder, *Farmer Boy*, 286.
42. Eloise Jarvis McGraw, "Always Ask Why," unpublished manuscript (author's copy), 2.
43. Wilder, *Farmer Boy*, 16–18.
44. Wilder, *Farmer Boy*, 372.
45. Wilder, *Little House in the Big Woods*, 238.
46. Wilder, *Farmer Boy*, 372.

47. LIW, "Detroit Book Fair Speech," 1937, p. 2, box 13, Lane Papers.
48. Wilder, *Farmer Boy*, 189.
49. RWL to George Bye, March 20, 1933, box 13, Lane Papers.

6. *Little House on the Prairie*, Part One

1. RWL, diary #37 (1931–35), April 9, 1933, box 22, Laura Ingalls Wilder Series, Lane Papers.
2. Woolf, *Diary of Virginia Woolf*, ix.
3. Marjorie Vitense to LIW, February 22, 1933, folder 14, LIW Papers.
4. LIW to RWL, August 17, 1938, box 13, file 189, Lane Papers.
5. Miscellaneous correspondence and rough manuscript notes, folder 14, LIW Papers.
6. LIW, *Little House on the Prairie* manuscript, p. 1, folder 15, LIW Papers.
7. Cather, *O Pioneers!*, 5.
8. Lane, *Let the Hurricane Roar*, 3.
9. Wilder, *Little House on the Prairie*, 1.
10. LIW, "Pioneer Girl," 1930, folder 1, LIW Papers.
11. Wilder, *Little House in the Big Woods*, 3.
12. Wilder, *Little House on the Prairie*, 2.
13. Wilder, *Little House on the Prairie*, 3.
14. Wilder's family may have moved from Wisconsin to Chariton County, Missouri, in 1869, and from there to the Osage Diminished Indian Reserve. In 1868 Charles Ingalls sold his farm in Wisconsin and with his brother-in-law, Henry Quiner, bought land in Chariton County, in the northeast part of the state. The historical record doesn't reveal why the men chose to buy land in Missouri, or if either attempted to settle their families there. But after the Civil War ended in 1865, settlers, many whose lives had been disrupted by years of guerilla warfare in Missouri, swept west into Kansas. It's possible that the Ingalls family was part of that general westward movement out of Missouri.
15. Wilder, *Little House on the Prairie*, 1.
16. Wilder, *Little House on the Prairie*, 2.
17. Wilder, *Little House on the Prairie*, 13.
18. Wilder, *Little House on the Prairie*, 54, 280, 166, 275.
19. Wilder, *Little House on the Prairie*, 247–48.
20. Wilder, *Little House on the Prairie*, 174.
21. Wilder, *Little House on the Prairie*, 74.
22. Wilder, *Little House on the Prairie*, 174.
23. Wilder, *Little House on the Prairie*, 75.
24. Wilder, *Little House on the Prairie*, 9.
25. Wilder, *Little House on the Prairie*, 6.
26. Wilder, *Little House on the Prairie*, 49.
27. Wilder, *Little House on the Prairie*, 47.

28. Wilder, *Little House on the Prairie*, 7.
29. Wilder, *Little House on the Prairie*, 21.
30. Wilder, *Little House on the Prairie*, 22.
31. Wilder, *Little House on the Prairie*, 23.
32. Wilder, *Little House on the Prairie*, 24–25.
33. Wilder, *Little House on the Prairie*, 25. In a dramatic scene in the following chapter, Jack returns to the family.
34. Wilder, *Little House on the Prairie*, 24.
35. Brink, *Caddie Woodlawn*, 188.
36. Wilder, *Little House on the Prairie*, 204.
37. Wilder, *Little House on the Prairie*, 60–62.
38. Wilder, *Little House on the Prairie*, 157.
39. Wilder, *Little House on the Prairie*, 66.
40. Wilder, *Little House on the Prairie*, 69.
41. In 1936, the year *Little House on the Prairie* qualified for a Newbery designation, the committee awarded honor titles to *Honk, the Moose* by Phil Strong, *The Good Master* by Kate Seredy, *Young Walter Scott* by Elizabeth Janet Gray, and *All Sail Set: A Romance of the Flying Cloud* by Armstrong Sperry.
42. Wilder, *Little House on the Prairie*, 9.
43. Wilder, *Little House on the Prairie*, 308.
44. Wilder, *Little House on the Prairie*, 310.
45. Wilder, *Little House on the Prairie*, 311.
46. Wilder, *Little House on the Prairie*, 14.
47. Wilder, *Little House on the Prairie*, 37.
48. Wilder, *Little House on the Prairie*, 96–97.
49. Wilder, *Little House on the Prairie*, 98.
50. Wilder, *Little House on the Prairie*, 321.
51. Wilder, *Little House on the Prairie*, 324–25.
52. Wilder, *Little House on the Prairie*, 335.
53. Wilder, *Little House on the Prairie*, 317.
54. Wilder, *Little House on the Prairie*, 320–21.
55. Wilder, *Little House on the Prairie*, 124.
56. Wilder, *Little House on the Prairie*, 328.
57. Wilder, *Little House on the Prairie*, 331.
58. Wilder, *Little House on the Prairie*, 331.
59. Wilder, *Little House on the Prairie*, 330.
60. Wilder, *Little House on the Prairie*, 327.
61. Wilder, *Pioneer Girl*, 112.
62. Wilder, *Little House on the Prairie*, 332.
63. Ida Louise Raymond to LIW, August 27, 1934, box 13, Lane Papers.
64. McAuliffe, *The Deaths of Sybil Bolton*, 109.

7. *Little House on the Prairie*, Part Two

1. Wilder, *Little House on the Prairie*, 183.

2. Wilder, *Little House on the Prairie*, 1.
3. LIW, quoted in a letter from Ursula Nordstrom to unidentified reader, October 14, 1952, in Marcus, *Dear Genius*, 54.
4. Ursula Nordstrom to Garth Williams, February 11, 1954, quoted in Marcus, *Dear Genius*, 75.
5. Meagan Flynn, "Laura Ingalls Wilder's Name Stripped from Children's Book Award over 'Little House' Depictions of Native Americans," *Washington Post*, July 5, 2018.
6. Hazel Rochman, "Children's Books, Salamancha's Journey," *New York Times*, May 21, 1995.
7. Wilder, *Little House on the Prairie*, 47.
8. Wilder, *Little House on the Prairie*, 237.
9. Wilder, *Little House on the Prairie*, 284.
10. Wilder, *Little House on the Prairie*, 211.
11. Wilder, *Little House on the Prairie*, 237.
12. Wilder, *Little House on the Prairie*, 311.
13. Wilder, *Little House on the Prairie*, 262.
14. Wilder, *Little House on the Prairie*, 262.
15. Wilder, *By the Shores of Silver Lake*, 64.
16. In *On the Banks of Plum Creek*, Mr. Nelson comes to the family's aid to put out a tumbleweed fire while Pa is away, earning money in the East after the grasshopper plague. Mr. Nelson's actions don't upstage Pa since he is absent.
17. Wilder, *Little House on the Prairie*, 137, 233, 134.
18. Wilder, *Little House on the Prairie*, 135, 140.
19. Wilder, *Little House on the Prairie*, 142.
20. Wilder, *Little House on the Prairie*, 139.
21. Wilder, *Little House on the Prairie*, 38.
22. Wilder, *Little House on the Prairie*, 141.
23. Wilder, *Little House on the Prairie*, 143.
24. Wilder, *Little House on the Prairie*, 142.
25. Wilder, *Little House on the Prairie*, 143–44.
26. Wilder, *Little House on the Prairie*, 230.
27. Wilder, *Little House on the Prairie*, 230–31.
28. Wilder, *Little House on the Prairie*, 232.
29. Wilder, *Little House on the Prairie*, 233.
30. Wilder, *Little House on the Prairie*, 234.
31. Burns, *History of the Osage People*, 283.
32. Chapman, "Removal of the Osages from Kansas," 305n8.
33. W. G. Cutler, "Montgomery County," in *A History of the State of Kansas*.
34. Isaac Gibson to Enoch Hoag, January 8, 1870, quoted in Linsenmayer, "Kansas Settlers," 178.

35. Enoch Hoag to the Office of Indian Affairs, January 28, 1870, quoted in Linsenmayer, "Kansas Settlers," 178.
36. Wilder, *Little House on the Prairie*, 146.
37. Wilder, *Little House on the Prairie*, 283.
38. Wilder, *Little House on the Prairie*, 284.
39. Wilder, *Little House on the Prairie*, 285.
40. Wilder, *Little House on the Prairie*, 285.
41. Wilder, *Little House on the Prairie*, 212.
42. *Pioneer Girl* follows the chronology of the historical record, which indicates that Wilder made a conscious, artistic choice when she rearranged the sequence of events in *Little House on the Prairie*.
43. Wilder, *Little House on the Prairie*, 191.
44. Wilder, *Pioneer Girl*, 14.
45. Wilder, *Pioneer Girl*, 5.
46. As historian Brooks Blevins writes, only Springfield in Greene County, Missouri, approximately sixty miles from Wilder's Rocky Ridge Farm, supported a "fully realized" African American community. Most rural Ozark counties "housed minute populations" of African Americans in the early twentieth century. Blevins, *History of the Ozarks*, 107.
47. Wilder, *Little House on the Prairie*, 189.
48. Wilder, *Little House on the Prairie*, 192.
49. Wilder, *Little House on the Prairie*, 192.
50. W. G. Cutler, "Montgomery County," in *A History of the State of Kansas*.
51. LIW, diary, August 14, 1894, folder 33, LIW Papers.
52. Wilder, "Laura Ingalls Wilder," in Kunitz and Haycroft, *Junior Book of Authors*, 299.
53. "The Congregational Christian Tradition," Congregational Library and Archives, accessed January 25, 2019, www.congregationallibrary.org.
54. L'Engle, *Herself*, 180.
55. L'Engle, *Herself*, 174.

8. *On the Banks of Plum Creek*

1. RWL, diary #37 (1931–35), March 28, 1933, box 22, Laura Ingalls Wilder Series, Lane Papers.
2. RWL, diary #37, December 6, 1932, box 22, Lane Papers.
3. RWL, diary #37, January 11, 1933, box 22, Lane Papers.
4. RWL, diary #37, June 11, 1933, box 22, Lane Papers.
5. In 1935 Lane published *Old Home Town* with Longmans, Green. The book featured many of the short stories that had originally appeared in the *Saturday Evening Post* and the *Ladies Home Journal* during the early 1930s. Several were inspired by characters and plot lines from "Pioneer Girl."

6. The Rock House initially stood empty after the Wilders returned to the farmhouse. Over time, however, the Rock House became a rental property and provided the Wilders with additional income. They sold the Rock House in 1943.
7. George Bye to LIW, May 31, 1939, Brown Collection.
8. Wilder, *On the Banks of Plum Creek*, 9–10.
9. Wilder, *On the Banks of Plum Creek*, 192, 195.
10. LIW to RWL, August 6, 1936, folder 19, LIW Papers.
11. Wilder, *On the Banks of Plum Creek*, 17.
12. Wilder, *On the Banks of Plum Creek*, 16–17.
13. Wilder, *On the Banks of Plum Creek*, 53.
14. Wilder, *On the Banks of Plum Creek*, 62.
15. Wilder, *On the Banks of Plum Creek*, 66.
16. Wilder, *On the Banks of Plum Creek*, 6.
17. Wilder, *On the Banks of Plum Creek*, 6.
18. Wilder, *On the Banks of Plum Creek*, 7.
19. Wilder, *On the Banks of Plum Creek*, 189.
20. Wilder, *On the Banks of Plum Creek*, 146.
21. Wilder, *On the Banks of Plum Creek*, 108.
22. Wilder, *On the Banks of Plum Creek*, 111–14.
23. Wilder, *On the Banks of Plum Creek*, 116.
24. Wilder, *On the Banks of Plum Creek*, 109.
25. Wilder, *On the Banks of Plum Creek*, 117.
26. Wilder, *On the Banks of Plum Creek*, 193.
27. Wilder, *On the Banks of Plum Creek*, 193.
28. Wilder, *On the Banks of Plum Creek*, 194–95.
29. Wilder, *On the Banks of Plum Creek*, 196.
30. Wilder, *On the Banks of Plum Creek*, 202.
31. Wilder, *On the Banks of Plum Creek*, 208–9.
32. Wilder, *On the Banks of Plum Creek*, 7.
33. Wilder, *On the Banks of Plum Creek*, 17.
34. Wilder, *On the Banks of Plum Creek*, 82.
35. Wilder, *On the Banks of Plum Creek*, 107.
36. Wilder, *On the Banks of Plum Creek*, 120.
37. Wilder, *On the Banks of Plum Creek*, 203.
38. Wilder, *On the Banks of Plum Creek*, 304.
39. Wilder, *On the Banks of Plum Creek*, 203.
40. Wilder, *On the Banks of Plum Creek*, 47.
41. Wilder, *On the Banks of Plum Creek*, 64.
42. Wilder, *On the Banks of Plum Creek*, 156.
43. Wilder, *On the Banks of Plum Creek*, 17.
44. Wilder, *On the Banks of Plum Creek*, 79.
45. Wilder, *On the Banks of Plum Creek*, 136–37.

46. Wilder, *On the Banks of Plum Creek*, 138.
47. Wilder, *On the Banks of Plum Creek*, 102.
48. Wilder, *On the Banks of Plum Creek*, 103–4.
49. Wilder, *On the Banks of Plum Creek*, 105.
50. Wilder, *On the Banks of Plum Creek*, 106.
51. Wilder's depiction of the West and the natural world also has much in common with the literary agrarian movement of the late nineteenth and early twentieth centuries. Agrarian writers considered the family farm as a fundamental social unit, and farming itself represented a kind of idealized occupation, one that fostered independence and democracy. Wilder's Little House books clearly reflect these tenets.

    At the heart of the agrarian tradition, however, was the idea that nature is a dynamic force, indifferent toward human life. Although Wilder sometimes personifies nature (and by extension, the West), she doesn't romanticize it. It is a powerful, unpredictable force over which Wilder's characters have no control, whether it's a flooded creek or a glittering cloud of grasshoppers. Laura and Pa admire the beauty, wildness, and spirit of the natural world but also respect its strength, power, and volatility.
52. Hall, "Children's Reading," 124–25.
53. Nilsen and Donelson, *Literature for Today's Young Adults*, 55. Two years before Laura Ingalls was introduced to the reading public, another iconic American literary heroine made her debut: Nancy Drew. Like Laura, Nancy wasn't afraid to roam outside the house. She drove her own convertible, knew how to change its tires, and eagerly took on a traditionally male role (i.e., solving mysteries). Still, by 1931 a new management team was in place at the Stratemeyer Syndicate, the publishing company that had created Nancy, and it believed the reading public wanted a softer, more conventionally feminine main character. This new, "less abrasive" Nancy made her debut in the fourth Nancy Drew novel, *The Mystery at Lilac Inn*. Benson, "The Nancy I Knew," n.p.
54. Wilder, *Pioneer Girl*, 85.
55. RWL to LIW, June 13, 1936, folder 19, LIW Papers.
56. LIW to RWL, n.d. [1936], folder 19, LIW Papers.
57. LIW to RWL, July 2, 1936, folder 19, LIW Papers.
58. LIW to RWL, n.d. [1936], folder 19, LIW Papers.
59. LIW to RWL, n.d. [1936], folder 19, LIW Papers.
60. LIW to RWL, July 2, 1936, folder 19, LIW Papers.
61. Wilder, *On the Banks of Plum Creek*, 305–6.
62. LIW to RWL, January 26, 1938, box 13, Lane Papers.

9. *By the Shores of Silver Lake*

1. Lane also consulted her father for essential details about the pioneering experience as she wrote *Free Land*.

2. LIW to RWL, February 5, 1937, box 17, Lane Papers.
3. Lane, *Free Land*, 107.
4. Lane, *Free Land*, 130. Lane also fictionalized her mother's family. They appear as the Peters in *Free Land*, a family of six—Mr. and Mrs. Peters, Nettie, Flora, Lucy, and Charley. Wilder herself appears as Nettie.
5. Wilder, *By the Shores of Silver Lake*, 64–65.
6. Wilder, *On the Banks of Plum Creek*, 338.
7. Wilder, *Pioneer Girl*, 97.
8. Wilder, *Pioneer Girl*, 142.
9. LIW to RWL, n.d. [1937], box 13, Lane Papers.
10. Wilder, *By the Shores of Silver Lake*, 1.
11. Wilder, *By the Shores of Silver Lake*, 13.
12. Wilder, *By the Shores of Silver Lake*, 14.
13. *Little Women*'s Beth has no future. She dies in volume 2 of the novel, which Louisa May Alcott published in 1869.
14. Alleen Pace Nilsen and Kenneth L. Donelson, quoted in Cart, *From Romance to Realism*, 4.
15. Rioux, *Meg, Jo, Beth, Amy*, 48.
16. Louisa May Alcott, quoted in Jehlen, "Banned in Concord," 93.
17. One of the most successful American middle grade novels dates from this period—*The Wonderful Wizard of Oz* by L. Frank Baum, published in 1900.
18. Rubio, *Lucy Maud Montgomery*, 525.
19. Lane, *Old Home Town*, 21.
20. The Elsie Dinsmore series, written by Martha Finley, focuses on Elsie's determination to adhere to Christian values and yet remain devoted to her family. Published between 1867 and 1905, the books take place on southern plantations and follow Elsie's growth and maturity from the pre–Civil War era through adulthood. The Five Little Peppers series was written by Harriett Lothrop under the pseudonym of Margaret Sidney and follows the lives of the five Pepper children as they grow up. The twelve books in the series were published between 1881 and 1916.
21. Rioux, *Meg, Jo, Beth, Amy*, 60.
22. RWL to George Bye, October 5, 1931, box 13, Lane Papers.
23. Natalie Babbit, quoted in Cart, *From Romance to Realism*, 5.
24. LIW to RWL, January 26, 1938, box 13, Lane Papers.
25. LIW to RWL, January 26, 1938.
26. The existing editorial correspondence between Wilder and Lane doesn't directly reveal why Wilder chose not to include the birth and death of her baby brother in the Little House series—other than her assessment, as we've seen, that her family's experience when they moved east to Iowa was "a story in itself." But it's likely that Wilder

felt the death of a nine-month-old infant in the book's opening pages would add another layer to the "recital of discouragement and calamities" she already had to navigate in *By the Shores of Silver Lake.*

27. LIW to RWL, January 26, 1938, box 13, Lane Papers.
28. LIW, *By the Shores of Silver Lake* manuscript, pp. 1–2, folder 25, LIW Papers.
29. RWL to LIW, December 19, 1937, box 13, Lane Papers.
30. LIW to RWL, January 25, 1938, box 13, Lane Papers.
31. Wilder, *By the Shores of Silver Lake*, 2–3.
32. For more insights into the editorial compromise Wilder and Lane reached for the opening chapter of *By the Shores of Silver Lake*, see my discussion in Hill, *Laura Ingalls Wilder*, 175–77.
33. Wilder, *By the Shores of Silver Lake*, 2.
34. Wilder, *Pioneer Girl*, 142.
35. LIW to RWL, March, 23, 1937, box 13, Lane Papers.
36. Allexan et al., "Blindness in Walnut Grove," 2.
37. RWL to LIW, December 19, 1937, box 13, Lane Papers.
38. Scarlet fever was a dreaded and sometimes fatal disease in the nineteenth and early twentieth centuries. It touched families from all walks of life. Wilder, her sisters, and cousins had scarlet fever in 1874. See Wilder, *Pioneer Girl*, 55.
39. Wilder, *By the Shores of Silver Lake*, 2.
40. Wilder, *By the Shores of Silver Lake*, 2.
41. LIW to RWL, n.d. [1937], box 13, Lane Papers.
42. Wilder, *By the Shores of Silver Lake*, 54.
43. Wilder, *By the Shores of Silver Lake*, 50. Teenage marriage was a somewhat daring topic for Wilder to address in fiction for young readers in 1939, when *By the Shores of Silver Lake* was published; it is even more so today.
44. Wilder, *By the Shores of Silver Lake*, 47.
45. Wilder, *By the Shores of Silver Lake*, 51.
46. Wilder, *By the Shores of Silver Lake*, 166.
47. Wilder, *By the Shores of Silver Lake*, 165.
48. Wilder, *By the Shores of Silver Lake*, 172.
49. Wilder, *By the Shores of Silver Lake*, 59.
50. Wilder, *By the Shores of Silver Lake*, 60.
51. Wilder, *By the Shores of Silver Lake*, 61.
52. Wilder, *By the Shores of Silver Lake*, 61–62.
53. Wilder, *By the Shores of Silver Lake*, 131.
54. Wilder, *By the Shores of Silver Lake*, 30.
55. LIW to RWL, n.d. [1937], box 13, Lane Papers.
56. LIW to RWL, January 25, 1938, box 13, Lane Papers.
57. Wilder, *By the Shores of Silver Lake*, 107.

58. Wilder, *By the Shores of Silver Lake*, 106.
59. Wilder, *By the Shores of Silver Lake*, 65.
60. Wilder, *By the Shores of Silver Lake*, 58.
61. George Bye to RWL, Western Union telegram, June 25, 1939, Brown Collection.
62. In the late 1940s, Harper & Brothers engaged Garth Williams to illustrate new editions of the Little House books, and these versions, released in 1953, became iconic. The books had a uniform design, shape, and style, which masked the differences in readership between the first four books in the series (for middle grade readers) and the last four (for young adults).
63. Wilder, *Pioneer Girl*, 174.
64. Wilder, *By the Shores of Silver Lake*, 271.
65. Charles Ingalls initially purchased two lots and built a pair of buildings as De Smet, South Dakota, took shape in 1880. See Wilder, *Pioneer Girl*, 189–90.
66. Wilder, *By the Shores of Silver Lake*, 285.

10. *The Long Winter*, Part One

1. George Bye to LIW, April 30, 1940, Brown Collection.
2. *New York Herald Tribune*, November 10, 1940, clipping, box 15, Lane Papers.
3. Wilder, *Long Winter*, 87.
4. LIW to RWL, June 3, 1939, box 13, Lane Papers.
5. LIW to George Bye, May 7, 1940, Brown Collection.
6. As Herbert S. Schell points out in his *History of South Dakota*, the winter of 1880–81 became widely known as "the hard winter" by the pioneers who had endured it and by early twentieth-century historians who wrote about it later. Schell, *History of South Dakota*, 180.
7. Wilder, *Pioneer Girl*, 207.
8. LIW to RWL, February 19, 1938, box 13, Lane Papers.
9. *Pioneer Girl* records that the Masters baby—a boy—was born after the blizzard that struck while Wilder and her sister Carrie were in school, during the fall of 1880. For more details about the birth, see Wilder, *Pioneer Girl*, 207.
10. LIW to RWL, March 7, 1938, box 13, file 194, Lane Papers.
11. LIW to RWL, March 7, 1938, box 13, file 194, Lane Papers.
12. LIW to RWL, February 19, 1938, box 13, Lane Papers.
13. Wilder, *Long Winter*, 34–35.
14. Wilder, *Long Winter*, 1.
15. Wilder, *Long Winter*, 6–7.
16. Wilder, *Long Winter*, 12.
17. Wilder, *Long Winter*, 13
18. Wilder, *Long Winter*, 14.

19. Wilder, *Long Winter*, 335.
20. Wilder, *Long Winter*, 4.
21. Wilder, *Long Winter*, 9.
22. Wilder, *Long Winter*, 186, 188.
23. Wilder, *Long Winter*, 85.
24. Mr. Foster's character in *The Long Winter* is based on Wilder's memory of a man she identifies as "Mr. Holms" in *Pioneer Girl*. See Wilder, *Pioneer Girl*, 207.
25. Wilder, *Long Winter*, 88.
26. Wilder, *Long Winter*, 88.
27. Wilder, *Long Winter*, 90.
28. Wilder, *Long Winter*, 91.
29. Wilder, *Long Winter*, 95.
30. Wilder, *Long Winter*, 187.
31. Wilder, *Long Winter*, 224.
32. Wilder, *Long Winter*, 226.
33. Wilder, *Long Winter*, 227.
34. Wilder, *Long Winter*, 288–89.
35. Wilder, *Long Winter*, 290.
36. Wilder, *Long Winter*, 291–92.
37. Wilder, *Long Winter*, 77.
38. Wilder, *Long Winter*, 78.
39. Wilder, *Long Winter*, 95. Oscar Edmund (Cap) Garland was roughly two years older than Wilder. Born in Wisconsin, he, his mother, and two sisters moved to Dakota Territory in 1880. Cap never married, and he died in 1891 in a gruesome accident when a threshing machine exploded. He was twenty-six.
40. Wilder, *Long Winter*, 23–24.
41. Wilder, *Long Winter*, 24.
42. Wilder, *Long Winter*, 21.
43. Wilder, *By the Shores of Silver Lake*, 53–54.
44. Wilder, *Long Winter*, 24.
45. Wilder, *Pioneer Girl*, 241, 243.
46. LIW to RWL, June 26, 1938, box 13, Lane Papers.
47. LIW to RWL, February 19, 1939, box 13, Lane Papers. For more details on the ideas Wilder and Lane discussed on this subject, see Wilder, *Pioneer Girl*, 243n41.
48. Wilder, *By the Shores of Silver Lake*, 262–63. Almanzo's family left Malone, New York, in 1875 and settled in Spring Valley, Minnesota. Four years later, Almanzo, Royal, and their sister Eliza Jane filed adjoining homestead claims in Dakota Territory, northwest of De Smet. All three also had tree claims in the area. Royal opened a feed store in town.

49. Wilder, *Long Winter*, 99. The Homestead Act dates from 1862 and allowed adults over twenty-one (including women) to claim up to 160 acres of public land for a minimal registration fee. To assume full ownership of the property, homesteaders were required to build a home (no matter how primitive) on the land, plant crops, and live there for five years.
50. Wilder, *Long Winter*, 59.

11. *The Long Winter*, Part Two

1. RWL to George Bye, July 30, 1932, Brown Collection.
2. Lane, *Free Land*, 153.
3. Wilder, *Pioneer Girl*, 217.
4. LIW to RWL, March 7, 1938, box 13, file 194, Lane Papers.
5. LIW to George Bye, May 7, 1940, Brown Collection.
6. RWL to George Bye, June 5, 1940, Brown Collection.
7. Wilder, *Long Winter*, 224.
8. Wilder *Long Winter*, 98.
9. Wilder, *Long Winter*, 98.
10. Wilder, *Long Winter*, 123.
11. Wilder, *Long Winter*, 98.
12. Wilder, *Long Winter*, 163.
13. Wilder, *Long Winter*, 163–64.
14. Wilder, *Long Winter*, 164.
15. LIW to RWL, March 7, 1938, box 13, file 194, Lane Papers.
16. Wilder, *Long Winter*, 255.
17. Wilder, *Long Winter*, 307.
18. Wilder, *Long Winter*, 304.
19. Wilder, *Long Winter*, 303.
20. Wilder, *Long Winter*, 308.
21. Wilder, *Long Winter*, 216.
22. Wilder, *Long Winter*, 223.
23. Wilder, *Long Winter*, 61. The illustration of this scene in the classic Garth Williams edition of *The Long Winter* illustrates this point very clearly. The Native American man stands apart from the other men gathered in the store. A plow is positioned between them, and in the background are all the supplies civilization can furnish, thanks to modern technology and the railroad. These supplies will soon be gone, and for the length of the Hard Winter, they will be irreplaceable. Civilization and its technologies will be no match for the cold and snow and wind yet to come.
24. Wilder, *Long Winter*, 61.
25. Wilder, *Long Winter*, 62.
26. Wilder, *Long Winter*, 63.
27. Wilder, *Long Winter*, 61.

28. Meek, "And the Injun Goes 'How!,'" 95; Flanigan, "American Indian English in History and Literature," 174–75.
29. Wilder, *Pioneer Girl*, 203. A brief discussion of similar encounters in Dakota Territory and across the border in Minnesota appears in Wilder, *Pioneer Girl*, 203n7.
30. Leechman and Hall, "American Indian Pidgin English Attestations," 417, 418.
31. Flanigan, "American Indian English in History and Literature," 119.
32. Mark Twain published a scathing essay that faulted Fenimore Cooper for, among other things, his depiction of Native Americans and his masterless "construction of dialogue." Yet Twain didn't fault Cooper for the way his Native American characters speak. Instead, Twain levels his criticism of Cooper's dialogue against his white protagonists, whose speech patterns are inconsistent. See Twain, "Fenimore Cooper's Literary Offenses," 553. In her dissertation on American Indian English, Beverly Olson Flanigan maintains that "Cooper's 'Indian talk,' whether real or feigned, is generally consistent and credible." See Flanigan, "American Indian English in History and Literature," 118–19.
33. Kelly, *Narrative of My Captivity among the Sioux Indians*, vi.
34. Wilder, *Long Winter*, 62. Charles L. Cutler, however, questions the authenticity of the word "heap" as an American Indian pidgin synonym for "a lot" or "plenty." He argues that this usage may have been pure literary invention. See C. L. Cutler, *O Brave New Words!*, 132.
35. Underhill and Littlefield, *Hamlin Garland's Observations on the American Indian*, 124.
36. Wilder, *Pioneer Girl*, 203. *The Jazz Singer*, released in October 1927, is generally recognized as the first talking motion picture, but the transition to sound in films was gradual and began in 1926 with several films that featured recorded music and sound effects.
37. *The Long Winter*'s "very old Indian" would have likely been a Dakota, Lakota, or Nakota man, living on a reservation in Dakota Territory.
38. Garland visited the Standing Rock Reservation in 1897 and again in 1900. On both visits, he relied on Louis Primeau, "a half-blood trader," to serve as interpreter. See Underhill and Littlefield, *Hamlin Garland's Observations on the American Indian*, 20, 37.
39. Wilder, *Long Winter*, 62.
40. LIW to RWL, March 7, 1938, box 13, file 194, Lane Papers.
41. Wilder, *Long Winter*, 272.
42. Wilder, *Long Winter*, 273.
43. Wilder, *Long Winter*, 276.
44. Wilder, *Long Winter*, 277.
45. Wilder, *Long Winter*, 275.

46. Wilder, *Long Winter*, 277–79.
47. Wilder, *Long Winter*, 279.
48. Wilder, *Long Winter*, 285.
49. Wilder, *Long Winter*, 285.
50. Wilder, *Long Winter*, 263.
51. Wilder, *Long Winter*, 263.
52. Wilder, *Long Winter*, 285.
53. Wilder, *Long Winter*, 286.
54. Wilder, *Long Winter*, 286–87.
55. Wilder, *Long Winter*, 291.
56. Wilder, *Long Winter*, 294.
57. Wilder, *Long Winter*, 298.
58. Wilder, *Pioneer Girl*, 217.
59. Wilder, *Long Winter*, 225.
60. Wilder, *Long Winter*, 138.
61. Wilder, *Long Winter*, 310.
62. Wilder, *Long Winter*, 309–10.
63. Wilder, *Long Winter*, 239.
64. Wilder, *Long Winter*, 253.
65. Wilder, *Long Winter*, 312.

12. *Little Town on the Prairie*

1. LIW to RWL, June 3, 1939, box 13, Lane Papers.
2. LIW to RWL, June 3, 1939, box 13, Lane Papers.
3. LIW, "Prairie Girl" outline, box 16, Lane Papers.
4. LIW to RWL, March 7, 1938, box 13, file 194, Lane Papers.
5. LIW to RWL, March 15, 1938, box 13, Lane Papers. Stella Gilbert was about three years older than Wilder. Her family arrived in Dakota Territory during the Great Dakota Land Boom. Genevieve Masters—Genieve—was a few months younger than Wilder and part of the Masters clan the Ingalls family had first met in Minnesota.
6. LIW to RWL, August 17, 1938, box 13, Lane Papers. Caroline Ingalls's brother Tom Quiner was one of twenty-six men and one woman who followed John Gordon into the Black Hills illegally in 1874. The group built a stockade and planned to prospect for gold but was escorted out by the cavalry in April 1875. At that time, the Black Hills were part of the Great Sioux Reservation, which had been set aside exclusively for the Sioux nation under the Treaty of Fort Laramie in 1868.
7. William T. Anderson in Wilder, *Selected Letters*, xviii.
8. LIW to Miss Crawford, September 16, 1940, quoted in Wilder, *Selected Letters*, 225.
9. Ursula Nordstrom to LIW, July 1941, quoted in Wilder, *Selected Letters*, 230.
10. Wilder, *Little Town on the Prairie*, 1.

11. LIW, "Detroit Book Fair Speech," 1937, box 13, Lane Papers.
12. Wilder, *Little Town on the Prairie*, 10.
13. Wilder, *Little Town on the Prairie*, 2.
14. RWL to LIW, n.d. [late October 1937], box 13, Lane Papers.
15. Wilder, *Little Town on the Prairie*, 4.
16. Wilder, *Little Town on the Prairie*, 10.
17. Wilder, *Little Town on the Prairie*, 8.
18. Wilder, *Little Town on the Prairie*, 11.
19. Wilder, *Little Town on the Prairie*, 31.
20. Wilder, *Little Town on the Prairie*, 27.
21. Wilder, *Little Town on the Prairie*, 34.
22. Tolkien, *The Hobbit*, 47.
23. Wilder, *Little Town on the Prairie*, 35.
24. Wilder, *Little Town on the Prairie*, 34.
25. Wilder, *Little Town on the Prairie*, 35.
26. Wilder, *Little Town on the Prairie*, 2.
27. LIW to RWL, n.d. [1937], box 13, Lane Papers.
28. LIW, "Detroit Book Fair Speech."
29. Wilder, *Little Town on the Prairie*, 35–37.
30. Wilder, *Little Town on the Prairie*, 28.
31. Wilder, *Little Town on the Prairie*, 29.
32. Wilder, *Little Town on the Prairie*, 37. Wilder not only worked in the De Smet dry goods store, she boarded with the family, sleeping in the attic with the owner's mother-in-law. See Wilder, *Pioneer Girl*, 236–37.
33. Wilder, *Little Town on the Prairie*, 45.
34. Wilder, *Little Town on the Prairie*, 42.
35. Wilder, *Little Town on the Prairie*, 44.
36. Wilder, *Little Town on the Prairie*, 46.
37. Wilder, *Little Town on the Prairie*, 48.
38. Wilder, *Little Town on the Prairie*, 49.
39. Wilder, *Little Town on the Prairie*, 57.
40. Wilder, *Little Town on the Prairie*, 112.
41. Wilder, *Little Town on the Prairie*, 112.
42. Wilder, *Little Town on the Prairie*, 153.
43. Wilder, *Little Town on the Prairie*, 155.
44. Wilder, *Little Town on the Prairie*, 161.
45. Wilder, *Little Town on the Prairie*, 163, 164.
46. Wilder, *Little Town on the Prairie*, 167.
47. Wilder, *Little Town on the Prairie*, 180.
48. Wilder, *Little Town on the Prairie*, 93. For a more complete discussion of late nineteenth-century corsets, see Wilder, *Pioneer Girl*, 299n58.
49. Wilder, *Little Town on the Prairie*, 94.
50. Wilder, *Little Town on the Prairie*, 266.
51. Wilder, *Little Town on the Prairie*, 129.

52. Wilder, *Little Town on the Prairie*, 92.
53. Wilder, *Little Town on the Prairie*, 129.
54. Wilder, *Little Town on the Prairie*, 148, 147.
55. Wilder, *Little Town on the Prairie*, 148.
56. Wilder, *Little Town on the Prairie*, 148–49.
57. Wilder, *Little Town on the Prairie*, 149.
58. Wilder, *Little Town on the Prairie*, 185.
59. Wilder, *Little Town on the Prairie*, 187.
60. Wilder, *Little Town on the Prairie*, 188.
61. Wilder, *Little Town on the Prairie*, 250.
62. Wilder, *Little Town on the Prairie*, 252.
63. Wilder, *Little Town on the Prairie*, 200.
64. Wilder, *Little Town on the Prairie*, 236.
65. Wilder, *Little Town on the Prairie*, 260.
66. Wilder, *Little Town on the Prairie*, 259.
67. David S. Reynolds observes, "Today the inherent racism in minstrel shows is widely understood, which has made it difficult for Lincoln biographers to talk about his [Lincoln's] love of 'darky' performances." See Reynolds, *Abe*, 236. For more perspectives on minstrelsy in the United States, see Wilder, *Pioneer Girl*, 254n62.
68. Wilder, *Pioneer Girl*, 252.
69. Wilder, *Little Town on the Prairie*, 259.
70. Basinger, *Movie Musical*, 113.
71. The additional lyrics appear in Wilder, *Little Town on the Prairie* (New York: Harper & Brothers, 1941), 253. Wilder identifies the song in both the 1941 and the 1953 editions of *Little Town on the Prairie* as "The Mulligan Guards," but the lyrics are actually from the song "The Skidmore Guards." Lyrics for both songs were written by Edward Harrigan. See Wilder, *Pioneer Girl*, 254n63.
72. Ursula Nordstrom to Zena Sutherland, November 18, 1969, in Marcus, *Dear Genius*, 289. The manuscript in question was *The First Four Years*, published in 1971.
73. Viet Thanh Nguyen, "My Young Mind Was Disturbed by a Book: It Changed My Life," *New York Times*, January 29, 2022.
74. LIW, "Detroit Book Fair Speech."
75. LIW, "Prairie Girl" outline, box 16, Lane Papers.
76. For a detailed examination of American Libertarian influences in the Little House series, see Woodside, *Libertarians on the Prairie*.
77. Wilder, *Little Town on the Prairie*, 73.
78. Holtz, *Ghost in the Little House*, 383.
79. Brink, *Caddie Woodlawn*, 26. Adult fiction from this period contains similar patriotic or political themes. A striking example is Bess Streeter Aldrich's *A Lantern in Her Hand*, published in 1929. Set on the Nebraska frontier, it follows the life of a pioneer heroine, and

like *Caddie Woodlawn* and the Little House series, Aldrich's novel is constructed around autobiographical elements.

80. Wilder, *Little Town on the Prairie*, 76.
81. Wilder, *Little Town on the Prairie*, 68.
82. Wilder, *Little Town on the Prairie*, 84.
83. Wilder, *Little Town on the Prairie*, 225. Best known for his raid on the federal armory at Harpers Ferry, Virginia, in 1859, John Brown launched his militant abolitionist activities on the Missouri-Kansas border in the late 1850s. Following the Harpers Ferry raid, Brown was convicted of treason and hanged.
84. Wilder, *Little Town on the Prairie*, 225.
85. Wilder, *Little Town on the Prairie*, 277.
86. Wilder, *Little Town on the Prairie*, 279.
87. Wilder, *Little Town on the Prairie*, 147.
88. Wilder, *Little Town on the Prairie*, 211.
89. Wilder, *Little Town on the Prairie*, 271.
90. Wilder, *Little Town on the Prairie*, 212.
91. Wilder, *Little Town on the Prairie*, 262.
92. Wilder, *Little Town on the Prairie*, 274.
93. Wilder, *Little Town on the Prairie*, 279.
94. Wilder, *Little Town on the Prairie*, 279.
95. Wilder, *Little Town on the Prairie*, 291.
96. Wilder, *Little Town on the Prairie*, 293.
97. Wilder actually received her teaching certificate when she was sixteen, on December 10, 1883. Her original teacher's certificate, part of the Laura Ingalls Wilder Home and Museum's collection, confirms the date. Why then was her fictional counterpart in *Little Town on the Prairie* a full year younger? The existing editorial correspondence is unclear. For a fuller discussion of these subjects, see Wilder, *Pioneer Girl*, 260–62.
98. Wilder, *Little Town on the Prairie*, 307.

13. *These Happy Golden Years*, Part One

1. George Bye to LIW, September 29, 1942, Brown Collection.
2. Wilder, *These Happy Golden Years*, 2.
3. Wilder, *These Happy Golden Years*, 2.
4. Wilder, *These Happy Golden Years*, 3.
5. Wilder, *These Happy Golden Years*, 4.
6. Wilder, *These Happy Golden Years*, 4.
7. Wilder, *These Happy Golden Years*, 5.
8. Wilder, *These Happy Golden Years*, 8–9.
9. Wilder, *These Happy Golden Years*, 7.
10. Rolvaag, *Giants in the Earth*, 37–38.
11. Wilder, *These Happy Golden Years*, 9.

12. Wilder, *These Happy Golden Years*, 6.
13. Wilder, *These Happy Golden Years*, 10.
14. Wilder, *These Happy Golden Years*, 6.
15. Wilder, *These Happy Golden Years*, 22.
16. Wilder, *These Happy Golden Years*, 13.
17. Wilder, *These Happy Golden Years*, 24.
18. Wilder, *These Happy Golden Years*, 28.
19. Wilder, *These Happy Golden Years*, 29.
20. Wilder, *These Happy Golden Years*, 47.
21. Wilder, *These Happy Golden Years*, 35.
22. Wilder, *These Happy Golden Years*, 33.
23. Wilder, *These Happy Golden Years*, 46.
24. Wilder, *These Happy Golden Years*, 61.
25. Wilder, *These Happy Golden Years*, 61.
26. Wilder, *These Happy Golden Years*, 23.
27. Wilder, *These Happy Golden Years*, 52.
28. Wilder, *These Happy Golden Years*, 39.
29. Wilder, *These Happy Golden Years*, 31.
30. Wilder, *These Happy Golden Years*, 32.
31. Wilder, *These Happy Golden Years*, 31.
32. Wilder, *These Happy Golden Years*, 55.
33. Wilder, *These Happy Golden Years*, 55.
34. Wilder, *These Happy Golden Years*, 52.
35. Wilder, *These Happy Golden Years*, 61.
36. Wilder, *These Happy Golden Years*, 55.
37. Wilder, *These Happy Golden Years*, 61.
38. Wilder, *These Happy Golden Years*, 62.
39. Wilder, *These Happy Golden Years*, 62.
40. Wilder, *These Happy Golden Years*, 62–63, 64.
41. Wilder, *These Happy Golden Years*, 64.
42. Wilder, *These Happy Golden Years*, 64–65.
43. Wilder, *These Happy Golden Years*, 66.
44. Wilder, *These Happy Golden Years*, 67–68.
45. Wilder, *These Happy Golden Years*, 67–68.
46. Wilder, *These Happy Golden Years*, 67–68.
47. Wilder, *These Happy Golden Years*, 77.
48. Wilder, *These Happy Golden Years*, 70.
49. Wilder, *These Happy Golden Years*, 69.
50. Wilder, *These Happy Golden Years*, 72.
51. Wilder, *These Happy Golden Years*, 73.
52. Wilder, *These Happy Golden Years*, 71–72.
53. Wilder, *These Happy Golden Years*, 73.
54. Wilder, *These Happy Golden Years*, 74.

55. Wilder, *These Happy Golden Years*, 74.
56. Wilder, *These Happy Golden Years*, 75.
57. Wilder, *These Happy Golden Years*, 76.
58. Wilder, *These Happy Golden Years*, 78.
59. Wilder, *These Happy Golden Years*, 82.
60. Wilder, *These Happy Golden Years*, 85.
61. Wilder, *Pioneer Girl*, 297. In September 1937 the *Saturday Evening Post* published Rose Wilder Lane's short story "Home over Saturday." The story was based on details Wilder included in "Pioneer Girl" and essentially follows the same outline as "A Cold Ride" in *These Happy Golden Years*. Lane's retelling, however, puts a different spin on this episode. A love triangle is the central focus of "Home over Saturday," and Lane's butcher knife scene is far less menacing than her mother's account in both "Pioneer Girl" and *These Happy Golden Years*. As in most of Lane's fiction, her characters' emotional motivations in "Home over Saturday" are less subtle and more melodramatic than Wilder's.
62. LIW to RWL, February 2, 1938, box 13, Lane Papers.
63. Wilder, *These Happy Golden Years*, 88.

14. *These Happy Golden Years*, Part Two

1. RWL to Clarence Day, June 26, 1928, box 5, Lane Papers.
2. LIW to RWL, March 17, 1939, in Wilder, *Selected Letters*, 196.
3. Petersen, *Bess Streeter Aldrich*, 184.
4. Stuart Roge to Bess Streeter Aldrich, August 27, 1941, in Petersen, *Bess Streeter Aldrich*, 184.
5. LIW to Alvilda Sorenson, December 29, 1941, in Wilder, *Selected Letters*, 236.
6. LIW, "Detroit Book Fair Speech," 1937, box 13, Lane Papers.
7. LIW to George Bye, September 28, 1942, Brown Collection.
8. George Bye to LIW, May 5, 1943, Brown Collection.
9. Marjorie Vitense to LIW, February 22, 1933, folder 14, LIW Papers.
10. Wilder, *These Happy Golden Years*, 144.
11. Maureen Daly, quoted in Cart, *From Romance to Realism*, 16. Like Laura Ingalls and Jo March, Angie Morrow in *Seventeenth Summer* is one of four sisters. The parallel is pronounced, especially to *Little Women*. Angie's father is a traveling salesman and is often away from his family, just as Jo's father is absent for much of *Little Women*.
12. Wilder, *These Happy Golden Years*, 39.
13. Wilder, *These Happy Golden Years*, 62.
14. Wilder, *These Happy Golden Years*, 89.
15. Wilder, *These Happy Golden Years*, 91.
16. Wilder, *These Happy Golden Years*, 91.
17. Wilder, *These Happy Golden Years*, 91–92.

18. Wilder, *These Happy Golden Years*, 92
19. Wilder, *These Happy Golden Years*, 92
20. Wilder, *These Happy Golden Years*, 101
21. Wilder, *These Happy Golden Years*, 121.
22. Wilder, *These Happy Golden Years*, 136.
23. Wilder, *These Happy Golden Years*, 143.
24. Wilder, *These Happy Golden Years*, 144. In the Little House series, the fictional Laura Ingalls appears interested in only Cap Garland and Almanzo Wilder. But several young men caught the eye of the real Laura Ingalls. See Wilder, *Pioneer Girl*, 252, 255–57, 259.
25. Wilder, *These Happy Golden Years*, 187.
26. Wilder, *These Happy Golden Years*, 145.
27. Wilder, *These Happy Golden Years*, 188.
28. Wilder, *These Happy Golden Years*, 214.
29. Wilder, *These Happy Golden Years*, 215.
30. Wilder, *These Happy Golden Years*, 186.
31. Wilder, *These Happy Golden Years*, 92.
32. Wilder, *These Happy Golden Years*, 209–10.
33. Wilder, *These Happy Golden Years*, 216.
34. Wilder, *These Happy Golden Years*, 240.
35. Wilder, *These Happy Golden Years*, 248–49.
36. Wilder, *These Happy Golden Years*, 250.
37. Daly, *Seventeenth Summer*, 52.
38. Wilder, *These Happy Golden Years*, 67.
39. By contrast, Angie Morrow in *Seventeenth Summer* appears to have no serious ambition other than pursuing her romance with Jack Duluth. Although the novel ends as Angie speeds away on a train to college, her desire to further her education isn't a serious theme in the novel.
40. In *These Happy Golden Years*, Laura teaches at the Perry school, just south of Pa's homestead claim, and the Wilkins school, where she boards with the Wilkins family and shares a room with her friend Florence. Wilder herself taught at four schools between 1882 and 1885: the Bouchie school (the Brewster school in *These Happy Golden Years*), the Perry school, and the Wilkins school. She also was a substitute teacher for the lower grades at the De Smet school in 1884.
41. Wilder, *These Happy Golden Years*, 152.
42. Wilder, *These Happy Golden Years*, 96.
43. Wilder, *These Happy Golden Years*, 96–97.
44. Wilder, *These Happy Golden Years*, 98.
45. Wilder, *These Happy Golden Years*, 98.
46. Wilder, *These Happy Golden Years*, 136.
47. Wilder, *These Happy Golden Years*, 262.
48. Wilder, *These Happy Golden Years*, 262.

49. Wilder, *These Happy Golden Years*, 263.
50. Wilder, *These Happy Golden Years*, 138–39.
51. Wilder, *These Happy Golden Years*, 139.
52. Wilder, *These Happy Golden Years*, 264.
53. Wilder, *These Happy Golden Years*, 169.
54. Wilder, *These Happy Golden Years*, 254.
55. Wilder, *These Happy Golden Years*, 258.
56. Wilder, *Little Town on the Prairie*, 131.
57. Wilder, *Little Town on the Prairie*, 135. Nellie Oleson's character in her final scenes in *These Happy Golden Years* is based on the real Stella Gilbert. See Wilder, *Pioneer Girl*, 290n37, 301.
58. Wilder, *These Happy Golden Years*, 171–72.
59. Wilder, *These Happy Golden Years*, 172.
60. Wilder, *These Happy Golden Years*, 172–73.
61. Wilder, *These Happy Golden Years*, 173.
62. Wilder, *These Happy Golden Years*, 174.
63. Wilder, *These Happy Golden Years*, 175.
64. Wilder, *These Happy Golden Years*, 180.
65. Wilder, *These Happy Golden Years*, 175.
66. Wilder, *These Happy Golden Years*, 168.
67. Wilder, *These Happy Golden Years*, 269.
68. Wilder, *These Happy Golden Years*, 270.
69. Wilder, *These Happy Golden Years*, 266.
70. Wilder, *These Happy Golden Years*, 271.
71. Wilder, *These Happy Golden Years*, 271.
72. The real Laura Ingalls and Almanzo Wilder were married on Tuesday, August 25, 1885, at the home of Reverend Brown. Ida Brown and Elmer McConnell were witnesses. In *Pioneer Girl*, Wilder confirms that Reverend Brown did not use the word "obey" in the ceremony. See Wilder, *Pioneer Girl*, 322.
73. Wilder, *These Happy Golden Years*, 289.
74. LIW to Mrs. Phraner, May 10, 1943, in Wilder, *Selected Letters*, 248.

15. *The First Four Years*

1. LIW to George Bye, May 10, 1943, Brown Collection.
2. LIW to George Bye, May 10, 1943.
3. Ursula Nordstrom to Virginia Haviland, April 8, 1969, in Marcus, *Dear Genius*, 267–68.
4. Ursula Nordstrom to Zena Sutherland, November 18, 1969, in Marcus, *Dear Genius*, 267–68.
5. Wilder, *First Four Years*, 4.
6. Wilder, *First Four Years*, 3–4.
7. Wilder, *Little Town on the Prairie*, 34.

8. Wilder, *First Four Years*, 5.
9. Roger Lea MacBride in the introduction to Wilder, *First Four Years*, xiv.
10. Holtz, *Ghost in the Little House*, 6, 7–8.
11. LIW to RWL, August 17, 1938, box 13, Lane Papers.
12. LIW to RWL, August 17, 1938.
13. Holtz, *Ghost in the Little House*, 65, 279.
14. Holtz, *Ghost in the Little House*, 278.
15. LIW, "The First Four Years, Pages 81–161," p. 135, box 16, Lane Papers. Archivists gave the manuscript its title, "The First Four Years," apparently to conform to its published title. Wilder, in her own handwriting, titled the manuscript "The First Three Years." She didn't number pages. Page numbers were added later to aid research and documentation.
16. LIW, "The First Four Years, Pages 81–161," 135.
17. LIW, "The First Four Years, Pages 81–161," 136. The full text of this draft letter reads: "Mansfield, Mo, Jan. 26, 1933[,] Federal Land Bank[,] St. Louis[,] E.C. Lips, Treas. Dept. Dear Sir, Your letter of Jan. 17th with ~~statemt~~ correct statement received."
18. RWL, journal, January 25, 1933, box 23, Lane Papers.
19. LIW, "The First Four Years, Pages 1–80," p. 13, box 16, Lane Papers.
20. LIW, "The First Four Years, Pages 1–80," 15.
21. Wilder, *These Happy Golden Years*, 273.
22. LIW, "The First Four Years, Pages 1–80," 13.
23. Wilder, *First Four Years*, 9. MacBride used far less restraint in the mid-1980s when he developed a version of Wilder's original "Pioneer Girl" manuscript for young readers. He pulled from Wilder's letters, rough drafts of the Little House books, and interviews to create "new material" for this edition, which, he said, would be "reflective of the past" (Roger Lea MacBride to William Anderson, July 24, 1985, private collection). Far from duplicating the voice of Wilder's original "Pioneer Girl" manuscript, MacBride's composite version attempted to mimic the style and tone of the Little House series. He titled the project "Pioneer Girl: More Stories from the 'Little Houses' by Laura Ingalls Wilder." The manuscript, which is part of the Laura Ingalls Wilder Memorial Society's archives in De Smet, South Dakota, was never published.
24. Wilder, *First Four Years*, xix.
25. See Wilder, *Pioneer Girl*, 306–8. The song's lyrics also appear in *These Happy Golden Years* when Almanzo asks Laura if she would "like an engagement ring." See Wilder, *These Happy Golden Years*, 213–14. The melody to "In the Starlight" is by Stephen Glover, lyrics by Joseph E. Carpenter.

26. Wilder, *First Four Years*, xx.
27. Lane, *Let the Hurricane Roar*, 6.
28. LIW, "The First Four Years, Pages 1–80," 15.
29. Lane, *Let the Hurricane Roar*, 5–6.
30. LIW, "The First Four Years, Pages 1–80," 11. In both Wilder's original manuscript and in the published version of *The First Four Years*, Laura's parents aren't identified by their first names. Since "Caroline" and "Charles" appear in *Let the Hurricane Roar*, as well as *Little House in the Big Woods*, Wilder may have intentionally chosen not to repeat those names in "First Three Years."
31. Wilder, *First Four Years*, 12, 14, 16.
32. Lane, *Let the Hurricane Roar*, 15. Lane based her depiction of the dugout along Wild Plum Creek on her mother's descriptions of the Ingalls family's Plum Creek dugout in "Pioneer Girl."
33. Wilder, *First Four Years*, 14.
34. Wilder, *First Four Years*, 11
35. Wilder, *First Four Years*, 25.
36. Wilder, *First Four Years*, 27.
37. Lane, *Let the Hurricane Roar*, 17.
38. Wilder, *Pioneer Girl*, 83.
39. Lane, *Let the Hurricane Roar*, 18.
40. Lane, *Let the Hurricane Roar*, 19.
41. Lane, *Let the Hurricane Roar*, 20.
42. Aldrich, *Lantern in Her Hand*, 81.
43. LIW, "The First Four Years, Pages 81–161," 81.
44. LIW, "The First Four Years, Pages 81–161," 82.
45. LIW, "The First Four Years, Pages 81–161," 83.
46. LIW, "The First Four Years, Pages 81–161," 83.
47. Lyrics to "Angel Band" are by Jefferson Hascall, melody by William Batchelder Bradbury. This hymn dates from the 1860s. Its original title was "My Latest Sun Is Sinking Fast."
48. Wilder, *First Four Years*, 70.
49. LIW, "The First Four Years, Pages 81–161," 84.
50. Lane, *Let the Hurricane Roar*, 20.
51. Wilder, *First Four Years*, 72.
52. Lane, *Let the Hurricane Roar*, 28.
53. Lane, *Let the Hurricane Roar*, 37.
54. Lane, *Let the Hurricane Roar*, 38.
55. Lane, *Let the Hurricane Roar*, 43.
56. Lane, *Let the Hurricane Roar*, 64.
57. Wilder, *First Four Years*, 48.
58. Wilder, *First Four Years*, 49.
59. Wilder, *First Four Years*, 54.

60. Wilder, *First Four Years*, 55.
61. Lane, *Let the Hurricane Roar*, 85.
62. Lane, *Let the Hurricane Roar*, 88.
63. Lane, *Let the Hurricane Roar*, 106.
64. Wilder, *Pioneer Girl*, 81.
65. Lane, *Let the Hurricane Roar*, 152. A similar passage appears in Bess Streeter Aldrich's *A Lantern in Her Hand* when the main character, like Caroline, is expecting her second child and for the first time fully embraces her husband's homesteading dream: "A revival of hope and courage possessed her. This was their own land. They, who had never owned a foot of ground, were now the sole owners of one hundred and sixty acres. . . . A farm of their own upon which to make a home,—a home for Mack [their son],—and one other!" Aldrich, *A Lantern in Her Hand*, 77–78.
66. Wilder, *First Four Years*, 89.
67. Wilder, *First Four Years*, 90–91.
68. Wilder, *First Four Years*, 93.
69. Lane, *Let the Hurricane Roar*, 142.
70. Lane, *Let the Hurricane Roar*, 143. Caroline's encounter with the timber wolves in *Let the Hurricane Roar* was inspired by Wilder's account of her own encounter with a pair of "big buffalo wolves" in *Pioneer Girl*, 181–83.
71. Lane, *Let the Hurricane Roar*, 144.
72. Wilder, *First Four Years*, 105.
73. Wilder, *First Four Years*, 106.
74. Wilder, *First Four Years*, 133.
75. Wilder, *First Four Years*, 133–34.
76. LIW, "The First Four Years, Pages 1–80," 15.
77. LIW to RWL, n.d. [1932], box 13, Lane Papers.
78. Lane, *Let the Hurricane Roar*, 76–77.
79. Wilder, *First Four Years*, 89.
80. Wilder, *First Four Years*, 127. Wilder's description of the death of her unnamed baby in *The First Four Years* is remarkably similar to her depiction in *Pioneer Girl* of her baby brother's death: "Little Brother was not well and the Dr. came. I thought that would cure him. . . . But little Brother got worse instead of better and one awful day he straightened out his little body and was dead" (97).
81. Wilder, *First Four Years*, 35.
82. Wilder, *First Four Years*, 111.
83. Wilder, *First Four Years*, 63.
84. Lane, *Let the Hurricane Roar*, 121–22.
85. Wilder, *First Four Years*, 25.
86. Wilder, "Whom Will You Marry?" in *Little House Reader*, 131.

87. Wilder, "Whom Will You Marry?," 133.
88. Wilder, "Whom Will You Marry?," 132.
89. Wilder, "Whom Will You Marry?," 133.
90. Wilder, "Whom Will You Marry?," 141.
91. Wilder, *These Happy Golden Years*, 289.
92. RWL to LIW, November 11, 1930, box 13, Lane Papers.
93. LIW to RWL, February 5, 1937, box 17, Lane Papers.
94. LIW to Ida Louise Raymond, December 13, 1937, in Wilder, *Selected Letters*, 137.
95. Ida Louise Raymond to LIW, December 18, 1937, and RWL to LIW, December 20, 1937, box 13, Lane Papers.
96. RWL to LIW, December 20, 1937.
97. RWL to LIW, December 20, 1937.
98. LIW to RWL, n.d. [1937], box 13, Lane Papers.
99. LIW to George Bye, June 21, 1940, Brown Collection.
100. Anderson, introduction to Wilder, *Selected Letters*, xviii–xix.
101. Lucille Morris Upton, "True Stories That Read Like Fiction Brought Fame to Laura Ingalls Wilder," *Springfield (MO) News Leader*, n.d. [1949], author's collection.
102. LIW, "The First Four Years, Pages 81–161," 159. Sill's poem, which was originally written in the late 1800s, was reprinted in its entirety in the November 1932 issue of the *Atlantic*. Could Wilder have read Sill's poem in the *Atlantic* that fall? It's an intriguing idea and not entirely outside the realm of possibility. Wilder read the *Atlantic* regularly and stored issues in her library at Rocky Ridge Farm, where they remain today. The full text of Sill's poem appears at www.theatlantic.com/magazine/archive/1932/11/the-fools-prayer-april-1879/650550.
103. Ida Louise Raymond to LIW, December 18, 1937, box 13, Lane Papers.
104. RWL to LIW, n.d. [October 1937], box 13, Lane Papers.
105. RWL to LIW, n.d. [October 1937].

Bibliography

Archives and Manuscript Materials

Ellis Library, University of Missouri, Columbia
Western Historical Manuscript Collection

Herbert Hoover Presidential Library, West Branch, Iowa
Laura Ingalls Wilder Series, Rose Wilder Lane Papers

Laura Ingalls Wilder Historic Home and Museum, Mansfield, Missouri
Laura Ingalls Wilder Papers

Laura Ingalls Wilder Memorial Society, De Smet, South Dakota

Rare Book and Manuscript Library, Columbia University, New York
James Oliver Brown Collection

Utah State University Special Collections and Archives, Logan
Jack and Charmian London Correspondence and Papers

Published Works

Aldrich, Bess Streeter. *A Lantern in Her Hand*. New York: D. Appleton, 1928.

Allexan, Sarah S., et al. "Blindness in Walnut Grove: How Did Mary Ingalls Lose Her Sight?" *Pediatrics* 131, no. 3 (March 2013): 1–3.

Anderson, William T., ed. *The Horn Book's Laura Ingalls Wilder*. Boston: Horn Book, 1987.

Basinger, Jeanine. *The Movie Musical*. New York: Alfred A. Knopf, 2019.

Benson, Mildred Wirt. "The Nancy I Knew." In *The Mystery at Lilac Inn*, by Carolyn Keene. Bedford MA: Applewood Books, 1994.

Blevins, Brooks. *A History of the Ozarks: The Ozarkers*. Vol. 3. Urbana: University of Illinois Press, 2021.

Brantley, Billy C. "History of the *Missouri Ruralist*, 1902 through 1955." Master's thesis, University of Missouri, 1958.

Brink, Carol Ryrie. *Caddie Woodlawn*. New York: Simon & Schuster Books for Young Readers, 1973.

Burns, Louis. *A History of the Osage People*. Tuscaloosa: University of Alabama Press, 2004.

Cart, Michael. *From Romance to Realism: Fifty Years of Growth and Change in Young Adult Literature*. New York: HarperCollins, 1996.

Cather, Willa. *O Pioneers!* New York: Barnes & Noble Classics, 2003.

Chapman, Berlin B. "Removal of the Osages from Kansas." *Kansas Historical Quarterly* 7, no. 3 (August 1938): 287–305.

Cutler, Charles L. *O Brave New Words! Native American Loanwords in Current English*. Norman: University of Oklahoma Press, 1994.

Cutler, William G. *A History of the State of Kansas*. Chicago: A. T. Andreas, 1883.

Daly, Maureen. *Seventeenth Summer*. New York: Dodd, Mead, 1952.

Flanigan, Beverly Olson. "American Indian English in History and Literature." PhD diss., University of Indiana, 1981.

Hall, G. Stanley. "Children's Reading: As a Factor in Their Education." *Library Journal* 33 (April 1908): 123–28.

Hill, Pamela Smith. *Laura Ingalls Wilder: A Writer's Life*. Pierre: South Dakota State Historical Society Press, 2007.

Hines, Stephen W., ed. *Laura Ingalls Wilder, Farm Journalist: Writings From the Ozarks*. Columbia: University of Missouri Press, 2007.

Holtz, William. *The Ghost in the Little House: A Life of Rose Wilder Lane*. Missouri Biography Series. Columbia: University of Missouri Press, 1993.

Jehlen, Myra. "Banned in Concord: *Adventures of Huckleberry Finn* and Classic American Literature." In *The Cambridge Companion to Mark Twain*, edited by Forrest G. Robinson. New York: Cambridge University Press, 1995.

Kelly, Fanny. *Narrative of My Captivity among the Sioux Indians*. Cincinnati: Wilstach, Baldwin, 1871.

Kirkus, Virginia. "The Discovery of Laura Ingalls Wilder." *Horn Book Magazine* 29 (December 1953): 423–30.

Kunitz, Stanley J., and Howard Haycroft, eds. *Junior Book of Authors*. 2nd ed. New York: H. W. Wilson, 1951.

Lane, Rose Wilder. *Free Land*. New York: Longmans, Green, 1938.

———. *Let the Hurricane Roar*. New York: Longmans, Green, 1933.

———. *Old Home Town*. Lincoln: University of Nebraska Press, 1985.

Leechman, Douglas, and Robert Hall Jr. "American Indian Pidgin English Attestations and Grammatical Peculiarities." *American Speech* 30, no. 3 (October 1955): 163–71.

L'Engle, Madeleine. *Herself: Reflections on a Writing Life*. Edited by Carole F. Chase. Colorado Springs CO: Shaw Books, 2001.

Linsenmayer, Penny. "Kansas Settlers on the Osage Diminished Reserve: A Study in Laura Ingalls Wilder's *Little House on the Prairie*." *Kansas History* 24, no. 3 (Autumn 2001): 168–85.

MacNicol, Glynnis. "The Problem with Laura." *Wilder*. Iheart Media audio podcast, July 20, 2023. www.iheart.com/podcast/1119-wilder-112847598/episode/7-the-problem-of-laura-119295852/.

Marcus, Leonard S., ed. *Dear Genius: The Letters of Ursula Nordstrom*. New York: HarperCollins, 1998.

McAuliffe, Dennis, Jr. *The Deaths of Sybil Bolton: Oil, Greed, and Murder on the Osage Reservation*. Chicago: Council Oaks Books, 2021.

Means, Florence Crannell. *A Candle in the Mist: A Story for Girls*. Boston: Houghton Mifflin, 1931.
Meek, Barbra A. "And the Injun goes 'How!': Representations of American Indian English in White Public Space." *Language in Society* 35, no. 1 (January 2006): 93–128.
Miller, John E. *Becoming Laura Ingalls Wilder: The Woman behind the Legend*. Missouri Biography Series. Columbia: University of Missouri Press, 1998.
Nilsen, Alleen Pace, and Kenneth Donelson. *Literature for Today's Young Adults*. 6th ed. New York: Longman, 2001.
Petersen, Carol Miles. *Bess Streeter Aldrich*. Lincoln: University of Nebraska Press, 1995.
Reynolds, David S. *Abe: Abraham Lincoln in His Times*. New York: Penguin, 2020.
Rioux, Anne Boyd. *Meg, Jo, Beth, Amy: The Story of Little Women*. New York: W. W. Norton, 2018.
Robinson, Forrest G., ed. *The Cambridge Companion to Mark Twain*. New York: Cambridge University Press, 1995.
Rolvaag, O. E. *Giants in the Earth*. New York: Harper & Row, 1955.
Rubio, Mary Henley. *Lucy Maud Montgomery: The Gift of Wings*. Toronto: Doubleday Canada, 2008.
Schell, Herbert S. *History of South Dakota*. Rev. ed. Lincoln: University of Nebraska Press, 1968.
Tolkien, J. R. R. *The Hobbit or, There and Back Again*. Boston: Houghton Mifflin, 1984.
Twain, Mark. "Fenimore Cooper's Literary Offenses." In *The Portable Mark Twain*. New York: Viking Press, 1984.
Underhill, Lonnie E., and Daniel F. Littlefield Jr., eds. *Hamlin Garland's Observations on the American Indian, 1895–1905*. Tucson: University of Arizona Press, 1976.
Wilder, Laura Ingalls. *By the Shores of Silver Lake*. New York: Harper Trophy, 1971.
———. *Farmer Boy*. New York: Harper Trophy, 1971.
———. *The First Four Years*. New York: Harper Trophy, 1971.
———. *Little House in the Big Woods*. New York: Harper Trophy, 1971.
———. *Little House on the Prairie*. New York: Harper Trophy, 1971.
———. *A Little House Reader: A Collection of Writings*. Edited by William T. Anderson. New York: Harper Trophy, 1998.
———. *A Little House Traveler: Writings from Laura Ingalls Wilder's Journeys across America*. New York: Harper Collins, 2006.
———. *Little Town on the Prairie*. New York: Harper Trophy, 1971.
———. *The Long Winter*. New York: Harper Trophy, 1971.
———. *On the Banks of Plum Creek*. New York: Harper Trophy, 1971.
———. *On the Way Home*. New York: Harper & Row, 1962.

———. *Pioneer Girl: The Annotated Autobiography*. Edited by Pamela Smith Hill. Pierre: South Dakota State Historical Society Press, 2014.

———. *The Selected Letters of Laura Ingalls Wilder*. Edited by William T. Anderson. New York: HarperCollins, 2016.

———. *These Happy Golden Years*. New York: Harper Trophy, 1971.

Wilder, Laura Ingalls, and Rose Wilder Lane. *A Little House Sampler*. Edited by William T. Anderson. Lincoln: University of Nebraska Press, 1988.

Wilson, Jeffrey R. "Historicizing Presentism: Toward the Creation of a Journal of Public Humanities." MLA *Profession*, Spring 2019. https://profession.mla.org/historicizing-presentism-toward-the-creation-of-a-journal-of-the-public-humanities/.

Woodside, Christine. *Libertarians on the Prairie: Laura Ingalls Wilder, Rose Wilder Lane, and the Making of the Little House Books*. New York: Arcade, 2016.

Woolf, Virginia. *The Diary of Virginia Woolf*. Vol. 1. Edited by Anne Olivier Bell. New York: Harcourt Brace Jovanovich, 1977.

Index